D1617373

Feminist
Legal Literature

GARLAND REFERENCE LIBRARY
OF SOCIAL SCIENCE
(VOL. 671)

Feminist
Legal Literature

A Selective Annotated Bibliography

compiled by

F. C. DeCoste

K. M. Munro

Lillian MacPherson

GARLAND PUBLISHING, INC. • NEW YORK & LONDON
1991

Library of Congress Cataloging-in-Publication Data

DeCoste, F.C., 1946–
    Feminist legal literature : a selective annotated bibliography /
compiled by F.C. DeCoste, K.M. Munro, Lillian MacPherson.
      p. cm. — (Garland reference library of social science ; vol.
671)
    Includes indexes.
    ISBN 0–8240–7117–4 (alk. paper)
    1. Women—Legal status, laws, etc.—Bibliography. 2. Sex and law—
Bibliography. 3. Women—Bibliography. 4. Feminism—Bibliography.
I. Munro, K.M. II. MacPherson, Lillian. III. Title. IV. Series.
K644.A12D43 1991
016.34601'34—dc20
[016.3426134]
                                          91–9731
                                              CIP

Printed on acid-free, 250-year-life paper
Manufactured in the United States of America

CONTENTS

INTRODUCTION

This bibliography was compiled in order to provide organized access to multi-disciplinary materials dealing with issues of interest to feminists, written from a feminist perspective, and of relevance to law. While the scope of the bibliography is largely defined by those issues upon which law has an impact, we did not limit ourselves to legal periodicals. We chose also from alternative press, social science journals, and international human rights literature.

The period covered by this bibliography is, generally, the decade of the 1980's. For the period of January, 1980 to June 30, 1990, we completed a systematic search of materials; for the period from June 30, 1990 to November 30, 1990, our search was less systematic, but we nonetheless were as comprehensive as was possible.

Computer searches were done on the following databases: Westlaw's *Texts and Periodicals, Canadian Legal Literature, Legal Resource Index, Index to Legal Periodicals, PAIS International, Philosopher's Index, Humanities Index, Sociological Abstracts* and *Woman-Source.*

Manual searches were conducted in the *Index to Canadian Legal Periodical Literature, Alternative Press Index* and *Women Studies Abstracts.*

This bibliography attempts to include all relevant English language journal articles, as well as articles written in French which are published in French Canadian publications. We have not included works which are published in edited monographs; nor have we included treatises. We have, however, chosen to publish annotations of book review essays. We made this choice for two reasons. Firstly, book review essays give the reader a sense of the books published during a specific time frame; and by including review essays, we have attempted to give the reader notice of various tools of analysis which are available in monograph form. In addition, and in our view, more importantly, book reviews are frequently the location of emerging debate in feminist analysis; they are frequently more creative and innovative forms of analysis than the later articles which refine these earlier points of analysis.

While we are aware that in any legal writing, and most particularly in feminist legal writing, there are seldom discrete areas of interest, we have attempted to categorize the materials in order to make them more easily accessible. When it was necessary to locate a particular article in more than one category, we have indicated the overlap by including the cite, but not repeating the annotation, in the second category.

We have, in addition, included three indices in order to ensure that the reader can locate a particular text. Firstly, we have indexed the material according to author's name. This index includes not only references to the writing by that author, but also references to the author in other writing.

Secondly, we have indexed the materials by periodical name. This will allow the reader to ascertain all materials published in a certain journal, and we think it will be especially helpful to those researching in a limited library in order to quickly establish which articles are available to them.

Lastly, we have included a topical index, in which certain keywords are indexed to the page upon which they appear. We trust that the combination of these three indices, and the categories specified under the Table of Contents, will provide sufficient guidance with respect to the location of individual articles or certain topics.

We must define some forms of our categorization. We have chosen to include analysis of human rights agreements made on an international basis within the Constitutional Law category. We adopted this practice simply because the arguments respecting the one are similar to the arguments respecting the other, namely, both are rights-based.

We have chosen to classify separately two issues of special concern. The first is writing done with respect to First Nations women; the second is writing with respect to lesbian women. Our choice to provide a separate category for annotations in either of these topics is not based on a belief that such writing is of interest only to First Nations or lesbian women. On the contrary, the strongest and most powerful critique of much feminist writing comes from the doubly disadvantaged women who are the subject of such writing, and, in our view, any theory of feminism must account for both of these concerns.

We have chosen, also, to combine First Nations and Race as a category. Again, this decision was difficult, insofar as the issues raised are certainly not identical. However, there are substantial similarities, and for this reason we chose to combine these two categories.

We do not purport to have a comprehensive record of legal literature related to women. This is so because we chose materials for their feminist perspective -- not merely because they dealt with what are commonly referred to as "women's issues." The few exceptions to this method of selection are articles annotated and included which were written in response to a feminist article; we were of the opinion that without such inclusion, the complementary annotation was of less value to the reader.

It is without doubt impossible to exhaust the literature in a search for any bibliography. We have made a serious effort, and have been very thorough, but would urge our readers to view bibliographies on similar topics as complementary to each other, not as redundant. Thus, we have included a chapter in which we recognize similar work done by others.

We have followed the most commonly used Canadian legal style guide as the form for our citations (McGill Law Journal, _Canadian Guide to Uniform Legal Citation_, 2d ed. (Toronto: Carswell, 1988)). We have made some exceptions to McGill's guidelines, one of which is that we have not abbreviated the names of journals. This was done to assist the non-legal reader. We have also followed the Canadian practice of identifying the author of notes and comments.

As with any text of this scope, we received generous assistance in the compilation of these materials.

We would like to acknowledge the financial support of the Small Faculties Endowment Fund of the University of Alberta.

We wish to thank the following law students, who annotated articles: Tom Bulmer, Kate Hurlburt, Peggy Kobly, Heather Paton, Susan Richardson, Kerry Rittich, and Elisabeth Van Vleit.

We are especially grateful for the assistance of members of the staff of the John A. Weir Memorial Law Library at the University of Alberta. Shelley McLeod and her Circulation staff located and retrieved items expeditiously; Francis Abiew helped find missing information. Over a two-year period, Caron Rollins did all the online and most of the manual searching, bringing the searches up-to-date regularly. She also was the resident expert on Notebook II, the software package we used to manage the data. Michael Storozuk supported us with his technical expertise, and resolved all the problems related to producing camera-ready copy. His hand (and computer) are responsible for the final appearance of this book.

F. C. DeCoste
K. M. Munro
Lillian MacPherson

December 1990

Feminist
Legal Literature

CHAPTER 1
ABORTION AND REPRODUCTION

"Rethinking (M)otherhood: Feminist Theory and State Regulation of Pregnancy" (1990) 103 *Harvard Law Review* 1306-1325

This paper argues that rights discourse is inappropriate for state regulation of pregnant women's activities such as drug use, especially in the absence of provision of effective pre-natal care or drug treatment to women at risk. It concludes with a suggestion that a better discussion would involve attempting to meet the needs of both the foetus and the mother, rather than privileging either maternal or foetal rights.

"Rumpelstiltskin Revisited: The Inalienable Rights of Surrogate Mothers" (1986) 99 *Harvard Law Review* 1936-1955

This article evaluates the constitutionality of statutory authorization for specific performance of surrogacy contracts. It concludes that neither the thirteenth amendment nor the right to privacy provides adequate grounds for such an assessment, and that an evaluation of rights central to personhood is the best method of choosing between two paternalistic options -- namely, the alienability or the inalienability of rights. An application of personhood analysis suggests that courts should not permit the alienation of the right to abortion, but should enforce the specific performance of consent to adoption due to the risk of comparable harm to the father.

Anita L. Allen, "Taking Liberties: Privacy, Private Choice, and Social Contract Theory" (1987) 56 *University of Cincinnati Law Review* 461-490

Part of a Symposium on Feminist Moral, Social, and Legal Theory, this article provides a defence of decisional privacy arguments -- i.e. arguments premised upon the value of freedom from coercive inter-ference with decision-making affecting intimate and personal affairs, and deployed by the U.S. Supreme Court in its reproductive rights decisions -- against, inter alia, the charge of male ideology, namely, that the articulation of reproductive rights as a matter of privacy for women is an instance of male ideology when men still dominate private life and ultimately decide women's procreative fates. The author argues that notwithstanding that in the past, privacy for women has meant dependence, wrongful patterns and instances of privacy can be rejected on moral grounds without abrogating privacy itself. For this reason, she claims, privacy rights are tools women can use to create opportunities for significant decisional privacy in private life, and privacy and decisional privacy cannot be dismissed as mere male ideology. The author concludes by illustrating how decisional privacy arguments for abortion rights justify permissive reproductive rights policies.

Susan Frelich Appleton, "Surrogacy Arrangements and the Conflict of Law" [1990] *Wisconsin Law Review* 399-482

The existence of a number of state legislative schemes dealing with surrogacy arrangements, ranging from restrictive to permissive, has created a conflict of laws situation. The author examines a number of hypothetical, multi-jurisdictional cases, and analyses the possible legal outcomes for both the restrictive state and the citizens who are attempting to evade the restriction. She concludes that the development of a federal legislative policy would provide uniformity, and prevent the use of evasion tactics.

Marie Ashe, "Law-Language of Maternity: Discourse Holding Nature in Contempt" (1988) 22 *New England Law Review* 521-559

This article outlines the current status of surrogacy law, and the public policy debate to which it has given rise. The author contrasts the medical model of childbirth with the natural and cultural experience of women during childbirth, and argues that the desired legislative response is neither to prevent surrogacy, nor to enforce surrogacy contracts when broken. The author concludes that the law has not incorporated women's experience.

Marie Ashe, "Review Essay: Conversation and Abortion -- Book Review: Mary Ann Glendon, ABORTION AND DIVORCE IN WESTERN LAW (1987)" (1987) 82 *Northwestern University Law Review* 387-402

For annotation, see Chapter 16: BOOK REVIEWS.

Mary E. Becker, "From Muller v. Oregon to Fetal Vulnerability Policies" (1986) 53 *University of Chicago Law Review* 1219-1268

This article examines the justification and legality of restricting employment opportunities to women in order to protect existing and potential foetuses. The author notes the similarity between current arguments on this issue and those once proposed to support sex-specific labour legislation, and counsels against the casual acceptance of policies that put the interests of the next generation above those of women. The author concludes that such decisions are better left with Congress than with individual employers.

Suzanne Bélanger, "Le Retrait Préventif de la Travailleuse Enceinte" (1986) 1 *Canadian Journal of Women and the Law* 498-504

This article reviews the Quebec Occupational Health and Safety Act which provides pregnant and nursing women protection from workplace hazards to the foetus and child. The author concludes that its effectiveness is reduced by workers' ignorance of the law, lack of co-operation by the medical profession, and risk of job loss by workers who exercise their rights. Research into the workplace, greater publicity, and complementarity between federal and provincial laws, is advocated.

Janet Benshoof, "The Establishment Clause and Government-Funded Natural Family Planning Programs: Is the Constitution Dancing to a New Rhythm?" (1987-88) 20 *New York University Journal of International Law and Politics* 1-33

Part of a Symposium on the Civil Liberties and Human Rights Implications of United States International Population Policy, this article claims that because natural family planning is so inextricably intertwined with Roman Catholic doctrine, government grants to its institutions for programs is unconstitutional under the establishment clause of the first amendment of the Constitution. The author discusses American policy related to the Agency for International Development, the secular purpose test, and the unacceptable risk of advancing religious doctrine.

Joan Bercovitch, "Civil Law Regulation of Reproductive Technologies: New Laws for the New Biology?" (1986) 1 *Canadian Journal of Women and the Law* 385-407

The author analyzes the impact of new reproductive technologies,

such as artificial insemination and in-vitro fertilization, on Quebec civil
law, particularly in the areas of contract, affiliation, and medical liability.
Issues such as donor consent, legal status of embryos and of children
born as a result of the process, and civil suits for damages are considered. She concludes that the legal implications of the techniques
require greater scope than the courts are currently applying.

**Randall P. Bezanson, Sheldon F. Kurtz, and Beverly Hovenkamp,
"Model Human Reproductive Technologies and Surrogacy Act" (1987)
72 *Iowa Law Review* 943-1013**
    This model act is the product of a university class entitled, "The
Status of Children of the New Biology Drafting Seminar". The act covers
artificial insemination, in vitro fertilization and surrogacy, and includes
extensive comments on the policy decisions and rationales underlying the
specific provisions. Highlights include: judicial pre-authorization of contracts, counselling requirements, restriction of surrogacy to married
couples, rights of and obligations to the child, confidentiality requirements, and liability provisions.

**L. Binet, "La Maternité Instituée Comme Phénomène Social et
Politique" (1986) 1 *Canadian Journal of Women and the Law* 313-323**
    The author claims that maternity can only be understood through
the institutions that produce it, and she argues that the female body and
its reproductive capacity determine women's social inferiority.   An
analysis of motherhood as a social and political state through legal, medical and scientific institutions will, she concludes, enable women to
comprehend the ramifications of new reproductive technologies for
women.

**Somer Brodribb, "Off the Pedestal and Onto the Block? Motherhood,
Reproductive Technologies, and the Canadian State" (1986) 1 *Canadian
Journal of Women and the Law* 407-423**
    The author argues that reproductive technologies have appropriated
childbearing for the patriarchal medical profession, and will threaten
women's right to bear children. She concludes that artificial insemination,
surrogacy, and in vitro fertilization are all regulated by traditional family
policies, which result in a technological and ideological warfare over
women's procreativity.

James Burr, "Collins v. Eli Lilly & Company: The DES Causation Problem and Risk Contribution Theory" (1985) 1 *Wisconsin Women's Law Journal* 69-96

The author discusses the difficulty faced by female DES-users in civil actions against the drug manufacturers, namely, the inability to identify the company which manufactured the medication consumed by that individual plaintiff. The inequities inherent in this situation, the author claims, led courts to fashion new theories of causation, for instance, allowing the plaintiff to shift the burden of actual causation (i.e. identification of manufacturer) to the defendant manufacturer. The author argues that individualized civil actions, based on either a market share or a risk contribution theory, are staggeringly expensive, and may be an "over-deterrence" with respect to drug manufacturers, and concludes that no-fault legislation would better protect victims of dangerous drugs.

June K. Burton, "Human Rights Issues Affecting Women in Napoleonic Legal Medicine Textbooks" (1987) 8 *History of European Ideals* 427-434

This article deals with the application of medical opinions and knowledge to judicial proceedings. The article describes how legal medicine became established in the French Revolutionary/Napoleonic era, supplanting the Church as the arbiter of women's bodies. The author discusses the opinions of the first professor of legal medicine, specifically with regard to the prohibition of marriage, rape, conception, abortion and infanticide. The medical and legal considerations surrounding each issue are canvassed, illustrating how men in the Napoleonic medical and legal professions worked together to ensure that justice for women was not always fairness, and that the regime's policies would result in a population increase regardless of the human cost to women.

Denise Kenneally Cahalane, "Court-Ordered Confinement of Pregnant Women" (1989) 15 *New England Journal on Criminal and Civil Confinement* 203-223

Part of a Women's Symposium, this article provides an analysis of the confinement of pregnant women by court order to protect the foetus, proposes a model for court intervention, and recommends a procedure for that intervention. With respect to the second matter, the author concludes that courts should intervene only under egregious circumstances, namely, where the woman is clearly in her third trimester, and her viable foetus is in clear danger.

Sharon Camp, "The Impact of the Mexico City Policy on Women and Health Care in Developing Countries" (1987-88) 20 *New York University Journal of International Law and Politics* **35-51**

Part of a Symposium on the Civil Liberties and Human Rights Implications of United States International Population Policy, this article provides historical background on the Reagan administration's Mexico City policy, which denies U.S. contributions to family planning programs if the donee country supports abortion activities. It also reports on a research project which assessed the policy's impact. The author concludes that the policy will "eventually destroy many good family planning programs."

Natalie Loder Clark, "New Wine in Old Skins: Using Paternity-Suit Settlements to Facilitate Surrogate Motherhood" (1986-1987) 25 *Journal of Family Law* **483-508**

The author draws an analogy between surrogacy contracts and paternity legislation, and proposes the use of the latter to allow payments during pregnancy, and to recognize both biological parents until adoption by the legal mother. She includes a sample proposed contract.

Jennie A. Clarke, "The Chinese Population Policy: A Necessary Evil?" (1987-88) 20 *New York University Journal of International Law and Politics* **321-354**

Part of a Symposium on the Civil Liberties and Human Rights Implications of United States International Population Policy, this article examines the Chinese one-child policy, and abuses which have occurred, and suggests alternatives "which might be less intrusive and potentially more effective."

Mary Anne Coffey, "Of Father Born: A Lesbian Feminist Critique of the Ontario Law Reform Commission Recommendations on Artificial Insemination" (1986) 1 *Canadian Journal of Women and the Law* **424-433**

For annotation, see Chapter 12: LESBIANISM AND SEXUAL ORIENTATION.

Cynthia Price Cohen, "International Fora for the Vindication of Human Rights Violated by the U.S. International Population Policy" (1987-88) 20 _New York University Journal of International Law and Politics_ 241-266

This is part of a Symposium on the Civil Liberties and Human Rights Implications of United States International Population Policy. Concerned with the adverse effects of the Mexico City policy -- under which the U.S. denies contributions to family planning projects if the donee country supports abortion -- the author describes its possible health effects and resulting human rights violations. She reviews the international fora in which the policy might be challenged, and concludes that although these may not be successful, they would highlight the adverse effects of the policy, and give impetus to any movement to reverse it.

Sandra Coliver and Frank Newman, "Using International Human Rights Law to Influence United States Foreign Population Policy: Resort to Courts or Congress?" (1987-88) 20 _New York University Journal of International Law and Politics_ 53-91

Part of a Symposium on the Civil Liberties and Human Rights Implications of United States International Population Policy, this article discusses three ways in which U.S. federal and state courts might apply international rights law, and assesses which would be most effective in attacking the legality of the Reagan Administration's Mexico City policy on abortion and family planning. That policy denies aid to family planning projects where the donee country supports abortion.

Ruth Colker, "Feminism, Theology, and Abortion: Toward Love, Compassion, and Wisdom" (1989) 77 _California Law Review_ 1011-1075

The author advocates a feminist-theological dialogue as a method of discovering the authentic self by uniting the aspirational strength of theology with the critical strength of feminism. Using the abortion issue as an example, she contends that sensitivity to the aspirations of love, compassion, and wisdom would require both pro-choice and pro-life advocates to modify their positions. She argues that the value of foetal life should be recognized by the state, but that criminalizing abortion is not a necessary means to achieving this end. Some state regulation, she concludes, is needed for a fully informed abortion decision.

Rebecca Cook, "U.S. Population Policy, Sex Discrimination, and Principles of Equality Under International Law" (1987-88) 20 *New York University Journal of International Law and Politics* 93-142

Part of a Symposium on the Civil Liberties and Human Rights Implications of United States International Population Policy, this article reveals that maternal mortality rates are 200 times higher in developing countries than in industrialized countries. The author argues that the Mexico City policy on abortion and family planning -- which prohibits U.S. aid to family planning projects where the donee country supports abortion -- causes the U.S. to "violate its obligations under international treaty law and customary international law," because " the denial of the choice of abortion violates internationally protected human rights."

Brenda Cossman, "The Precarious Unity of Feminist Theory and Practice: The Praxis of Abortion" (1986) 44 *University of Toronto Faculty of Law Review* 85-108

The author claims that abortion has become the site of open gender conflict. Pro-choice proponents view it as fundamental to the emancipation of women, while anti-abortionists regard it as a symbol of the traditional patriarchal family. However, a pro-choice victory would be short-lived unless the protagonists understand the theoretical and ideological implications of the issue. The author analyzes Catharine MacKinnon's work with reference to other feminist writers such as Mary O'Brien, and concludes that an analysis of sexuality must be accompanied by an analysis of the relation of reproduction to the means of production. Four potentially problematic concepts underlying the current abortion arguments are examined: liberty, rights, individualism, and equality.

Dawn H. Currie, "Book Review: Lydia O'Donnell, THE UNHER-ALDED MAJORITY: CONTEMPORARY WOMEN AS MOTHERS (1985)" (1989) 3 *Canadian Journal of Women and the Law* 313-316

For annotation, see Chapter 16: BOOK REVIEWS.

Nancy Davis, "Abortion and Self-Defense" (1984) 13 *Philosophy and Public Affairs* 175-207

This article distinguishes the views of Moderates, Permissives, and Restrictives regarding the justification for abortion. The author claims that the justification of abortion on the grounds of self-defence is problematic as the foetus cannot be regarded as an aggressor and the victim's response is deliberate. She analyzes the role of third-party assistance in terms of the pregnant woman's permission to favour the preservation of her own life. Finally, the relationship between the foetus and the woman is characterized as asymmetrical; it cannot give rise to a vision of abortion as an act of self defence.

Mary DeLano, "The Conflict Between State Guaranteed Pregnancy Benefits and the Pregnancy Discrimination Act: A Statutory Analysis" (1986) 74 _Georgetown Law Journal_ **1743-1768**
This article contributes to the debate over the interpretation of the federal Pregnancy Discrimination Act in light of state laws guaranteeing pregnancy leave and job security. Legislative history, Equal Employment Opportunity Commission guidelines, and Supreme Court decisions on the Act are all canvassed. After stating that it would be possible either to prohibit or to permit such laws, the author concludes that laws which guarantee job security only to pregnant workers do conflict with the PDA. She suggests that the best response to pregnancy discrimination in the workplace is to ensure that all workers have adequate disability benefits.

Molly Diggins, "Paternal Interests in the Abortion Decision: Does the Father Have a Say?" [1989] _University of Chicago Legal Forum_ **377-398**
The author argues that legislation to balance paternal and maternal rights in pregnancy and the decision about abortion would be constitutional under the due process and equal protection clauses in the United States Constitution. She further argues that the state has a strong interest in maintaining marriage and family relationships, a role which would protect many paternal rights.

Ruth Dixon-Mueller, "U.S. International Population Policy and "The Woman Question"" (1987-88) 20 _New York University Journal of International Law and Politics_ **143-167**
In this article, which is part of a Symposium on the Civil Liberties and Human Rights Implications of United States International Population Policy, the author reviews U.S. international population policy from the 1950s through the 1980s, and analyzes it from the dual perspective of human rights and impact on women's lives. She concludes that the

patriarchal system may "impede a woman's ability to exercise her rights within the familial domain."

Janet L. Dolgin, "Status and Contract in Surrogate Motherhood: An Illumination of the Surrogacy Debate" (1990) 38 *Buffalo Law Review* 515-550
The author examines the law of surrogacy, which she claims reflects the ambivalence with respect to the two opposing claims of status and contract. Where contract is the basic unit of social reality, the individual is defined by her ability to contract with another, equally situated individual. Status, however, is based on inherent distinctions such as age or sex. Surrogacy contracts define a baby as either a commodity (i.e. contract) or a gift (i.e. status), and the relationships between the parties is affected by this choice. The author examines the BABY M case [IN THE MATTER OF BABY M, 537 A. 2d 1128 (1987) aff'd in part in rev'd in part, 537 A. 2d 1227 (1988)] with respect to assumptions about contract versus status, and concludes that this ambivalence ought to be resolved by allowing, but regulating, surrogacy contracts.

Nancy E. Dowd, "Maternity Leave: Taking Sex Differences into Account" (1986) 54 *Fordham Law Review* 699-705
This article provides an overview of current U.S. maternity leave policies, and focuses on restructuring the workplace in order to take sex differences into account. Sex specific legislation is recommended to deal with the issue, and it is justified on public policy grounds as an essential way to achieve the goal of equal opportunity.

Mary C. Dunlap, "Toward Recognition of 'A Right to be Sexual'" (1982) 7 *Women's Rights Law Reporter*
Part of a Symposium on Reproductive Rights, The Emerging Issues, this article employs rights analysis to discuss the problems inherent in the legal system in determining a right to be sexual. The author analyzes United States Supreme Court decisions in her examination of the issue.

Ellen Faulkner, "The Case of 'Baby M'" (1989) 3 *Canadian Journal of Women and the Law* 239-245

This paper discusses the role of the patriarchal legal system in denying women rights as parents, with specific reference to the Baby M surrogacy case [see: IN THE MATTER OF BABY M, 109 N.J. 396, 537 A.2d. 1227 (1988)]. There, the surrogate mother, because of "non-motherly" behaviour, such as a divorce, remarriage, and a subsequent pregnancy, was deemed an unfit mother, and denied even visitation rights to her child. The biological father, who needed the child to carry on his patriarchal line, gained custody of the child in a case, the author concludes, that demonstrates that the legal system exists for men, and treats children as property of men.

Martha A. Field, "Controlling the Woman to Protect the Foetus" (1989) 17 _Law, Medicine and Health Care_ 114-129
This article examines the extent to which control may be exercised over a woman during her pregnancy in order to protect the foetus. The author rejects governmental coercion in favour of the woman's right to control her own destiny, and advocates such measures as education, free prenatal care, and drug abuse rehabilitation as appropriate measures for protection of the foetus.

Judy Fudge, "The Privatization of the Costs of Social Reproduction: Some Recent Charter Cases" (1989) 3 _Canadian Journal of Women and the Law_ 246-314
This article examines seemingly disparate case decisions with respect to mothering and reproduction. The author argues that the decisions are consistent insofar as they all represent the state's attempt to shift childrearing costs from the public sphere to the private, and that this attempt increases women's economic dependence on men. She recommends alternative publicly funded support schemes, and challenges feminist lawyers to question the use of equality rhetoric in litigation strategies to end the sexual and economic subordination of women by men.

Janet Gallagher, "Prenatal Invasions & Interventions: What's Wrong with Fetal Rights" (1987) 10 _Harvard Women's Law Journal_ 9-58
The author discusses the emergence of foetal rights, and claims that the abstract status of foetal rights must remain secondary to the central issue of the rights of the pregnant woman. She rejects ROE v. WADE (410 U.S. 113 (1973)) as authority for disregarding women's objections

to medical treatment, noting that there is a common law tradition of judicial refusal to subordinate the interests of one individual to those of another. Even limited foetal rights, she concludes, may be a springboard for new intrusive state actions against pregnant women.

Helen Garfield, "Privacy, Abortion, and Judicial Review; Haunted by the Ghost of Lochner" (1986) 61 _Washington Law Review_ 293-371

This article is a response to Ely's critique (Ely, "The Wages of Crying Wolf: A Comment on ROE v. WADE" (1973) 82 Yale Law Journal 920) of ROE v. WADE (410 U.S. 113 (1973)) on the basis of interpretivist and non-interpretivist models of judicial review. Ely urges that ROE v. WADE be rejected as it poses a threat of the return of unbridled judicial discretion over the legislative process. The author discusses the history of the right to privacy, focusing on Brandeis and his view of the court's role in protecting the individual against the state. She notes that substantive due process has not been confined to rights mentioned in the BILL OF RIGHTS, and advocates development of a constitutional rationale for protecting privacy rights in the context of abortion.

Shelley Gavigan, "On 'Bringing on the Menses': The Criminal Liability of Women and the Therapeutic Exception in Canadian Abortion Law" (1985-1986) 1 _Canadian Journal of Women and the Law_ 279-312

The author looks beyond the legal and medical professions' approaches towards abortion to discuss women's historical feelings and actions in regards to their own fertility. Against this background, she discusses the possibilities of post-coital birth control (i.e. the morning-after pill), and the development of the therapeutic exception in Canadian abortion law. Her emphasis throughout is on women, and how they have consistently insisted on maintaining control of their fertility.

Ruth Bader Ginsburg, "Some Thoughts on Autonomy and Equality in Relation to Roe v. Wade" (1985) 63 _North Carolina Law Review_ 375-386

The author contrasts equality adjudication in gender-based classification and in reproductive autonomy, and claims that while gender decisions are uncontroversial, ROE v. WADE (410 U.S. 113 (1973)) was controversial at judgment, and remains so. The author thinks that ROE, which allowed women the personal autonomy to abort, went too far in the change ordered, and that the decision was not adequately justified.

This resulted in legislatures' undertaking measures to minimize the impact of the decision, and in courts' failing to acknowledge the equality aspect of the abortion issue, specifically regarding public assistance cases. The author concludes that the ROE opinion is weakened by the concentration on 'medically approved autonomy', to the exclusion of a sex-equality perspective.

Barbara Gregoratos, "Tempest in the Laboratory: Regulation of Medical Research on Spare Embryos From In Vitro Fertilization" (1986) 37 _Hastings Law Journal_ 977-1006
Part of a Symposium on Issues in Procreational Autonomy, this article examines the ethical and legal question raised by in vitro fertilization (IVF), and specifically discusses the non-therapeutic use of "spare embryos" in research. The author notes that the legal status of the embryo is uncertain, surveys American legislation which regulates research, but suggests that this legislation is inadequate to deal with the issue of IVF and the use of embryos in research. She concludes with suggested guidelines for future legislation to regulate such use.

Jiri F. Haderka, "Czechoslovakia: Abortion and Social Security Reforms" (1988-89) 27 _Journal of Family Law_ 91-100
This article discusses changes in the laws on abortion and pregnant women, as well as court decisions relating to guardianship, adoption and maintenance.

Joan Fitzpatrick Hartman, "The Impact of the Reagan Administration's International Population Policy on Human Rights Relating to Health and the Family" (1987-88) 20 _New York University Journal of International Law and Politics_ 169-191
In this article, which forms part of a Symposium on the Civil Liberties and Human Rights Implications of United States International Population Policy, the author argues that the Mexico City policy -- under which the U.S. denies aid to family planning projects if the donee country supports abortion -- violates international human rights. She considers the general right to health under international law, raises the issue that its implementation infringes "the sovereignty of recipient nations," and questions the "utility of litigation premised on international standards."

Virginia Held, "Birth and Death" (1989) 99 *Ethics* 362-368
This article is part of a Symposium on Feminism and Political Theory. The author claims that birth should not be considered "natural," but rather as distinctively human. She shows how "the standard conceptions are awry," and concludes that the experiences of birth and mothering must be taken into account to achieve the post-patriarchal society.

Berend Hovius, "The Morgentaler Decision: Parliament's Options" (1988) 3 *Canadian Family Law Quarterly* 137-165
This article explores options with respect to the regulation of abortion available to the Canadian Parliament following the Supreme Court of Canada's decision in R. v. MORGENTALER [1988] 1 S.C.R. 161 which struck down the regulatory provision in section 251 of the Canadian CRIMINAL CODE. In the author's view, the options now available to Parliament are to decline to enact new criminal law, and allow the provinces to regulate health care services; to enact criminal law; to enact legislation by gestation period; or to enact a reformed version of s. 251 to ensure that the system operates fairly without unnecessary delay.

Ruth Hubbard, "Legal and Policy Implications of Recent Advances in Prenatal Diagnosis and Fetal Therapy" (1982) 7 *Women's Rights Law Reporter* 201-218
Part of a Symposium on Reproductive Rights, this article examines the health risks to the foetus, and to the pregnant woman, the risks of legal intervention, and some social and economic concerns. Brief responses to this article follow.

Albert R. Jonsen, "Transition From Fetus to Infant: A Problem for Law and Ethics" (1986) 37 *Hastings Law Journal* 697-702
In this article, written as an Introduction to the Symposium on Issues in Procreational Autonomy, the author discusses varying roles of the courts, lawyers, philosophers, and theologians in the debate with respect to the rights of the foetus, infant, parents, and the state. The author concludes that any debate must be a discourse including voices of both lawyers and ethicists.

James M. Jordan III, "Incubating for the State: the Precarious Autonomy of Persistently Vegetative and Brain-Dead Pregnant Women" (1987) 22 _Georgia Law Review_ 1103-1164

In this paper on "the principle of bodily autonomy," the author discusses the gaps in the law which allow courts to "commandeer the body of any pregnant woman who loses consciousness and use her as an incubator, without regard to her known preferences, or those of her family, or the restriction on state action recognized by ROE and QUINLAN." He claims that the CONSTITUTION, existing law, and public policy do not support disregarding the privacy rights of unconscious pregnant women, reviews the law on right to abortion and the right to die, and challenges the assumption that a woman who has suffered brain death has lost her right of bodily control.

Denise Kaiser, "Artificial Insemination: Donor Rights in Situations Involving Unmarried Recipients" (1988) 26 _Journal of Family Law_ 793-811

This piece examines the legal status of semen donors in Artificial Insemination by Donor for unmarried women. The author examines case law and legislation, and argues for judicial recognition of the more creative parenting situations prevalent with today's technology.

Herma Hill Kay, "Equality and Difference: The Case of Pregnancy" (1985) 1 _Berkeley Women's Law Journal_ 1-38

The author discusses traditional models for dealing with pregnancy in the context of equality, and argues that they are an inadequate response to the problems faced by pregnant women. The author suggests a new model which would avoid penalizing women for their reproductive capacities and behaviour.

Sally J. Kenney, "Reproductive Hazards in the Workplace: the Law and Sexual Difference" (1986) 14 _International Journal of the Sociology of Law_ 393-414

The author canvasses the theoretical and strategic questions facing feminist jurisprudence with respect to the use of potential reproductive hazards as justification for the exclusion of women in certain jobs. British protective legislation is outlined, and the growing awareness of potential hazards amongst workers is contrasted with the state of current scientific knowledge. Cases from Britain and America are reviewed, and the author concludes that both jurisdictions apply the "difference" approach, despite the desirability of the "equality" approach. Feminists should operate from the equality model, and advocate one standard for both sexes in protection from reproductive hazards.

Kathryn Kolbert, "A Reproductive Rights Agenda" (1989) 1 _Yale Journal of Law and Feminism_ **3-4**
   This article outlines a feminist agenda for reproductive rights that emphasizes choice, particularly the right to meaningful choice. The agenda includes such political and economic goals as ensuring affordable access to reproductive technology, child care, birth control, and pre-natal care, as well as the economic means for all families to provide adequately for themselves and their children.

Kathryn Kolbert, "Webster v. Reproductive Health Services: Reproductive Freedom Hanging by a Thread" (1989) 11 _Women's Rights Law Reporter_ **153-162**
   This article is an introduction to an issue containing the best of the thirty-two pro-choice amici curiae briefs presented to the Supreme Court in WEBSTER v. REPRODUCTIVE HEALTH SERVICES (109 S.Ct. 3040 (1989)). The author analyzes the case, and concludes that it was because of the amici effort and the public outcry that the Court did not completely overturn ROE v. WADE [410 U.S. 113 (1973)].

Sylvia A. Law and Lisa F. Rackner, "Gender Equality and the Mexico City Policy" (1987-88) 20 _New York University Journal of International Law and Politics_ **193-228**
   This article is part of a Symposium on the Civil Liberties and Human Rights Implications of United States International Population Policy. The authors argue that the Mexico City policy -- under which the U.S. denies aid to family planning projects if the donee country supports abortion -- has an anti-egalitarian and anti-woman bias, and is "contrary to the evolving international principle of gender equality," because state denial of reproductive freedom injures women "economically, emotionally, physically and morally." After reviewing the American historical record, the authors do a gender equality analysis of the Mexico City policy.

Mindy J. Lees, "I Want a New Drug: RU-486 and the Right to Choose" (1990) 63 _Southern California Law Review_ 1113-1150

RU-486 is a new drug which induces abortions without surgical intervention. The author discusses how the drug works and its safety, and the reasons for the drug's unavailability in the U.S. Possible legal means of making it available are explored. The author claims that the opposition of the anti-abortionists should not determine this issue since (a) they are a minority, albeit a highly vocal one, and (b) the U.S. Supreme Court has stated that an abortion is a matter between a woman and her doctor.

Marianne Levitsky, "Protecting Workers from Reproductive Hazards" (1986) 1 _Canadian Journal of Women and the Law_ 488-497

The author outlines some of the major considerations in developing safe and equitable approaches to reproductive hazards at work, and offers directions for change. Policies that focus on the hazard to women's reproduction, she claims, have clear implications for equality of opportunity, and often fail to recognize similar risks to men. Regulations applied to "non-traditional" work have generally ignored traditionally female jobs. She gives examples of different approaches by employers, and discusses policy issues regarding exposure limits, definitions of "susceptible" workers, assessment of risk, and the rights of workers to disclosure.

Jennifer Beulah Lew, "Terminally Ill and Pregnant: State Denial of a Woman's Right to Refuse a Cesarean Section" (1990) 38 _Buffalo Law Review_ 619-645

The author examines case law with respect to forced Caesareans, and argues that the law reflects conflict between the cultural norms of individual autonomy and maternal self-sacrifice. She criticizes judicial decisions to order Cesarean section operations because they are based on incorrect findings of fact, and fail to account for the constitutionally recognized zones of privacy of contraception, reproduction, and family relationships. The author draws an analogy between forced Cesarean surgery and bone marrow transplants, where courts have rightly refused to intrude into an individual's right to refuse treatment, and concludes that forced medical treatment of a woman to save her foetus ought to similarly rule in order to defer to individual and family decisions.

Jane Lewis and Fenella Cannell, "The Politics of Motherhood in the 1980s: Warnock, Gillick and Feminists" (1986) 13 *Journal of Law and Society* 321-342

This article discusses two related debates in England -- the first concerning a case on contraception and parental control over the sexuality of minors, and the second a report on access to artificial reproduction techniques. The authors raise the issues of assumptions regarding the nature of motherhood, and of the relationship between mothers and the medical profession. These are discussed against the backdrop of the prevailing legal decisions and political policies on the family and social welfare.

Abby Lippman, "Access to Prenatal Screening Services: Who Decides?" (1986) 1 *Canadian Journal of Women and the Law* 434-445

This article deals with the explicit and implicit assumptions underlying access to prenatal screening. The author describes common techniques for prenatal screening, such as amniocentesis and chorionic villi sampling. She identifies two philosophies guiding the operation and delivery of these services: the "public health" model, and the "reproductive autonomy" model. Current decisions rest in the hands of professionals, and do not necessarily serve either end. She concludes that discussion of the legal, social, and ethical questions underlying screening are essential to maximize both individual autonomy and social equity.

Catharine MacKinnon, "Complicity: An Introduction to Andrea Dworkin -- Book Review: Andrea Dworkin, RIGHT WING WOMEN (1983)" (1983) 1 *Law and Inequality* 89-93

For annotation, see Chapter 16: **BOOK REVIEWS**.

Isabel Marcus, "A Sexy New Twist: Reproductive Technologies and Feminism -- Book Review" (1990) 15 *Law and Social Inquiry* 247-269

For annotation, see Chapter 16: **BOOK REVIEWS**.

Sally Markowitz, "Book Review: Kristin Luker, ABORTION AND THE POLITICS OF MOTHERHOOD (1984)" (1985) 2 *Wisconsin Women's Law Journal* 151-157

For annotation, see Chapter 16: **BOOK REVIEWS**.

Sheilah L. Martin, "Canada's Abortion Law and the Canadian Charter of Rights and Freedoms" (1986) 1 _Canadian Journal of Women and the Law_ 339-384

This article evaluates the impact of the Canadian CHARTER OF RIGHTS AND FREEDOMS on the abortion provisions of the CRIMINAL CODE. The author canvasses the arguments that could be invoked by both pro-choice and pro-life movements, and concludes that ss. 1, 7 and 12 of the CHARTER would be at issue, as well as the sex equality provisions of ss. 15 and 28. Such a situation would provide an opportunity to examine both the judiciary's acceptance of its new role in the wake of the CHARTER, and its views on reproductive freedom for women.

Sheilah L. Martin, "The New Abortion Legislation" (1990) 1:2 _Constitutional Forum: Forum Constitutionnel_ 5-7, 20

The author examines Canadian Bill C-43, which both criminalizes abortion and provides a specific defence to the criminal charge. She discusses possible CHARTER OF RIGHTS AND FREEDOMS challenges to this legislation, and compares the proposed legislation to an earlier provision of the Canadian CRIMINAL CODE which was declared unconstitutional by the Supreme Court of Canada. The author concludes that the question of the proposed legislation's constitutionality will be dependent upon the way the "legislation works in practice."

Gwen C. Mathewson, "Security of the Person, Equality and Abortion in Canada" [1989] _University of Chicago Legal Forum_ 251-280

This article discusses the constitutional basis of the abortion provisions in the Canadian CRIMINAL CODE as decided in MORGENTALER [1988] 1 S.C.R. 30. The author reviews the history of the Canadian CHARTER OF RIGHTS AND FREEDOMS, and the jurisprudence that has developed concerning its interpretation. The three majority opinions in MORGENTALER are compared, with particular focus on the analysis in each of the meaning of "person" in the context of s. 7 of the CHARTER. The author observes that the constitutional basis of the right to abortion remains unsettled, and she concludes that future legislation may find a more stable foundation on the CHARTER guarantees of gender equality.

M. L. McConnell, "'Even by Commonsense Morality': MORGEN-TALER, BOROWSKI and the Constitution of Canada" (1989) 68 *Canadian Bar Review* 765-796
The author attempts to reconcile judicial action in MORGEN-TALER ([1988] 1 S.C.R. 30), and BOROWSKI ([1989] 92 N.R. 110), recommendations for reform of the law regarding the foetus by the Law Reform Commission of Canada, and developments in reproductive technology. She compares laws of other countries with Canadian developments, and expresses concern that women's rights may be pitted against foetal rights, instead of "characterizing the issue as a question of personal autonomy and equality."

Thelma McCormack, "Public Policies and Reproductive Technology: A Feminist Critique" (1988) 14 *Canadian Public Policy* 361-375
Sociobiology and technological determinism underlie the debate surrounding reproductive technologies, in a political climate where women aspire to "achieve control over their own fertility." The author identifies the main participants in the debate as the Catholic Church, legal and scientific scholars, and feminists. She proposes a new paradigm on which "a set of feminist guidelines for a public policy on reproductive technology can be indicated."

Marie-Therese Meulders-Klein, "The Position of the Father in European Legislation" (1990) 4 *International Journal of Law and the Family* 131-153
This article surveys recent developments in the laws of western European countries which regulate the position of fathers vis-a-vis their children. The author observes that scientific and cultural developments have reversed the historical position so that now it is the mother who controls the conception and birth of children, and she questions how far mothers should also control the extent to which fathers may become legally involved in the lives of their children. She examines the position of both married and unmarried fathers, and concludes by putting the question within a framework of children's rights.

Karen A. Morrisey, "Artificial Insemination By Donor: Practical and Legal Issues Involved in Single Motherhood" (1985) 1 *Wisconsin Women's Law Journal* 97-119

This article canvasses the kinds of artificial insemination -- namely, artificial insemination by husband (AIH), artificial insemination by donor (AID), and combined artificial insemination (AIC) -- as well as the methods of actual insemination employed by sperm banks, medical facilities, or women alone. The author discusses the practical, medical, and legal issues raised by AID using a known donor, several known donors, or an unknown donor. She pays particular attention to parental rights arguments, and possible infection with the HIV virus for lesbian women. The author claims that unmarried women have a constitutionally protected right to conceive a child by AID and to raise that child without any involvement by the donor of the sperm, and concludes that lawmakers, judges, and physicians must recognize a "single woman's rights to motherhood through AID" within our enlarged concept of the meaning of "family." A sample contract between a sperm donor and recipient is included.

Aryeh Neier, "The Right to Free Expression Under International Law: Implications of the Mexico City Policy" (1987-88) 20 *New York University Journal of International Law and Politics* 229-240

Because the U.S. Mexico City policy will forbid speech about abortion in the counselling and medical contexts, the author claims that it "poses a serious threat to the future of free expression." This is part of a Symposium on the Civil Liberties and Human Rights Implications of United States International Population Policy.

Lawrence J. Nelson, Brian P. Buggy and Carol J. Weil, "Forced Medical Treatment of Pregnant Women: 'Compelling Each to Live as Seems Good to the Rest'" (1986) 37 *Hastings Law Journal* 703-764

Part of a Symposium on Issues in Procreational Autonomy, this article examines whether a woman should be legally compelled to undergo medical treatment for the benefit of her foetus. The authors identify clinical conditions in which this conflict might arise, and examine the ethical questions raised by a physical compelling a woman to undergo treatment. They also discuss the legal implications of forced treatment, both for the foetus and for the mother, and conclude that pregnant women should not be legally, or socially, compelled to accept medical treatment for the sake of the foetus.

Laurie Nsiah-Jefferson, "Reproductive Laws, Women of Color, and Low-Income Women" (1989) 11 *Women's Rights Law Reporter* 15-38
For annotation, see Chapter 6: FIRST NATIONS AND RACE.

Madalyn O'Hair, "Abortion" (1988) 30:3 *American Atheist* 8
The author gives a history of abortion, suggests that the real issue is sex education, surveys court activity over the years, and is very critical of the pro-life movement.

S. O'Rourke, "Family Law in a Brave New World: Private Ordering of Parental Rights and Responsibilities for Donor Insemination" (1985) 1 *Berkeley Women's Law Journal* 140-174
The author discusses the question of donor rights within the context of new reproductive technologies, especially artificial insemination by donor. She examines the legal, constitutional, and medical perspectives which these technologies raise. The author concludes that a model of increased private ordering through contracting provides the optimal legal response for ensuring equal access to donor insemination by nontraditional families, and that law should not impair parental obligations in opposition to the parties' agreement.

Frances Olsen, "Unravelling Compromise" (1989) 103 *Harvard Law Review* 105-135
This article examines American legislation and case law regarding abortion, with particular emphasis on the analyses utilized in cases of the United States Supreme Court. The author discusses the traditional liberal view both of abortion generally (that the issue is whether a foetus is a legally protected person) and of the case law in particular (that the abortion cases are part of a series of "privacy" cases), and evaluates the advantages for women of this method of analysis. She argues that decisions about the legality of abortion have been made primarily by men, that because they have the power to describe and name the experience, their views become "the truth," and that the debate occurring within the rubric of privacy ignores the coercive nature of sexuality as it is experienced by women. She concludes with a challenge to the Court to "show intellectual honesty and integrity" in an open acknowledgment of the gender politics involved in the abortion question.

C. Overall, "Reproductive Ethics: Feminist and Non-Feminist Approaches" (1986) 1 _Canadian Journal of Women and the Law_ 271-277
   The author argues that non-feminist approaches have dominated the debate on reproductive technology, that the debate has been characterized by a failure to examine underlying social assumptions, and that this has practical implications in the areas of infertility treatment, surrogacy, and foetal sex selection. A feminist approach, on the other hand, contemplates the huge range of issues connected to reproduction, and the author advocates that approach to circumvent the existing inequities, and to place reproductive power with women.

Lynn M. Paltrow, "Book Review: Rita Arditti, Renate Duelli Klein and Shelley Minden, TEST-TUBE WOMEN: WHAT FUTURE FOR MOTHERHOOD? (1984)" (1985) 8 _Women's Rights Law Reporter_ 303-307
   For annotation, see Chapter 16: BOOK REVIEWS.

Donna M. Peizer, "A Social and Legal Analysis of the Independent Practice of Midwifery: Vicarious Liability of the Collaborating Physician and Judicial Means of Addressing Denial of Hospital Privileges" (1986) 2 _Berkeley Women's Law Journal_ 139-240
   For annotation, see Chapter 10: LEGAL HISTORY.

Margaret Jane Radin, "Market-Inalienability" (1987) 100 _Harvard Law Review_ 1849-1936
   For annotation, see Chapter 14: PROSTITUTION.

John W. Ratcliffe, "The Reagan Population Policy: An Error of the Third Kind" (1987-88) 20 _New York University Journal of International Law and Politics_ 267-299
   In this article, which is part of a Symposium on the Civil Liberties and Human Rights Implications of United States International Population Policy, the author identifies two underlying misconceptions adopted by the Reagan administration as reason for the failure of its population policies. He concludes that free choice of birth control methods and access to abortion are necessary as part of the resolution of global problems of overpopulation.

Nancy K. Rhoden, "The Judge in the Delivery Room: The Emergence of Court-Ordered Caesareans" (1986) 74 *California Law Review* 1951-2030

This article deals with the increase in court-ordered Caesarean sections. Arguing that child neglect law is irrelevant to the issue, the author discusses the general right of the individual to refuse treatment. She proposes the use of the law of rescue as the appropriate model for analysis. She concludes that women should not be forced to undergo significant risks in order to save foetuses, and that a proper interpretation of abortion law precludes non-consensual surgery.

Sarah Ricks, "The New French Abortion Pill: The Moral Property of Women" (1989) 1 *Yale Journal of Law and Feminism* 75-99

This article discusses the legal implications of the new French abortion pill, RU486, in the United States. The author gives a brief history of the pill's development, and the legal furore it created in both France and United States, and discusses the process involved in its eventually becoming available in the U.S. She thinks that the law on abortion, outlined in ROE v. WADE (410 U.S. 113 (1973)), and based on privacy and non-interference by the state in the patient/doctor relationship, would probably cover the use of RU486. The right to privacy in the home, outlined in GRISWOLD v. CONN. (381 U.S. 479 (1965)), could be used to support the use of the pill in the home. One important element in the discussion is often ignored, namely, the safety and health of the women involved, which should not be overlooked in the desire to secure the right to obtain the pill.

Stephanie Ridder and Lisa Woll, "Transforming the Grounds: Autonomy and Reproductive Freedom" (1989) 2 *Yale Journal of Law and Feminism* 75-98

This article examines the application of theories of privacy and equal protection to cases involving reproductive freedom for women. Following the gains made by women in the 1970's, the authors argue that legislatures and courts are joining the backlash against women's empowerment. Due to ambivalence or hostility to the recent changes in women's role, women are currently vulnerable to erosion of their reproductive rights through the expansion of foetal rights and father's rights. The authors conclude that an analysis of reproductive freedom as fundamental to the rights of women could provide adequate constitutional protection to women.

John A. Robertson, "Procreative Liberty and the Control of Conception, Pregnancy, and Childbirth" (1983) 69 _Virginia Law Review_ 405-464
This article identifies the freedom to procreate as one of the reproductive freedoms that is ill-defined and unprotected by law. The author attempts to address the scope of this positive right, and to reconcile reproductive techniques with humanist traditions. Five issues are raised: the nature of the right and its meaning in the context of controls on conception, and the management of pregnancy, parturition, and childrearing.

S. Rodgers, "Fetal Rights and Maternal Rights: Is There a Conflict?" (1986) 1 _Canadian Journal of Women and the Law_ 456-469
This article discusses the trend in both American and Canadian case law to give priority to the rights of the foetus over the mother's right to refuse medical treatment. Arguments raised by the proponents of both foetal rights and maternal rights are contrasted in the context of abortion legislation, actions for wrongful birth, informed consent, and child welfare legislation. The author concludes that a balancing of appropriate criteria will almost invariably result in giving priority to the mother's decision over foetal rights.

Albert J. Rosenthal, "International Population Policy and the Constitution" (1987-88) 20 _New York University Journal of International Law and Politics_ 301-319
Part of a Symposium on the Civil Liberties and Human Rights Implications of United States International Population Policy, this article describes the effects of the U.S.'s policy on right of privacy, freedom of speech, and freedom of the press, and suggests that the policy is unconstitutional. Under the policy, the U.S. denies aid to family planning projects if the donee country supports abortion.

C. Rushevsky, "Legal Recognition of Surrogate Gestation" (1982) 7 _Women's Rights Law Reporter_ 107-142
This article examines the desirability of various alternatives to the legal issues raised by surrogate motherhood, and the author focuses on

the potential of existing law to resolve the difficulties. Three major areas are considered: the power of the state to intervene in private contracts in the interests of public policy; the legal status of the child; and the rights of the contracting parties. The Michigan bill on surrogate gestation contracts is used as a model to evaluate the problems and benefits of legislation. The author concludes that any legislative action is likely to be prohibitory, but argues that surrogacy will continue nonetheless, and thus should be regulated.

G. Schachter, "A Private Cause of Action for Abortion Expenses Under State Paternity Statutes" (1982) 7 *Women's Rights Law Reporter* 63-90

In most American states, women who become pregnant outside of marriage may recover pregnancy-related expenses through state paternity proceedings. This article explores whether these provisions also permit recovery for abortion expenses, and if not, whether such legislation could survive a constitutional challenge. The author reviews the history of the current statutes, and the interests they were designed to protect. She discusses the language of the statutes, the effect of an abortion decision on the woman's right to proceed under the statute, and problems of proof of paternity. The latter part of the article deals with constitutional questions, including equal protection, due process, and free exercise of religion.

Paul Schwartz, "Baby M in West Germany -- Book Review: Michelle Stanworth, REPRODUCTIVE TECHNOLOGIES: GENDER, MOTHERHOOD AND MEDICINE (1987); and Goerhard Amendt, DER NEUE KLAPPERSTORCH: DIE PSYCHISCHEN UND SOZIALEN FOLGEN DER REPRODUKTIONSMEDIZIN (1987)" (1989) 89 *Columbia Law Review* 347-367

For annotation, see Chapter 16: BOOK REVIEWS.

Robyn S. Shapiro and Richard Barthel, "Infant Care Review Committees: An Effective Approach to the Baby Doe Dilemma?" (1986) 37 *Hastings Law Journal* 827-862

Part of a Symposium on Issues in Procreational Autonomy, this article examines American legislation regarding withholding treatment of disabled newborns, and authors argue that uncertainty with respect to diagnosis, prognosis, and the possible outcomes of treatment enure in both ethical and legal dilemmas for medical personnel. The authors suggest a solution lies in the formation of infant care review committees, and propose a model statute which addresses the problem.

Andrea M. Sharrin, "Potential Fathers and Abortion: A Woman's Womb is Not a Man's Castle" (1990) 55 _Brooklyn Law Review_ 1359-1404
This article examines the assertion by potential fathers of constitutional rights in the foetus and, more particularly, the arguments put forward seeking to restrain a woman from having an abortion. The author concludes that in this context, the assertion of paternal rights operates to exclude the constitutional right of the woman, and furthermore constitutes sex discrimination.

Josephine Shaw, "Wrongful Birth and the Politics of Reproduction: West German and English Law Considered" (1990) 4 _International Journal of Law and the Family_ 52-82
This article surveys West German and English law relating to compensation in tort and contract for failed sterilizations and failed abortions leading to the birth of an unplanned but healthy child. The author argues that the limitations which have been placed on the recovery of damages reflect gender stereotyped notions of female and male behaviour and sexuality, and she criticizes existing literature for failing to take into account gender divisions in society. She concludes that there is an urgent need to reconsider the categories of the law of obligations, such as damage and compensation, in order to reveal their gendered content and differential effects.

Marjorie Maguire Shultz, "Reproductive Technology and Intent-based Parenthood: An Opportunity for Gender Neutrality" [1990] _Wisconsin Law Review_ 297-398
The development of modern reproductive technologies has raised a number of new legal issues, including the parental status of each participant in a surrogacy agreement. The author argues that legal rules regarding parenthood should recognize the individual's intention about procreation and parenting because intention is a sex-neutral criterion which recognises the individual's right to choice and control. She discusses the benefits of and objections to the new reproduction technolo-

gies, proposes a new legal policy regarding parenthood, and examines possible arguments against it. The BABY M case is used to illustrate her analysis.

Reva B. Siegel, "Employment Equality Under the Pregnancy Discrimination Act of 1978" (1985) 94 *Yale Law Journal* 929-955
The Pregnancy Discrimination Act of 1978 amends Title VII of the Civil Rights Act of 1964 so that sex based discrimination now includes discrimination on the basis of pregnancy. This article challenges the "comparable treatment" interpretation of the PDA, which allows pregnancy to be treated comparably with disability. According to the author, this approach means that no discrimination will be found to exist in a "facially neutral leave policy," despite its being inadequate for child-bearing and its ensuring the termination of the pregnant employee. The author argues that pregnancy be treated as a normal condition of employment because this could acknowledge that "the primary detriments of their economic status are social, not biological in origin."

Steven R. Smith, "Disabled Newborns and the Federal Child Abuse Amendments: Tenuous Protection" (1986) 37 *Hastings Law Journal* 765-826
Part of a Symposium on Issues in Procreational Autonomy, this article examines American child protection legislation which attempts to scrutinize decisions by parents to withhold medical treatment from disabled newborn babies. The author argues that there are limits to a parent's right to make treatment decisions, and suggests a test for defining when treatment of impaired newborns may be legally withheld. He concludes with a recommendation that multi-disciplinary teams monitor decisions by parents of newborns to not treat medically, in order to ensure protection of the infant.

Margaret A. Somerville, "Reflections on Canadian Abortion Law: Evacuation and Destruction: Two Separate Issues" (1981) 31 *University of Toronto Law Journal* 1-26
The author explores the separate legal rights of the foetus on the assumption that the woman's right to abortion is primary. She concludes that the purpose of an abortion must be limited to the evacuation of the uterus, and that the foetus should be entitled to a legal right not to be

killed unnecessarily. Amendments to the Canadian CRIMINAL CODE
are proposed.

Barbara Stark, "Constitutional Analysis of the Baby M Decision"
(1988) 11 _Harvard Women's Law Journal_ 19-52
While Baby M ruled that surrogacy contracts are not constitutionally protected, the author argues that the judge mistakenly assumed such
relationships to be a single event, rather than a multi-faceted relationship
which changes over time. She suggests an alternative formulation of
privacy rights as the right to decisional control over reproduction, and a
right to bodily integrity. She further argues that such rights cannot
constitutionally be waived in advance, or alienated for future selves, and
that the parental rights of a surrogate mother cannot be terminated
without due process protection.

Lorraine Stone, "Neoslavery -- 'Surrogate' Motherhood Contracts v.
The Thirteenth Amendment" (1988) 6 _Law and Inequality_ 63-73
This article is a critique of surrogate motherhood contracts, using
the Baby M case as a reference point. The author examines the problems with contract, property, and class analyses of the issue, and
discusses the problem of legal language in relation to who gets to define
the issue.

Andrea E. Stumpf, "Redefining Mother: A Legal Matrix for New
Reproductive Technologies" (1986) 96 _Yale Law Journal_ 187-208
This article provides a comprehensive legal matrix to accommodate
the shift in parental rights and obligations caused by new reproductive
technologies, especially surrogacy. The author argues that parental
rights should vest in the contracting parents immediately upon birth; and
that courts should facilitate this placement, and should recognize that the
contracting parents' mental conception of the child prior to the surrogacy
is important in the granting of such rights.

Janice J. Tait, "Reproductive Technologies and the Rights of Disabled
Persons" (1985-86) 1 _Canadian Journal of Women and the Law_ 446-455
The author claims that mainstream feminism has almost totally
ignored the concerns of women with disabilities. This article explores

the reasons for feminism's ambivalence toward disabilities. It discusses women's struggle to be perceived as capable of rational thought, women's experience of otherness in a patriarchal system, and the ethical dilemmas surrounding reproduction and disabilities. The author suggests that issues such as abortion be reframed by the integration of disabled women into the dialogue.

Nadine Taub, "Report: Symposium on Reproductive Rights: The Emerging Issues" (1982) 7 *Women's Rights Law Reporter* 169-173
The author reviews the issues discussed at this symposium on reproductive rights, including pregnancy in the workplace, the rapid escalation of birth-related technology, and unspoken premises underlying child custody decisions. The author reports that the tension between women's immediate interests and the ultimate goal of altering sex roles and power relations was a recurring theme in the discussions.

Nadine Taub, "Surrogacy: Sorting Through The Alternatives" (1989-90) 4 *Berkeley Women's Law Journal* 285-299
This article deals with possible legislative responses to surrogacy arrangements, which the author identifies as ranging from permissive to restrictive. The author analyzes each with respect to gender equality and reproductive choice, and then proposes a moderate legislative approach of court-determined custody with a presumption in favour of the birth mother.

Nadine Taub and Lisa McCauley Parles, "Amicus Brief: In the Matter of Baby M" (1987) 10 *Women's Rights Law Reporter* 7-24
In her introduction, Ms. Parles summarizes the Baby M case, and discusses the issues involved in a situation where the gestational mother changes her mind about a surrogacy arrangement. The bulk of the article is the Amicus Brief presented in the case by Nadine Taub for the Rutgers Women's Rights Litigation Clinic. There are three main arguments in the brief. The first is that before terminating parental rights under New Jersey law, the court must be sure that the child has been intentionally abandoned. The second argument is that an agreement made to terminate parental rights before birth is against public policy. The third argument is that the contract should not be enforced without a consideration both of possible unconscionability -- especially,

undue influence or misrepresentation -- and of the child's best interests.

Patricia A. Timko, "Exploring the Limits of Legal Duty: A Union's Responsibilities with respect to Fetal Protection Policies" (1986) 23 _Harvard Journal on Legislation_ 159-210
   The author describes foetal protection programs, the current state of scientific knowledge, legislation, and case law concerning Title VII discrimination protections and a trade union's duty of fair representation. Though it is unlawful for a union to avoid dealing with discriminatory foetal protection policies under both Title VII and under the duty of fair representation, the author feels unions may not have the resources necessary adequately to address this complicated issue.

Gilles Trudeau et Jean-Pierre Villaggi, "Le Retrait Préventif de la Femme Enceinte en Vertu de la Loi sur la Santé et la Securité du Travail: Où en Sommes-nous?" (1986) 46 _Revue du Barreau_ 477-490
   The authors review the right to preventive withdrawal from hazardous work environments, and the requirements for benefits for pregnant women under the Quebec Health and Employment Safety Act. They identify legal issues which remain unsettled such as the validity of medical certificates and their judicial weight, and conclude that the 1985 modifications to the law will not greatly affect the jurisprudence that has developed around the legislation.

Madelaine Vallée, "De la contraception à l'avortement: outrage à l'autonomie des femmes" (1989-1990) 3 _Canadian Journal of Women and the Law_ 483-509
   This article examines the role of contraception in women's lives from an historical and a contemporary perspective. The author examines Canada's legislation and case law with respect to abortion, and concludes with a discussion about the significance of both the majority decision and Madame Justice Wilson's reasons, in the Supreme Court of Canada decision in R. v. MORGENTALER ([1988] 1 S.C.R. 30).

Anne T. Vitale, "Inmate Abortions - The Right to Government Funding Behind the Prison Gates" (1980) 48 _Fordham Law Review_ 550-567

As the state is the only source of abortion funding for incarcerated women, state refusal to aid inmates requiring abortions may constitute an unconstitutional burden. This article explores the nature of the inmate's right to abortion, distinguishing it from the Supreme Court decision on funding of medically necessary abortions for free women. Among the issues discussed are the right to privacy, the eighth amendment entitlement of prison inmates to medical treatment, and questions related to funding.

Michael Vitiello, "Baby Jane Doe: Stating a Cause of Action Against the Officious Intermeddler" (1986) 37 _Hastings Law Journal_ 863-908
Part of a Symposium on Issues in Procreational Autonomy, this article examines the role of intervenors in a parental decision to withhold medical treatment of a newborn. The author claims that pro-life advocates resort to litigation to prevent parents of impaired newborns from refusing or discontinuing treatment of the infant. He suggests that a privacy action on behalf of the infant would fail, but that a privacy action on the parents' behalf would be appropriate, and concludes that parents of profoundly impaired neonates should begin a cause of action in the tort of invasion of privacy in order to protect against officious intermeddlers.

Maria F. Walters, "Who Decides? The Next Abortion Issue: A Discussion of Father's Rights" (1988-89) 91 _West Virginia Law Review_ 165-191
The author analyzes the extent of "a father's notification and prohibitory rights" in the mother's decision to have an abortion. Her analysis encompasses constitutional rights and court decisions before and after ROE v. WADE. She predicts that the West Virginia Supreme Court of Appeals would declare any statute requiring the father be notified or consent unconstitutional although she is not sure whether a "balancing" of rights would be required. With regard to the Supreme Court of the United States, she concludes that its decision would depend substantially on the make-up of the court.

Joanna K. Weinberg, "The Politicization of Reproduction -- Book Review: Sherrill Cohen and Nadine Taub, REPRODUCTIVE LAWS FOR THE 1990s (1989)" (1989-90) 5 _Berkeley Women's Law Journal_

197-213
For annotation, see Chapter 16: **BOOK REVIEWS.**

Marjorie Weinzweig, **"Pregnancy Leave, Comparable Worth, and Concepts of Equality"** (1987) 2 _Hypatia: A Journal of Feminist Philosophy_ 71-101
Feminists are divided as to whether special treatment for women will promote equality or reinforce sex stereotypes and gender based discrimination in the workplace. The author argues that to make possible a more human life for both men and women, the workplace must be radically restructured and she articulates. the restructuring necessary in terms of the concepts of equality as "participation" or "incorporation" of all individuals into a community, and androgyny.

Norma Juliet Wikler, **"Society's Response to the New Reproductive Technologies: The Feminist Perspectives"** (1986) 59 _Southern California Law Review_ 1043-1057
Two themes regarding reproductive technologies are emerging in feminist literature: first, the view that it is likely that social changes resulting from the new technology will reflect the existing power imbalance between men and women; and second, the feminist fear that the use of the techniques will be manipulated by experts working within the framework of the patriarchal system to limit women's autonomy with regard to reproductive choice.

Charles Wolfson, **"Midwives and Home Birth: Social, Medical, and Legal Perspectives"** (1986) 37 _Hastings Law Journal_ 909-976
Part of a Symposium on Issues in Procreational Autonomy, this article examines the increasing use of home births, explores the medical advantages and disadvantages of home birthing, and discusses the legal position of home birth and lay midwives who participate in home births. The author questions whether the decision to choose an alternative birthing circumstance is a constitutionally protected right, and concludes that it is not. He goes on to recommend the establishment of medical standards for midwives, in order to allow freedom of choice to expectant parents.

**Judith T. Younger, "What the Baby M Case is Really All About"
(1988) 6 _Law and Inequality_ 75-82**

This article is a defence of the decision in the BABY M case. The
author takes a traditional contract approach to the problem of surrogacy
contracts, and argues such contracts should be allowed, based on
common law contract principles. She concludes that in custody cases
arising from surrogacy contracts, the best interests of the child should be
the only consideration.

CHAPTER 2
CONSTITUTIONAL LAW

"Anti-Pornography Laws and First Amendment Values" (1984) 98 *Harvard Law Review* 460-481
This article analyzes the feminist conception of pornography with a view to determining whether it encompasses expression entitled to first amendment protection. The author suggests that the appropriate focus of the debate is the value of such expression and the relevant standard of review. Anti-pornography legislation may be justified by looking at the reasons underlying constitutional toleration of obscenity and libel laws. In addition, the evidence of pornography's harm to women is sufficient to support any reasonable legislative determination of its threat to safety and social equality.

"Rumpelstiltskin Revisited: The Inalienable Rights of Surrogate Mothers" (1986) 99 *Harvard Law Review* 1936-1955
For annotation, see Chapter 1: ABORTION AND REPRODUCTION.

"To Have and to Hold: The Marital Rape Exception and the Fourteenth Amendment" (1986) 99 *Harvard Law Review* 1255-1273
This paper discusses the marital rape exemption as a manifestation of and vehicle for the continued subordination of women. The adverse effects and legislative history of the exemption reveal an unconstitutional discriminatory intent based on the theory of implied consent. Rights - based arguments for challenging the constitutionality of the exemption are contrasted with a gender discrimination analysis which conceptualizes the issue in terms of collective power.

Rosalie Silberman Abella, "The Social and Legal Paradigms of Equality" (1989) 1 *Windsor Review of Legal and Social Issues* 5-16
This is the text of a paper which the author presented to the Canadian Judicial Council in September, 1987 at the Canadian-American

Legal Exchange, Osgoode Hall. In it, the author offers a legal paradigm
of equality based upon a social model of equality. According to her, the
social model is that equality is realized in the reduction of inequality, and
that inequality is the existence of discrimination, while the legal model
is that equality requires justice and liberty for individuals, not equal
treatment.

**Anita L. Allen, "Taking Liberties: Privacy, Private Choice, and Social
Contract Theory" (1987) 56** _University of Cincinnati Law Review_ **461-490**
    For annotation, see Chapter 1: ABORTION AND REPRODUC-
TION.

**Doris Anderson, "The Canada Act 1982 -- Aftermath and Consequen-
ces for Women's Rights" [1983]** _Canadian Community Law Journal_
128-135
    The author reports on the pressures Canadian women applied to
constitutional negotiations in an attempt to influence decisions specifically relevant to them. The Canadian CHARTER OF RIGHTS AND
FREEDOMS was drafted without women's input, and with the an-
nouncement of the final wording, women had to fight for change. The
article describes how women succeeded in strengthening the equality
provisions, including the removal of a restraining clause on s. 28, and the
events leading to Anderson's resignation as president of the Canadian
Advisory Council on the Status of Women. She concludes with accounts
of several notorious Supreme Court cases which confirm that the court
has not historically advanced the causes of women.

Doris Anderson, "The Supreme Court and Women's Rights" (1980) 1
Supreme Court Law Review **457-460**
    The author argues the Supreme Court of Canada's position has
been a cautious, traditional one, and that with respect to women, the
Court has at times played a very negative role. She notes that while the
proper function of the Court is to interpret legislation "as it is," the
response of the general public to harsh and inequitable decisions is to
criticize the Court for its lack of humanity. The author concludes that
the Supreme Court should not be a socially activist court, "in effect, to
legislate themselves," but does call upon the Court to "take judicial notice
of the social values of the people."

Elvia Rosales Arriola, "Sexual Identity and the Constitution: Homosexual Persons as a Discrete and Insular Minority" (1988) 10 _Women's Rights Law Reporter_ 143-176

For annotation, see Chapter 12: LESBIANISM AND SEXUAL ORIENTATION.

Gordon B. Baldwin, "Pornography: The Supreme Court Rejects A Call for New Restrictions" (1985) 2 _Wisconsin Women's Law Journal_ 75-83

For annotation, see Chapter 13: PORNOGRAPHY.

Jennifer K. Bankier, "Equality, Affirmative Action, and the Charter: Reconciling 'Inconsistent' Sections" (1985) 1 _Canadian Journal of Women and the Law_ 134-151

Canadian courts have favoured a "literalist" interpretation of statutes, but, the author claims, such an inflexible approach is not appropriate for a constitutional document. Recognizing the underlying constitutional goal of increased social equality, she applies a policy-oriented analysis to reconcile the Canadian CHARTER OF RIGHTS AND FREEDOMS provisions which appear to be in conflict. Section 15(2) affirmative action, is discussed with reference to s. 15(1) equality, s. 25 aboriginal rights, s. 27 multiculturalism, s. 28 equality, and s. 29 separate schools. She concludes that affirmative action is an important remedial social tool, and cannot be considered discrimination.

Anne F. Bayefsky, "The Jamaican Woman Case and the Canadian Human Rights Act: Is Government Subject to the Principle of Equal Opportunity?" (1980) 18 _University of Western Ontario Law Review_ 461-492

This article discusses the case law which arose when several domestic workers from Jamaica were threatened with deportation because of non-disclosure of their parenthood. The women laid a complaint to the Canadian Human Rights Commission, and sought an injunction to stop the deportation until it could be determined whether this was discrimination based on race or sex. This was the first time the Canadian Human Rights Act was considered in the courts, and the facts of the case are used to discuss whether the Act allows the Commission to investigate claims against the government and to provide remedy.

Michael J. Bazyler, "The Rights of Women in the Soviet Union" (1987) 9 _Whittier Law Review_ 423-430

An address to the Symposium on Women's Rights in International Law, this piece provides an historical survey of the rights of women in the Soviet Union beginning with Tsarist Russia. The author reports that in the post-Stalinist period, Soviet women have legal equality, but have not achieved social and economic equality. He also reports that the Gorbachev regime is not enlightened in its approach to women.

Clare F. Beckton, "The Impact on Women of Entrenchment of Property Rights in the Canadian Charter of Rights and Freedoms" (1985) 9 _Dalhousie Law Journal_ 288-312

The Progressive Conservative Opposition, in the Canadian Parliament, proposed in 1983 that s.7 of the proposed CHARTER OF RIGHTS AND FREEDOMS include the right to property. The author explores different philosophies of property, including Locke's, Rousseau's, and Marx's, and addresses what constitutes property. She examines the American experience with guaranteed property rights, and compares it with Canadian requirements for fairness and natural justice. She claims that entrenchment of property rights would probably not be of benefit to women, and discusses the possible impact on matrimonial property law and other forms of property, such as pension rights.

Janet Benshoof, "The Establishment Clause and Government-Funded Natural Family Planning Programs: Is the Constitution Dancing to a New Rhythm?" (1987-88) 20 _New York University Journal of International Law and Politics_ 1-33

For annotation, see Chapter 1: **ABORTION AND REPRODUCTION.**

Diane M. Bessette, "Getting Left Behind: The Impact of the 1986 Immigration Reform and Control Act Amnesty Program on Single Women with Children" (1990) 13 _Hastings International and Comparative Law Review_ 287-314

The author argues that single women with children are discriminated against when they apply under the Immigration and Reform Act for amnesty to attain permanent residency status in the United States. This occurs because the Immigration and Naturalization Service has promulgated regulations on public charge exclusions which have the effect of leaving behind this category of undocumented person. She claims these regulations are contrary to the Equal Protection clause of the Constitution and international human rights treaties, and offers proposals to rectify the misinterpretation by the Immigration and Naturalization Service.

Kay Boulware-Miller, "Female Circumcision: Challenges to the Practice as a Human Rights Violation" (1985) 8 *Harvard Women's Law Journal* 155-177

This article describes the practice of female circumcision, including the procedure's three primary variations. The author identifies attempts from within and without Africa to regulate this practice, as well as the influence of international organizations and governments. The views of African women who support circumcision must be considered in any successful campaign to eradicate the practice. She discusses, in light of these views, human rights arguments that circumcision violates the Rights of the Child under the 1959 U.N. Declaration, The Right of a Woman to Sexual and Corporal Integrity and the Right to Health. She concludes that the argument most likely to succeed is the right to health which best considers the issue from the African perspective.

Christine Boyle, "Home Rule for Women: Power-Sharing Between Men and Women" (1983) 7 *Dalhousie Law Journal* 790-809

The author examines the constitutional and political science issues of the Canadian "first-past-the-post" electoral system, which results in decision making by a minority. She notes that women are conspicuously under-represented, and appear to be unwilling to participate in the system as they find it. She advocates a movement away from geographical constituencies towards a "mirror" theory of representation, which would involve electing representatives from a variety of interest groups, such as women and disadvantaged minorities.

Paul Brest and Ann Vandenberg, "Politics, Feminism, and the Constitution: The Anti-Pornography Movement in Minneapolis" (1987) 39 *Stanford Law Review* 607-661

This article traces developments leading to the Minneapolis Ordinance proposed by MacKinnon and Dworkin, which treats pornography as a civil rights infringement. The authors claim that community activism pressured Minneapolis to consider the proposal to provide civil remedies for persons harmed by pornography, and report that public hearings were held before the ordinance was passed by city council, but vetoed by the mayor. Similar provisions passed in Indianapolis were struck down by the United States Supreme Court as an unconstitutional violation of first amendment rights.

Margaret Buist, "Elusive Equality: Women and the Charter of Rights and Freedoms" (1988) 17:3 *Resources for Feminist Research: Documentation sur la Recherche Féministe* **103-105**
      This article briefly discusses the history of the entrenchment of equality rights in the CHARTER OF RIGHTS AND FREEDOMS of the Canadian Constitution, and then analyzes the trends in equality cases in the first three years that s. 15 was in force. The author notes that more men than women are bringing claims under the section, frequently to the detriment of women. She is also disturbed by the courts' narrow definition of equality.

Eloise A. Buker, "How Does the Constitution Constitute Women Citizens?" (1988-89) 24 *Gonzaga Law Review* **107-133**
      On the assumption that language orders values, the author analyzes the interpretive and political language of the U.S. Supreme Court during the 1970s. She claims that this language establishes the rules and norms for society, and provides an effective means to understand the American collective consciousness. She argues that the court proceeded with three assumptions about women's roles: that married women are primarily economic dependents of husbands; that it is acceptable to treat individual women as members of a class, rather than as individual persons; and that women as a class are not able to render public judgments as estate representatives or jury members. These assumptions also construct sex discrimination: that women who receive special benefits are extra burdens; and that with respect to abortion, a women is a patient under the authority of her doctor, rather than a citizen with her own private judgment. The author concludes that it is important to examine these values in order to change them.

M. Caron, "Les Travaux du Comité pour l'élimination de la Discrimi-

nation à l'égard des Femmes" (1985) 2 _Revue Québecoise de Droit International_ 295-303

This article reviews the history of the United Nations Convention on Women. The author focuses on the work of the Committee for the elimination of discrimination against women which was created to examine the legislative and administrative measures implemented by signatory nations to turn the ideals of the Convention into reality. A review of the findings of the Committee is included. She concludes that the work of the Committee has had a favourable effect on discrimination. However, she claims, legislation is not enough; changes in personal attitudes about gender throughout society are necessary to ensure the elimination of the problem.

Edward A. Carr, "Feminism, Pornography, and the First Amendment: An Obscenity-Based Analysis of Proposed Antipornography Laws" (1987) 34 _UCLA Law Review_ 1265-1304

This article examines the civil rights approach to anti-pornography ordinances innovated by MacKinnon and Dworkin. The author concludes that the proposed ordinances fail to include speech-protective criteria mandated by the United States Supreme Court, and offers a reconciliation of the ordinances with constitutional mandates.

Lorenne M. G. Clark, "Liberalism and the Living-Tree: Women, Equality, and the Charter" (1990) 28 _Alberta Law Review_ 384-395

The author reviews criticisms of the Canadian CHARTER OF RIGHTS AND FREEDOMS' ability to effect change and move towards equality in a liberal state. She believes that because Canada's origins coincided with a broader liberal view, the CHARTER could be effective in promoting "positive" rights in a social democracy, including the elimination of discrimination on the basis of sex.

David Cole, "Strategies of Difference: Litigating for Women's Rights in a Man's World" (1984) 2 _Law and Inequality_ 33-95

For annotation, see Chapter 5: FEMINIST THEORY -- GENERAL.

Sandra Coliver, "United Nations Commission on the Status of Women:

Suggestions for Enhancing Its Effectiveness" (1987) 9 *Whittier Law Review* 435-443

In an address to the Symposium on Women's Rights in International Law, the author compares the working methods and resources of the U.N. Commission on Human Rights and the U.N. Commission on the Status of Women, both formed in 1946. She comments that the Human Rights Commission has been more successful, and suggests ways of improving the effectiveness of the Women's Commission.

Ruth Colker, "Anti-Subordination Above All: Sex, Race, and Equal Protection" (1986) 61 *New York University Law Review* 1003-1063

For annotation, see Chapter 6: FIRST NATIONS AND RACE.

Ruth Colker, "The Anti-Subordination Principle: Applications" (1985) 3 *Wisconsin Women's Law Journal* 59-80

For annotation, see Chapter 6: FIRST NATIONS AND RACE.

Ruth Colker, "Legislative Remedies for Unauthorized Sexual Portrayals: A Proposal" (1984-85) 20 *New England Law Review* 687-720

Part of a Symposium on Pornography, this article recommends a legislative model which would give civil remedies for invasion of privacy to models, actresses, and others who are subject to unauthorized sexual portrayals. The author argues that these portrayals "violate the sex-based civil rights of the individuals portrayed," surveys common law actions which have been brought, and shows how her proposed legislation would survive constitutional challenge.

Rebecca Cook, "Human Rights and Development: Are Women Still Separate and Unequal?" [1986] *Canadian Council on International Law: Proceedings* 315-347

The United Nations Convention on the Elimination of All Forms of Discrimination Against Women is "the definitive international legal instrument requiring respect for and observance of the rights of women to be equal to men". However, at least 39 countries have already filed reservations, some of which run contrary to the objectives. The author asks how far countries should be allowed to derogate from the Convention on cultural and religious grounds. Offering evidence and empirical data on discrimination against women and their disadvantage, the author discusses the challenges presented by cultural difference, and the legal obstacles to progress and enforcement. Opportunities for resolution are identified, including targeting foreign aid to implement minimum standards.

Mary Irene Coombs, "Shared Privacy and the Fourth Amendment, or the Rights of Relationships" (1987) 75 _California Law Review_ 1593-1663
Important events in human life occur in situations of "shared privacy," where chosen individuals share places and experiences we care about. The author claims that fourth amendment jurisprudence neglects the reality of how privacy embodies chosen sharing, and assumes that expectations of privacy belong only to individuals, unless joint claims are legally formalized. She seeks to use feminist insights to reconceptualize fourth amendment values based upon the assumption that shared privacies are a part of ordinary human behaviour, that people have an expectation that such privacy should be respected, and that we need safely to share privacy with others to become fully human. She discusses when and why the third-party consent of one person should allow for the search of a place shared by others, and argues that certain relationships between a defendant and the primary rightholder (i.e. shared households), should give rise to the rebuttable presumption that the defendant has a claim under the fourth amendment.

Katherine de Jong, "On Equality and Language" (1985) 1 _Canadian Journal of Women and the Law_ 119-133
The author argues that the language of legal communications reflects and affects the status of women because of the connections between male domination, language, and law. The sexual equality provisions of the Canadian CHARTER OF RIGHTS AND FREEDOMS provide an opportunity to eliminate the problems of generic nouns; the linguistic status of generic words, which justify legal norms that discriminate against women; and interpretation statutes which entrench imbalance through the rules of grammar which reflect and enforce the power of the creators. She concludes that the CHARTER will be effective only if substantive equality is sought.

David S. Dooley, "Immoral Because They're Bad, Bad Because They're

Wrong: Sexual Orientation and Presumptions of Parental Unfitness in Custody Disputes" (1989-1990) 26 *California Western Law Review* 397-424
  For annotation, see Chapter 12: **LESBIANISM AND SEXUAL ORIENTATION.**

Andrea Dworkin, "The ACLU: Bait and Switch" (1989) 1 *Yale Journal of Law and Feminism* 37-39
  The author, in a previously unpublished paper dating from 1981, argues that the ACLU is corrupt. She begins with her own experiences as the recipient of repeated requests for support, apparently endorsed by many leading women and feminists. After sending a donation, she found that the organization had virtually no women in responsible positions or with their names on the letterhead. The article goes on to discuss the ACLU's support for such groups as the Nazis and the Ku Klux Klan, and argues that there is great danger in defending a pure principle without consideration of the context. She concludes by pointing out that free speech which promotes equality or objects to discrimination is very different from free speech aimed at hurting another group.

Betty G. Elder, "The Rights of Women: Their Status in International Law" (1986) 25 *Crime and Social Justice* 1-39
  Evaluating the effectiveness of the international community in furthering the equality of women, the author examines the role of the United Nations in fostering sexual equality through its various organs. She also discusses the United Nations as a source of human rights and corrective international action, as well as a source of law for women's rights. She gives the U.N. Decade for Women, 1976-1985 a general appraisal, including the three World Conferences which produced programs of action for women to the year 2000.

Debra Evenson, "Women's Equality in Cuba: What Difference Does a Revolution Make?" (1986) 4 *Law and Inequality* 295-326
  This article examines the advancement of women's equality in Cuba since the revolution, and reports that there is evidence that judicial and legislative support have improved the position of women, although certain barriers such as paternalism continue to impede progress towards full equality.

Nan Feyler, "The Use of the State Constitutional Right to Privacy to Defeat State Sodomy Laws" (1986) 14 _New York University Review of Law and Social Change_ 973-994

For annotation, see Chapter 12: LESBIANISM AND SEXUAL ORIENTATION.

Owen M. Fiss, "Coda" (1988) 38 _University of Toronto Law Journal_ 229-244

This paper is the text of the Cecil A. Wright Lecture delivered at the University of Toronto in March 1987. The author contrasts two models of adjudication in constitutional law: corrective justice and structural reform. He argues that since the corrective model is based on the concept that individuals are equal and any inequality is a result of a particular transaction, it does not recognize the claims of women or any other social movement. He urges that the structural reform model be adopted as this approach classifies problems in group terms, and would seek to "reform the institution responsible."

David Fraser, "And Now for Something Completely Different: Judging Interpretation and the Canadian Charter of Rights and Freedoms" (1987) 7 _Windsor Yearbook of Access to Justice_ 66-78

This piece examines the interpretive role of judges, and the increase of legal power over the daily lives of citizens which the Canadian CHARTER OF RIGHTS AND FREEDOMS has engendered. The author cautions that any attempt to use the law, a powerful form of interpretation and discourse, as a method of liberation, will fail due to the hegemonic nature of legal discourse. He argues for communicative action between excluded or marginalized groups, and concludes with a discussion of options for women engaged in the struggle to celebrate male-female differences outside the rule of law and present institutions.

Jody Freeman, "Justifying Exclusion: A Feminist Analysis of the Conflict Between Equality and Association Rights" (1989) 47 _University of Toronto Faculty of Law Review_ 269-316

The author claims that the exclusion of women from private men's business clubs violates section 15 of the Canadian CHARTER OF RIGHTS AND FREEDOMS, and is not protected by section 2(d), freedom of association. The equality provisions are overriding in this case because the existence of these clubs insulates women from political and economic networks, and therefore lessens their chances of mainstream success. She argues that the public/private distinction should be extended to include "public-like" matters within the purview of the CHARTER. This approach would also allow the application of human rights legislation to these clubs. She concludes that a subordination/participatory perspective should be applied to both equality and association. She also argues in favour of women-only clubs.

Marsha A. Freeman, "Measuring Equality: A Comparative Perspective on Women's Legal Capacity and Constitutional Rights in Five Commonwealth Countries" (1989-90) 5 *Berkeley Women's Law Journal* **110-138**
    The author examines equality in Commonwealth countries, including Kenya, Tanzania, Zimbabwe, Jamaica, and Canada, and reports that each still has an underlying belief that men are the only fully adult persons in the population. African women live with customary and religious law, and Jamaican women with invisibility. In Canada, she concludes, the "legal community has a unique opportunity to shape the equality discussion with a new language."

Jacques Frémont, "Droit Public Assurance-chômage, maternité et adoption: les récents modifications et leur validité" (1982-1983) 17 *Chroniques Sectorielles* **497-506**
    This article looks at recent changes to the Canadian unemployment insurance legislation in regard to maternity and adoption benefits. The changes in both areas are deemed to be positive in light of the Canadian CHARTER OF RIGHTS AND FREEDOMS, because they make benefits available to either sex (in the case of adoption) and special time requirements are eliminated (in the case of maternity leave).

Judy Fudge, "The Public/Private Distinction: The Possibilities of and the Limits to the Use of Charter Litigation to Further Feminist Struggles" (1988) 25 *Osgoode Hall Law Journal* **485-554**
    The author argues that the struggle for equality rights is a mobilizing, radicalizing process, but that the continued use of the public/private dichotomy and the formal equality typical of liberal jurisprudence perpetuates a subordinate status for women. She examines case law which recognizes and regulates only a specific type of family, and the

feminist view that the traditional family is merely a replication of societal inequalities. She argues for true equality in marriage, non-patriarchal naming of wives and children, and non-discrimination against same sex partners. Because of the dangers of formal equality, the author advises feminists to use Canadian CHARTER OF RIGHTS AND FREEDOMS with great trepidation.

Mary Ellen Gale, "Unfinished Women: the Supreme Court and the Incomplete Transformation of Women's Rights in the United States" (1987) 9 _Whittier Law Review_ 445-490
   This article is part of the Symposium on Women's Rights in International Law. Following an overview of women's rights in the United States, the author discusses three women's rights cases in the 1986-87 term of the Supreme Court. She surveys several feminist stances on equality, and determines which the court applied in its decisions.

Janet Gallagher, "Prenatal Invasions & Interventions: What's Wrong with Fetal Rights" (1987) 10 _Harvard Women's Law Journal_ 9-58
   For annotation, see Chapter 1: ABORTION AND REPRODUC-TION.

Jeffrey M. Gamso, "Sex Discrimination and the First Amendment: Pornography and Free Speech" (1986) 17 _Texas Tech Law Review_ 1577-1602
   The author discusses the issues of discrimination and demonstrable harm to women underlying anti-pornography legislation, and the failure of the courts to come to grips with them. He concludes that the governments' compelling interest in protecting the equality of women may override constitutionally protected speech.

Helen Garfield, "Privacy, Abortion, and Judicial Review; Haunted by the Ghost of Lochner" (1986) 61 _Washington Law Review_ 293-371
   For annotation, see Chapter 1: ABORTION AND REPRODUC-TION.

Beth Gaze, "Pornography and Freedom of Speech: An American

Feminist Approach" (1986) 11 *Legal Services Bulletin* 123-127

The author argues that the recent pornography controversy in North America parallels the rise of the 'new right' in an alarming way. Feminist attempts to suppress pornography might create a dangerous alliance, though feminists are aligned with conservatives in practice only, and do not subscribe to the conservative emphasis on moral standards. Feminists, she suggests, are more aligned with liberal theory because they agree that harm to women justifies the restriction of pornography. Feminism defines harm broadly, contemplating psychological harm and general adverse societal effects. The author discusses implications of this for the Australian BILL OF RIGHTS, in which the recent enshrinement of freedom of speech raises questions about acceptable restrictions. The fate of the Indianapolis ordinance, she concludes, suggests restriction of pornography may be found to be contrary to the Australian BILL OF RIGHTS.

Ruth Bader Ginsburg, "Remarks on Women Becoming Part of the Constitution" (1988) 2 *Law and Inequality* 19-25

Part of a Symposium on the American Constitution and Equality, this article reviews legal history from 1961 to 1971 in relation to judicial comments on women. It was during this time that the courts were incorporating an equality analysis into decisions. The author views the courts as an "amplifier" of societal changes in the U.S.'s economic and social life, rather than as pioneers of social change.

Ruth Bader Ginsburg, "Some Thoughts on Autonomy and Equality in Relation to Roe v. Wade" (1985) 63 *North Carolina Law Review* 375-386

For annotation, see Chapter 1: ABORTION AND REPRODUC-TION.

Robert Goodman, "Substantive Due Process Comes Home to Roost: Fundamental Rights, GRISWOLD to BOWERS" (1988) 10 *Women's Rights Law Reporter* 177-208

For annotation, see Chapter 12: LESBIANISM AND SEXUAL ORIENTATION.

Donna Greschner, "Book Review: Kenneth H. Fogarty, EQUALITY

RIGHTS AND THEIR LIMITATIONS IN THE CHARTER (1987)"
(1988) 2 _Canadian Journal of Women and the Law_ 463-467
For annotation, see Chapter 16: BOOK REVIEWS.

Sandra J. Grove, "Constitutionality of Minnesota's Sodomy Law"
(1984) 2 _Law and Inequality_ 521-556
For annotation, see Chapter 12: LESBIANISM AND SEXUAL
ORIENTATION.

Billie Heller, "International Convention on Women's Rights:
Bringing About Ratification in the United States" (1987) 9 _Whittier Law Review_ 431-433
In an address to the Symposium on Women's Rights in Inter-
national Law, the author describes the work of the National Committee
on the United Nations Convention on the Elimination of Discrimination
Against Women, formed in 1985, which is dedicated to "bringing about
the United States' ratification or accession to the Convention." The
committee also educates the public about the Convention.

Kathy E. Hinck, "Second Class Prisoners: New Hampshire's Place-
ment Policy for Female Offenders" (1989) 15 _New England Journal on Criminal and Civil Confinement_ 225-241
Part of a Women's Symposium, this article examines New
Hampshire's treatment of female offenders in its correctional system.
The author provides an historical overview of the state's treatment of
female offenders, analyzes the constitutional ramifications of the statutes
New Hampshire uses to send female prisoners out of state, and proposes
programs which the state will need to develop for female inmates once
its first women's prison opens in 1989.

Anita Hodgkiss, "Petitioning and the Empowerment Theory of
Practice" (1987) 96 _Yale Law Journal_ 569-592
Legal theorists have largely forgotten about the petition for redress
clause in the U.S. First Amendment when addressing issues of freedom
of speech and assembly. The author provides a history of the first
amendment petition clause, which is a demand from a group for a particular government action, describes the liberal, radical, and post-Marxist

interpretations of this right, and claims that petitioning adds to empowerment, local control, and collective action. She concludes with a discussion of the radical lawyer's role in working against the hierarchy and towards social change.

Joan Hoff-Wilson, "The Unfinished Revolution: Changing Legal Status of U.S. Women" (1987) 13 *Signs: Journal of Women in Culture and Society* 7-36
   For annotation, see Chapter 10: **LEGAL HISTORY.**

Catherine Hoskyns, "Women, European Law and Transnational Politics" (1986) 14 *International Journal of the Sociology of Law* 299-314
   This article examines the importance of addressing women's issues within the European Community because of the interdependence of the states and the internationalization of capital. The author explains the formal legal basis which already exists in Article 119 of the Treaty of Rome, and subsequent legislation and policy. She examines the aims and demands of the woman's movement, the development of the Community provisions on women's rights, and their impact in the United Kingdom. The article concludes with a discussion of the difficulties in establishing a grassroots political movement.

Berend Hovius, "The Morgentaler Decision: Parliament's Options" (1988) 3 *Canadian Family Law Quarterly* 137-165
   For annotation, see Chapter 1: **ABORTION AND REPRODUCTION.**

Judith L. Hudson, "Book Review: Jane J. Mansbridge, WHY WE LOST THE ERA (1986)" (1988) 86 *Michigan Law Review* 1408-1413
   For annotation, see Chapter 16: **BOOK REVIEWS.**

Patricia Hughes, "Feminist Equality and the Charter: Conflict with Reality?" (1985) 5 *Windsor Yearbook of Access to Justice* 39-101
   The author reviews the fundamentals of feminist theory from the liberal, socialist, androgynous, and separatist perspectives, and builds a theory of equality based upon radical feminist themes, namely, that the

basic divisions in society are sexual, not economic, and that society is more fundamentally patriarchal, than capitalist. The author then applies a feminist theory of equality to the Canadian CHARTER OF RIGHTS AND FREEDOMS, and argues that s. 15 and s. 28 should be interpreted to recognize differences and not to mean same treatment; that discrimination should encompass both intentional and unintentional discrimination; that the affirmative action exemption should be used to ensure appropriate provisions for reproduction; that s. 28 be paramount in any conflicts between ss. 25 and 27; and that sexual equality in s. 15(1) not be subject to ss. 1 or 33.

A. Jacomy-Millette, "Réflexions sur la condition féminine au Canada à l'aube des années 80: égalité ou discrimination" (1983) 1 _Canadian Human Rights Yearbook_ 195-204
   The author identifies two tasks to be faced in the search for sexual equality in law. The first is to examine the laws and their effects; and the second is to define, collectively and individually, the needs of women. She claims that despite legislation and affirmative action programmes directed at sexual equality, women still play a limited role in the political life of Canada, and exert influence only indirectly. Women are increasingly present in the professions, but the double burden of work and family carried by most women, and the ghetto-ization of women in low-paying jobs, remain areas of concern.

M. J. B. Jones, "Sexual Equality, The Constitution and Indian Status: A Comment on s. 12(1)(b) of the Indian Act" (1984) 4 _Windsor Yearbook of Access to Justice_ 48-72
   For annotation, see Chapter 6: FIRST NATIONS AND RACE.

James M. Jordan III, "Incubating for the State: the Precarious Autonomy of Persistently Vegetative and Brain-Dead Pregnant Women" (1987) 22 _Georgia Law Review_ 1103-1164
   For annotation, see Chapter 1: ABORTION AND REPRODUCTION.

Rimma Kalistratova, "Legislatively Guaranteed Equality" (1989) 10 _Canadian Woman Studies_ 38-40

The author examines equality law in the Soviet Union beginning with Lenin's revolutionary call to bring women from "their stupefying house and kitchen environment" into the public and political realm. Though Article 35 of the Constitution of the U.S.S.R. guarantees equality between men and women, she notes that a conflict still exists between "the role of a woman worker in production and her role at home." While there are provisions for "easier jobs for expectant mothers while retaining average earnings of their former office," a disproportionate number of higher government positions go to men, with only 8-11% of those jobs occupied by women.

Masako Kamiya, "Women in Japan" (1986) 20 *University of British Columbia Law Review* 446-469
This article discusses the concept of equality as it is perceived in Japan, which the author claims to be de jure equality rather than de facto equality; that is, women are treated in a like fashion to men through the use of sex-neutral laws. She examines the law with respect to education, traditional patterns of life for men and women, the Japanese constitution as it relates to women, the civil code, and social security for women, and canvasses the impact of international covenants respecting equal rights for women. She concludes with a discussion of the minimal role feminism plays within Japanese political discourse, which she attributes to the fact that financial autonomy offered by feminism is of little interest to women who "live with the reality" of poor jobs at low wages with minimal prospects for better employment.

Kenneth L. Karst, "Women's Constitution" (1984) 3 *Duke Law Journal* 447-508
The author explores the idea of woman as a social construct, and suggests that law is constructed around the needs of men. He claims that this masculine identification is built on a bipolar ideology which sees femininity as submissiveness, dependence, and domesticity, and reinforces male control of sexuality and maternity. He discusses the role of constitutional law in the reconstruction of social order, and women as a living metaphor of society's problems with autonomy. The alternative conception which he proposes would modify the system's orientation and account for women's values. He reviews Gilligan's care/justice paradigm, the interdependence of the new language, and doctrines and labels in constitutional law, and discusses consciousness raising in the

larger social process.

Jean E. Keet, "Women and the Law: the Charter of Rights and Freedoms" (1985) 7 _Canadian Criminology Forum_ **103-115**

The author evaluates the potential and limitations of the Canadian CHARTER OF RIGHTS AND FREEDOMS to combat discrimination against women through an examination of the relationship between capitalism, the state, and the law, and the way these structures give rise to substantive inequality. She reviews case law which illustrates historical barriers to equality and women's struggles for minimal gain. She warns that "extra-legal variables," such as the fact that the CHARTER was written, and will be interpreted, mainly by men, are important to consider. The article concludes that there are a variety of socially based myths and ideologies, with the common theme of patriarchy, which form the foundation of law and legal interpretation.

Celia Laframboise and Leigh West, "The Case of All-Male Clubs: Freedom to Associate or License to Discriminate?" (1987-1988) 2 _Canadian Journal of Women and the Law_ **335-362**

The fact that exclusionary practices of all-male clubs have prevented women from full commercial and political participation in their communities has recently been recognized by the U.S. Supreme Court. The authors think that a Canadian constitutional challenge is likely to come in the form of a CHARTER OF RIGHTS AND FREEDOMS attack on provincial Human Rights legislation. They outline legal arguments for such a challenge, as well as the possible defenses by male clubs, and predict women's equality rights will prevail where a club is not truly private and where its commercial purpose is predominant over its "expressive" function.

Kathleen A. Lahey, "The Canadian Charter of Rights and Pornography: Toward a Theory of Actual Gender Equality" (1984-5) 20 _New England Law Review_ **649-685**

Part of a Symposium on Pornography, this article discusses the split, both personal and political, in the feminist position on pornography. The author contends that the liberal pursuit of freedom cannot be accomplished without the subjection of women and the use of pornography. The role of the state in achieving feminist goals is viewed differently by libertarians, who oppose state intervention; marxists who think that state domination will result in more domination of women; and radical feminists who believe that the empowerment of women will occur with minimizing the role of the state. She concludes that the equality provisions of the Canadian CHARTER OF RIGHTS AND FREE-DOMS may be available for arguments against pornography as discrimination, not as a form of speech.

Kathleen A. Lahey, "Feminist Theories of (In)Equality" (1985) 3 *Wisconsin Women's Law Journal* 5-27
Part of the 1986 Feminism and Legal Theory Conference, this article discusses the meaning of "equality," and judicial interpretation of equality in the United States and Canada. The author argues that sexist, racist, classist, and heterosexist biases have compelled an "inherently conservative" interpretation of equality, which is, in fact, actual inequality pronounced in the name of abstract theoretical equality. Within this interpretation, elimination of actual equality is reasoned to be special treatment, and "affirmative action" -- the means to ameliorate the material consequences of inequality -- was and is contained by narrow interpretation by the judiciary. She concludes that only a theory of inequality is acceptable for challenging the complex causes of oppression and subordination.

Sylvia A. Law, "Rethinking Sex and the Constitution" (1984) 132 *University of Pennsylvania Law Review* 955-1039
The author develops a constitutional test for the legitimacy of laws which distinguish between men and women in terms of sex-based biological differences. She examines the conceptual and historical reasons that courts scrutinize explicit sex-based classifications, while ignoring sex-specific biological classifications. The Supreme Court, she reports, now justifies scrutiny of explicit sex-based classifications based upon "real" differences between men and women. Her central thesis is that a sex equality doctrine must reconcile the reality of categorical biological differences with the ideal of human equality by distinguishing between laws that classify on the basis of sex and those which govern reproduction, recognizing that laws governing reproduction implicate equality concerns. She proposes the following two-part test which she applies to the case law: (1) does the law have a significant impact on perpetuating the inequality of women and; (2) can it be justified as the

best means of serving a compelling state purpose?

Legal Theory Students, University of Victoria, "Understanding Equality: A Reply to Dale Gibson" (1990) 1:3 *Constitutional Forum: Forum Constitutionnel* **18-19**

This is a response to an earlier article by Dale Gibson [see:Gibson, "The Nature of Equality: Apples and Oranges/Chests and Breasts" (1989) 1:1 *Constitutional Forum: Forum Constitutionnel* 3]. Following class discussion of the article, the students summarized their collective comments, which include a criticism that Gibson conceded "an awful lot to the status quo of inequality," questioned his underlying assumptions, which they claim to be primarily heterosexual and male, and criticized his trivialization of the equality issue in both his choice of title and his choice of hypotheticals.

Margaret Leopold and Wendy King, "Compulsory Heterosexuality, Lesbians, and the Law: The Case for Constitutional Protection" (1985-1986) 1 *Canadian Journal of Women and the Law* **163-186**

For annotation, see Chapter 12: **LESBIANISM AND SEXUAL ORIENTATION.**

Angela A. Liston, "Pornography and the First Amendment: The Feminist Balance" (1985) 27 *Arizona Law Review* **415-435**

This article examines the legal distinction between pornography and obscenity, and its roots in religious values. The author reviews the Indianapolis anti-pornography ordinance and the grounds on which it was deemed unconstitutional. In its place, she proposes a model statute creating a narrow category of actionable speech based on a finding of "violent depictions" of women. Principles of free speech require the burden of proof to be on the plaintiff; however, the author proposes grounds both for finding harm to women and satisfying the MILLER obscenity test [MILLER v. CALIFORNIA (413 U.S. 15 (1973))]. The author concludes that remedies in pornography actions serve a dual function: they are incentives to women, and deterrents to pornographers.

Marilyn J. Maag, "The Indianapolis Pornography Ordinance: Does the Right to Free Speech Outweigh Pornography's Harm to Women?" (1985)

54 University of Cincinnati Law Review 249-269
    This article describes the alleged harmful effects of pornography on
women, and examines the Indianapolis ordinance which characterizes
pornography as a form of sex discrimination and allows civil actions by
those harmed by it. The author analyzes the United States Supreme
Court's decision that the ordinance was unconstitutional, and concludes
that it was correct. She advocates the use of other legal methods of
reducing the presence and effect of pornography that do not abridge the
right to free speech.

**Catharine MacKinnon, "Pornography, Civil Rights, and Speech" (1985)
20 *Harvard Civil Rights and Civil Liberties Law Review* 1-70**
    This is a feminist critique of pornography which defines por-
nography as a civil rights violation. The author claims the modern
formulation of obscenity is a male definition of morality, perpetuated and
legitimized because men are in power. Pornography constructs the social
reality of gender, and renders invisible gender subordination and gender
inequality. This inequality has become institutionalized in law. The
Minneapolis ordinance drafted by MacKinnon and Dworkin defines pornography as a practice of sex discrimination, and gives women who are
injured by it civil remedies against those who benefit from the harm.
The author argues that women are harmed as participants, viewers, and
victims of pornography, and claims that because women are victims of
systemic inequality perpetuated by pornography, institutional support for
sexual equality is essential.

**Catharine MacKinnon, "Sex Equality and Nation-Building in Canada:
The Meech Lake Accord" (1990) 25 *Tulsa Law Journal* 735-757**
    For annotation, see Chapter 10: **LEGAL HISTORY.**

**Catharine MacKinnon, "Unthinking ERA Thinking -- Book Review:
Jane J. Mansbridge, WHY WE LOST THE ERA (1986)" (1987) 54
University of Chicago Law Review 759-771**
    For annotation, see Chapter 16: **BOOK REVIEWS.**

**Deborah L. Markowitz, "In Pursuit of Equality: One Woman's Work
to Change the Law" (1989) 11 *Women's Rights Law Reporter* 73-97**

For annotation, see Chapter 10: **LEGAL HISTORY.**

Thurgood Marshall, "Justice Thurgood Marshall's Remarks on the Bicentennial of the U.S. Constitution" (1987) 13 _Signs: Journal of Women in Culture and Society_ **2-6**
For annotation, see Chapter 6: **FIRST NATIONS AND RACE.**

Sheilah L. Martin, "Canada's Abortion Law and the Canadian Charter of Rights and Freedoms" (1986) 1 _Canadian Journal of Women and the Law_ **339-384**
For annotation, see Chapter 1: **ABORTION AND REPRODUCTION.**

Sheilah L. Martin, "The New Abortion Legislation" (1990) 1:2 _Constitutional Forum: Forum Constitutionnel_ **5-7, 20**
For annotation, see Chapter 1: **ABORTION AND REPRODUCTION.**

Gwen C. Mathewson, "Security of the Person, Equality and Abortion in Canada" [1989] _University of Chicago Legal Forum_ **251-280**
For annotation, see Chapter 1: **ABORTION AND REPRODUCTION.**

Ann Elizabeth Mayer, "Law and Women in the Middle East" (1984) 8:2 _Cultural Survival Quarterly_ **49**
The author argues that under Islamic law, Middle Eastern women enjoy relative equality in political rights, access to education, professional opportunities, and salaries, and that property and business rights existed before they were available to western women. It is in the area of family law and inheritance, she claims, that Middle Eastern women are severely disadvantaged and dominated. She reports, however, that except in Saudi Arabia, the male political elite has attempted some reform in order to modernize society, often in advance of social evolution. The resurgence of Islamic fundamentalism and a move towards religious conservatism not only threatens the reform, but also the removal of established women's rights. Some fundamentalists are calling for rigid

sexual segregation, the elimination of coeducation and jobs outside the home, restriction of political rights, prohibition on birth control and abortion, imposition of dress codes, and the removal of women from the legal profession and the judiciary.

Sandra K. McCallum, "Women and the Charter of Rights and Freedoms" (1986) _DeNovo Printemps_ 12-14

The author examines the equality provisions in the Canadian CHARTER OF RIGHTS AND FREEDOMS, the historical problems with the meaning of equality within the Canadian BILL OF RIGHTS, and the potential application of these provisions for obtaining equality. She argues that CHARTER interpretation must in some way accommodate the "womb factor," that is, that the female alone has the capacity to bear children.

A. Anne McLellan, "Legal Implications of the Persons Case" (1989) 1:1 _Constitutional Forum: Forum Constitutionnel_ 11-14

This article discusses the PERSONS CASE [see: RE SECTION 24 OF THE B.N.A. ACT [1930] 1 D.L.R. 98] in which the word "persons" in the Canadian Constitution was held to include female persons. The author examines aspects of this case which are of continuing relevance to women -- namely, the hostile stance of the federal government to the claims made by women, the court's non-employment of originalist interpretive techniques, and the potential lobbying strategies which are of continued assistance to women. She also discusses the change in women's goals from formal equality as sought in the PERSONS CASE, to substantive equality as presently sought by women in modern society.

M. L. McConnell, "'Even by Commonsense Morality": MORGEN- TALER, BOROWSKI and the Constitution of Canada" (1989) 68 _Canadian Bar Review_ 765-796

For annotation, see Chapter 1: ABORTION AND REPRODUC- TION.

Jennifer McKenna, "Symposium on Women's Rights in International Law" (1987) 9 _Whittier Law Review_ 407-411

Part of a Symposium on Women's Rights in International Law, this article provides a fifteen year history of how the United Nations has dealt with the issue of women's "globally systemic unequal status" through international legal mechanisms. It outlines the contents of the "World Plan of Action" adopted during the 1975 U.N. conference in Mexico City, as well as some of the elements in the U.N. Convention on the Elimination of All Forms of Discrimination Against Women adopted by the General Assembly in 1979.

Theodor Meron, "Enhancing the Effectiveness of the Prohibition of Discrimination Against Women" (1990) 84 _American Journal of International Law_ 213-217
This Editorial Comment examines the adoption of the Convention on the Elimination of All Forms of Discrimination Against Women by the General Assembly of the United Nations. The Convention's weaknesses are discussed, and four possible kinds of improvement are suggested.

Martha Minow, "Speaking of Silence -- Book Review: Kristin Bumiller, THE CIVIL RIGHTS SOCIETY: THE SOCIAL CONSTRUCTION OF VICTIMS (1988)" (1988) 43 _University of Miami Law Review_ 493-511
For annotation, see Chapter 16: **BOOK REVIEWS.**

Martha Minow, "The Supreme Court 1986 Term, Foreword: Justice Engendered" (1987) 101 _Harvard Law Review_ 10-45
The author describes the varieties of individualism, including categories like gender, race, ethnicity, and class, which are used to presume real differences, and claims that unfairness can result under the guise of objectivity. In her view, the dilemma of difference has three versions: the re-creation of difference by noticing it or ignoring it; the riddle of neutrality; and the choice between broad discretion and individualized decisions. She examines the 1986 decisions of the U.S. Supreme Court using the difference framework, and finds that gender, colour, and class continue to present challenges. The persistence of the assumption that men are the standard moves the author to argue for a commitment to approach questions of difference differently, seeking out our unstated assumptions, and she recommends two exercises to help to deepen and broaden our perspective. This is crucial, she suggests, for judges who debate the coercive forces of law. For there is no simple answer, and it

is important that they welcome complexity and challenge complacency, and render judgments in a way that is committed to making meaning.

Selene Mize, "A Critique of a Proposal by Radical Feminists to Censor Pornography Because of its Sexist Message" (1988) 6 *Otago Law Review* 589-614

This article analyzes the feminist arguments advanced by Women Against Pornography that pornography be regulated due to its false and damaging depiction of female sexuality. The author takes the view that WAP's definition of pornography is overly broad. She claims that feminists have not substantiated their position that pornography perpetuates inequality, and rejects the view that its characters are perceived as representative of all women. She concludes that WAP's proposed legislative changes would unduly restrict free speech. Furthermore, she suggests, it may cause a backlash which would hinder future progress toward sexual equality, and re-enforce the notion that women require legislative protection from men.

Martha J. Morgan, "Founding Mothers: Women's Voices and Stories in the 1987 Nicaraguan Constitution" (1990) 70 *Boston University Law Review* 1-107

For annotation, see Chapter 10: **LEGAL HISTORY.**

Karen A. Morrisey, "Artificial Insemination By Donor: Practical and Legal Issues Involved in Single Motherhood" (1985) 1 *Wisconsin Women's Law Journal* 97-119

For annotation, see Chapter 1: **ABORTION AND REPRODUCTION.**

David W. Mossop, "A Discussion of Systemic Discrimination in a Constitutional Forum" (1985) 43 *Advocate* 779-784

Section 15 of the Canadian CHARTER OF RIGHTS AND FREEDOMS raises the question whether the doctrine of systemic discrimination has been entrenched. The author's definition is "a legally protected action which is neutral on its face but which has a disproportionate adverse impact on a specified group that is protected by a civil rights statute or constitutional amendment." He discusses its origins in the equal protection clause of the U.S. Constitution, and the public issues it raised. He proposes a legal test for violation of s. 15 through systemic discrimination.

Mary Beth Norton, "The Constitutional Status of Women in 1787" (1988) 6 _Law and Inequality_ 7-15
    For annotation, see Chapter 10: **LEGAL HISTORY.**

Karen O'Connor and Lee Epstein, "Sex and the Supreme Court: An Analysis of Judicial Support For Gender-Based Claims" (1983) 64 _Social Science Quarterly_ 327-331
    For annotation, see Chapter 6: **FIRST NATIONS AND RACE.**

Christopher Osakwe, "Equal Protection of Law in Soviet Constitutional Law and Theory -- A Comparative Analysis" (1985) 59 _Tulane Law Review_ 974-1013
    The author examines the Soviet conception of equal justice, which has as its purpose de facto equality of all persons. The scheme distinguishes various forms of equality: individual and group; procedural and substantive; social, economic, and cultural; and civil and political equality. He concludes that the Soviet equality regime is closer to the American conservative-majoritarian trend, than it is to the liberal-activist position.

Lynne Pearlman and T. Brettel Dawson, "The Shaping of Equality" (1989) 10:5 _Broadside_ 8-9
    The authors examine the decade of the 80's in Canadian law relating to equality, the formation of the Women's Legal Education and Action Fund (LEAF), and the successes and failures of equality litigation. They conclude that while the Supreme Court of Canada is showing increasingly sophisticated analysis of equality issues, feminists cannot rely solely on the courts, but must maintain political lobbying and strong female coalitions.

Marilyn L. Pilkington, "The Canadian Charter of Rights and Freedoms: Impact on Economic Policy and Economic Liberty Regarding Women in Employment" (1988) 17 _Manitoba Law Journal_ 267-289

The Canadian CHARTER OF RIGHTS AND FREEDOMS does not guarantee equality, nor does it impose affirmative obligations on governments to achieve equality. In an analysis of s.15(1), the author argues that "discrimination" be defined as simple "distinction," in order to ensure that justification of inequality comply with s. 15(2), or with the onus and standard of proof required by ss. 1 and 28. She analyzes each of these sections; discusses the impact of the CHARTER on wage equity and pensions; and outlines the nature of the inequality between men and women in employment.

Deborah C. Poff, "Feminism and Canadian Justice: How Far Have We Come?" (1990) 2:1 _Journal of Human Justice_ 93-104

This paper discusses the impact of the Canadian CHARTER OF RIGHTS AND FREEDOMS on women's social and economic status, and the role that feminists can play in changing the Canadian justice system. The author argues that the CHARTER has done little to improve the status of women, and recommends that despite this, and even though the ultimate goals of feminism require a radical transformation of the theories of justice, feminists should continue to channel at least some of their energy through the Supreme Court of Canada.

Deana Pollard, "Regulating Violent Pornography" (1990) 43 _Vanderbilt Law Review_ 125-159

The article examines the research used by the 1986 Attorney General's Commission on Pornography in concluding that a causal relationship exists between violent pornography and men's aggression towards women. On basis of this evidence, the author concludes that there is a need for the regulation of such material, but she submits that the ordinance proposed by Catharine MacKinnon and Andrea Dworkin is too vague. She proposes an alternative ordinance for the regulation of violent pornography, and examines the extent to which it will survive constitutional challenge.

Robert C. Post, "Cultural Heterogeneity and Law: Pornography, Blasphemy, and the First Amendment" (1988) 76 _California Law Review_ 297-335

This article considers the question of the kinds of values the first amendment should protect in light of feminist demands for pornography regulation. The author describes three types of legal structures possible in a heterogeneous society: assimilationism, pluralism, and individualism. After concluding that the first amendment is strongly individualist in character, he suggests that the success of the feminist drive for pornography regulation will lie in its ability to provide a convincing pluralist vision of the first amendment.

Mathias Reimann, "Prurient Interest and Human Dignity: Pornography Regulation in West Germany and the United States" (1987-88) 21 _University of Michigan Journal of Law Reform_ 201-253
Part of a Symposium on Pornography, this article compares the regulation of pornography in West Germany and the United States. The standard used in West Germany is "human dignity," whereas the current standard in the United States is "appeal to prurient interest." The American approach views pornography as objectionable because it offends traditional morality. The "human dignity" approach, on the other hand, regulates the material because it is dangerous, not because it is immoral. The author argues that this approach is more consistent with classic American liberal constitutional theory, since it does not require that pornography be found to lie outside the ambit of the first amendment.

Deborah L. Rhode, "Equal Rights in Retrospect" (1983) 1 _Law and Inequality_ 1-72
For annotation, see Chapter 10: **LEGAL HISTORY.**

Deborah L. Rhode, "It May have been Fruitless, but in the Long Run, the Tough Fight over the ERA may have been the Best Thing to Happen to Feminist Politics Since the Suffragette" (1984) 12 _Student Lawyer_ 12-15
For annotation, see Chapter 10: **LEGAL HISTORY.**

David A. J. Richards, "Constitutional Privacy and Homosexual Love" (1986) 14 _New York University Review of Law and Social Change_ 895-905
For annotation, see Chapter 12: **LESBIANISM AND SEXUAL ORIENTATION.**

Stephanie Ridder and Lisa Woll, "Transforming the Grounds: Autonomy and Reproductive Freedom" (1989) 2 *Yale Journal of Law and Feminism* 75-98

For annotation, see Chapter 1: ABORTION AND REPRODUCTION.

S. Rodgers, "Fetal Rights and Maternal Rights: Is There a Conflict?" (1986) 1 *Canadian Journal of Women and the Law* 456-469

For annotation, see Chapter 1: ABORTION AND REPRODUCTION.

Michel Rosenfeld, "Affirmative Action, Justice, and Equalities: A Philosophical and Constitutional Appraisal" (1985) 46 *Ohio State Law Journal* 845-922

This article provides philosophical and constitutional justifications for affirmative action, in terms of a stated conceptual framework of equality. The author justifies the pursuit of affirmative action even when less qualified individuals are given preference over more qualified competitors, under a principle of justice as "reversibility". Though affirmative action may seem radical, it is actually conservative because it "reshuffles" individuals, while keeping existing power structures and hierarchies intact. He concludes that affirmative action is a necessary remedial step toward a system of genuine equality of opportunity.

Albert J. Rosenthal, "International Population Policy and the Constitution" (1987-88) 20 *New York University Journal of International Law and Politics* 301-319

For annotation, see Chapter 1: ABORTION AND REPRODUCTION.

D. Sanders, "Indian Status: A Women's Issue or an Indian Issue?" (1984) 3 *Canadian Native Law Reporter* 31-40

For annotation, see Chapter 6: FIRST NATIONS AND RACE.

Judy Scales-Trent, "Black Women and the Constitution: Finding Our Place, Asserting Our Rights" (1989) 24 *Harvard Civil Rights-Civil Liberties*

Law Review 9-44
For annotation, see Chapter 6: FIRST NATIONS AND RACE.

G. Schachter, "A Private Cause of Action for Abortion Expenses Under State Paternity Statutes" (1982) 7 Women's Rights Law Reporter 63-90
For annotation, see Chapter 1: ABORTION AND REPRODUC-TION.

Lynn Hecht Schafran, "Women in the Courts Today: How Much Has Changed" (1988) 2 Law and Inequality 27-34
Part of a Symposium on the American Constitution and Equality, this article takes an anecdotal approach in an attempt to demonstrate the problems women face as judges, litigators, and participants in the legal process.

Patricia Schulz, "Institutional Obstacles to Equality Between the Sexes" (1986) 9 Women's Studies International Forum 5-11
The author argues that, despite the passage of constitutional amendments conferring equal status on women, practice in Switzerland will not change for years to come. Switzerland is a patriarchal state, where institutions are dominated by men, and women are expected to be in the private sphere. She concludes that change requires that women be treated as a group, and not as individuals.

Andrea J. Seale, "Can the Canada Pension Plan Survive the Charter? Section 15 and Sex (In)Equality" (1985) Queen's Law Journal 441-474
With the advent of the Canadian CHARTER OF RIGHTS AND FREEDOMS, government must ensure that pension plans do not discriminate on the basis of sex. The author looks at s. 15 as it applies to discrimination in benefit eligibility, size of benefits, and survivorship benefits, and compares it to the U.S. BILL OF RIGHTS. She concludes that the Canada Pension Plan must be changed to ensure both that it does not mirror inequality which exists in the workplace, and that its provisions are not based on stereotypical concepts of spousal dependency.

Elizabeth Sheehy, "Canadian Judges and the Law of Rape: Should the Charter Insulate Bias?" (1989) 21 *Ottawa Law Review* 151-197
For annotation, see Chapter 3: CRIMINAL LAW -- RAPE.

Dinah Sheldon, "Address Given at the Fourth Annual International Law Symposium: Improving the Status of Women Through International Law" (1987) 9 *Whittier Law Review* 413 - 418
The author's address to the Symposium on Women's Rights in International Law, entitled IMPROVING THE STATUS OF WOMEN THROUGH INTERNATIONAL LAW, describes the 1979 U.N. Convention on the Elimination of All Forms of Discrimination Against Women, and puts it into context of other U.N. initiatives on freedom from discrimination. She deplores the U.N.'s record in the practice of eliminating discrimination against women, and criticizes the lack of machinery for enforcing the Convention. She nonetheless urges that the United States ratify it.

N. Colleen Sheppard, "Equality, Ideology and Oppression: Women and the Canadian Charter of Rights and Freedoms" (1986) 10 *Dalhousie Law Journal* 195-223
This article examines the tensions between the liberal concept of equality, post-liberal influences, and conservatism, and their relationship to the Canadian CHARTER OF RIGHTS AND FREEDOMS. The legal treatment of women historically is reviewed in light of these contrasting theories. The author notes that anti-discrimination laws often only advance "exceptional" individual women who succeed within a male-defined structure, and that this devalues women's traditional work and values. CHARTER interpretation must consider whether law or social practice injures women and contributes to their subordination. She concludes that interpretation of this sort is dependent more on the ability of the judiciary to develop compassion and empathy for those discriminated against than on any particular theory of equality.

N. Colleen Sheppard, "Recognition of the Disadvantaging of Women" (1990) 35 *McGill Law Journal* 207-234
The author examines the Supreme Court of Canada's approach to constitutional equality, and finds its "purposive" approach -- which rejects "sameness" and embraces "effects" -- encouraging for women concerned

with gender equality.

Suzanna Sherry, "Civic Virtue and the Feminine Voice in Constitutional Adjudication" (1986) 72 Virginia Law Review 543-616

The author uses what she terms a feminine rather than a feminist analysis. In modern jurisprudence, she claims, the masculine vision parallels liberal pluralist theory, while the feminine vision parallels classical republican theory. In contemporary constitutional interpretation the liberal pluralist individualist underlies the theme of autonomy and separation where relationships are secondary. In this non-teleological view of human nature, there is no unitary end. The concept of the good life or abstract idealization of the universal human telos requires an infrastructure of independence tied together by the necessity of society. In the classical paradigm, on the other hand, the central theme is connection. The intersubjective vision of self and self-knowledge as a communal project, with the community shaping of aspirations and shared telos, results in the conscious selection and ordering of values. The author argues that republicanism values the good of the whole over the good of individuals. The role of government is to define communal values. Women's unique perspective in law and jurisprudence -- that they have a functionally different world view -- is republican, because the feminine perspective sees the individual as an interconnected member of a community. The feminine voice in jurisprudence may aid in ameliorating distortions which have been brought about by the overly individualistic liberal paradigm.

Suzanna Sherry, "An Essay Concerning Toleration" (1987) 71 Minnesota Law Review 963-989

For annotation, see Chapter 5: FEMINIST THEORY -- GENERAL.

Suzanna Sherry, "Two Hundred Years Ago Today" (1988) 2 Law and Inequality 43-61

For annotation, see Chapter 10: LEGAL HISTORY.

Salina M. Shrofel, "Equality Rights and Law Reform in Saskatchewan: An Assessment of the Charter Compliance Process" (1985) 1 Canadian

Journal of Women and the Law 108-118

After the Canadian CHARTER OF RIGHTS AND FREEDOMS was declared in 1982, there was a three year delay in the enactment of s. 15 (equality rights) to allow governments to review their legislation and have it conform. The article examines the process followed in Saskatchewan, and comments on the Review Committee's success in identifying discriminatory legislation and the effectiveness of its recommendations and subsequent changes. The author reports that the Committee was not composed of people with expertise in women's and human rights issues, that it concentrated primarily on making gender neutral wording changes to statutes, that it made erroneous assumptions about women's equality, and that it failed to consider the interrelatedness of statutes and their culminative effect on women. She concludes that the Committee lacked imagination, and failed to understand the nature and extent of systemic discrimination.

Lynn Smith, "Could the Meech Lake Accord Affect the Protection of Equality Rights for Women and Minorities in Canada?" (1990) 1:2 *Constitutional Forum: Forum Constitutionnel* **12, 17-20**

The author examines a proposed Canadian Constitutional amendment -- the Meech Lake Accord -- and discusses the potential impact this amendment would have on women's equality rights as guaranteed in the Canadian CHARTER OF RIGHTS AND FREEDOMS. She discusses both the political arguments initiated by the amendment, as well as the legal arguments with respect to interpretation of the Accord and the CHARTER.

Elizabeth Spahn, "On Sex and Violence" (1984-85) 20 *New England Law Review* **629 - 647**

Part of a Symposium on Pornography, this article examines the feminist anti-pornography program, and its main critics, advocates of civil rights, free speech, and gender neutrality. The author concludes by suggesting that the debate focus on a new value about sex: "Taking sexual pleasure in another person's pain is wrong."

Christina Spaulding, "Anti-Pornography Laws as A Claim for Equal Respect: Feminism, Liberalism and Community" (1988-89) 4 *Berkeley Women's Law Journal* **128-165**

The author argues that anti-pornography ordinances have challenged the absolutist theory underlying the civil libertarian position on the First Amendment, and that this challenge permits, for the first time, a direct assessment of the conflict between free speech and equality. The author submits that this conflict should not automatically be resolved in favour of speech rights. Analyzing male dominance as the power which defines reality from no apparent perspective, she proposes a broader notion of equal respect that cannot be dismissed simply by the privileged justification of liberal principles.

Barbara Stark, "Book Review: Malvina Halberstam and Elizabeth F. Defeis, WOMEN'S LEGAL RIGHTS: INTERNATIONAL COVENANTS; AN ALTERNATIVE TO THE ERA? (1987)" (1990) 12 _Women's Rights Law Reporter_ 51-57
For annotation, see Chapter 16: BOOK REVIEWS.

Barbara Stark, "Constitutional Analysis of the Baby M Decision" (1988) 11 _Harvard Women's Law Journal_ 19-52
For annotation, see Chapter 1: ABORTION AND REPRODUCTION.

V. Sterling, "Pension Plans and Sex Discrimination" (1985) 3 _Canadian Journal of Insurance Law_ 66-78
Women on average live longer than men, and therefore must either contribute more to pension plans or receive a lower monthly pension on retirement. Pension plans treat each individual as having the same characteristics as the class, even though only one woman in six will actually live longer than the average male. The Employment Standards Act of Ontario appears to adopt sexual equality, but in fact allows employers to discriminate. Using liberal jurisprudential theory, the author discusses the constitutionality of such discrimination, with reference to the equality provisions of the Canadian CHARTER OF HUMAN RIGHTS AND FREEDOMS. American constitutional and civil rights law is compared.

Marcy Strauss, "Sexist Speech in the Workplace" (1990) 25 _Civil Liberties Law Review_ 1-51

This article examines whether sexist speech could be protected under the First Amendment. The author canvasses the value of free speech, and the state's interest in eliminating sexist speech from the workplace, and proposes a solution for the regulation of such speech which is compatible with First Amendment protection of free speech.

David B. Sugarman and Murray E. Straus, "Indicators of Gender Equality for American States and Regions" (1988) 20 _Social Indicators Research_ 229-270

The authors measured gender equality in the political, economic, and legal spheres state by state, and prepared an overall Gender Equality Index. They report that women measured from a low of 19% to a high of 60% as against men. In the political sphere, participation in the legislatures, courts, and municipalities was studied, while in the legal sphere certain laws calling for equality were examined.

Cass R. Sunstein, "Pornography and the First Amendment" [1986] _Duke Law Journal_ 589-626

This article discusses the nature and desirability of "viewpoint neutrality" in the adjudication of pornography and the First Amendment. Pornography is characterized as both a significant social problem and "low-value" speech which is entitled to less constitutional protection than other forms of speech. The author argues that anti-pornography legislation enhances free speech; and he rejects the argument that anti-pornography legislation is based on the suppression of a viewpoint.

Cass R. Sunstein, "Six Theses on Interpretation" (1989) 6 _Constitutional Commentary_ 91-95

The author argues that the American Supreme Court's privacy cases also involve discrimination on the basis of sex. He reviews the decision in GRISWOLD v. CONNECTICUT (381 U.S. 479 (1965)) on the use of contraceptives, and the decision in ROE v. WADE (410 U.S. 113 (1973)) on abortion, and claims that they can be "understood in terms of social subordination or ... discriminatory intent."

Bruce A. Taylor, "Hard-Core Pornography: A Proposal for a Per Se Rule" (187-88) 21 _University of Michigan Journal of Law Reform_ 255-281

Part of a Symposium on Pornography, this article discusses the current American test for obscenity, and provides a detailed description of the terms used in it. The author argues that current obscenity laws should be supplemented by a per se rule regarding hard-core pornography, which he defines as any visual material in which penetration, manipulation, or ejaculation of the genitals is clearly visible. Distribution or possession of such material should be banned outright. He concludes that concerns for freedom of expression are outbalanced by the evil that results from permitting circulation of this material.

Sherry Teachnor, "The U.N. Convention on The Elimination of All Forms of Discrimination Against Women: An Effective Tool to Combat Discrimination in the 20th Century" (1987) 9 *Whittier Law Review* 419-422
This is a summary of the remarks of Sherry Teachnor to the Inter-American Bar Association Convention in Buenos Aires May 10, 1987. Part of a Symposium on Women's Rights in International Law, the address focuses on the U.N. Convention on the Elimination of All Forms of Discrimination Against Women, and its importance to IABA members and their clients. The Convention can "provide a definition of what equality for women and men means under a constitutional provision for this equality; provide a description of what are discriminatory practices or effects; and, provide a mechanism for the international supervision of obligations that have been accepted by those states of the Americas which have ratified the Convention."

Rosemarie Tong, "Women, Pornography, and the Law" (1987) 73(5) *Academe: Bulletin of the American Association of University Professors* 14
The author argues that law is not the weapon with which feminists ought to fight pornography, and that feminists must re-examine political alliances, legal theories, and philosophical assumptions. In the author's view, judicial commitment to free speech is so strong, that without positive proof that pornography incites men to abuse women sexually, immediately and directly, they will not ban it. The defamation approach is unsatisfactory because intent is difficult to prove. She concludes that since the civil rights approach has been properly declared unconstitutional, the real weapon is education and not law.

Jill McCalla Vickers, "Majority Equality Issues of the Eighties" (1983) 1 _Canadian Human Rights Yearbook_ 47-72
This article provides the author's speculations with respect to how the Canadian CHARTER OF RIGHTS AND FREEDOMS will be used by different groups to further their equality demands. The author claims that the CHARTER is the first impetus for Canadian society to consider seriously equality issues, and she provides a brief explanation of the major equality theories.

Anne T. Vitale, "Inmate Abortions - The Right to Government Funding Behind the Prison Gates" (1980) 48 _Fordham Law Review_ 550-567
For annotation, see Chapter 1: ABORTION AND REPRODUCTION.

Deborah A. Wean, "Real Protection for African Women? The African Charter on Human and Peoples' Rights" (1988) 2 _Emory Journal of Dispute Resolution_ 425-457
The author compares the provisions of the African CHARTER ON HUMAN AND PEOPLES' RIGHTS to other regional and international instruments, and analyzes its procedural provisions. She looks at the CHARTER in relation to marriage, the family, and genital operations in English speaking sub-Saharan countries, and finds that women's rights are in conflict with protection of religious freedom, and duties to traditional family structure and the community. She suggests amendments which would strengthen the CHARTER as a tool for resolving women's human rights concerns.

Robin West, "The Authoritarian Impulse in Constitutional Law" (1988) 42 _University of Miami Law Review_ 531-552
Many theorists have argued for greater public participation in constitutional debates, where questions of morality are decided. The author agrees that methods for resolving moral questions in the United States are flawed, but does not agree that the solution is greater community involvement in existing debates. Her view is that the process of constitutional debate is itself flawed, because it is based on an authoritarian, not a normative, tradition. This is so because the courts deny that they are debating moral issues, and claim to be applying an

already existing authority, the Constitution, to the case at hand.

Robin West, "Equality Theory, Marital Rape, and the Promise of the Fourteenth Amendment" (1990) 42 _Florida Law Review_ 45-79

Part of a Symposium on Women and the Law: Goals for the 1990s, this article claims that the marital rape exemption, whether statutory or common law, is a denial of a women's constitutional right to equal protection under the law. Within this context, the author raises issues of equal protection ideology and equality theory, and argues that the endurance of the marital rape exemption illustrates both the inadequacies of modern equal protection law, and how the adjudicative context has skewed an understanding of equal protection laws. She argues that the marital rape exception is unconstitutional under any meaning of equality protection: dominant rationality, antisubordination, or the author's "pure protection" understanding. She concludes with the claim that the exemption is simply the most brutal of indications of the trivialization of women's interest in physical and sexual security; acquaintance rape and date rape are other manifestations. However, until women have this security, their public lives and private contributions will be limited by legal vulnerability built on social and legal inferiority and individualized sovereignty.

Robin West, "The Supreme Court 1989 Term -- Foreword: Taking Freedom Seriously" (1990) 104 _Harvard Law Review_ 43-106

Using Czechoslovak President Vaclav Havel's post-democratic political philosophy as an alternative to the liberal legalism on which American liberalism's commitment to the individual has been defended, this article offers "a strategy for maintaining the freedom of the individual" which is based upon civic and communitarian responsibility, instead of upon liberal legalism's rights. The author describes recent United States Supreme Court decisions from both traditional liberal commitments and liberal jurisprudence; contrasts Havel's post-democratic liberal theory with liberal legalism and with modern American civic republicanism; offers a limited critique of Havel's liberalism; and urges the adoption of "responsibility-based liberalism" as a basis for criticizing the Supreme Court's retreat from liberal values. The article concludes with the author's speculations with respect to the consequences of reformulating American liberal ideals in a fashion that joins responsibility with rights.

Wendy Williams, "The Equality Crisis: Some Reflections on Culture, Courts, and Feminism" (1982) 7 *Women's Rights Law Reporter* **175-200**

Part of a Symposium on Reproductive Rights, this article discusses the role of the United States Supreme Court in equality issues and the effect of the male cultural standard on the determination of these issues. It also examines the cultural limits on the woman's side. In conclusion, the author questions whether feminists should strive for equality or justice.

Bertha Wilson, "Law In Society: The Principle of Sexual Equality" (1983) 13 *Manitoba Law Journal* **221-233**

The author, now a Supreme Court of Canada Justice, argues that the main impediment to the implementation of the sexual equality provisions in the Canadian CHARTER OF RIGHTS AND FREE-DOMS is prevailing social attitudes with respect to women. These attitudes are the result of conditioning by church, school, and family, each of which plays a key role in the formation of attitudes inimical to sexual equality. She concludes with a discussion of two subsidiary impediments -- the provision of adequate enforcement mechanisms, and the difficulty inherent in the concept of social equality itself.

Ernest H. Wohlenberg, "Correlates of Equal Rights Amendment Ratification" (1980) 60 *Social Science Quarterly* **676-684**

Writing at the time that thirty-five of the required thirty-eight states had ratified the Equal Rights Amendment, the author develops eight hypotheses on the characteristics which affect passage of the amendment. He looks at the states for such things as innovation, religious fundamentalism, liberal orientation, and historical record for ratifying amendments, and then attempts to predict the final outcome of the ratification process.

CHAPTER 3
CRIMINAL LAW

General

Roy L. Austin, "Liberation and Female Criminality in England and Wales" (1981) 21 *British Journal of Criminology* 371-385
This article is a critique of the method and conclusions of feminist researcher Carol Smart. Smart's research rejected the theory that increases in the rate of female criminality were related to the women's movement.

Roy L. Austin, "Women's Liberation and Increases in Minor, Major and Occupational Offences" (1982) 20 *Criminology* 407-409
The author outlines and graphs statistical information related to such factors as increased female participation in the work force, rising divorce statistics, and increased female criminal behaviour rates. His research starts in 1966, the year that he concludes marks the beginning of the women's movement. His thesis is that the increase of female independence, promoted by the women's movement and indicated by the first two sets of statistics, is causally related to the more rapid increase in female criminality, as compared to the increase in male criminality over the same period.

R. Beaudry, "Survol Bibliographique de la Littérature Criminologique Féminine" (1983) 16:2 *Criminologie* 121-125
The author discusses the revolution in the recent literature on the approach to treating female criminality, noting that earlier studies were coloured by preconceptions about the natural characteristics of women. She surveys the current debates on the effects of feminism, and the changes in economic opportunities and the psycho-social milieu, on the rate of female criminality. The paternalism of judges, and inequality of treatment for female offenders, are identified as major themes in the

literature.

M. A. Bertrand, "Femmes et justice: Problèmes de l'intervention"
(1983) 16:2 *Criminologie* 77-87

The author claims that problems of morality and legitimacy surround the imposition of penal sanctions. Observing that sanctions are not applied equally, the author discusses the absence of the four "fundamentals of criminality" in most infractions committed by women. Penal interventions against women, she concludes, are a method of confirming women in their inferior social roles.

Steven Box and Chris Hale, "Liberation and Female Criminality in
England and Wales" (1983) 23 *British Journal of Criminology* 35-49

This article is a sociological study of female criminality. Its authors attack the methodology of many researchers, for failing to control for factors such as the changing population base of females available to commit crimes. Their study detected no statistical relationship between four identified measures of female liberation and female crime rates in England and Wales, and conclude that factors like the rate of unemployment and the changing practices of processing female criminals do appear to be related to female crime rates.

Maureen Cain, "Towards Transgression: New Directions in Feminist
Criminology" (1990) 18 *International Journal of the Sociology of Law* 1-17

This is the revised text of Cain's speech when she was presented with the Sellin-Glueck Award by the American Society of Criminology in November 1988. She is concerned that feminist criminology continues to be marginalized and reviews the three traditional approaches -- namely, unequal treatment, female criminology, and women as victims. She then offers the transgressive alternative which incorporates three strategies, reflexivity, de-construction, and re-construction. She describes her alternative, through the example of policing the sexuality of girls and women, and emphasizes the need to do "women only" studies, because the questions are about women, not about crime. She claims that "criminological discourse cannot think gender ... [it] does not see maleness ...," and concludes that feminists have to transgress criminology "in order to understand men and women as offenders, victims, defendants and prisoners."

Meda Chesney-Lind, "Girl's Crime and Women's Place: Toward a Feminist Model of Female Delinquency" (1989) 35 *Crime and Delinquency* 5-29

The author first describes how the traditional approaches towards delinquency have focused on male delinquency, and how this androcentric approach ignores the different causes of female delinquency. She further criticizes the juvenile justice system, which she says has sexualized and oppressed female delinquents, many of whom became involved in the system when fleeing abuse. She describes the feminist perspective on the problem, and notes that young women shaped by the patriarchal society often become involved in crimes that exploit their femaleness.

Dorothy E. Chunn and Robert J. Menzies, "Gender Madness and Crime: The Reproduction of Patriarchal and Class Relations in a Psychiatric Court Clinic" (1990) 1:2 *Journal of Human Justice* 33-54

This article examines how forensic clinicians, especially psychiatrists, help maintain the "constructed normality" of capitalist, patriarchal relations in contemporary liberal democratic states, through a comparison of decision-making about accused women and men at a Canadian pre-trial clinic. Using quantitative and qualitative data, the authors argue that while clinicians rarely express overt bias towards "clients," their assessments for the courts are shaped by intertwined assumptions about class and gender embodied in familial ideology which condemn most of the assessors to negative outcomes and which transform moral judgements about accused persons into "scientific" ones. In this way, the authors conclude, clinicians individualize and depoliticize the deviance of their "clients," and provide the rationale for decisions made by other cercarial agents to sanction offenders.

Lorenne M. G. Clark, "Boys Will Be Boys: Beyond the Badgley Report" (1986) 2 *Canadian Journal of Women and the Law* 135-149

The author focuses on what she calls the paternalistic attitude of the Badgley Report (Report of the Committee on Sexual Offences Against Children and Youths), and its lack of emphasis on the fact that almost all offenders are male. She suggests that the report's sense of outrage, while not misplaced, fails to consider that the problem is part of the existing social structure, and not just the isolated deviance of a few men. She argues that despite the pervasiveness of the problem, the authors of the report do not recognize that the entire male sexual socialization process is implicated. She further points out that the report's proposed solutions are superficial, and designed to reduce, not eliminate, the problem.

Michelle Clark and Sally Smith, "Canada's Female Young Offenders: Isolated and Ignored" (1987) *Breaking the Silence* **18-21**
The authors argue that females charged under the Canadian YOUNG OFFENDER'S ACT face a corrections system ill prepared to handle their special needs. Because their numbers are low in comparison to males charged, they are often isolated and ignored. The lack of appropriate programs is the largest problem facing those in custody or on probation, as most young women are simply put into existing services established for males. There is a need for special programs for retraining for dealing with health matters such as pregnancy, and for counselling. The number of young female offenders is rising, and longer and harsher sentences are being given females as opposed to males.

R. Collette-Carrière and L. Langelier-Biron, "Du Côté des Filles et des Femmes, Leur Délinquance, Leur Criminalité" (1983) 16:2 *Criminologie* **27-45**
This article contains an overview of recent theories and studies concerning female criminality. Among the issues raised are the difficulty of evaluating criminality among girls due to the paucity of official data, and the disparate conclusions reached by researchers. Noting that property crimes account for most of the increase in crime among adult women, the author advocates further research leading to a theory adapted to the contemporary realities of women.

Daniel J. Curran, "The Myth of the 'New' Female Delinquent" (1984) 30 *Crime and Delinquency* **386-399**
The author disputes the argument that there has been an increase in female delinquent activity as a result of the women's movement. He identifies three relevant periods: paternalistic (1960-67); due process (1968-76); and law and order (1977-80). During these periods, he argues, there were significant political and legal shifts in attitude and procedure that resulted in an apparent increase in the rate of female delinquency. His research in the Philadelphia Family Court System reveals that the increase was, in fact, caused by a legal reclassification of

juvenile offences.

Liba Duraj, "The Concept of Female Juvenile Delinquency: A Feminist or Non-Feminist Approach?" (1982) 33 *Juvenile and Family Courts Journal* 25-31

This article discusses the possible causal factors influencing female juvenile delinquency. The author concludes that women's increased participation in the work force, the erosion of sexual stereotypes, and women's greater participation in social development result in a discontinuity between reality and perception. She relates this discontinuity, and the rapid changes in the quality of life, to the increase in female delinquency.

Josefina Figueira-McDonough, "Feminism and Delinquency: In Search of an Elusive Link" (1984) 24 *British Journal of Criminology* 325-343

This article discusses research derived from self-administered questionnaires completed by high school students. The research attempted to test three hypotheses regarding the impact of feminist aspirations on behaviour: equal opportunity theory; frustration theory; and competitive theory. The competitive theory held that a high level of feminist aspiration would lead to high levels of legitimate activity by females seeking to compete with males. This theory received the most support from the research; however the other two hypotheses also received limited support, depending upon certain variables. The author concludes that the benefits of pro-feminist attitudes outweigh the costs, but on the basis of the research, she suggests ways to minimize even those limited costs.

Nancy Finley, Deborah Glaser and Harold Grasmick, "Labor Force Participation, Sex-Role Attitudes, and Female Crime" (1984) 65 *Social Science Quarterly* 703-722

This article analyzes the effect of adult female labour force participation and non-traditional sex-role attitudes on female crime rates. The authors hypothesize that employed females and those with non-traditional sex role attitudes will be more involved in crime than other women, and that their illegal activity rates will be similar to male rates. They conclude that there is a convergence of male and female rates for economic crimes, but not for violent or other types of crime. They discuss the viewpoints of subjectivists, who suggest female crime is linked to masculine traits, and objectivists, who argue that female crime increases are the result of increased opportunity. They conclude that the results of their studies support the objectivist theory.

Geraldine Finn, "Taking Gender Into Account In The 'Theatre of Terror': Violence, Media, and the Maintenance of Male Dominance" (1989-1990) 3 *Canadian Journal of Women and the Law* 375-393
This article examines the relationship between the media and terrorism, and the aspect of terrorism about which there is systematic silence, terrorism against women. The author examines the risk of violence which women face, merely because of being female, namely, assault by "our own" men during "peace," and by "the enemy," when "our own men are at war." She examines media representation of stranger assaults versus affinity assaults, intrafamilial killings by men of women and children, and rape. She concludes that these representations are a form of social control: they ensure women are subordinate and submissive to men.

Nancy Frank, "Book Review: Eleanor M. Miller, STREET WOMEN (1986)" (1985) 4 *Wisconsin Women's Law Journal* 129-133
For annotation, see Chapter 16: BOOK REVIEWS.

Gwen Fraser, "Taking Spousal Assault Seriously: A Philosophical View of Legal Contradiction" (1985) 5 *Windsor Yearbook of Access to Justice* 368-380
The author argues that to deal with spousal assault in Family Court, rather than in criminal proceedings, is to discriminate institutionally, on the basis of sex, against victims of domestic violence. Attempts to justify such a division are not defensible, and are based on archaic, and no longer justifiable, attitudes.

Sylvie Frigon, "Femmes et Héroïnes: Bilan des Connaissances, Limites et Perspectives Nouvelles" (1989) 22:1 *Criminologie* 85-109
This article summarizes results of the current research literature on women and heroin. The author suggests that the research poses several problems, including the use of the male norm in drug addiction studies,

and the consequent marginalization of women. She proposes an analysis of women heroin users as an independent group, and advocates the construction of a general plan to analyze the marginality, deviance, and criminality of women, using radical materialist feminism and theories of social reaction.

Shelley Gavigan, "Women's Crime and Feminist Critiques: A Review of the Literature" (1982) 5:1 *Canadian Criminology Forum* 40-53
The author examines recent criminological literature dealing with women as offenders and victims, and attempts to assess the significance of that work in understanding the oppression of women in capitalist society. She considers the issues of how the disparity in crime rates between men and women have been addressed, the ideology of "women" in various theoretical perspectives, and the relationship between the women's movement and the increase in women's criminal activity. She also includes a brief critique of recent feminist critiques of criminology.

Gloria Geller, "Feminism and Criminal 'Justice': An Uneasy Partnership" (1988) 17:3 *Resources for Feminist Research: Documentation sur la Recherche Féministe* 100-104
This article asks challenging questions about the future goals of the feminist movement in regard to the criminal justice system. The author discusses the public/private dichotomy that exists now in law, and which often serves to subjugate and ignore women's voices. The questions for the future include whether the traditional patriarchal system can ever be modified sufficiently to end women's oppression. Four feminist perspectives -- egalitarianism, integration, radicalism, and socialism -- are outlined, and the author emphasizes that each perspective is an important tool in continuing to analyze the relationship between the state, criminal law, the criminal justice system, and women.

Loraine Gelsthorpe, "Towards a Sceptical Look at Sexism" (1986) 14 *International Journal of the Sociology of Law* 125-152
This article describes a study of a Juvenile Liaison Office in a police station. The author reports that officers view boys and girls differently, and that their perceptions are not compatible with precinct records. The idea that girls are more likely to shoplift, for instance, is not substantiated by records; nor is the assumption that they are becoming

more violent as part of 'women's liberation'. She argues that 'essential truths' must be related to social, political, and cultural contexts, and that recorded behaviour is not sufficient evidence. The micropolitics of the organization, and the sexism mediated by administrative and organizational factors, must also be considered. She reviews current theories, and concludes that the gender oppression of women is a relatively autonomous element of social formation.

Margaret T. Gordon, Stephanie Riger, Robert K. LeBailly, and Linda Heath, "Crime, Women, and the Quality of Urban Life" (1980) 5 *Signs: Journal of Women in Culture and Society* 144-160

This is the report of an empirical study of women's fear of crime, and their increased use of safety precautions in order to avoid becoming a crime victim. The authors conclude that crime rates alone do not explain the study results -- namely, that women report more fear of crime than do men, and that women fear most being victims of rape. They suggest that social policies to reduce women's fears should focus on women's perceived risk of rape, and consequent feelings of vulnerability.

John Hagen, "Toward a Structural Theory of Crime, Race, and Gender: The Canadian Case" (1985) 31 *Crime and Delinquency* 129-146

For annotation, see Chapter 6: FIRST NATIONS AND RACE.

Timothy F. Hartnagel, "Modernization, Female Social Roles, and Female Crime: A Cross National Investigation" (1982) 23 *Sociological Quarterly* 477-489

The author attempts to define a sociological relationship between modernization and female crime rates. Using INTERPOL data from forty countries to derive crime rate statistics, and data from a variety of sources to measure female social role participation, he tests the hypothesis that modernization has a positive effect on female crime rates. The results generally did not support the hypothesis, with only a small effect noted in some types of crime and a negative effect in others. He discusses some of the possible reasons for the unpredicted results, including the suggestion that the level of urbanity chosen was too low. He also concludes that inequality, not poverty, is the important variable impacting on crime rates, either male or female.

Frances Heidensohn, "Models of Justice: Portia or Persephone? Some Thoughts on Equality, Fairness, and Gender in the Field of Criminal Justice" (1986) 14 _International Journal of the Sociology of Law_ 287-297

The article reviews feminist legal literature to determine what in feminist terms is meant when it is claimed that a court has been "unfair" or "unjust" towards women. In a criminal context, the author examines what "justice for women" means, what exists now, and what alternatives are available. She compares the "Portia" model of justice with the "Persephone" model, explaining the values and characteristics of each, and their concepts of justice. She concludes that there is clear evidence of feminist dissatisfaction with traditional concepts of justice. Feminists, she reports, claim that justice for women cannot be measured simply in terms of fair and open treatment of women in the courts. Procedural justice, rather, must be seen in a wider social context, in relation to the disadvantages women experience before they encounter the law.

Kirk Heilbrun, Patricia Griffin Heilbrun and Melwyn Griffin, "Comparing Females Acquitted by Reason of Insanity, Convicted, and Civilly Committed in Florida" (1988) 12 _Law and Human Behavior_ 295-311

This article compares the three groups mentioned in the title from a controlled sample in Florida in order to determine what characteristics are common to the women who successfully use the insanity defense, how long they are hospitalized in comparison to the convicted and civilly committed groups, and what types of psychiatric disorders are most common in each group. The authors conclude that in most of the areas they studied, the group which was acquitted by reason of insanity fell in between the other two groups.

Danielle Laberge and Shirley Roy, "Femmes et criminalité: Le contrôle social est-il sexué? Une analyse des données statistiques québecoises" (1989-1990) 3 _Canadian Journal of Women and the Law_ 457-463

Female offenders are often portrayed stereotypically as victims, as prostitutes, or as committing infanticide. The authors examine the 1977-1985 Quebec statistics with respect to female crime, as compared to male crime, and conclude that behaviour is considered intolerable for different reasons between men and women; that there is an absence of neutrality in regulation of social deviance; and that social control is

carried out in a gendered fashion.   They conclude that criminal
marginality is related to gender.

Reva Landau, "Status Offences: Inequality Before the Law" (1981) 39
University of Toronto Faculty of Law Review 149-168
   The article examines the problems of status offences, particularly
as they apply to children under the Canadian JUVENILE DELIN-
QUENTS ACT (since repealed), and the various provincial child
protection acts. The author notes that more female juvenile offenders
are sentenced to training schools than male, although their rates of arrest
are similar, and she points out that child protection laws, particularly as
they are applied to girls, are discriminatory, ignore due process, and are
open to procedural and human rights abuses, all under the guise of
protection.

Carol Pitcher LaPrairie, "Selected Criminal Justice and Socio-Demo-
graphic Data on Native Women" (1984) 26 _Canadian Journal of_
Criminology 161-169
   For annotation, see Chapter 6: FIRST NATIONS AND RACE.

Lori Leu, "Book Review: Ellen Hawks, FEMINISM ON TRIAL: THE
GINNY FOAT CASE AND ITS MEANING FOR THE FUTURE OF
THE WOMEN'S MOVEMENT (1986); Jean Harris, STRANGER IN
TWO WORLDS (1986)" (1987) 10 _Harvard Women's Law Journal_
327-333
   For annotation, see Chapter 16: BOOK REVIEWS.

M. Los, "Les femmes, le pouvoir et le crime en Pologne" (1983) 16:2
Criminologie 47-66
   This article contains an analysis of the social and economic changes
in Poland since the end of the Second World War, and their relation to
female criminality. The author notes that the greatest part of women's
criminal activity consists of economic crimes against the state; and she
cautions that it is important to recognize that the application of such laws
is very selective, and often politically influenced. Women may function
as scapegoats in such situations, as they rarely occupy the positions of
power that allow men to commit economic crimes with relative impunity.

Catharine MacKinnon, "Toward Feminist Jurisprudence -- Book Review: Ann Jones, WOMEN WHO KILL (1980)" (1982) 34 _Stanford Law Review_ 703-737
>For annotation, see Chapter 16: BOOK REVIEWS.

Otwin Marenin, "Nations not Obsessed with Crime -- Book Review: Freda Alder, NATIONS NOT OBSESSED WITH CRIME (1984)" (1985) 31 _Crime and Delinquency_ 332-333
>For annotation, see Chapter 16: BOOK REVIEWS.

Janice Dickin McGinnis, "Book Review: Christine L. M. Boyle et al., A FEMINIST REVIEW OF CRIMINAL LAW (1985)" (1987) 21 _University of British Columbia Law Review_ 241-246
>For annotation, see Chapter 16: BOOK REVIEWS.

Steven F. Messer and Scott J. South, "The Sex Ratio and Women's Involvement in Crime: A Cross-National Analysis" (1987) 28 _Sociological Quarterly_ 171-186
>This article reports the findings of an international study seeking to link the sex ratio of women to men in sixty countries to women's involvement in crime in three areas: women's victimization, women's protection in the criminal justice system, and women's criminal offences. The results suggest that an undersupply of women decreases women's offending rates significantly, and may protect women from criminal victimization to a certain extent. However it did not seem to influence the female homicide victimization rate.

Eleanor M. Miller, "International Trends In The Study of Female Criminality: An Essay Review" (1983) 7 _Contemporary Crises_ 59-70
>This article provides the author's reflections on monograph and journal contributions to the debate surrounding the statistical increase in criminal offences generally, and to the hypothesis that the "women's liberation movement" has caused the increase.

Judith A. Osborne, "The Crime of Infanticide: Throwing out the Baby with the Bathwater" (1987) 6 _Canadian Journal of Family Law_ 47-59

The author discusses the law of infanticide in Canada, its common law and statutory history, and the recent recommendations that ss. 216 and 590 of the Canadian CRIMINAL CODE relating to infanticide be abolished. She agrees that the law should be abolished, but only for the right reasons. The removal of the crime of infanticide, she insists, must be accompanied by a change in societal values towards women, namely, that they be accorded full responsibility for their actions. The court's traditional leniency towards women who killed their infants, she claims, was based in part on the myth of women's inherent biological weakness. The author concludes that the law should consider women's culpability for infanticide based on the standard insanity defense, and not on some special separate standard for women.

Danuta Plenska, "La Criminalité Féminine en Pologne" (1980) 22 *Canadian Journal of Criminology* 464-475

The author reviews the evolution of female criminality in Poland over a fifty year period. Noting its sharp increase after the Second World War and its subsequent decrease, she concludes that the changes are related to the socio-economic conditions of women. There is a discussion of the factors which induced women to enter the paid work force; and the increase in crime is identified as primarily property crime against the state. The church and other cultural factors are also identified as affecting women's criminal behaviour.

Barbara Raffel Price, "Book Review: Freda Adler, THE INCIDENCE OF FEMALE CRIMINALITY IN THE CONTEMPORARY WORLD (1981); S. K. Mukherjee and Jocelynne A. Scutt, (eds.), WOMEN AND CRIME (1981); Dorothy Zeitz, WOMEN WHO EMBEZZLE OR DEFRAUD: A STUDY OF CONVICTED FELONS (1981)" (1982) 8 *Signs: Journal of Women in Culture and Society* 718-721

For annotation, see Chapter 16: **BOOK REVIEWS**.

Nicole Hahn Rafter and Elena M. Natalizia, "Marxist Feminism: Implications for Criminal Justice" (1981) 27 *Crime and Delinquency* 81-98

The authors argue that sexism in the criminal justice system -- sexism against victims, offenders, and system personnel -- is rooted in sexism in capitalism, and they urge resistance and challenge to the contradictions of capitalism. The oppression of women preserves the economic status quo and includes, for women in prison, differential sentencing statutes, drugging into passivity and resocialization into "proper" gender roles, and morality status for juveniles. The failure to respond to issues of critical importance to especially poor, working class women -- including incest, unsafe birth control, rape, and wife abuse -- is rooted, they claim, in the patriarchal concept of women as sexual chattels. They conclude by recommending a shift in focus from individual deviance to a focus on systemic oppression and exploitation.

Marge Reitsma-Street, "More Control Than Care: A Critique of Historical and Contemporary Laws for Delinquency and Neglect of Children in Ontario" (1989-1990) 3 _Canadian Journal of Women and the Law_ 510-529

This article examines the two major frameworks with respect to social welfare policies and laws for delinquent or neglected youth -- the parens patriae framework which was dominant until the mid-twentieth century, and the presently dominant rights framework. The author examines delinquency legislation passed in Ontario from each perspective, and argues that neither operates from a perspective of care so much as they do from a perspective of control. She criticizes each framework because care and control can be linked to the privatized economy, the family, and women's role within the family.

Marguerite Russell, "A Feminist Analysis of the Criminal Trial Process" (1989-1990) 3 _Canadian Journal of Women and the Law_ 552-562

The author examines masculinist thinking which underlies all aspects of criminal process: the purported dichotomy between substance and procedure, and the roles played by judges, counsel, and juries. She concludes that women must lay a foundation for a society which truly values all, rather than privileging a minority, and that this will in turn eradicate the substantive/procedural dichotomy, and the adversarial hierarchical roles now present in our patriarchal judicial system.

Shirley Sagawa, "A Hard Case for Feminists: People v. Goetz" (1987) 10 _Harvard Women's Law Journal_ 253-273

This article discusses sexism and criminal law, and in particular gender neutrality and separate standards for women, which, in the author's view, may perpetuate stereotypes, and punish women by holding them to the reasonable man standard. The author examines the successful invocation of an individualized defense of self-defense in the case of a white male shooting four black males, and compares it to the reasonable man test in cases of battered women, the majority of which are unsuccessful. She argues for the individualization of the defense for battered women, in order to correct the white male biases which the law presently incorporates.

Sally S. Simpson, "Why Can't a Woman Be More Like A Man?" (1989) 27 *Criminology* 605-630
This article is an introduction to feminist criminology. The author provides an overview of feminist theory -- liberal, socialist, and radical -- and notes the alternate framework of women of colour. She then reviews the application of feminist theory to criminology, including the study of the female offender, the female victim, and the criminal justice process, specifically race and gender discrimination by police, the courts, and corrections. She targets for further research, race and crime, elite crime (white collar), and deterrence.

Elizabeth Stanko, "What's a Nice Girl like You Doing in a Place Like This?" (1981) 7/8 *Crime and/et Justice* 220-225
The author discusses her experiences while doing a sociological study of individuals involved in the criminal justice system. She was an observer in a police precinct and a prosecutor's office, watching day to day activity and interaction over an extended period. She discusses the advantages and disadvantages of being a female researcher in a virtually all male environment. She concludes that gender differences raise many obstacles, but that these obstacles are worth overcoming, because of the value of new female insights into how the system operates.

Victor L. Striel and Lynn Sametz, "Executing Female Juveniles" (1989) 22 *Connecticut Law Review* 3-59
For annotation, see Chapter 10: **LEGAL HISTORY.**

Jim Thomas, "Criminal Justice -- Book Review: Allison Morris, WOMEN, CRIME AND CRIMINAL JUSTICE (1987)" (1988) 38 *Journal of Legal Education* 437-450

For annotation, see Chapter 16: **BOOK REVIEWS.**

Robert B. Ward, "A Kinder, Gentler System: An Examination of How Crime Victims Have Benefitted From the Women's Movement" (1989) 15 _New England Journal on Criminal and Civil Confinement_ 171-175
Part of a Women's Symposium, this article discusses the relationship between what the author refers to as the Women's Movement and the Crime Victims' Rights Movement, and argues that issues first raised by feminists made possible the Victims' Movement.

R. A. Weisheit, "Women and Crime: Issues and Perspectives" (1984) 11:7 _Sex Roles_ 567-580
This article examines various approaches, theories, and research dealing with female criminality, including macro-level explanations, which study how the social structure affects crime. The author notes that both the two leading macro-level theories, the opportunity and the socialization theories, derive from the macro theory of convergence, which claims that as social roles equalize, the crime rate differences between men and women will disappear. The individual level explanations have a more biological and psychological focus, and she presents a historical overview of the development of these theories. The third type of explanation is derived from a relatively new mode of analysis, micro-level, which examines the effect of the peer group on the individual. She concludes by noting that there is still much disagreement about which mode of analysis is the most appropriate in studying female criminality.

Conna Wood, "Book Review: Mary Eaton, JUSTICE FOR WOMEN?: FAMILY, COURT AND SOCIAL CONTROL" (1988) 79 _Journal of Criminal Law & Criminology_ 261-263
For annotation, see Chapter 16: **BOOK REVIEWS.**

Battering

**"Domestic Violence and Custody -- 'To Ensure Domestic Tranquillity'"
(1984) 14 *Golden Gate University Law Review* 623-638**
    This is a panel presented to the National Association of Women
Judges, and included in the Symposium Issue. The panellists review joint
custody, mediation, and domestic violence, concluding that the best
interests of the child must be the governing factor in deciding difficult
cases.

**Beverly Balos and Katie Trotzky, "Enforcement of the Domestic Abuse
Act in Minnesota: A Preliminary Study" (1988) 6 *Law and Inequality* 83--
125**
    This article evaluates the effectiveness of the Order for Protection
in Minnesota, the response of the legal system, and the variables that
may influence their enforcement, especially race. The author's recommendations focus on simplified procedures, and increased police training
and sensitivity to the problem of domestic violence.

**Micheline Baril, Marie-Marthe Cousineau, and Sylvie Gravel, "Quand
Les Femmes Sont Victimes...Quand Les Hommes Appliquent La Loi"
(1983) 16:2 *Criminologie* 89-100**
    The authors argue that the justice system views domestic assaults
as a less serious threat to public order than other assaults, and fails to
protect victims. Contrary to popular belief, data indicates that women
do leave violent relationships, although they are not necessarily protected
when they do so. The reaction of the police in classifying the gravity of
complaints is, they suggest, an important factor in the victim's decision
to pursue the complaint. They conclude that the majority of those
accused of assault escape the criminal justice system relatively unscathed,
and that the gravity of the offence seems to have little effect on the
sentence.

**Julie Blackman, "Emerging Images of Severely Battered Women and
the Criminal Justice System" (1990) 8 *Behavioral Sciences and the Law*
121-130**

For annotation, see Chapter 6: FIRST NATIONS AND RACE.

Brenda Boswell, "The Perpetuation of Wife Assault" (1983) 4 _Canadian Woman Studies_ 69-71

The history of wife assault, and the attitudinal and societal circumstances which encourage its existence, are explored. Some ways to change attitudes and behaviour are suggested.

Christine Boyle, "Violence Against Wives -- The Criminal Law in Retreat?" (1980) 31 _Northern Ireland Legal Quarterly_ 35-57

The author examines the law's impact on the family, through analysis of the role of criminal law in relation to wife abuse, specifically regarding marital rape, compellability of spouses, and the defense of provocation. Her examination includes analysis from radical and liberal feminism, and involves analyses of case law in the area of wife abuse. She concludes with a call for consistency in both criminal law content and in enforcement.

Wini Breines and Linda Gordon, "The New Scholarship on Family Violence" (1982) 8 _Signs: Journal of Women in Culture and Society_ 490-531

The authors examine literature from many disciplines regarding family violence, specifically child abuse, wife battering, and incest. They argue that while each of these forms of violence merits separate analysis, it is nonetheless important to discuss all generally as related to our understanding of the family, gender, and power. Violence, they argue, must be viewed within the context of a gendered social context, because violence is not "necessarily deviant or fundamentally different" from other methods of exerting power. They conclude with the recommendation that qualitative research is necessary for a full understanding of any act of family violence, with the claim that the task of feminist analyses must be to defend women against victim-blaming, and with a demand for the application of gender analysis to all discussion of family violence.

Gary Richard Brown, "Battered Women and the Temporary Restraining Order" (1989) 10 _Women's Rights Law Reporter_ 261-267

This article evaluates the effectiveness of civil restraining orders as remedies for domestic violence. The author discusses how women's ability to get restraining orders is limited by financial, housing, and legal considerations, and how these limits are being overcome, and he explores the current and ideal enforcement of these orders. He concludes that to be effective in helping battered women, restraining order legislation must provide for ready access and consistent enforcement.

Rick Brown, "Limitations on Expert Testimony on the Battered Woman Syndrome in Homicide Cases: The Return of the Ultimate Issue Rule" (1990) 32 _Arizona Law Review_ 665-689

This article examines the Battered Woman Syndrome (BWS), and the use of expert testimony in a woman's defense to homicide, as proof of the woman's perception of imminent danger. The author argues that in cases where the court has determined that expert evidence regarding BWS is helpful for the jury, then the opinion of that expert with respect to whether the accused woman fits within the diagnosis of BWS should also be admissible. He concludes that the expert in such circumstances is not determining an ultimate legal issue, but is only identifying the woman as subject to the BWS, and allowing the jury to determine her mental state.

Lorenne M. G. Clark, "Feminist Perspectives on Violence Against Women and Children: Psychological, Social Service, and Criminal Justice Concerns" (1989-1990) 3 _Canadian Journal of Women and the Law_ 420-431

This article examines the pervasiveness of physical, sexual, and emotional violence against women and children, and suggests that the fragmented approach presently taken with respect to detection, punishment, and treatment is indicative of institutional acceptance of male authority over women. The author claims that the serious harm which occurs must be acknowledged, and that violent behaviour must be de-legitimized, and she recommends prevention should involve a broader and more integrated mandate to the social service delivery system, based upon a recognition that incarceration of offenders will not solve the problem. The correctional systems, she suggests, should be dismantled, and the social service delivery system should be re-mantled as the appropriate response to crime.

Roger Cranfield and Elizabeth Cranfield, "Female Circumcision: An Assault" (1983) 227 _Practitioner_ 816-817

This article examines whether female circumcision constitutes an illegal assault, and whether public policy concerns, regarding upholding the traditions of certain ethnic groups, can be reconciled with the law on consent and assault.

Dawn H. Currie, "Battered Women and The State: From the Failure of Theory to a Theory of Failure" (1990) 1:2 _Journal of Human Justice_ 77-96

The Battered Wife Movement (BWM) has divided feminists on the question of criminal justice as a desirable component of a feminist agenda. In the author's view, this division provides a good example of the dilemmas of developing a feminist theory of the state as the basis for informed practice. The article surveys the way in which the BWM has been transformed from a radical demand for the redistribution of social power into an expansion of current patriarchal institutions. However, she rejects explanations of this transformation as simply ideological by the state, and argues that it occurs through, and not against, feminist discourse. She concludes that this means that feminists must acknowledge theory as practice, if they are to develop a truly subversive and libratory discourse within feminist scholarship.

Franklyn W. Dunford, David Huizinga, and Delbert S. Elliott, "The Role of Arrest in Domestic Assault: The Omaha Police Experiment" (1990) 28 _Criminology_ 183-206

This article reports on a replication of the Minneapolis Domestic Violence Experiment (see: Lawrence W. Sherman and Richard A Berk, THE MINNEAPOLIS DOMESTIC VIOLENCE EXPERIMENT (19-84)), in Omaha, Nebraska. Suspects who were eligible for the experiment were randomly assigned to one of three police dispositions -- mediation, separation, or arrest. The authors report that no difference by disposition was found in prevalence or frequency of repeat offending, using five measures of recidivism to assess outcome six months after police intervention.

Desmond Ellis, "Marital Conflict Mediation and Post-Separation Wife Abuse" (1990) 8 _Law and Inequality_ 317-339

The author examines factors which increase the likelihood a woman in mediation will be physically abused after separation -- namely, power differences between the husband and wife, pre-separation violence, privacy norms which define reporting of violence as "snitching," and alcohol and drug abuse. He cautions that mediators can perpetuate abuse of wives unless post-separation assault is treated seriously, and concludes with the recommendation that stopping the abuse must be viewed as an important objective of mediation, and that mediation must be viewed as an empowering process or it is not appropriate.

Timothy A. O. Endicott, "The Criminality of Wife Assault" (1987) 45 *University of Toronto Faculty of Law Review* **355-393**
The author surveys the legal and social aspects of assault of wives, and possible non-legal and civil remedies for wife abuse, proposes criminalization of the offence, and discusses what effect that step will have on the family.

Amy Eppler, "Battered Women and the Equal Protection Clause: Will the Constitution Help Them when the Police Won't?" (1986) 95 *Yale Law Journal* **788-809**
The author argues that the police practice of non-arrest of battering husbands is a violation of the woman's right to equal protection of the laws, and constitutes sex discrimination based on the stereotypical view that it is men's right to beat women. She argues that this is exemplified by a policy of non-intervention, which has been viewed as related to an important state interest, as discriminatory in intent, or as an inappropriate intrusion into family privacy. She concludes with recommendations for policy changes.

M. D. A. Freeman, "Violence Against Women: Does the Legal System Provide Solutions or Itself Constitute the Problem" (1980) 3 *Canadian Journal of Family Law* **377-401 (Alternate Citation: (1980) 7** *British Journal of Law & Society* **215-241)**
The author argues that there is no need for husbands to have a formal right to beat their wives, because the ideology of patriarchy is sufficient to subordinate and control women. He argues that lawyers must dismantle both patriarchal ideology and the legal structure erected upon the ideology in order to effect any real change. The battle for

battered women is in reality a battle for all women.

Pauline W. Gee, "Ensuring Police Protection of Battered Women: The SCOTT v. HART Suit" (1982) 8 _Signs: Journal of Women in Culture and Society_ **554-567**
    The author examines the legal challenge to obtain police protection for battered women, and to educate police, the criminal justice system, and the public about domestic violence: SCOTT v. HART (C-76-2395 N.D. Cal.). This challenge argued that police policy of non-intervention and arrest-avoidance was invidious discrimination which encouraged violence against women, as it was based on sexist assumptions about a man's right to punish or restrain his wife. The cause of action was discontinued when a settlement was reached rescinding the police policy, and requiring the municipality to provide support services for battering victims. She concludes with litigation strategies for similar suits, yet cautions that domestic violence requires solutions beyond merely legal and policy changes. However, she claims, the legal system reflects what is considered wrongful behaviour, and has more power than do women and children, and is thus a large part of the solution.

Robert Geffner and Mildred Daley Pagelow, "Mediation and Child Custody Issues in Abusive Relationships" (1990) 8 _Behavioral Sciences and the Law_ **151-159**
    The authors argue that the legal system must come to understand the ramifications of joint custody and mediation in abusive relationships, discuss the effects of each on the children and adults, and conclude with a number of recommendations for dealing with power and other issues in abusive relationships.

Charlotte Germane, Margaret Johnson, and Nancy Lemon, "Mandatory Custody Mediation and Joint Custody Orders in California: The Danger for Victims of Domestic Violence" (1985) 1 _Berkeley Women's Law Journal_ **175-200**
    California's no-fault divorce legislation makes mediation of custody mandatory, and presumes joint custody. The authors examine the legislation's impact on families in which the husband is a batterer. They conclude that the lack of legislative or judicial recognition of spousal abuse, as a factor in custody determination, places the wife at risk of

losing custody completely within the context of the "friendly parent" rule. They argue for reform to make domestic violence a factor in custody/visitation determinations.

Edward W. Gondolf, "Anger and Oppression in Men Who Batter: Empiricist and Feminist Perspectives and Their Implications for Research" (1985) 10 *Victimology* 311-324

The author examines psychological research with respect to battering, and characterizes it as either empiricist (anger-induced battering) or feminist (battering as oppression). He suggests further research to mediate these conflicting perspectives, and concludes that research with battering men is necessary to ascertain whether batterers perceive the same cycle of violence and low self-esteem as do the women they batter.

Anita L. Grant, "The Battered Woman: When a Woman's 'Place' is in the Courts" (1988) 10 *Criminal Justice Journal* 273-305

This article examines the response of the criminal justice system to battered women. The author argues that the courts have failed to recognize battering as a potentially deadly assault, and suggests that this failure may cause courts to be sceptical of the cause of criminal actions committed by women under threat of abuse. She advocates the use of expert testimony in prosecutions arising from such actions, in order to allow the court to see the woman's actions in the context of such abuse.

Aled Griffiths, "The Legacy and Present Administration of English Law: Some Problems for Battered Women in Context" (1980) 2 *Cambrian Law Review* 29-39

The author reviews the nature of domestic violence in Wales, and argues that legislation exhibits a symbolic, rather than instrumental function, with respect to domestic violence, as is demonstrated by the inadequate and varying responses from the legal community. She recommends increased contact with other agencies, police encouragement of civil suits where criminal prosecution is unavailable, and emergency availability of legal counsel.

Jalna Hanmer and Elizabeth Stanko, "Stripping Away the Rhetoric of

Protection: Violence to Women, Law and the State in Britain and the U.S.A." (1985) 13 _International Journal of the Sociology of Law_ 357-374

The authors examine the relationship between various forms of violence toward women, and conclude that the idea that the criminal justice system provides protection from male violence is actually indifference masked by rhetoric. They challenge social scientists to analyze women's increased vulnerability, which is well-recognized as a condition of gender, as an issue of gender inequality, and call for a juncture of the specialized areas of criminology and research on violence toward women.

Katherine Lynn Held, "Law Enforcement and Prosecutor Responses to Domestic Violence: Non-Involvement to the Application of Criminal Justice Sanctions" (1985) 2 _Wisconsin Women's Law Journal_ 95-124

This article examines police policy and methods of dealing with battering, and the author claims that police officers' responses to incidents of domestic violence are shaped by ill-conceived, patriarchal, and frequently racist or ethnocentric beliefs. She argues that mediation policies are seriously limiting, because these policies are wrongly based on an assumption of equality between the batterer and the battered woman, and expect the woman to compromise her right to be free from physical harm. She examines a pro-arrest and prosecution policy by police in Wisconsin, which she claims a success in promoting victims' access to law enforcement protection, as well as community resources, while ensuring that the batterer is criminally accountable for his behaviour. An Appendix includes a copy of the policies employed by the Dane County and Madison Police departments.

Helen Rubenstein Holden, "Does the Legal System Batter Women? Vindicating Battered Women's Constitutional Rights to Adequate Police Protection" (1989) 21 _Arizona State Law Journal_ 705-728

This article examines the nature and extent of wife battering, and discusses the social, legal, and criminal justice aspects of the problem. The author argues that battered women can claim for damages, on constitutional grounds, against police departments who have provided inadequate protection. This argument is based on the equal protection clause of the fourteenth amendment, which she concludes will result in necessary public policy changes such as police policy reforms, stricter enforcement of existing law, and mandatory arrest schemes.

Pamela Jenkins and Barbara Davidson, "Battered Women in the Criminal Justice System: An Analysis of Gender Stereotypes" (1990) 8 *Behavioral Sciences and the Law* **161-170**
  This article presents a gender analysis of the social construction of the trial setting in ten court cases of battered women charged with the death of their partners. The analysis includes the structure of the trial, the language of the trial, the participants in the process and the role played by the accused in her defense.

Sybille Kappel and Erida Leuteritz, "Wife Battering in the Federal Republic of Germany" (1980) 5 *Victimology* **225-239**
  The authors describe the role of the West German women's aid movement in developing homes and programs for battered women. They also depict the need for collective, non-hierarchical work in implementing the programs, carrying out theoretical analysis, and lobbying for legal change. The paper includes data with respect to the women who were program recipients.

Linda R. Keenan, "Domestic Violence and Custody Litigation: The Need for Statutory Reform" (1985) 13 *Hofstra Law Review* **407-441**
  This article examines the interrelationship between domestic violence and custody litigation, within the context of California's divorce legislation. The author argues that children of abusive marriages suffer serious negative effects both in the short term and intergenerationally, and that custody litigation can be and is used as a battering weapon. She concludes that evidence of wife beating should create a presumption of the abuser's unfitness as a parent, because the rights of the abuser must be subverted to the rights of the victim to autonomy and an absence of battering.

Nancy Lemon, "Book Review: Cynthia K. Gillespie, JUSTIFIABLE HOMICIDE: BATTERED WOMEN, SELF-DEFENSE, AND THE LAW (1989)" (1989-90) 5 *Berkeley Women's Law Journal* **227-235**
  For annotation, see Chapter 16: **BOOK REVIEWS.**

Lisa G. Lerman, "Mediation of Wife Abuse Cases: The Adverse Impact of Informal Dispute Resolution on Women" (1984) 7 *Harvard*

Women's Law Journal 57-113

The author criticizes family violence mediation from the standpoint of the law enforcement model. The conciliation model is premised on the idea that family problems should be solved within the family, and therefore focuses on the role of the victim, as well as the perpetrator, in the violence. She recommends, instead, the law enforcement model which focuses on the causes for violence within the abuser and society. She concludes that if mediation is used, the procedure should offer protection for the victim, place all the responsibility for stopping the violence on the abuser, and allow for the enforcement of the mediation agreement.

Christine A. Littleton, "Women's Experience and the Problem of Transition: Perspectives on Male Battering of Women" [1989] *University of Chicago Legal Forum* 23-57

The author discusses different perspectives within feminist legal theory, and then particularizes the discussion to battered wives, whom she claims are battered by the batterer, society, and the legal system. She discusses the difference between the legal view of the woman and the woman's experience in the relationship through feminist reconstructive jurisprudence, and concludes that women have to learn forms of connectedness other than traditional marriage.

Susan Maidment, "The Relevance of the Criminal Law to Domestic Violence" [1980] *Journal of Social Welfare Law* 26-32

This paper discusses the general trend toward decriminalization of socially unacceptable behaviour, specifically as it relates to decriminalization of domestic violence. The author identifies arguments for criminal sanction (including social condemnation of violence, and forcing personal accountability by the offender) and arguments against it (including evidentiary problems, exacerbating the violence, and the unavailability of treatment during incarceration.) In conclusion, she recommends that the decision to pursue criminal sanction should not be made by either the wife or the police, but instead by a professional decision-maker in consultation with a social worker.

A. Orlando, "Exclusive Possession of the Family Home: The Plight of Battered Cohabitees" (1987) 45 *University of Toronto Faculty of Law*

Review 152-178

The author examines the differential treatment with respect to exclusive possession of the family home for married women and cohabitees who are battered. She argues that cohabitees are, statistically, more financially vulnerable, and recommends that the same protection as is provided to married women be extended to cohabitees. She concludes that legal reform can only marginally alleviate domestic violence, and that a change in the structural position of women is necessary in order seriously to protect women from exploitative relationships.

Mary Lassance Parthun and Gloria Hart, "Domestic Violence Intervention: A Generic Service Model" (1983) 4 *Canadian Woman Studies* **73**

This paper describes the domestic violence program of Catholic Family Services of Toronto.

Maria K. Pastoor, "Police Training and the Effectiveness of Minnesota 'Domestic Abuse' Laws" (1984) 2 *Law and Inequality* **557-606**

This article discusses the reluctance of the criminal justice system and the police to interfere in domestic violence. The author argues that wife-battering is not treated as a crime in order to maintain male dominance in the family, and that police training procedures must be changed if legislative reforms requiring arrests are to be effective. Based on her studies in Minnesota, she criticizes training programs which regard wife-battering as a crime against the family, rather than the person, and which emphasize mediation, a process which ignores the woman's injuries and places some of the blame for the "disturbance" on her. She recommends a restructuring of training programs to recognize the criminal nature of battering.

D. Pedlar and L. Wilcox, "The Women's Advocacy Program and Other Services Available to Battered Women, Batterers and their Children" (1987) 5 *Crown Counsel Review* **11-13**

The Women's Advocacy Program is a unique program which provides an interdisciplinary support group to women who are the victims of spousal abuse. Copies of all Winnipeg police arrest reports are sent to the staff; the progress through the criminal justice system of all cases involving domestic violence is monitored. The program provides the

woman with a legal advocate and a counsellor, as well as training to
professionals in the detection of abuse and in how to treat victims of
abusive relationships. The related services available in Winnipeg, including various shelters and programs, are summarised.

Teresa Godwin Phelps, "Stories of Women in Self-Defense -- Book
Review: Cynthia K. Gillespie, JUSTIFIABLE HOMICIDE: BAT-
TERED WOMEN, SELF-DEFENSE, AND THE LAW (1989)" (1989)
2 _Yale Journal of Law and Feminism_ 189-197
       For annotation, see Chapter 16: **BOOK REVIEWS**.

Christopher J. Pibus, "Civil Remedies for Interspousal Violence in
England and Ontario: A Comparative Study" (1980) 38 _University of
Toronto Faculty of Law Review_ 33-51
       This article discusses the legislative provisions and practices with
respect to domestic violence in Ontario, and concludes that they offer
less relief than obstacles. The author recommends a more flexible interpretation of the current legislation in Ontario, and refers to the English
system as offering a more suitable range of options for ensuring physical
security of the battered woman.   He also identifies areas requiring
immediate legislative reform, namely, the lack of power of arrest for
non-molestation/ possession orders, the absence of a remedy for unmarried victims, and the restricted access to court in an emergency
situation.

Katharine E. Renison, "Book Review: Marion Boyd, ed., HAND-
BOOK FOR ADVOCATES AND COUNSELLORS OF BATTERED
WOMEN (1985)" (1986) 2 _Canadian Journal of Women and the Law_
214-218
       For annotation, see Chapter 16: **BOOK REVIEWS**.

Vincent F. Sacco and Meena Trotman, "Public Information Programming and Family Violence: Lessons from the Mass Media Crime
Prevention Experience" (1990) 32 _Canadian Journal of Criminology_
91-105
       This article canvasses the literature on public information program-
ming, and in particular mass media crime prevention, in order to provide

a preliminary assessment of the applicability of such approaches to family violence prevention. The authors identify three general strategies -- problem definition, offender deterrence, and the teaching of risk-reducing skills -- and conclude that a tentative interpretation of available data suggests that policies directed toward problem definition will be most successful. The article concludes with a discussion of the limitations of public information approaches to family violence.

Jocelynne A. Scutt, "Going Backwards: Law 'Reform' and Women Bashing" (1986) 9 *Women's Studies International Forum* 49-55
This article contrasts the recent trend in Australia to claim the rights of women victims of domestic violence with the need to combat violence. The author argues that the discourse is misdirected because present emphasis on the need to give police more powers would be better directed toward forcing the police to use existing powers of intervention/arrest for criminal assault in domestic violence cases. To treat domestic violence differently than violence against strangers is, she concludes, to ignore masculine destruction in women's own homes.

Jocelynne A. Scutt, "In Support of Domestic Violence: The Legal Basis" (1980) 3 *Family Law Review* 23-32
The author discusses various frameworks which have been employed in dealing with wife abuse: treating abuse as no crime, as a special crime, totally ignoring it, or creating a special venue for adjudicating disputes related to the abuse. She claims that resolution of the ongoing conflict between the mysticism adhering to the family unit and the reality of that unit, will define which framework will be employed in dealing with abuse. She concludes that those seeking to preserve the family unit are, by definition, also seeking to preserve the greater rights of the husband/father with an unequal sharing of power.

Dianna R. Stallone, "Decriminalization of Violence in the Home: Mediation in Wife Battering Cases" (1984) 2 *Law and Inequality* 493-519
The author examines the use of mediation in cases of wife beating, paying particular attention to battering by men of colour, and argues that mediation can be evaluated positively, only if compared to the criminal system which simply ignores battering. The author claims that mediation permits a dodging of the pervasive violence in the family, is ineffective

in stopping battering, and may exacerbate the problem. She concludes with suggestions for reform which would more effectively serve the needs of battered women.

Sue Stapely, "Judicial Attitudes Towards Domestic Violence" (1980) 10 _Kingston Law Review_ 156-182

This article reviews the courts' reluctance to grant injunctions preventing a battering husband's entry to the matrimonial home in the United Kingdom. The author argues that the ambivalence of the court decisions occurs because of the necessary balance between protection of property rights and protection of the battered spouse. She reports, however, that domestic violence legislation has been used to grant injunctions where there is a risk of real injury to the woman or her children, or where molestation affects the mental or physical health of the woman and/or children.

Michael Steinman, "Lowering Recidivism Among Men Who Batter Women" (1990) 17 _Journal of Police Science and Administration_ 124-132

This article reports the findings of a study undertaken to evaluate the effects of a coordinated effort to lower recidivism among men who batter women, by the Domestic Violence Coalition of Lincoln and Lancaster Counties in Nebraska.

Judith Vega, "Coercion and Consent: Classic Liberal Concepts in Texts on Sexual Violence" (1988) 16 _International Journal of the Sociology of Law_ 75-87

The feminist view of sexual violence is closely related to classic liberal theory's description of absolutism. Both regard the violence of the person in power as being opposed by the natural rights of the subject/victim. The author traces the influence of the theory of natural rights in the works of Susan Brownmiller and Catharine MacKinnon, and argues for re-adoption of the classic liberal consent theory. She concludes that consent is a complex part of the male-female power relationship, and a fact which derives from the social construction of gender.

Kathleen Waits, "The Criminal Justice System's Response to Battering:

Understanding the Problem, Forging the Solutions" (1985) 60 *Washington Law Review* 267-329

The author describes the extent and dynamics of wife abuse, argues that the law must seriously condemn abuse by challenging current reluctance to interfere in family privacy, and recommends changes which will protect the victim and deter the batterer. She concludes with a challenge to lawyers and the judiciary to develop firm and strict sentencing guidelines, to encourage the creative use of judicial discretion, and to treat recidivism harshly.

Frances Wasoff, "Legal Protection From Wifebeating: The Processing of Domestic Assaults by Scottish Prosecutors and Criminal Courts" (19-82) 10 *International Journal of the Sociology of Law* 187-204

For annotation, see Chapter 10: **LEGAL HISTORY.**

Evidence

Shira Bernholtz, "The Best Defence: Women, Self-Defence and the Law" (1987) *Breaking the Silence* 20-22

This article, written by a lawyer, discusses the law of self-defense in layman's language. She briefly describes the principles necessary to establish self-defense, and some issues of particular interest to women, including rape and spousal battering. She also provides guidelines for women to use when faced with assault.

Eugene Borgida, and Patricia Frazier, "Rape Trauma Syndrome Evidence in Court" (1985) 40 *American Psychologist* 984-993

The authors discuss the admissibility of expert evidence in the United States, including the different and conflicting standards emerging in various American jurisdictions. The article describes the cases where rape trauma syndrome evidence has been ruled to be inadmissible, and those where it has been admitted, and concludes that the deciding factor has been the perceived helpfulness of the evidence to the jury. The second part of the article examines this factor and others, including the scientific status of rape trauma syndrome, the possible prejudicial effect, and the kind of weight juries are believed to give to expert evidence.

Diana Brahms, "Premenstrual Tension and Criminal Responsibility" (1983) 227 _Practitioner_ 807-813
The author examines whether premenstrual tension (PMS) should be available as a defense, noting among other problems, the difficulty in determining the difference between the defendant "did not resist her impulse" and she "could not resist her impulse". The article begins with a description of two recent English cases in which the defense was successfully used to reduce murder charges to manslaughter by reason of diminished responsibility, and examines the implications of these cases for English law.

Kathee Rebernak Brewer, "Missouri's New Law on 'Battered Spouse Syndrome': A Moral Victory, A Partial Solution" (1988) 33 _Saint Louis University Law Journal_ 227-255
The article discusses the elements of the Battered Woman Syndrome, its relevance to self-defense, and the requirements for admissibility under state legislation. The author discusses the legislation's applicability to other self-defense claims, e.g. battering relationship with a male victim, the statute's potential for illegitimate use, and its potential use in insanity defenses. She concludes with recommendations for legislative amendments.

Daniel J. Brodsky, "Educating Juries: The Battered Woman Defence in Canada" (1987) 25 _Alberta Law Review_ 461-476
The author describes the Battered Woman's Syndrome, the history of the defense as it developed in the United States, and the availability of the defense in Canada. He argues that the defense should be applicable under the interpretation of admissibility of expert testimony, and concludes with the recommendation that the problem of family violence must be addressed by protecting the rights of the woman to act reasonably in self-defense.

Jenae R. Bunyak, "Battered Wives Who Kill: Civil Liability and the Admissibility of Battered Woman's Syndrome Testimony" (1986) 4 _Law_

and Inequality 603-636

This article examines the admissibility of expert testimony regarding Battered Woman's Syndrome in civil actions in wrongful death. The author reports that unlike criminal actions, the self-defense standards and burdens of proof established by wrongful death statutes vary from state to state, as does the applicability of the doctrine of interspousal tort immunity.

Linda R. Chait, "Premenstrual Syndrome & Our Sisters in Crime: A Feminist Dilemma" (1986) 9 _Women's Rights Law Reporter_ 267-293

Pre-menstrual Syndrome (PMS) as a criminal defense is viewed as a double-edged sword by feminists. The author attempts to separate the myth from the reality of PMS. She reviews the history of medical theories about the social inferiority of women, touching on Darwinism, Freudian psychology, the discovery of hormones, and the present debate on the nature and causes of PMS. She concludes that the unwarranted use of the PMS defense is a threat to the goals of women's liberation. Where appropriate, it should be treated as a diminished capacity defense based on organic illness, and not forced to fit the insanity model. Mitigation of sentence alternatives and trial techniques to neutralize harmful stereotypes are also discussed.

Andrew B. Clarke, "Corroboration in Sexual Cases" [1980] _Criminal Law Review_ 362-371

This article examines the Canadian and Australian departure from the established common law principle of corroboration in sexual assault cases. In a brief case survey, the author examines cases from BASKER-VILLE [1916] 2 K.B. 658 to MURPHY (1976) 9 N.R. 329, and suggests that the latter case results in the merger of the concepts of relevant and corroborative evidence. He suggests that there are three possible alternatives that English law might take, and concludes that a gradual approach that reduces the "artificially enhanced value" of corroboration is the most desirable.

Cynthia L. Coffee, "A Trend Emerges: A State Survey on the Admissibility of Expert Testimony Concerning the Battered Woman Syndrome" (1987) 25 _Journal of Family Law_ 373-396

This piece surveys the admissibility of expert testimony on the

Battered Woman Syndrome by state in the United States. The trend appears to be to admit such evidence to some degree, though judicial decisions are rationalized differently in different jurisdictions.

Phyllis L. Crocker, "The Meaning of Equality for Battered Women Who Kill Men in Self-Defense" (1985) 8 _Harvard Women's Law Journal_ **121-153**

This article discusses the feminist theory of self-defense for battered women who kill their batterers, and analyzes the judicial response to this theory. The author examines the judicial reception of expert testimony regarding the Battered Woman Syndrome, and concludes that the goal of advancing self-defense claims as equal to those of men has not succeeded. She argues that feminist theory has resulted in perpetuation of the stereotyping it was to eliminate.

Peter R. Dahl, "Legal and Psychiatric Concepts and the Use of Psychiatric Evidence in Criminal Trials" (1985) 73 _California Law Review_ **411-442**

The author examines the use of psychiatric evidence in criminal trials, and argues that this evidence must not encroach or diminish the decision-making role of the courts. He identifies the use of psychiatric evidence in battered women's syndrome and diminished capacity as problem areas. In the former, he argues, the evidence is merely explanatory not exculpatory, and therefore the law retains its control of policy decisions. In the latter, he outlines cases where psychiatric evidence seems to have removed the decision-making power from the legal system, and he suggests extreme caution in accepting such evidence.

Katherina Dalton, "Premenstrual Syndrome" (1986) 9 _Hamline Law Review_ **141-151**

This article, by one of the leading medical specialists in the area of premenstrual syndrome (PMS), provides a comprehensive description of the syndrome, including its historical background, definition, diagnosis, and methods of treatment. The author also describes the character of PMS criminal activity, and outlines ways in which evidence of PMS might be collected.

John Dent, "Postpartum Psychosis and the Insanity Defence" [1989]
University of Chicago Legal Forum 355-374

This article provides an historical overview of the insanity defense, the M'Naghten test, and the test proposed by the American Legal Institute, and then discusses the subsequent rejection of the latter test in many American jurisdictions after several controversial acquittals. The author then analyzes the availability of the defense for postpartum psychosis, and notes that the traditional common law burden of proof is a difficult standard for defendants claiming temporary insanity. Using the rational connection test and the relative convenience standard, he demonstrates that in cases of postpartum psychosis, a less onerous standard is more appropriate.

Susan Edwards, "Mad, Bad, or Pre-menstrual?" (1988) 138 *New Law Journal* 456-458

The author provides a short history of pre-menstrual tension (PMT) in British law, from the nineteenth century practice of accepting evidence of PMS as a defense to the 1982 English Court of Appeal decision to reject PMT as a substantive defense. Since that time, evidence of PMT and of pre-menstrual syndrome (PMS) has been accepted as a factor in mitigation of sentence, and has even had some uneven influence in non-criminal proceedings, including family cases. She concludes with the warning that while PMT has an obvious place in mitigation, along with other social, economic, and psychological factors, introduction of evidence of PMT may obscure those other factors as well as defenses available, and pathologise the offender.

David L. Faigman, "The Battered Woman Syndrome and Self-Defense: A Legal and Empirical Dissent" (1986) 72 *Virginia Law Review* 619-647

The author argues that the uniqueness of the battering relationship requires that the application of the self-defense claim be carried out in a flexible manner, and that the Battered Woman Syndrome has little evidentiary value in self-defense claims. Scientific research, he claims, is of limited use in determining why an abused woman strikes out at her mate when she does. He concludes that courts should admit into evidence empirical findings with respect to economic and social factors forcing women to remain in violent relationships, as well as testimony about the deceased husband's history of violence, in order to permit a just hearing of the criminal charge against the battered woman.

David L. Faigman, "Discerning Justice When Battered Women Kill --
Book Review: Charles P. Ewing, BATTERED WOMEN WHO KILL:
PSYCHOLOGICAL SELF-DEFENSE AS LEGAL JUSTIFICATION
(1987)" (1987) 39 _Hastings Law Journal_ 207-227
    For annotation, see Chapter 16: **BOOK REVIEWS.**

**Shelley Gavigan, "Petit Treason in Eighteenth Century England:
Women's Inequality Before the Law" (1989-1990) 3 _Canadian Journal of
Women and the Law_ 335-374**
    This piece examines the English law of petit treason as it was
specifically related to wives accused of murdering their husbands. Until
1790, a woman so convicted was publicly executed by burning at the
stake. The author asserts that the law of petit treason was a logical
extension of women's subordination by sex and by marriage. The form
of conviction and the punishment of these wives proved a "powerful
moral lesson for both husbands and wives." Formal equality was won for
women in the change in the charge from petit treason to wilful murder,
and in the change in punishment from burning at the stake to hanging.
However, through this change, the patriarchal family was both transformed and renewed in the new ideology of public and private spheres.

**J. Greene, "A Provocation Defence For Battered Women Who Kill?"
(1989) 12 _Adelaide Law Review_ 145-163**
    A successful defense of provocation reduces murder to manslaught-
er. In this article, the author proposes a policy basis for the law of
provocation which would extend the defense to battered women who kill
their abusers and who are subsequently charged with murder. The
article also contains an analysis of the various approaches the law has
taken to killings by battered women, and suggestions for the implementation of the provocation defense in these cases.

**Jessica P. Greenwald, Alan J. Tomkins, Mary Kenning and Denis
Zavodny, "Psychological Self-Defense Jury Instructions: Influence on
Verdicts for Battered Women Defendants" (1990) 8 _Behavioral Sciences
and the Law_ 171-180**
    This article examines the effect of the "psychological self-defense"
which would provide a legal justification for a killing committed under
the threat of extremely serious psychological injury. One hundred and

ninety-six subjects issued verdicts after reading two vignette cases in which a battered woman killed her abuser, and a series of jury instructions (psychological self-defense only, physical self-defense only, psychological and physical self-defense, or none of these). The authors report that only psychological self-defense instructions significantly influenced verdict patterns, by shifting what would have been voluntary manslaughter convictions to acquittals.

Kay A. Heggstad, "The Devil Made Me Do It: The Case Against Using PMS as a Defence in a Court of Law" (1986) 9 *Hamline Law Review* 155-163

This article opposes the use of premenstrual syndrome (PMS) as a defense, because it is not a well-defined phenomenon. The author argues that diagnosis is subjective, and that there is no proven cause or treatment. She describes the numerous treatments as ineffective, noting that the proposed progesterone therapy had been brought into question by controlled studies. Her concerns about PMS as a defense focus on the possibility of a criminal "faking" symptoms, the difficulties of proof, and the problem that PMS is unlikely to be the sole cause of the criminal behaviour.

William R. Keye and Eric Trunell, "PMS: A Medical Perspective" (1986) 9 *Hamline Law Review* 165-181

This article, written by gynaecologists, discusses the medical issues involved in premenstrual syndrome (PMS), including guidelines for diagnosis of PMS, its prevalence, its symptoms, and the common classifications. The authors propose a biopsychosocial model of PMS, arguing that the syndrome does not have a single cause, and must be considered in light of cultural, social, psychological, and biological factors. They also suggest strategies for identifying and classifying PMS symptoms, and list the wide variety of therapies currently in use.

Kit Kinports, "Defending Battered Women's Self-Defense Claims" (1988) 67 *Oregon Law Review* 393-465

This article examines the use of the self-defense claim for battered women who kill their batterers. The author first examines the Battered Woman Syndrome, and then discusses the potential use of the defense in limited circumstances, including instructions to the jury to consider the psychological traits of a battered woman and the conditions of battering. She then discusses and rejects criticisms of the use of self-defense by battered women, and concludes that in some cases, self-defense is an appropriate claim.

Robert R. Lawrence, "Checking the Allure of Increased Conviction Rates: The Admissibility of Expert Testimony of Rape Trauma Syndrome in Criminal Proceedings" (1984) 70 *Virginia Law Review* 1657-1705

This article discusses the possibility that the admission of evidence on Rape Trauma Syndrome (RTS) may negate the effects of rape law reforms. It examines briefly the nature of rape law reform, and notes that although there has been no increase in conviction rates, the reforms have been successful in alleviating the complainants' trauma, and in having rape treated like other violent crimes. The author discusses the scientific background of RTS, the factors relating to its admissibility as evidence, and its reliability. He contrasts its value with the constitutional requirement that would allow the defense to focus on the victim's character and conduct. He concludes that there will always be tension between civil libertarians and those advocating enlightened sexual assault legislation, and that a delicate balance must be maintained. This balance, he suggests, would be upset by the admission of RTS evidence.

Victoria Mikesell Mather, "The Skeleton in the Closet: The Battered Woman Syndrome, Self-Defense, and Expert Testimony" (1988) 39 *Mercer Law Review* 545-589

The author argues that while traditional notions of self-defense do not translate well to the Battered Woman Syndrome, it is important to take a realistic view of the physical and social differences between men and women in considering a battered woman's self-defense claim. She recommends that courts admit expert testimony which explains the Syndrome, and that they do so on basis of the helpfulness of the evidence to the jury, and not upon whether the woman exactly fits the symptoms of the Syndrome. She claims that the theory is well-recognized by psychology professionals, but would require an expert's explanation to the jury. She concludes that not to admit such evidence would do injustice to battered women.

Karen M. McArthur, "Through Her Looking Glass: PMS on Trial"

(1989) 47 *University of Toronto Faculty of Law Review* 825-873

The author claims that, in its present biological determinist form, the pre-menstrual syndrome defense is a male construct, arising from the male centred medical and legal views, and perpetrates societal myths surrounding menstruation. She examines the medical approach to menstruation, canvasses the legal concerns -- criminal, evidentiary, and constitutional -- on the PMS defense, and offers a "workable premenstrual change defense which is less problematic for feminist justice." She concludes with a plea for reconstruction of traditional gender roles, and a move toward "more subjectivism" in the criminal law.

Eugene Meehan and Katherine MacRae, "Legal Implications of Premenstrual Syndrome: A Canadian Perspective" (1986) 135 *Canadian Medical Association Journal* 601-608

Through analysis of the leading English cases and several Canadian cases, the authors address the issue of the legal recognition of premenstrual tension. They discuss PMS as it has been historically encountered, its symptoms and treatment, and the possible legal implications. They conclude that PMS is unlikely to become a substantive defense, but that it has been and should continue to be used to mitigate sentences. See also (1986) 135 *Canadian Medical Association Journal* 1340 for a reader's response to the article.

Richard T. Oakes, "PMS: A Plea Bargain Does Not a Rule of Law Make" (1986) 9 *Hamline Law Review* 203-216

This article discusses the state of the law in regard to premenstrual syndrome (PMS) as a defense, and argues that it has not been accepted as an affirmative defense in any jurisdiction, although there has been limited admission of PMS evidence. The author suggests that it is unlikely that PMS will be accepted as a defense in the United States, due to the restrictions of the FRYE test, and (in the federal courts) the INSANITY DEFENCE REFORM ACT of 1984 (18 USCA s.20 [Supp 1985]), which excludes lack of capacity from the insanity defense. He discusses several ways in which PMS might be used outside the federal courts, including limiting the defense to first degree murder, reducing the degree of homicide from premeditated to unmeditated, limiting the defense to specific intent crimes, or to mitigating sentence.

Judith A. Osborne, "Perspectives on Premenstrual Syndrome: Women, Law and Medicine" (1989) 8 _Canadian Journal of Family Law_ 165-184

This article canvasses the history of the medical recognition of premenstrual syndrome (PMS), and discusses studies which have questioned the validity of PMS research. The author argues that legal recognition of PMS can be a "double-edged sword." Positively, it recognizes a real female experience, but negatively it may result in the presentation of a normal experience as pathological. Her legal analysis includes a discussion of the Canadian law of insanity, automatism, and infanticide. She concludes that it would be difficult to fit PMS as a substantive defense within present legal categories, and argues that it may be necessary to create a new category. She cautions that the tendency to "medicalize" women's deviance may reinforce the perception of women as inferior.

Susan L. Podebradsky and Mary E. Triggiano-Hunt, "An Overview of Defense of Battered Women from a Postconviction Perspective" (1985) 4 _Wisconsin Women's Law Journal_ 95-115

The authors discuss the practical and legal concerns for a defense attorney of a women who has been battered. They examine the battering relationship, the battered woman, and the Battered Woman Syndrome (BWS), in which the woman "interrupts the cycle of violence with a violent response of her own." They urge lawyers to maintain creativity and sensitivity in dealing with women who have been battered, and to use all available legal and psychological resources in order to most effectively help their clients.

Thomas L. Riley, "PMS as a Legal Defence" (1986) 9 _Hamline Law Review_ 193-201

The author presents the historical background of Pre- Menstrual Syndrome (PMS), its definition, and the problems associated with its diagnosis and treatment. He also discusses the role of the expert witness, noting that because most women suffer some type of PMS, the expert must be able to state that PMS was a factor in the commission of the crime, not just that the defendant has PMS. He suggests a variety of factors that the expert can gather to provide objective proof, including employment and criminal records that demonstrate periodic erratic behaviour that can be linked to PMS. Other sources include blood tests and medical history.

Cathryn Jo Rosen, "The Excuse of Self-Defense: Correcting a Historical Accident on Behalf of Battered Women Who Kill" (1986) 36 *American University Law Review* 11-56

The author discusses the controversy which arises when battered women kill their batterers, and argues that difficulty arises in such cases because such women do not fit within the traditional categories of good and evil in the criminal law. She claims women who are subject to Battered Woman Syndrome and kill have no defense if the law is strictly applied, because it promotes a weighing of relative value of the abuser and victim. She concludes that an excuse principle would allow a more realistic focus on the pressure faced by the individual defendant and her lack of perceived options, while nonetheless discouraging such self-help actions.

J. A. Tanford and A. J. Bocchino, "Rape Victim Shield Laws and the Sixth Amendment" (1980) 128 *University of Pennsylvania Law Review* 544-600

The authors examine the various rape shield laws in place in most of the states, and conclude that many of them are unconstitutional. They argue that these laws prevent a defendant from presenting relevant evidence and from confrontation, both violations of the Sixth Amendment, and that the rules of evidence prior to the new laws were sufficient, because these rules prevented evidence from being presented to the jury if their prejudicial value outweighed their probative value. They further argue that the complainant's sexual history is potentially relevant in some cases, and that an absolute prohibition, therefore, violates federal constitutional standards, regardless of legislative intent or desire.

Jane A. Trimble and Margaret Furay Fay, "PMS In Today's Society" (1986) 9 *Hamline Law Review* 183-191

This article provides an historical overview of the syndrome, and discusses the variety of effects PMS may have on an individual. The authors, who are involved in running a PMS clinic, discuss the effect of PMS on the attorney-client relationship, and suggest how an attorney could determine if there is a possibility that their client has PMS. They also recommend factors which should be considered by an attorney if the client suffers from PMS.

Jeffrey T. Waddle, Mark Parts, "Rape Trauma Syndrome: Interest of the Victim and Neutral Experts" [1989] _University of Chicago Legal Forum_ 399-420

The authors discuss the nature of rape trauma syndrome (RTS) as a frequent result of nonconsensual sexual intercourse. Some jurisdictions have allowed the prosecution to introduce expert evidence to prove the absence of consent. This raises the issues of the defendant's right to use of RTS evidence under due process and confrontation, and of compulsory process and statutory rights under rape shield laws. They conclude that the defendant should have the right to introduce negative evidence of RTS when the prosecution introduces positive evidence of RTS results. They further suggest that to limit the victim's trauma, a neutral expert should be appointed, rather than having several experts examine her.

Pamela A. Wilk, "Expert Testimony on Rape Trauma Syndrome: Admissibility and Effective Use in Criminal Rape Prosecution" (1984) 33 _American University Law Review_ 417-461

The author analyzes the admissibility of expert evidence of rape trauma syndrome on the issue of consent in rape trials. She provides an historical and descriptive sketch of the syndrome, and discusses the use of expert testimony, and the legal recognition of rape trauma syndrome in different jurisdictions. She considers the positive and negative implications of its legal recognition, including its value in proving absence of consent, and the possibility that the defense might require a complainant to undergo further psychological examination once the prosecution has introduced the syndrome as evidence.

Howard V. Zonana, Roxanne L. Bartel, James A. Wells, Josephine A. Buchanan and Marjorie A. Getz, "Sex Differences in Persons Found Not Guilty by Reason of Insanity: Analysis of Data From the Connecticut NGRI Registry (Part II)" (1990) 18 _Bulletin of the American Academy of Psychiatry and the Law_ 129-142

For annotation, see Chapter 6: FIRST NATIONS AND RACE.

Rape

"To Have and to Hold: The Marital Rape Exception and the Fourteenth Amendment" (1986) 99 *Harvard Law Review* 1255-1273
For annotation, see Chapter 2: CONSTITUTIONAL LAW.

Zsuzsanna Adler, "Rape -- The Intention of Parliament and the Practice of the Courts" (1982) 45 *Modern Law Review* 664-674
This article examines the relationship between the intention of the British Parliament in passing reform legislation with respect to rape offences, and the practices of the courts. The author reports the findings of a study of conviction rates, especially noting the use of mistaken belief defense, and cross-examination of the victim on past sexual conduct. She concludes that the intention of legislators that the legislation would improve procedure in rape trials, eliminate prejudices to the victim, and thus encourage more reporting of sexual assaults was not fulfilled. This discrepancy between the intention of Parliament and the actual practice of the courts is due to inadequacies of the reform legislation, as well as to the male dominated nature of the legal system. She recommends systematic monitoring of the law relating to rape as a method by which this discrepancy may be decreased.

Christine Alder, "An Exploration of Self-Reported Sexually Aggressive Behaviour" (1985) 31 *Crime and Delinquency* 306-331
Part of a special issue on Rape, this article found that the most important factor in determining sexually aggressive behaviour was the influence of sexually aggressive friends. The author also reports that this factor interacted strongly with attitudes legitimizing sexual aggression and service in Vietnam.

H. E. Baber, "How Bad is Rape?" (1987) 2 *Hypatia: A Journal of Feminist Philosophy* 125-138
The author argues that to be compelled to do routine work is to be gravely harmed, and that pink-collar work is a more serious harm to women than rape. She urges feminists to arrange their priorities accordingly, and to devote their resources to the elimination of sex

segregation in employment.

Ronald J. Berger, Patricia Searles and W. Lawrence Neuman, "The Dimensions of Rape Reform Legislation" (1988) 22 _Law and Society Review_ 329-357
     This article examines the relative successes of feminist attempts at reform of rape legislation in the United States. The authors' research examines each state's rape legislation, identifying fifteen relevant elements and assigning a value code to each, to identify which values, ranging from traditional to feminist, are present in the legislation. They conclude that success has been mixed, and that feminist goals have been hampered by the ideologies of the criminal justice system and non-feminist political groups.

Sue Blay-Cohen and Dina L. Coster, "Marital Rape in California: For Better or for Worse" (1980) 8 _San Fernando Valley Law Review_ 239-261
     The authors trace the history of the common law doctrine prohibiting marital rape, discuss the justifications for the existence of spousal immunity, and describe the attempts to change the law in California. Finally, they assess the new law for its potential effect on spousal rape, and suggest possible changes.

Christine Boyle, "Book Review: Judith Rowland, RAPE: THE ULTIMATE VIOLATION (1986)" (1986) 14 _International Journal of the Sociology of Law_ 428-432
     For annotation, see Chapter 16: **BOOK REVIEWS**.

Christine Boyle, "Married Women -- Beyond the Pale of the Law of Rape" (1981) 1 _Windsor Yearbook of Access to Justice_ 192-213
     The author argues that the abolition of a husband's immunity to the offence of marital rape may not be sufficient to cure the problem, if the realities of the potential coercive nature of the husband/wife relationship are not taken into consideration.

Christine Boyle, "Sexual Assault and the Feminist Judge" (1985) 1 _Canadian Journal of Women and the Law_ 93-107

The author analyzes judging from a feminist standpoint, using different sexual assault scenarios as examples. Instead of choosing the male perspective, she suggests avoiding gender neutral abstraction when gender is significant, in order to acknowledge the underlying social problem. Feminist analysis, she concludes, is not necessarily monolithic -- there may be disagreement with respect to when gender is material.

Kristin Bumiller, "Fallen Angels: the Representation of Violence Against Women in Legal Culture" (1990) 18 *International Journal of the Sociology of Law* 125-141

Using as a focus for her research the New Bedford rape case, the author explores the media's role in the symbolic representation of victims and criminals in popular culture, and the way the reporting on "trials concerning sexual assault ... may actually reinforce dominant preconceptions about women, men and crimes of sexual violence." She describes the media attention given to the rape at the time it occurred, and later during the trial, and the difficulty the victim had in telling her story, given normal courtroom tactics. She discusses the implications for feminist strategies in a realist legal world.

Kristin Bumiller, "Rape as a Legal Symbol: An Essay on Sexual Violence and Racism" (1987) 42 *University of Miami Law Review* 75-91

Part of a symposium entitled Excluded Voices: Realities in Law and Law Reform, this article claims current rape law reform does not go far enough because it implicitly validates the current legal discourse about rape. The author argues that the current focus on consent denies the reality that victims are concerned with survival, and not with objectively demonstrating their nonconsent, and that what is needed is a new language to define the roles of the victim and the attacker. She concludes that otherwise, questioning of the sexist stereotypes inherent in rape trials will be controlled and limited by current legal definitions, and "may be cast within a class, race or sexist interpretation."

Duncan Chappell, "The Impact of Rape Legislation Reform: Some Contemporary Trends" (1984) 7 *International Journal of Women's Studies* 70-80

The author examines the impact of rape legislation reform in Canada and the United States, focusing on empirical data from

Washington State, and on Australian and American studies of the implementation of new rape laws. He examines the expressed purpose of rape law reform, and whether those goals have been achieved. The goals include recognition of rape as a crime of violence, increased conviction rates, and the improved treatment of rape victims. He concludes that most of the progress made was more symbolic than actual.

B.J. Cling, "Rape Trauma Syndrome: Medical Evidence of Non-Consent" (1988) 10 *Women's Rights Law Reporter* 243-259

Rape Trauma Syndrome (RTS) -- the clinically observed "traumatic psychological after-effects of rape" -- is a recognized psychological disorder. This article is an exploration of its acceptance by courts as proof of rape. The author reports that conflicting decisions have been rendered -- some allowing RTS as proof of rape, some allowing it only to rebut claims of "inconsistent victim behaviour," and some disallowing it completely. She calls for more research to confirm further its scientific reliability, and urges its admission in rape trials as evidence of the victim's non-consent.

Kenneth Cloke, "Date Rape and the Limits of Mediation" (1988) 21 *Mediation Quarterly* 77-83

The author describes a rocky relationship, an allegation of rape, and the resulting mediation by a therapist and an attorney team; and considers the effectiveness of mediation in such circumstances.

R. Collette-Carrière, "La Victimologie et le Viol: un Discours Complice" (1980) 13:1 *Criminologie* 60-79

The author has two goals in this article: to articulate the nature of rape, and to develop a theoretical and practical understanding of the victimology of rape. She traces the history of rape and discusses the contribution of radical feminists to the recent understanding of rape as an act of aggression. She reviews the pre-reform rape laws in the Canadian CRIMINAL CODE, the rate of under-reporting of the crime, and the disposition of rape cases in the judicial system. Finally, she discusses myths surrounding rape, rapists, and their victims, and the socialization of women which renders them "victimizable."

Eric T. Cooperstein, "Protecting Rape Victims from Civil Suits by Their Attackers" (1989) 8 *Law and Inequality* 279-308

Civil suits for defamation, as conducted by accused rapists against their victims, threaten to nullify the hard fought feminist successes in rape law reform by serving as a new and significant deterrent to women reporting sexual assault and rape. This article analyzes the impact of defamation suits on rape victims, going on to propose legislative and judicial solutions that "may prevent defamation suits from unduly burdening women and from pushing our jurisprudence back towards its sexist origins."

T. Brettel Dawson, "Sexual Assault Law and Past Sexual Conduct of the Primary Witness: The Construction of Relevance" (1988) 2 *Canadian Journal of Women and the Law* 310-334

The author discusses cross-examination of the complainant or primary witness in sexual assault cases, particularly about previous sexual history. She describes the common law evidentiary rules and the new Canadian rules embodied in ss. 246.6 and 246.7 of the CRIMINAL CODE, and argues that the new rules may actually allow more evidence of the complainant's past sexual history to be admitted. She compares legal liberalism, which disguises androcentrism with the concept of protecting civil liberties, and feminism, which seeks to counteract the biases that are built into the criminal justice system in general, and evidentiary rules in particular.

Anne Marie Delorey, "Rape Trauma Syndrome: An Evidentiary Tool" (1989-1990) 3 *Canadian Journal of Women and the Law* 531-551

The author traces the history of the use of Rape Trauma Syndrome (RTS) evidence in courts in the United States, where the prosecution is introducing such evidence as proof that the victim was forced to take part in non-consensual sexual activity, and discusses the possible use of such evidence within the context of Canadian criminal law. She suggests that the medicalization of rape as an individual woman's "problem" may not be a positive trend for women, insofar as it does not allow a view of rape as a crime of public proportions. Introducing evidence of RTS may allow even further questioning of a woman's background by defense, and lead to a battle of the experts over the woman's credibility. She concludes with the recommendation that RTS be used as a tool in the feminist project to eliminate sexual assault, but cautions of the hidden dangers in this legal reform.

Janet Drysdale, "Book Review: Sylvana Tomaselli and Roy Porter, RAPE (1986)" (1989-1990) 3 *Canadian Journal of Women and the Law* 644-647
For annotation, see Chapter 16: BOOK REVIEWS.

Megan Ellis, "Redefining Rape: Re-Victimization of Women" (1988) 17:3 *Resources for Feminist Research: Documentation sur la Recherche Féministe* 96-99
The author discusses how new sexual assault laws and rape law reform have failed to achieve feminist goals. She argues that the creation of a gender-neutral law reduced women to victims, shifted the problem to the concern of "crime victims," and ignored the gender-specific nature of the crime. The result was to remove the woman's voice from society's hearing, and return control to the bureaucrats and politicians of male hegemony.

Jim Galvin, "Rape: A Decade of Reform" (1985) 31 *Crime and Delinquency* 163-168
Part of a special issue on Rape, this article outlines the reforms to Michigan rape law. The author analyzes the changes, which he attributes to the increase in reporting of rape, and examines victim demands for changes and feminist analysis of rape.

L. Gibson, Stuart Johnson, and Rick Linden, "A Situational Theory of Rape" (1980) 22 *Canadian Journal of Criminology* 51-65
This article presents a sociological evaluation of the situational requirements that lead to rape. Situational theory, an alternative to genetic and victimological approaches, considers what circumstances are most conducive to the expression of deviant or criminal behaviour. The factors described by the authors as facilitating are times, places, hardware, others, actors, and circumstances. They address the issue of victim precipitation, and reject previous situational studies which view rape as a sexual act, rather than as assaultive, and victims as precipitators for behaviour that might "appear to invite sexual relations." They suggest that within the context of the situational theory, some factors of the

victim's behaviour will be relevant. They conclude that the theory is a useful framework for further research.

Jan M. Glasgow, "Marital Rape Exemption: Legal Sanction of Spouse Abuse" (1980) 18 *Journal of Family Law* 565-585
The author traces the history of the common law marital rape exemption, describes activity in relation to marital rape in the courts and legislatures in the United States, and poses some alternate solutions to law reform in this area.

Janet Gornick, Martha R. Burt, and Karen J. Pittman, "Structure and Activities of Rape Crisis Centers in the Early 1980s" (1985) 31 *Crime and Delinquency* 247-268
Part of a special issue on Rape, this article examines the evolution of rape crisis centers in the United States. The author reports that the centers have adapted to fit individual community needs, and that there is little uniformity among different centers in terms of the direct services they provide, or the community action and education they undertake.

Tan Cheng Han, "Marital Rape -- Removing the Husband's Legal Immunity" (1989) 31 *Malaysian Law Review* 112-128
This paper discusses the criminal code of Singapore and case law about marital rape. The author examines the arguments for the spousal immunity defense to a charge of rape, such as decreasing family unity, alternative remedies available, evidentiary difficulties, and floodgates problems. She then argues for legislative reform, at minimum to extend the rape offence to include non-cohabiting couples, or to allow for a rape offence with differentiation in sentencing between stranger rape and husband rape. The best result, she concludes, would be the complete abolition of the spousal immunity provision.

Ronald Hinch, "Inconsistencies and Contradictions in Canada's Sexual Assault Law" (1988) 14 *Canadian Public Policy* 282-294
The author examines three aspects of the sexual assault provisions of the Canadian CRIMINAL CODE -- the change of name from rape, the requirement (or lack thereof) for penetration of the vagina, and the reputation of the victim - in light of practice in the Halifax Police

Department. He concludes that although many feminist objectives were met by the revised legislation, some aspects continue to be anti-feminist and anti-woman.

Steven B. Katz, "Expectation and Desire in the Law of Forcible Rape" (1989) 26 *San Diego Law Review* 21-71
This article provides a critical review of the law of forcible rape. The author argues that rape law doctrine upholds the principle that a man is entitled to enforce his reasonable expectations of sexual access -- generated mainly by virtue of his personal relationship with his partner -- regardless of her willingness, subject only to the proviso that he must only use reasonable means of self-help. Various aspects of the law such as the marital exemption, evidence issues, and the mistake-of-fact defense, are examined. The author proposes that the present "property" conception of rape law be replaced by a "contract" conception, and concludes that it is difficult to determine whether it is ever possible for a woman truly to consent to sexual intercourse.

Catherine L. Kello, "Rape Shield Laws: Is it Time for Reinforcement?" (1987-88) 21 *University of Michigan Journal of Law Reform* 317-345
Michigan enacted the first American rape shield law (i.e. statute forbidding inquiry into a rape victim's past sexual conduct) in 1974. A new defense tactic has arisen whereby the accused, prior to the criminal proceedings, files a civil suit against the complainant for defamation, intentional infliction of emotional distress, and abuse of process. Since Michigan's civil discovery rules are very broad, the protection afforded by the rape shield law is effectively nullified. The author proposes a Model Statute which would provide that the civil action not be heard until after the termination of the criminal action.

Wayne A. Kerstetter, "Gateway to Justice: Police and Prosecutorial Response to Sexual Assaults Against Women" (1990) 81 *Journal of Criminal Law & Criminology* 267-313
This article reports the findings of a study of decisions made at two levels of the criminal justice system in cases of sexual assault -- namely, the police officer's decision to treat a woman's complaint as valid, and the prosecutor's decision to proceed with the charge. It suggests that

gender-based conflict theories account for differential levels of police protection, and that prosecution decisions can be explained both in terms of the "sexual property value" of some victims over others, and of the woman's conforming to sex-role norms. The author concludes, however, that the primary factor in official decision-making is instrumental or evidentiary, such as the victim's decision to press charges.

Michael R. Klatt, "Rape in Marriage: The Law in Texas and the Need for Reform" (1980) 32 *Baylor Law Review* 109-121
This article examines the arguments advanced in favour of the spousal exemption to rape charges, and concludes that while these arguments may have been valid at some point in history, they are no longer so. The author recommends the removal of the marital rape exemption in Texas.

H. Lane Kneedler, "Sexual Assault Law Reform in Virginia -- A Legislative History" (1982) 68 *Virginia Law Review* 459-505
The author describes the historic development of rape law under the common law in Virginia, and in particular the development of the requirement of "reasonable resistance," and the admission of evidence of the victim's past sexual conduct. He then describes the purpose and probable results of Virginia's reformed legislation.

Gary D. La Free, "Male Power and Female Victimization: Toward a Theory of Interracial Rape" (1982) 88 *American Journal of Sociology* 311-327
For annotation, see Chapter 6: **FIRST NATIONS AND RACE.**

C. Lacerte-Lamontagne, J. Giroux, R. Boyer and Y. Lamontagne, "L'article 142 du Code Criminel et les Victimes de viol" (1980) 40:3 *Revue du Barreau* 448-463
This article discusses the efficacy of s. 142 of the Canadian CRIMINAL CODE in protecting the interests of rape victims during the course of trial. Based on a two year study of rape and attempted rape cases in Montreal, the authors conclude that the provision has been successful in restraining the number of inquiries into the sexual conduct of victims. However, the credibility of the victim appears connected to

her sexual past, in the way that the credibility of the accused is connected to his criminal history.

Patricia Ladouceur and Mark Temple, "Substance Use Among Rapists: A Comparison with Other Serious Felons" (1985) 31 _Crime and Delinquency_ 269-294
For annotation, see Chapter 6: FIRST NATIONS AND RACE.

Barbara S. Lindemann, "'To Ravish and Carnally Know': Rape in Eighteenth-Century Massachusetts" (1984) 10 _Signs: Journal of Women in Culture and Society_ 63-82
For annotation, see Chapter 10: LEGAL HISTORY.

Alan J. Lizotte, "The Uniqueness of Rape: Reporting Assaultive Violence to the Police" (1985) 31 _Crime and Delinquency_ 169-190
Part of a special issue on Rape, this article compares rape to other forms of assault in relation to victim police reporting. The author reports that the reporting of rape is different from other assaults, and discusses factors which influence reporting.

Susan MacDonald-Caringella, "The Comparability in Sexual and Nonsexual Assault Case Treatment: Did Statute Change Meet the Objective?" (1985) 35 _Crime and Delinquency_ 206-222
Part of a special issue on Rape, this article compares the treatment of sexual and nonsexual assaults by victim and crime characteristics. The author reports that sexual assaults are pursued with less evidence than most nonsexual assaults, and that there is no difference in plea bargaining or acquittals.

Patricia Yancey Martin, Diana Dinitto, Sharon Maxwell, and Diane Blum Norton, "Controversies Surrounding the Rape Kit Exam in the 1980s:Issues and Alternatives" (1985) 31 _Crime and Delinquency_ 223-246
Part of a special issue on Rape, this article criticizes the use of rape kits as a method of evidence collection. Specifically mentioned are the lack of standards about what evidence is collected, where the exam occurs, and who performs the exam.

Paul Matthews, "Marital Rape" (1980) 10 *Family Law* 221-224

The paper discusses case law which deems it impossible for marital rape to occur because a wife's consent to sexual intercourse is implied in the marriage until such consent is specifically revoked. The author argues that the law is ridiculously outmoded, and that marital rape should be treated no differently from any other rape.

Maureen Mulligan, "Obtaining Political Asylum: Classifying Rape as a Well-Founded Fear of Persecution on Account of Political Opinion" (1990) 10 *Boston College Third World Law Journal* 355-380

For annotation, see Chapter 6: FIRST NATIONS AND RACE.

Frances Olsen, "Statutory Rape: A Feminist Critique of Rights Analysis" (1984) 63 *Texas Law Review* 387-432

The author argues that rights discourse encourages a partial and inadequate analysis of sexuality, because the issue is then viewed as one of discovering the line between freedom and social control. The real issue is not where to draw the line, but rather the substance and meaning given to sexuality in our society. She discusses feminism and women's rights, substantive vs. formal equality, and criticizes the pseudo-neutrality in law which uses a male norm. She looks at statutory rape laws which put young women unnecessarily under state-enforced sexual constraint and the debilitating stereotypes they embody. She calls for the empowerment of women and the disempowerment of the state. She claims that it is wrong to interpret women's sexuality as self-expression, as though sexism, which oppresses women, does not exist. Feminist jurisprudence must, instead, look at the broader issue of quality of sexual freedom and the nature of social control. Sexuality is socially constructed, and can be discovered.

Barbara Omolade, "Black Women, Black Men and Tawana Brawley -- The Shared Condition" (1989) 12 *Harvard Women's Law Journal* 11-23

For annotation, see Chapter 6: FIRST NATIONS AND RACE.

Toni Pickard, "Culpable Mistakes and Rape: Relating Mens Rea to the Crime" (1980) 30 *University of Toronto Law Journal* 75-98

The author argues that mistake as to consent should only be a valid defense if it is reasonable, and that culpable mens rea must depend upon the action to which it relates. The article, which was written before the Supreme Court of Canada decision in PAPPAJOHN [1980] 2 S.C.R. 120, answers three major objections to her position, namely, the requirement of reasonableness is unfair, that making a mistake is not sufficiently "bad" to impose a criminal sanction, and that there is authority that an honest mistake is sufficient to negative mens rea. She considers British and Canadian cases, and concludes that there is no convincing authority for any of these propositions.

Toni Pickard, "Culpable Mistakes and Rape: Harsh Words on 'PAPPAJOHN'" (1980) 30 *University of Toronto Law Journal* 415-419
This is a post-script to the author's first article on culpable mistakes (see: Pickard, "Culpable Mistakes and Rape: Relating Mens Rea to Crime" (1980) 30 *University of Toronto Law Journal* 75-98) following the Supreme Court's decision in PAPPAJOHN v. THE QUEEN [1980] 2 S.C.R. 120. She criticizes Justice Dickson's dissent for its subjective orthodoxy, and its superficial approach to the inter-related problems of recklessness and subjective and objective liability. She argues that his definition of recklessness as conscious risk-taking is tautological: under that definition a genuine mistake as to consent, however unreasonable, must always negate liability, because if the defendant believes there is consent, he can't be consciously taking a risk. She suggests that the defendant who consciously takes a risk is actually wilfully blind, not reckless, and concludes that the courts have yet to make a principled judgment on when to apply subjective or objective liability.

Stephen S. Pistono, "Rape in Medieval Europe" (1989) 14:2 *Atlantis* 36-42
For annotation, see Chapter 10: **LEGAL HISTORY.**

Kenneth Polk, "Rape Reform and Criminal Justice Processing" (1985) 31 *Crime and Delinquency* 191-205
Part of a special issue on Rape, this article discusses general reforms of rape law in the United States, and examines criminal justice processing. The author reports that while there has been no change in police clearance or in felony conviction of rape cases, there is now a greatly increased probability that offenders will be sentenced to state

institutions.

Kim Lane Schepple, "The Re-Vision of Rape Law -- Book Review: Susan Estrich, REAL RAPE: HOW THE LEGAL SYSTEM VICTIMIZES WOMEN WHO SAY NO (1987)" (1987) 54 *University of Chicago Law Review* **1095-1118**
For annotation, see Chapter 16: **BOOK REVIEWS**.

Martin D. Schwartz and Gerald T. Slatin, "The Law on Marital Rape: How do Marxism and Feminism Explain its Persistence" (1984) 8 *ALSA Forum* **244-264**
The authors discuss the difficulty of rationalizing Marxist and feminist analyses, specifically with respect to the persistence of law making marital rape impossible. They conclude that the spousal exemption arose because women were once viewed as property of men, and continues because the law continues to express male, patriarchal, and capitalist hegemony. This persistence can also be seen as the result of historical inertia; that is, no one group has heretofore lobbied for reform. They conclude that this latter view is supported by the fact that feminist groups have succeeded in lobbying for change in some jurisdictions.

Patricia Searles and Ronald J. Berger, "The Current Status of Rape Reform Legislation: An Examination of State Statutes" (1987) 10 *Women's Rights Law Reporter* **25-43**
Since the mid-1970s, most states' rape laws have been reformed. The authors provide tables categorizing states by sixteen characteristics of their rape laws. After examining the reforms that have been made, they suggest that the goals of rape reform legislation should be to increase reporting, prosecution, and conviction in rape cases, to provide better treatment for victims, to treat rape comparably with other violent crimes, to prohibit more "coercive sexual conduct," and to protect a broader range of persons.

Elizabeth Sheehy, "Canadian Judges and the Law of Rape: Should the Charter Insulate Bias?" (1989) 21 *Ottawa Law Review* **151-197**
The article discusses challenges under the Canadian CHARTER OF RIGHTS AND FREEDOMS to the rape shield provisions in ss. 276

and 277 of the Canadian CRIMINAL CODE, which deal with cross-examination of a victim of sexual assault on past sexual experiences. The author argues for survival of these sections, because the absence of their provisions would seriously threaten the integrity of the entire package of recent rape law reforms.

Mark A. Small and Pat A. Tetreault, "Social Psychology, 'Marital Rape Exemptions,' and Privacy" (1990) 8 _Behavioral Sciences and the Law_ 141-149
This article reports the results of a search of marital rape statutes in fifty American states. The author reports that states handle the question of marital rape in one of three ways: (1) by abolishing the exemption for husbands; (2) by qualifying the exemption; or (3) by allowing the exemption. The article concludes with a discussion of possible relationships between social psychology, marital rape exemptions, and privacy.

Carol Smart, "Law's Power, the Sexed Body, and Feminist Discourse" (1990) 17 _Journal of Law and Society_ 194-210
The author examines the relationship between knowledge and politics, and questions the "taken-for-granted assumptions" about knowledge, especially regarding its nature and validity. She claims the question of whether women have an authentic self from which to speak is especially important within law because law is both so powerful and so silencing of feminist interventions. A woman's body is sexualized within law, especially in rape trials, where her body "becomes literally saturated with sex," in the dominant (i.e. male, legal) account of rape. She concludes with a challenge to feminists to move away from the dominant and paradoxical account of sex as a measure of identity and an instrument of truth, and of women as eternal victims.

M. Dwayne Smith and Nathan Bennett, "Poverty, Inequality, and Theories of Forcible Rape" (1985) 31 _Crime and Delinquency_ 295-305
Part of a special issue on Rape, this article uses poverty and inequality as variables in examining community rape statistics. While poverty was found to be part of an ecological climate of a community with high rape statistics and poor people were more likely to be victims of rape, the authors report that a better predictor of rape statistics is the

rate of divorce in a community.

Keith Soothill, Sylvia Walby, and Paul Bagguley, "Judges, the Media, and Rape" (1990) 17 *Journal of Law and Society* 211-233
This article discusses media reporting of judges' comments in sexual assault cases in Britain. The authors report an increase in the number of assaults reported, as well as a change in the type of comments by the judiciary which were reported by newspapers following both acquittals and convictions for rape or attempted rape. They claim that, while the number of press reports of rape cases and judges' comments has risen, this is because of increased selectivity by the press, and a smaller number of cases receive much wider press coverage. They conclude that the feminist movement has done little to change remarks by the judiciary in rape cases.

Julie Taylor, "Rape and Women's Credibility: Problems of Recantations and False Accusations Echoed in the Case of Cathleen Crowell Webb and Gary Dotson" (1987) 10 *Harvard Women's Law Journal* 59-115
The author discusses the problems of rape victim credibility, the myth of false accusations, and the legal issues surrounding recantation. She focuses on the recantation of Webb and the subsequent release of Dotson, the man she had accused of raping her. She argues that the recantation was probably false, and the result of societal pressures which places blame on the victim. She also discusses how this lack of credibility is played out in the justice system, in terms of rapes which are unreported, dismissed by the police as unfounded, or not pursued by the prosecutor due to such factors as race, class, or circumstances.

Jennifer Temkin, "Towards a Modern Law of Rape" (1982) 45 *Modern Law Review* 399-418
This article deals with proposals for legal reform in Britain with respect to the law of rape which purported to assuage the controversy that treatment of rape victims in the legal process discourages reporting, and that the laws of evidence permit rapists to avoid conviction. The author argues that reform of the laws regarding the obtaining of consent by fraud, of the marital rape exemption, and of the requirement for corroboration, is crucial in order for the law to be seen to uphold the principle of freedom of choice to sexual intercourse for women.

Lucinda Vandervort, "Mistake of Law and Sexual Assault: Consent and Mens Rea" (1986-88) 2 *Canadian Journal of Women and the Law* 233-309

The author argues that the so-called mistakes of fact as to consent relied on by sexual assailants are actually mistakes of law which provide no defense to the attack. Common law defenses which encourage deference to customary norms in the interpretation and enforcement of statute law must be displaced by legislated norms, if the criminal law is to protect self-determination in sexual relationships. Social definitions of rape are based on myths, and focus on the type and degree of force, rather than on the absence of consent. She concludes that only the imposition of clear legal definitions of voluntariness and consent will significantly change the enforcement of rape laws.

Robin West, "Equality Theory, Marital Rape, and the Promise of the Fourteenth Amendment" (1990) 42 *Florida Law Review* 45-79

For annotation, see Chapter 2: CONSTITUTIONAL LAW.

Linda S. Williams, "The Classic Rape: When Do Victims Report?" (1984) 31 *Social Problems* 459-464

This article discusses the reasons why rape is so rarely reported, and describes the situation when a rape is most likely to be reported. The author's research indicates that a classic rape, defined as a sudden, violent attack by a stranger in a deserted public place, is the most likely to be reported. She identifies the relationship between the victim and the rapist as the most important factor in the victim's decision to report a rape. She claims that because women have been socialized to believe that the control of the male-female relationship is their responsibility, a rape victim is less likely to report a rape when she is in a close relationship with the rapist.

Sentencing and Prisons

L. Berzins and S. Cooper, "The Political Economy of Correctional Planning for Women: The Case of the Bankrupt Bureaucracy" (1982) 24 *Canadian Journal of Criminology* 399-416

This article describes the women's prison system in Canada, and includes an historical overview of prison planning and an explanation for the inadequate services provided for female offenders. The authors claim that because there are so few female offenders in the federal penitentiary system, their needs have not been met. They argue that the result has been a denial of equal opportunity for women offenders as contrasted with men offenders, and go on to suggest remedies and approaches that would be more appropriate to the unique needs of women prisoners.

Canadian Association of Elizabeth Fry Societies, "Male Guards in Women's Prisons" Pt.1: (1988) 4:3 *Justice Report* 10-15; Pt.2: (1988) 5:1 *Justice Report* 7-12

These articles discuss the problems associated with male guards in women's prisons, focusing on such issues as the possibilities of sexual coercion and rape, and the problems women may face in finding their own identity in a situation where men are present and stereotypical "female" behaviour is expected. The paper presents several recommendations to minimize the negative effects of male guards, including ensuring that their responsibilities are allocated in such a way that they aren't invading inmate privacy, regular review of female institutions with male guards, and further research on the role of male guards in women's institutions.

Pat Carlen, "Law, Psychiatry and Women's Imprisonment: A Sociological View" (1985) 146 *British Journal of Psychiatry* 618-621

The article addresses the problem of women held in British prisons who are emotionally disturbed and classified as having "psychopathic personality disorder", a classification which the author regards as a catch-all for authorities to evade responsibility. The combination of rigid discipline in the prisons, the repeated imprisonment of female petty offenders, the use of drugs, and inmate isolation from each other and the community, actually create the emotional problems that the prisons are intended to contain.

R. Collette-Carrière, "Réflexion Autour de la Notion de Services aux Femmes dans le Système de Justice" (1983) 16:2 _Criminologie_ 101-111
This article explores the services available to women in the justice system. The author reviews the broad-ranging contribution of women in the building of New France, and their role in the sphere of social services in particular. She concludes that the correctional system is conceived for men and is both discriminatory and unsuited to women. She discusses barriers to the development of services for women. In order to provide adequate services she advocates that female criminals be viewed as part of the community of women rather than part of the criminal population at large.

Estelle B. Freedman, "Sentiment and Discipline: Women's Prison Experiences in Nineteenth Century America" (1984) 16:4 _Prologue: The Journal of National Archives_ 249-259
This article examines the practices of American women's prisons, from their founding in 1873 to 1910, to determine how the goal of improving the treatment of women prisoners resulted in the establishment of traditional prison discipline. The author argues that the reformers' goal of creating strong, independent women through specialized female correctional treatment was defeated by the tension between the reformers' identification with the lot of prisoners as women and their identification with their professional role as helpers. This tension, she concludes, led the reformers to seek approval from the very male domination they had rejected as oppressive of women.

Sarah Gauch, "When Mothers Go To Prison" (1989) 16:2 _Human Rights_ 33-35
The author reports that the Dwight Correctional Centre in Illinois is attempting to create an atmosphere for inmates which promotes their independence, and encourages them to keep in contact with family. It provides academic educational programs, as well as job training in non--traditional occupations. As many offenses are connected with substance abuse, the facility offers a live-in therapeutic centre where constant counselling is available. Until society is ready to accept new alternatives

to incarceration, the author concludes, Dwight offers itself as a model of correctional reform for women.

**John Gruhl, "Women as Criminal Defendants: A Test for Paternalism"
(1984) 37** _Western Political Quarterly_ **456-467**
For annotation, see Chapter 6: **FIRST NATIONS AND RACE.**

**Alison Hatch and Karlene Faith, "The Female Offender in Canada: A
Statistical Profile" (1989-1990) 3** _Canadian Journal of Women and the
Law_ **432-455**
For annotation, see Chapter 6: **FIRST NATIONS AND RACE.**

**Penelope Dinneen Hillemann, "Gender and Privacy in the Prisons"
(1985) 1** _Wisconsin Women's Law Journal_ **123-140**
This article examines employment discrimination litigation generally, and civil actions with respect to employment in prisons specifically, and claims a special burden exists when a bona-fide occupational qualification (BFOQ) is based on prisoners' asserted privacy rights. The author examines case law dealing with privacy rights, in which inmates have had their privacy rights recognized, subject only to reasonable limits. She concludes that any reasonable conflict between prisoners' rights to privacy and the right to equal employment opportunities must be resolved in favour of the former.

**Kathy E. Hinck, "Second Class Prisoners: New Hampshire's Placement
Policy for Female Offenders" (1989) 15** _New England Journal on Criminal
and Civil Confinement_ **225-241**
For annotation, see Chapter 2: **CONSTITUTIONAL LAW.**

**Chris Hutton, Frank Pommersheim and Steve Feimer, "'I Fought the
Law and the Law Won': A Report on Women and Disparate Sentencing
in South Dakota" (1989) 15** _New England Journal on Criminal and Civil
Confinement_ **177-202**
For annotation, see Chapter 6: **FIRST NATIONS AND RACE.**

Candace Kruttschnitt and Daniel McCarthy, "Gender, Criminal Sentences and Sex Role Stereotypes" (1985) 5 _Windsor Yearbook of Access to Justice_ 306-313

This is a statistical analysis of whether and how the nature of the offence or prior criminal record mediates a woman's sentence. The sample was taken from the sixteen year period between 1965 and 1980, and was limited to property and drug offenses. The results show that the effect of sex on the decision to incarcerate is not contingent upon either the nature of the offense or the extent of the woman's prior record. The authors also report that women were more likely to be imprisoned before 1972 than after, and that there is some evidence that the traditional leniency toward female offenders is declining.

John Lowman, "Notions of Formal Equality Before the Law: The Experience of Street Prostitutes and Their Customers" (1990) 1:2 _Journal of Human Justice_ 55-76

In 1985, the Canadian Parliament amended the CRIMINAL CODE provisions with respect to prostitution in order to criminalize the activities of customers as well as prostitutes by prohibiting communication in a public place for the purpose of prostitution. This article examines: (a) the extent to which police in several jurisdictions across Canada have enforced the "communicating law" against customers as compared to prostitutes; (b) differentials in the sentencing of prostitutes and customers in Montreal, Toronto, and Vancouver; and (c) the social class characteristics of Vancouver men charged with communicating in a public place for the purpose of purchasing the sexual services of a prostitute.

Sue Mahan, "Book Review: Russel P. Dobash, R. Emerson Dobash, and Sue Goutteridge, THE IMPRISONMENT OF WOMEN (1986)" (1988) 79 _Journal of Criminal Law & Criminology_ 560-563

For annotation, see Chapter 16: **BOOK REVIEWS**.

Jo-Ann Mayhew, "Barred from Life: Canadian Women in Prison" (1988) _Breaking the Silence_ 20-23

Writing from the Prison for Women (P4W) in Kingston, Ontario, on her daughter's wedding day, the author describes the events in her life which led to her murder conviction, and incarceration in Canada's only women's penitentiary, which is located over a thousand miles from her home. She described her life inside, and the misery built into the corrections system for women, because it does not offer women the same opportunities as male prisoners. Meaningful programs such as job training and counselling for victims of battering and rape and substance abuse are required.

Renate M. Mohr, "Sentencing as a Gendered Process: Results of a Consultation" (1990) 32 _Canadian Journal of Criminology_ 479-485

This article examines the issue of sentencing reform from a feminist perspective. After canvassing the gender-neutrality of past sentencing reform efforts, the author draws on the results of a consultation conducted with the Canadian Association of Elizabeth Fry Societies which reveals that although a just desserts rationale may be the solution to unwarranted disparity in a society in which there is true equality, until that goal is attained, any reform model of sentencing must do more than treat unequals -- whether defined by gender, race or class -- equally.

Jessica Neuwirth, "Towards a Gender-Based Approach to Human Rights Violations" (1987) 9 _Whittier Law Review_ 399-406

Because both men and women are imprisoned for political activism, human rights violations have been generally subject to a "gender-blind approach." Part of a Symposium on Women's Rights in International Law, this article reveals some of the ways political imprisonment and torture affect women specifically. It should be recognized that women activists pay a heavy price for crossing political, racial, and traditional sexual barriers in their activism. The author reveals several alarming and graphic accounts of imprisonment and torture of women for their beliefs. Cases involving the torture of children, rape by prison officials, rape using dogs and rodents, torture during pregnancy, and other gender specific atrocities argue convincingly, she concludes, for a gender-based approach to human rights violations.

Barbara A. Owen, "Race and Gender Relations Among Prison Workers" (1985) 31 _Crime and Delinquency_ 147-159

For annotation, see Chapter 8: **LABOUR AND EMPLOYMENT -- AFFIRMATIVE ACTION.**

M. D. Pelka-Slugocka and Leszek Slugocki, "The Impact of Imprisonment on the Family Life of Women Convicts" (1980) 24 _International Journal of Offender Therapy and Comparative Criminology_ 249-259
This article reports findings of a Polish study of imprisoned women. The study attempted to uncover both prisoner perceptions about the impact of incarceration on their marriage and family life, and the reality of the impact. The study concludes that while women may have difficulties in the short term, ex-prisoners re-adjust to family life upon release, and suffer little social or familial stigma.

Susan A. Reid, "The 'Reproduction' of Women's Dependence as a Factor in 'Treating' the Female Offender" (1985) 7 _Canadian Criminology Forum_ 129-142
The author claims that policies and programs within women's penal institutions promote women's dependency, and are based upon retraining women for their "proper place" in society. This reproduction of women's dependency within capitalist society is examined through analysis of both class and patriarchal relations. She argues that it is because of class factors that incarcerated women suffer more than their male counterparts. However, she finds that the plight of inmate mothers separated from children is overstated. As most inmates have been separated from children before incarceration, this notion serves the interests of "mother's reform" as an extension of traditional views of "mother". She concludes that programs ought to focus on the realities of life for low income women, and stress social and economic independence.

Kathy Sigurdson and Dianne Fisher, "Women in Conflict with the Law" (1988) 5 _Justice Report_ 1-3
The authors discuss the goals, philosophy, and structure of a joint program sponsored by the Elizabeth Fry Society of Toronto and Opportunity for Advancement. The program is voluntary, open to women who are in some sort of conflict with the law, and is designed to meet their unique needs. The program focuses on experiential learning and mutual support aimed at helping these women, who tend to be poor, uneducated, and isolated.

Carolyn Strange, "'The Criminal and Fallen of Their Sex': The Establishment of Canada's First Women's Prison, 1874-1901" (1985-86)

1 *Canadian Journal of Women and the Law* 79-92
    For annotation, see Chapter 10: **LEGAL HISTORY.**

Fran Sugar and Lana Fox, "Nistum Peyako Seht'wawin Iskwewak:
Breaking Chains" (1989-1990) 3 *Canadian Journal of Women and the Law*
465-481
    For annotation, see Chapter 6: **FIRST NATIONS AND RACE.**

Deborah M. Tharnish, "Sex Discrimination in Prison Employment: The
Bona Fide Occupation Qualification and the Prisoners' Privacy Rights"
(1980) 65 *Iowa Law Review* 428-445
    This article discusses ways in a prison setting to balance female
guards' anti-discrimination employment rights under Title VII of the
Civil Rights Act of 1964 with male inmates' rights to privacy. Several
cases are examined which concern whether sex is a bona fide occupational qualification for a job involving the supervision of inmates in
showers and toilets, and performance of pat and strip searches are examined. The author concludes that rights must be balanced in a manner
which does not weaken anti-discrimination law, resulting in women being
excluded from certain jobs, but which also considers prisoners' rights.
She suggests that selective scheduling of duties between men and women
guards is a viable solution.

CHAPTER 4
FAMILY LAW

General

Abdullahi An-Na'im, "The Rights of Women and International Law in the Muslim Context" (1987) 9 *Whittier Law Review* 491-516
   In this article, which is part of a Symposium on Women's Rights in International Law, the author examines Shari'a and international standards on the rights of women, and the secularization of Muslim society along with its re-Islamization. She proposes an approach to the rights of Muslim women which recommends a combination of traditional and modern aspects, and internal reform. She asserts that women's rights "are an integral part of the individual and collective human rights of their men and children."

Alice Armstrong, "Zimbabwe: Away from the Customary Law" (1988-89) 27 *Journal of Family Law* 339-350
   The author surveys the rapid changes in family law since independence, discussing the complexities that arise in a dual system of customary and Roman-Dutch law.

W. R. Atkin, "New Zealand: Children Versus Families -- Is There Any Conflict?" (1988-89) 27 *Journal of Family Law* 231-242
   This article reports that recognition of traditional Maori practices in interpersonal relationships has been the subject of debate and government discussion papers in 1987.

Martha J. Bailey, "Book Review: Howard H. Irving and Michael Benjamin, FAMILY MEDIATION: THEORY AND PRACTICE OF DISPUTE RESOLUTION (1987)" (1989) 3 *Canadian Journal of Women and the Law* 303-312

139

For annotation, see Chapter 16: **BOOK REVIEWS.**

Nicholas Bala and Alistair Bissett-Johnson, "Canada: Supreme Court Thunder -- Abortion, Finality of Separation Agreements, Custody, and Access" (1988-89) 27 *Journal of Family Law* **35-56**
This article surveys Supreme Court and lower court judgments in 1987 and early 1988 on topics such as abortion, separation agreements, custody and access, pensions and professional degrees as part of matrimonial property, child protection legislation, and child abuse registers.

Vimal Balasulsrahmanyan, "Husbands Law Under Attack" (1984) 145 *Spare Rib* **15**
The author recounts the first challenge to the constitutional validity of Muslim personal law, which allows a husband to divorce unilaterally his wife, and leave her without alimony. She claims the lack of legislation protecting women is due to the perception that any change in Muslim personal law must come from within the Muslim religious community.

Virginia Bartley, "Book Review -- Shiela Kieran, THE FAMILY MATTERS (1986)" (1989) 3 *Canadian Journal of Women and the Law* **317-323**
For annotation, see Chapter 16: **BOOK REVIEWS.**

Frank Bates, "Australia: Towards the Familialization of Family Law" (1988-89) 27 *Journal of Family Law* **7-22**
The author discusses the FAMILY LAW AMENDMENT BILL, and the Australian Law Reform Commission's Report on Matrimonial Property, as well as developments in case law and state legislation during 1987.

Mario J. Bendersky, "Argentina: Divorce at Last!" (1988-89) 27 *Journal of Family Law* **1-5**
Divorce became part of the legal regime for the first time in June, 1987. The details and implications of the new act are described.

Christine Bradley and Sara Tovey, "Papua New Guinea: 'Lo Bilong Famili'" (1988-89) 27 _Journal of Family Law_ 261-273
The authors discuss the complexity of administering a legal system which includes introduced law and customary law.

David Bradley, "The Development of A Legal Status for Unmarried Cohabitation in Sweden" (1989) 18 _Anglo-American Law Review_ 322-334
This article examines the development of a legal status for unmarried cohabitation in Swedish law, and analyzes the significance of the COHABITEES (JOINT HOMES) ACT which was enacted in 1987.

Wini Breines and Linda Gordon, "The New Scholarship on Family Violence" (1982) 8 _Signs: Journal of Women in Culture and Society_ 490-531
For annotation, see Chapter 3: **CRIMINAL LAW -- BATTERING.**

W. E. Butler, "Mongolia: Coming to Terms with Family Legislation" (1988-89) 27 _Journal of Family Law_ 211-219
This article reports that although there is a FAMILY CODE, custom continues to play a large part in relationships.

W. E. Butler, "USSR: Divorce in Soviet Courts" (1988-89) 27 _Journal of Family Law_ 315-320
The Supreme Court of the Union of Soviet Socialist Republics has given particular attention to divorce, and the article describes recent developments.

Gabriel Garcia Cantera, "Spain: Family Law in the Eighties" (1988-89) 27 _Journal of Family Law_ 281-293
The author reports that constitutional reforms have fuelled extensive changes in family law between 1981 and 1987.

Phyllis Chesler, "Book Review: Miriam M. Johnson, STRONG MOTHERS, WEAK WIVES: THE SEARCH FOR GENDER EQUALITY (1988)" (1989) 3 _Canadian Journal of Women and the Law_

280-286
> For annotation, see Chapter 16: **BOOK REVIEWS.**

Elizabeth B. Clark, "Book Review: Michael Grossberg, GOVERNING THE HEARTH (1985)" (1985) 2 *Wisconsin Women's Law Journal* 159-167
> For annotation, see Chapter 16: **BOOK REVIEWS.**

Lorraine Code, "Book Review: Katherine O'Donovan, SEXUAL DIVISIONS IN LAW (1985)" (1986) 2 *Canadian Journal of Women and the Law* 190-198
> For annotation, see Chapter 16: **BOOK REVIEWS.**

The Collective of the Center for Women's Studies and Services, "Legislative Alert!" (1981) 6:1 *Longest Revolution* 5-6
> This brief article canvasses a number of legislative proposals with respect to their pro-feminist or anti-feminist directions.

Jane Connors, "Malaysia: Responding to Religious and Cultural Pluralism" (1988-89) 27 *Journal of Family Law* 195-209
> The author claims that it has been difficult to develop a uniform family law regime in a multi-racial and religiously plural society like Malaysia. She reports that THE LAW REFORM (MARRIAGE DIVORCE) ACT of 1982 has brought more certainty to the area.

Mary Irene Coombs, "Shared Privacy and the Fourth Amendment, or the Rights of Relationships" (1987) 75 *California Law Review* 1593-1663
> For annotation, see Chapter 2: **CONSTITUTIONAL LAW.**

Rose Laub Coser, "The Women's Movement and Conservative Attacks -- Book Review: Sylvia Ann Hewlett, A LESSER LIFE: THE MYTH OF WOMEN'S LIBERATION IN AMERICA (1986)" [1987] *Dissent* 259-262
> For annotation, see Chapter 16: **BOOK REVIEWS.**

Barbara J. Cox, "Alternative Families: Obtaining Traditional Family Benefits Through Litigation, Legislation and Collective Bargaining" (19-85) 2 _Wisconsin Women's Law Journal_ 1-51

This article canvasses protections and benefits available to traditional families, which the author claims are now viewed as "entitlements or rights," and suggests that seventy percent of the American population does not have such benefits available, because they live in alternative family forms. She examines lower court decisions which extend protection to alternative families, and suggests forms of protection which, in her view, should also be extended -- namely, zoning restriction to single family dwellings, employment benefits, loss of consortium, hospital visitation and treatment authorization, and family membership benefits in such organizations as the YWCA or a museum. She concludes with a recommendation for legislative reform.

Tove Stang Dahl, "Towards a Housewives' Law: The Case of National Insurance Provision for Handicapped Children in Norway" (1982) 10 _International Journal of the Sociology of Law_ 169-177

The author argues for a more effective housewives' law in Norway, by examining in particular a law with respect to payment for care of handicapped children. She identifies inequities in the current system for payment, which can result in a more qualified mother receiving less benefits. She cites this position as the worst example of society's exploitation of the housewife.

Ineke De Hondt and Nora Holtrust, "The European Convention and the 'Marckx-Judgment' Effect" (1986) 14 _International Journal of Sociology of Law_ 317-326

The authors examine the effect of the inclusion of family rights in the 1950 EUROPEAN CONVENTION ON HUMAN RIGHTS. This provision was historically viewed as protection from unwarranted interference by government authorities, specifically in the classic form of freedom for the father of the family. The authors examine the use of this provision in Dutch law, especially with respect to custody, access, and legitimacy of children, and conclude that interpretation of the provision has amounted to positive protection and support of the patriarchal marriage system in which the father has control over the children.

Molly Diggins, "Paternal Interests in the Abortion Decision: Does the Father Have a Say?" [1989] *University of Chicago Legal Forum* 377-398

For annotation, see Chapter 1: **ABORTION AND REPRODUCTION.**

Nancy E. Dowd, "Work and Family: The Gender Paradox and the Limitations of Discrimination Analysis in Restructuring the Workplace" (1989) 24 *Harvard Civil Rights-Civil Liberties Law Review* 79-172

Family and work responsibilities are in conflict, and this conflict cannot be entirely viewed as a women's issue and a gender issue. After describing the conflict -- namely, the paradox that these are and are not women's issues -- the author focuses on the "interface between childbirth and the workplace." She explores a means to get beyond the paradox, including discrimination analysis, and recommends ways to transform work and family. These "require a deconstruction of gender roles and an attack on patriarchy within family and work and within the relationship between work and family."

Virginia G. Drachman, "'My 'Partner' in Law and Life': Marriage in the Lives of Women Lawyers in Late 19th- and Early 20th-Century America" (1989) 14 *Law and Social Inquiry* 221-250

For annotation, see Chapter 10: **LEGAL HISTORY.**

William Duncan, "Ireland: The Status of Children and the Protection of Marriage" (1988-89) 27 *Journal of Family Law* 163-169

The author argues that in a legal regime such as Ireland's, which protects the marriage-based family, the equality of illegitimate children is an issue.

Rainer Frank, "Germany, Federal Republic of: Reflections on Joint Custody, Family Obligations, and the Entry of an Alien's Dependents" (1988-89) 27 *Journal of Family Law* 153-158

The author reports that joint custody after divorce, calculation of maintenance payments, and dependents of aliens were issues in German family law in 1987.

Michael D. A. Freeman, "England's Moral Quagmire" (1988-89) 27 _Journal of Family Law_ 101-125

The author reports that controversial ethical problems were the subject of judicial inquiry in 1987. These included involuntary sterilization, surrogacy, abortion, in vitro fertilization, and child sexual abuse. Other novel matters also reached the courts, and were the subject of inquiry.

Michael D. A. Freeman, "Ghana: Legislation for Today" (1988-89) 27 _Journal of Family Law_ 159-162

This article discusses three 1985 acts -- INTESTATE SUCCESSION LAW, CUSTOMARY MARRIAGE AND DIVORCE LAW, and HEAD OF FAMILY (ACCOUNTABILITY) LAW.

Alissa Friedman, "The Necessity for State Recognition of Same-Sex Marriage: Constitutional Requirements and Evolving Notions of Family" (1987-88) 3 _Berkeley Women's Law Journal_ 134-170

For annotation, see Chapter 12: LESBIANISM AND SEXUAL ORIENTATION.

Shelley Gavigan, "Petit Treason in Eighteenth Century England: Women's Inequality Before the Law" (1989-1990) 3 _Canadian Journal of Women and the Law_ 335-374

For annotation, see Chapter 3: CRIMINAL LAW -- EVIDENCE.

Margot Gebhardt-Benischke, "Family Law, Family Law Politics, and Family Politics" (1986) 9 _Women's Studies International Forum_ 25-33

The author examines family law reform in Germany, where there has been liberalization of divorce laws, culminating in drastically reduced maintenance awards. Reform has, in consequence, abandoned women to civic freedom with few rights and little protection. Patriarchal family ideology encourages women to submit, not fight; however, the author argues, women will fight because a family ideology offering protection, yet systematically decreasing protection, will not fool women. In this fashion, she concludes, liberalization offers hope for women to gain the position of active subject, and fight for legal change.

Judith Grbich, "The Position of Women in Family Dealing: The Australian Case" (1987) 15 _International Journal of the Sociology of Law_ 309-332

The author argues that taxation laws are a window on the family and the position of women in society, and that property is reified through taxation. She claims that the rationales for family dealing in property for tax purposes, sanctioned by the courts/state apparatus, contravene the formal individual unit of assessment prescribed by tax legislation. She argues that the position of women is not secured by rights to income or property as long as position is part of familial relations.

Anne Griffiths, "The Problem of Informal Justice: Family Dispute Processing Among the Bakwena -- A Case Study" (1986) 14 _International Journal of the Sociology of Law_ 359-376

This paper deals with three features of the informal justice model, namely, lack of specialists, party control, and party agreement. This framework is examined within the context of dispute resolution in the Bakwena tribe in Botswana, in order more fully to inform the Alternate Dispute Resolution debate in Britain. The author concludes that the relationship between formal and informal justice needs more study, but initial results show potential dangers which she recommends be dealt with post-haste.

Robert L. Griswold, "Sexual Cruelty and the Case for Divorce in Victorian America" (1986) 11 _Signs: Journal of Women in Culture and Society_ 529-541

The author examines case law to demonstrate the attitudes in Victorian United States to divorce, the family, and the differentiated roles of men and women in society.

Ilivier Guillod, "Switzerland: Hints of Things to Come" (1988-89) 27 _Journal of Family Law_ 305-313

The author surveys new and proposed legislative changes and developments in case law during 1987.

Monique Gysels and Mary Vogels, "Belgian Husbands and Wives: Equal in Patrimonial Matters?" (1982) 10 _International Journal of the_

Sociology of Law 205-216

This piece examines Belgian marriage legislation, which includes marriage regulation and laws with respect to matrimonial property, and reports study findings with respect to the law's impact on male and female roles. Recent reforms, the author concludes, have mandated autonomy in a wide range of behaviours, both decision-making and task execution.

Brenda Hoggett, "Recent Reforms in Family Law: Progress or Backlash?" (1987) 11 _Dalhousie Law Journal_ **5-20**

The author discusses legislative reform of family law. She argues that while progress has been achieved, specifically as regards sharing of matrimonial assets, there are still inequities in the law which require change.

Andrew Huxley, "Burma: It Works, but is it Law?" (1988-89) 27 _Journal of Family Law_ **23-34**

This is an outline of Burmese family law, which reflects "very little sexual discrimination," but restricts "parties to a narrow range of behaviour."

Claudia Kaufmann, "Marriage Law Revision -- Occasion for Hope?" (1986) 9 _Women's Studies International Forum_ **35-40**

The author reports that Switzerland's new marriage law (1987) will affect the role-image of women in a society which offered gender specific roles under the old legislation.

Sylvia A. Law, "Women, Work, Welfare, and the Preservation of Patriarchy" (1983) 131 _University of Pennsylvania Law Review_ **1249-1339**

The author argues that federal policy with respect to labour and welfare resolves the conflict between the reality of women employed outside the home and the traditional belief that they should not do so, in a fashion which is systematically harmful to women and children. This includes an examination of income security programs, and women's impeded access to the labour market. She concludes that welfare policy should recognize that women perform valuable work in the caring and nurturing of children, and that to fail to recognize the value of women's labour both inside the home and outside protects the patriarchal dominance of men in the wage market and home. She claims that current welfare laws place women in an impossible position, and that a radical restructuring of the view of the value of women's labour is necessary.

Jocelyne Legare, "La Condition Juridique Des Femmes ou L'Historique d'une 'Affaire de Famille'" (1983) 16:2 *Criminologie* 7-26
This article contains an overview and historical analysis of the absence of rights of women in Roman law, and its manifestation through "pater familias" in Quebec and Canadian law. The author proposes that the status of women has not improved due to both the role of the judiciary as guardian of traditional values, and the judicial definition of women through their roles as wives and mothers.

Peter Lodrup, "Norway: Reforming the Law of Matrimonial Property and Maintenance and Artificial Insemination" (1988-89) 27 *Journal of Family Law* 253-260
The author reports that uniform rules for the five Nordic countries have not been entirely successful as divergent practices in matrimonial property have emerged. Proposals for a new regime in Norway are discussed, as well as maintenance and artificial insemination.

Tukiya Mabula, "Zambia: Development or its Lack Since Independence" (1988-89) 27 *Journal of Family Law* 329-337
The author discusses the plurality of family laws upon independence, with customary law and English common law co-existing, and deals specifically with marriage, divorce, and succession.

Marie-Therese Meulders-Klein, "The Position of the Father in European Legislation" (1990) 4 *International Journal of Law and the Family* 131-153
For annotation, see Chapter 1: **ABORTION AND REPRODUCTION.**

Martha Minow, "Forming Underneath Everything That Grows: Toward

a History of Family Law" [1985] *Wisconsin Law Review* 819
    For annotation, see Chapter 10: LEGAL HISTORY.

Martha Minow, "The Properties of Family and the Families of Property -- Book Review: Mary Ann Glendon, THE NEW FAMILY AND THE NEW PROPERTY (1981)" (1982) 92 *Yale Law Journal* 376-395
    For annotation, see Chapter 16: BOOK REVIEWS.

Martha Minow, "Rights for the Next Generation: A Feminist Approach to Children's Rights" (1986) 9 *Harvard Women's Law Journal* 1-24
    Assumptions about differences between children and adults underlie the issue of children's rights, and the author argues that there is widespread societal neglect of children alleviated only by occasional outpourings of concern on a specific issue. She claims that a debate with respect to rights of children which joins the two goals of autonomy and affiliation is necessary to challenge existing societal neglect and the unrealistic splitting of private and public responsibility.

James C. Mohr, "Feminism and the History of Marital Law: Basch and Stetson on the Rights of Wives -- Book Review: D.M. Stetson, A WOMAN'S ISSUE: THE POLITICS OF FAMILY LAW REFORM IN ENGLAND (1982); N. Basch, IN THE EYES OF THE LAW: WOMEN, MARRIAGE AND PROPERTY IN NINETEENTH-CEN-TURY NEW YORK (1982)" [1984] *American Bar Foundation Research Journal* 223-228
    For annotation, see Chapter 16: BOOK REVIEWS.

F. L. Morton, "Sexual Equality and the Family in Tocqueville's Democracy in America" (1984) 17 *Canadian Journal of Political Science* 309-324
    For annotation, see Chapter 10: LEGAL HISTORY.

E. I. Nwogugu, "Nigeria: The Developing Family Law" (1988-89) 27 *Journal of Family Law* 243-252

The article reports that during the 1980's, there has been new legislation and case law with respect to marriage and matters relating to children.

Susan Moller Okin, "Justice and Gender" (1987) 16 _Philosophy and Public Affairs_ 42-72
The author examines theories of justice in relation to gender, and concludes that the family must be constructed in accordance with two principles of justice, namely, equal basic liberty and the difference principle combined with a requirement for fair equality of opportunity. She argues that if sharing is real and complete, not symbolic, the injustices inherent in the gender-structured family can be eliminated.

Susan Moller Okin, "Reason and Feeling in Thinking about Justice" (1989) 99 _Ethics_ 229-249
The author examines the work of Rawls and Kant, and proposes a re-interpretation with respect to principles of justice in moral and political theory. She argues that Rawls' view of the monogamous family as part of the basic structure of justice ignores the injustice in the gendered family, and the internal paradox in its assumption about the division of labour and women's role as nurturer. She proposes abiding by principles of justice which break away from the rationalist Kantian mode of thinking and recognize the individual and collective good, and which draw upon Rawls' acknowledgment of the importance of empathy, care, and concern.

Frances Olsen, "The Family and the Market: A Study of Ideology and Legal Reform" (1983) 96 _Harvard Law Review_ 1497-1578
The author argues that family law reform efforts have been limited by a structure of consciousness which emphasizes the separate and independent spheres of market and family -- the public and private. She further argues that this limited consciousness has decreased the range of strategy options able to be perceived by reformers. She recommends transcendence of the market/family and the male/female dichotomies to improve radically the lives of all, since women's involvement in the weak side of every dualism has produced a legacy of oppression.

Michael Palmer, "China: Problems of Marriage and Divorce" (1988-89) 27 _Journal of Family Law_ 57-79

The author reports that the Chinese state, in its attempts to "mold domestic institutions into a more definite socialist shape," continues to refine existing legislation and regulations, and study new legislative action.

Emily Patt, "Second Parent Adoption: When Crossing the Marital Barrier Is in a Child's Best Interests" (1987-88) 3 _Berkeley Women's Law Journal_ 96-133

The author argues that in cohabiting and coparenting relationships where marriage is either unwanted or impossible, an alternative method of giving legal protection to a child is through second parent adoption by the non-legal parent.

Maria Isabel Plata, "Colombia: Discriminating Against Women" (1988-1989) 27 _Journal of Family Law_ 81-89

In a society riddled with violence, women experience sexual discrimination despite legal reforms during the last two decades. The author outlines these changes.

Anika Rahman, "Religious Rights Versus Women's Rights in India: A Test Case for International Human Rights Law" (1990) 28 _Columbia Journal of Transnational Law_ 473-498

This article analyzes both the conflict between religious law and secular law, and the conflict between religious rights and women's rights, in the context of international human rights law and with emphasis on the right of an Indian Muslim woman to reasonable maintenance post-divorce. The author concludes that international human rights law cannot resolve the conflict between women's rights and religious rights in this context, and that the burden for dealing with the problem, therefore, falls on municipal law. The article concludes with the author's reflections on the likelihood of this happening in the Indian context.

Marge Reitsma-Street, "More Control Than Care: A Critique of Historical and Contemporary Laws for Delinquency and Neglect of Children in Ontario" (1989-1990) 3 _Canadian Journal of Women and the_

Law 510-529
  For annotation, see Chapter 3: **CRIMINAL LAW -- GENERAL.**

Madzy Rood-de Boer, "The Netherlands: Riding the Carousel of Family Law" (1988-89) 27 *Journal of Family Law* **221-229**
  Although de-regulation of personal life is the aim in the Netherlands, little progress has been made, as new legislation is slow to appear.

Nikolas Rose, "Beyond the Public-Private Division: Law, Power and the Family" (1987) 14 *Journal of Law and Society* **61-76**
  The author applies the analytical device of "genealogy" to feminist critique, and examines literature with respect to the public/private dichotomy. He concludes by challenging critical theorists to rethink the fundamental concepts of state, interest, ideology, and power.

Ariel Rosen-Zvi, "Israel: Proposed Reforms in Anticipation of a Political and Legal Contest" (1988-89) 27 *Journal of Family Law* **171-183**
  The author discusses moves towards reform in Israeli family law.

Jacqueline Rubellin-Devichi, "France: More Equality, More Solidarity in Family Relationships" (1988-89) 27 *Journal of Family Law* **143-151**
  The author reports that during 1987, equality before the law of married and cohabiting couples became near complete, and that the children of unmarried unions were achieving this equality, as autonomy in living arrangements became more of a reality. She also reports that issues surrounding paternity and in vitro fertilization and artificial insemination were litigated.

Ake Saldeen, "Sweden: More Rights for Children and Homosexuals" (1988-89) 27 *Journal of Family Law* **295-304**
  The article discusses Sweden's new MARRIAGE CODE, its HOMOSEXUAL COHABITATION ACT, two legislative reports on Children's Rights, and two committee reports on Conflict of Laws and Succession and Guardianship.

Matti Savolainen, "Finland: The New Marriage Act Enters Into Force" (1988-89) 27 _Journal of Family Law_ 127-141

The author reports that a new MARRIAGE ACT was passed in 1987, and entered into force January 1, 1988.

Carl E. Schneider, "Moral Discourse and the Transformation of American Family Law" (1985) 83 _Michigan Law Review_ 1803-1879

The author proposes that the transformation of family law in recent decades can be understood as a diminution in the law's discourse in moral terms about the relations between family members, and as a transfer of moral decision from the law to the people the law once regulated. He identifies four forces that have helped change family law and moral discourse within family law. They are: (1) the legal tradition of non-interference with family affairs; (2) the ideology of liberal individualism; (3) American society's changing moral beliefs; and (4) the rise of psychologic man. Using ROE v. WADE (410 U.S. 113 (1973)) as a case study, he explores the consequences of these four forces for family law.

Ferdinand Schoeman, "Book Review: L.D. Houlgate, FAMILY AND STATE: THE PHILOSOPHY OF FAMILY LAW (1988)" (1989) 99 _Ethics_ 651-655

For annotation, see Chapter 16: BOOK REVIEWS.

Selma Sevenhuijsen, "Fatherhood and the Political Theory of Rights: Theoretical Perspectives of Feminism" (1986) 14 _International Journal of the Sociology of Law_ 329-340

This article claims that family law provides the clearest example of the feminist claim that the principle of equality rights adversely affects women. The author reports that the Netherlands has proposed legislation favouring joint custody, which represents an astonishing rise of biologism. She concludes that it would be best for feminist theory to use equality as a political strategy only in areas where access has previously been denied to women, and make equality a private strategy in areas of childrearing. She suggests that it is crucial to develop public policy arguments which deal theoretically with the relationship between power and equality.

Ichiro Shimazu, "Japan: Trailing the West in Family Law" (1988-89) 27 *Journal of Family Law* **185-194**
    The author reports that during 1987, there were changes in the approach to divorce and adoption.

Carol Smart, "Regulating Families or Legitimating Patriarchy? Family Law in Britain" (1982) 10 *International Journal of the Sociology of Law* **129-147**
    The author argues that liberalization of divorce and family law has perpetuated the legal status of dependency of women, and reinforced the structures which oppress women. Family law now regulates women through the ideology of the primacy of the welfare of their children, through its extension of the dependent/breadwinner dichotomy, and through the engineered, but real popularity of marriage.

Amy Dru Stanley, "Conjugal Bonds and Wage Labour: Rights of Contract in the Age of Emancipation" (1988/89) 75 *Journal of American History* **471-500**
    For annotation, see Chapter 10: **LEGAL HISTORY.**

Wanda Stojanowska, "Poland: Cohabitation" (1988-89) 27 *Journal of Family Law* **275-280**
    The author discusses decisions of the Polish Supreme Court on cohabitation, and provides background information on cohabitation.

Lee E. Teitelbaum, "Family History and Family Law" [1985] *Wisconsin Law Review* **1135-1181**
    For annotation, see Chapter 10: **LEGAL HISTORY.**

Lee E. Teitelbaum, "The Legal History of the Family -- Book Review: Michael Grossberg, GOVERNING THE HEARTH: LAW AND THE FAMILY IN NINETEENTH-CENTURY AMERICA (1985)" (1987) 85 *Michigan Law Review* **1052-1070**
    For annotation, see Chapter 16: **BOOK REVIEWS.**

Lee E. Teitelbaum, "Moral Discourse and Family Law; Comment on 'Correspondence on Moral Discourse and the Transformation of American Family Law' (1985) 83 Michigan Law Review 1803" (1985) 84 _Michigan Law Review_ 430-441

This is a response to Carl E. Schneider's "Moral Discourse and the Transformation of American Family Law" [(1985) 83 _Michigan Law Review_ 1803] in which four forces were claimed to be shaping family law -- namely, the legal tradition of noninterference with the family; the ideology of liberal individualism; American society's changing moral beliefs; and the rise of 'psychologic man'. The present author claims that both the rules of family law and talk by the courts and legislatures have undergone a dramatic change, and proposes adding three further forces, namely: ambiguity of republican political and social theory, which results in the superiority of women within the household; a sense of social realism, in which the family is an extension of the larger community; and an assumption by the courts of authority over the family. He concludes that it is essential to consider families as relationships in order for other conceptualizations to emerge.

Vivienne H. Ullrich, "Equal but Not Equal -- A Feminist Perspective on Family Law" (1986) 9 _Women's Studies International Forum_ 41-46

The author discusses the role of family law in New Zealand, and claims that while women have formal equality rights within family law, they are disadvantaged in society and post-divorce. She specifically examines the economic impact of divorce, custody, and domestic violence, and concludes that a judicial system which purports to treat men and women as equals is in reality dominated by male values.

Walter Wadlington, "United States: The Continuing Debate About Surrogate Parenthood" (1988-89) 27 _Journal of Family Law_ 321-328

The author discusses surrogacy, the federal presence in family law, such as in the PARENTAL KIDNAPPING PREVENTION ACT, dying mothers of unborn children, and children and Acquired Immune Deficiency Syndrome (AIDS).

Custody

"Domestic Violence and Custody – 'To Ensure Domestic Tranquillity'" (1984) 14 *Golden Gate University Law Review* 623-638
For annotation, see Chapter 3: **CRIMINAL LAW – BATTERING.**

Katherine Arnup, "'Mothers Just Like Others': Lesbians, Divorce, and Child Custody in Canada" (1989) 3 *Canadian Journal of Women and the Law* 18-32
For annotation, see Chapter 12: **LESBIANISM AND SEXUAL ORIENTATION.**

Martha J. Bailey, "Unpacking the 'Rational Alternative': A Critical Review of Family Mediation Movement Claims" (1989) 8 *Canadian Journal of Family Law* 61-94
The author examines the claims made by family mediators, and argues each one fails independently on empirical grounds, because each is either unsupported or contradicted by available studies. These claims include the belief that joint custody is best for children; that mediation is less costly financially and emotionally; that higher levels of child support arise from negotiated agreements; and that mediation empowers the parties. She argues that the claims by family mediators are morally and politically dubious because of their stereotypical assumptions about women.

Katharine T. Bartlett and Carol B. Stack, "Joint Custody, Feminism and the Dependency Dilemma" (1986) 2 *Berkeley Women's Law Journal* 9-41
The authors argue that a maternal preference in custody determination, which is called for by many feminists, is antithetical to the feminist goal of reducing female dependency. A preference for joint custody should operate in custody determination, and feminists should concentrate on improving the life circumstances of women. They also argue that joint custody offers substantial benefits to children, and increases the equality between men and women, and therefore should not be rejected by feminists.

Susan B. Boyd, "Child Custody, Ideologies, and Employment" (1989) 3 _Canadian Journal of Women and the Law_ 111-133

The author argues that two inconsistent ideologies function to harm women in child custody disputes: the ideology of motherhood, and the ideology of equality. Employed mothers fail to satisfy either of these because they fail to stay at home with the children, and in addition are unable to compete economically at a rate which will enable post-divorce economic equality. In contrast, men are presumed to be as nurturing as women, despite familial histories of non-participation by the father. She concludes by calling for a primary care-giver presumption in custody determination.

Susan B. Boyd, "The Politics of Custody" (1987) _Breaking the Silence_ 8-10

The author reports on the issues discussed at a conference on the Politics of Child Custody held in Windsor, Ontario in July, 1986. Delegates from Canada and the United States debated the move toward joint custody as a "anti-woman backlash", a return to the time only sixty years ago when father's rights to custody prevailed. She discusses the effects of joint custody on a woman's income, as well as the special vulnerability of lesbian mothers. She argues that unless men participate in parenting in a more meaningful way, joint custody undervalues mothering, and legitimizes male control over women even after divorce.

Julia Brophy, "Parental Rights and Children's Welfare: Some Problems of Feminists' Strategy in the 1920s" (1982) 10 _International Journal of the Sociology of Law_ 149-168

The author discusses the battle by early feminists to change the automatic father-custody orders post-divorce. This examination is helpful because of the silences in the debate, and because it parallels present-day debates about custody determination. She concludes that custody and maintenance cannot be understood without considering the role the state plays in sustaining a particular family structure.

Kathryn A. Carver, "The 1985 Minnesota Indian Family Preservation Act: Claiming a Cultural Identity" (1986) 4 _Law and Inequality_ 327-354

For annotation, see Chapter 6: FIRST NATIONS AND RACE.

David L. Chambers, "The Abuses of Social Science: A Response to Fineman and Opie" [1987] *Wisconsin Law Review* 159-163
The author replies to issues raised in an article by Fineman and Opie (Martha Fineman and Annie Opie, "The Uses of Social Science Data in Legal Policy-making: Custody Determination at Divorce" [1987] *Wisconsin Law Review* 107) with respect to the use of social science research in legal decision-making.

David L. Chambers, "Rethinking the Substantive Rules for Custody Disputes in Divorce" (1984) 83 *Michigan Law Review* 477-569
The author presents a thorough examination of the rules for determining child custody disputes, including an analysis of the goals of custody determination, the needs of children and parents, and the information available about joint custody. This examination deals extensively with social science research on the needs of children and parents. He concludes by recommending a primary care-giver test for very young children, and the best interests test for older children.

Anne Marie Delorey, "Joint Legal Custody: A Reversion to Patriarchal Power" (1989) 3 *Canadian Journal of Women and the Law* 33-44
The author argues that the recent trend toward joint legal custody is negative because the result is a reinforcement of patriarchal power. Joint legal custody does not ensure equal sharing of childrearing responsibilities, and in fact, allows fathers to obtain lowered child support payments, control women and children post-divorce, and decreases the autonomy women need to discharge parental responsibilities. Mere legal custody of children without corollary care-giving responsibilities is an assignment of power to men over women, and reinforces patriarchy.

David S. Dooley, "Immoral Because They're Bad, Bad Because They're Wrong: Sexual Orientation and Presumptions of Parental Unfitness in Custody Disputes" (1989-1990) 26 *California Western Law Review* 397-424
For annotation, see Chapter 12: **LESBIANISM AND SEXUAL ORIENTATION**.

Janice Drakich, "In Search of the Better Parent: The Social Construc-

tion of Ideologies of Fatherhood" (1989) 3 *Canadian Journal of Women and the Law* 69-87

This article examines recent social scientific research on fathering, and the use of the findings by popular culture and father's rights groups to create a new ideology of fatherhood. The author cites alternate research regarding men's actual participation in childcare and housework, and argues that the father who participates meaningfully in the care of his child is statistically an anomaly. She concludes that the notion of a caring and nurturing father serves an ideological function in maintaining patriarchal control of women and children.

Germain Dulac, "Le Lobby des pères, divorce et paternité" (1989) 3 *Canadian Journal of Women and the Law* 45-68

The author argues that the current father's rights movement has appropriated the language of rights of victims in the attempt to re-assert traditional male authority over the family. While ostensibly promoting the interests of children and better relations between men and women, the movement is in effect trying to re-assert patriarchal power over women in response to perceived loss of power in the domain of the family. This desire for power and control over children exists despite a concurrent lack of interest in day to day custody and care.

Jon Elster, "Solomonic Judgments: Against the Best Interest of the Child" (1987) 54 *University of Chicago Law Review* 1-45

The author discusses the current best interest test used in custody determination, and argues that it is indeterminate and therefore unworkable. He recommends that two positions operate in every determination: no custody to an unfit parent; and pain and stress to the child be minimized. To comply with these requirements, he suggests use of either a strong maternal preference presumption, or a primary parent test.

Nancy S. Erickson, "The Feminist Dilemma Over Unwed Parents' Custody Rights: The Mother's Rights Must Take Priority" (1984) 2 *Law and Inequality* 447-472

This piece discusses various perspectives regarding methods of determining child custody, especially as they relate to a custody dispute between unmarried parents. The author claims that mainstream feminists argue for a sex-neutral test as an encouragement for fathers to take a more active role in care-giving, notwithstanding that such feminists agree that test operates to the detriment of women. She examines case law regarding unwed parents in custody disputes, and concludes that the unwed mother's rights must take priority over those of the unwed father, because the woman bears the physical and psychological stresses of pregnancy.

Ellen Faulkner, "The Case of 'Baby M'" (1989) 3 *Canadian Journal of Women and the Law* 239-245
For annotation, see Chapter 1: **ABORTION AND REPRODUCTION.**

Martha L. Fineman, "Custody Determination at Divorce: The Limits of Social Science Research and the Fallacy of the Liberal Ideology of Equality" (1989) 3 *Canadian Journal of Women and the Law* 88-110
The author seeks to demonstrate the inequities which result with the emergence of the equality ideal in family law. She argues that the use of biased social science data reinforces the trend toward formal equality, and that because such equality rules operate within a society which is deeply gendered, the emerging case law exacerbates the inequality of women. Furthermore, she suggests, these supposed equal, degendered rules are insulated from scrutiny by the ideology of equality inherent in liberalism, as well as the mantle of objectivity because of scientific research.

Martha L. Fineman, "Dominant Discourse, Professional Language, and Legal Change in Child Custody Decisionmaking" (1988) 101 *Harvard Law Review* 727-774
The author examines the changing process of decision-making in child custody disputes. While such decisions were historically made by legal decision-makers, a recent trend is for mediation and joint custody, which, the author argues, is an appropriation by the helping professions, and which is obscured by equality rhetoric and a focus on the process as against the outcome of the determination. She recommends a return to a legal decision-making model, and the use of the primary parent test within this model.

Martha L. Fineman, "A Reply to David Chambers" [1987] _Wisconsin Law Review_ 165-169

The author responds to David Chambers' response (see: David L. Chambers, "Rethinking the Substantive Rules for Custody Disputes in Divorce" (1984) 83 _Michigan Law Review_ 477; and David L. Chambers, "The Abuses of Social Science: A Response to Fineman and Opie" [1987] _Wisconsin Law Review_ 159) to her and Anne Opie's article concerning the use of social science data in custody determinations (see: Fineman and Opie, "The Uses of Social Science Data in Legal Policy Making: Custody Determinations at Divorce" [1987] _Wisconsin Law Review_ 107). In her response, she claims that Chambers' view exemplifies the misuse of social scientific research to enhance the role of the father in custody disputes.

Martha L. Fineman and Anne Opie, "The Uses of Social Science Data in Legal Policymaking: Custody Determination at Divorce" [1987] _Wisconsin Law Review_ 107-158

The authors discuss public policy for determination of child custody disputes, and criticize the use of selective social scientific studies to argue for certain legislative reforms. They discuss the history of custody and recent challenges to the mother-custody presumption, carefully examine new social science research on fatherhood, and discuss an earlier article by David Chambers ("Rethinking the Substantive Rules for Custody Disputes in Divorce" (1984) 83 _Michigan Law Review_ 477) as an instantiation of their criticisms with respect to legal reliance on such scientific data. They conclude that the result is legal and societal focus on fatherhood with a corollary devaluing of motherhood, and that this will further disadvantage women in child custody disputes.

Robert Geffner and Mildred Daley Pagelow, "Mediation and Child Custody Issues in Abusive Relationships" (1990) 8 _Behavioral Sciences and the Law_ 151-159

For annotation, see Chapter 3: **CRIMINAL LAW -- BATTERING.**

Charlotte Germane, Margaret Johnson, and Nancy Lemon, "Mandatory Custody Mediation and Joint Custody Orders in California: The Danger for Victims of Domestic Violence" (1985) 1 _Berkeley Women's Law Journal_ 175-200

For annotation, see Chapter 3: **CRIMINAL LAW -- BATTERING.**

**Linda K. Girdner, "Custody Mediation in the United States: Empower-
ment or Social Control?" (1989) 3** _Canadian Journal of Women and the_
Law **134-154**

The author discusses mediation in custody determination, especially
in the United States. Mediators differ in terms of professional orientation (i.e. mental health professional or lawyer) and in terms of
methodology (i.e. social control or empowerment). Mediation policy is
dependent upon the mediator's views of power. Some mediators have
as their goal joint custody, and perceive their role as mediator to
encourage a couple to choose this arrangement. She thinks that such a
view is inappropriate, and recommends custody mediation only if the
mediator's perceived role is within the empowerment model.

**Sheila M. Holmes, "Imposed Joint Legal Custody: Children's Interests
or Parental Rights?" (1987) 45** _University of Toronto Faculty of Law_
Review **300-322**

The author discusses the legal reform trend toward joint legal
custody, and the underlying assumption that mandated joint custody will
lead to equality between the sexes and fully co-operative child care. She
challenges this assumption by examining the historical context of custody,
the ideology of motherhood and fatherhood, and the reality of inequality
between mothers and fathers. She concludes with a recommendation
that joint custody be permitted where both parents agree, but that a
primary care-giver presumption should operate where parents disagree.
The advantages of this presumption are continuity, recognition of demonstrated parenting ability, and certainty of outcome.

**Linda R. Keenan, "Domestic Violence and Custody Litigation: The
Need for Statutory Reform" (1985) 13** _Hofstra Law Review_ **407-441**

For annotation, see Chapter 3: **CRIMINAL LAW -- BATTERING.**

**Patricia A. Monture, "A Vicious Circle: Child Welfare and the First
Nations" (1989) 3** _Canadian Journal of Women and the Law_ **1-16**

For annotation, see Chapter 6: **FIRST NATIONS AND RACE.**

Frances Olsen, "The Politics of Family Law" (1984) 2 *Law and Inequality* 1-19

The author claims that law, especially family law, contains both an apologetic (i.e. a status quo maintaining) and a utopian (i.e. a change orientated) aspect. The article provides a history of the political significance of family law case law and legislation, and examines the role of the tender years doctrine in custody determination, and how that concept, in its inception and its abolition, both helped and hurt women in families. She concludes that all legal reform ideas must be completely and carefully analyzed.

E. Diane Pask, "The Effect on Maintenance of Custody Sharing" (1989) 3 *Canadian Journal of Women and the Law* 155-181

While a major United States study found a clear relationship between shared legal custody of children and a decrease in child support, the author reports that no Canadian study has been undertaken which either confirms or rejects similar findings. The Canadian studies do, however, unequivocally reveal evidence of low levels of monthly child support awards. She makes specific recommendations with respect to fair allocation of child rearing costs where custody is shared.

Nancy Polikoff, "This Child Does Have Two Mothers: Redefining Parenthood to Meet the Needs of Children in Lesbian-Mother and Other Nontraditional Families" (1990) 78 *Georgetown Law Journal* 459-575

For annotation, see Chapter 12: LESBIANISM AND SEXUAL ORIENTATION.

Nancy D. Polikoff, "Why are Mothers Losing: A Brief Analysis of Criteria Used in Child Custody Determinations" (1982) 7 *Women's Rights Law Reporter*

Part of a Symposium on Reproductive Rights, this article discusses the factors, such as economic resources, employment, and remarriage, which favour fathers in custody disputes.

Dianne Post, "Arguments Against Joint Custody" (1989-90) 4 *Berkeley Women's Law Journal* 316-325

The author provides a framework of arguments and research for lawyers arguing against joint custody, and examines legislation and case law in California, Massachusetts, and other states. She concludes that the inequities of joint custody hurt both women and children, even occasionally when agreed to by the respective parents.

Mel Roman and Susan Dichter, "Fathers and Feminism: Backlash Within the Women's Movement" (1985) 23:2 *Conciliation Courts Review* 37-46

The authors argue that women and children are best served by a presumption of joint custody in post-divorce custody determination, and that shared physical custody is workable even with disputing parents. They conclude that feminist arguments against joint custody fatalistically accept the role of women as victims, and recommend equal parental rights as a method by which equality between men and women can be achieved.

Katherine C. Sheehan, "Post-Divorce Child Custody and Family Relocation" (1986) 9 *Harvard Women's Law Journal* 135-152

The author argues that instead of recognizing the realities of post-divorce families, custody law preserves stereotypical notions of the role of women and men in families. This is especially apparent in child custody disputes where the custodial parent wishes to relocate geographically, and often loses custody of the children. She argues for more creative shared custody schemes, and recommends that if a sole custody determination must be made, the best interests test or the primary care-giver test should be employed.

Annamay T. Sheppard, "Lesbian Mothers II: Long Night's Journey Into Day" (1985) 8 *Women's Rights Law Reporter* 219-245

For annotation, see Chapter 12: LESBIANISM AND SEXUAL ORIENTATION.

Annamay T. Sheppard, "Unspoken Premises in Custody Litigation" (1982) 7:2 *Women's Rights Law Reporter* 229-234

Part of a Symposium on Reproductive Rights, this article discusses women's role as mother, which the author argues continues to be perceived from a Victorian perspective, within which "non-motherly" behaviour as defined by this perspective is hazardous in custody disputes. She recommends the use of a custody theory which recognizes and balances the principle of equal parental rights with the realistic inequalities between men and women as parents.

Irene Thery, "The Interest of the Child and the Regulation of the Post-Divorce Family" (1986) 14 _International Journal of the Sociology of Law_ 341-358
For annotation, see Chapter 10: **LEGAL HISTORY.**

Marriage and Divorce

Rosalie Silberman Abella, "Economic Adjustment on Marriage Breakdown: Support" (1981) 4 _Family Law Review_ 1-15
The author argues that the inability to agree on a philosophy of post-divorce support derives from an inability to agree on the purpose of marriage. Marriage, once viewed as a dependency relationship, is now viewed as a partnership commitment, and this philosophy should be implemented by the judiciary in ascertaining spousal and child support obligations.

Katharine K. Baker, "Contracting for Security: Paying Married Women What They've Earned" (1988) 55 _University of Chicago Law Review_ 1193-1227
The author argues that the economic difficulties women experience following divorce have been exacerbated by the decrease in their bargaining power occasioned by changes in alimony and maintenance laws. Differing statutes between states prevent consistent application by the courts. She discusses partnership and contract paradigms as they relate to marriage, and why women are undercompensated using current alimony standards. She concludes with a method for determining spousal compensation which encourages appropriate compensation for women without encouraging dependency, and which provides for unambiguous guidance to the courts and ensures economic security for women.

Beverly Balos and Katie Trotzky, "Enforcement of the Domestic Abuse Act in Minnesota: A Preliminary Study" (1988) 6 *Law and Inequality* 83–125

For annotation, see Chapter 3: CRIMINAL LAW -- BATTERING.

Sandra Burman and Denise Rudolph, "Repression by Mediation: Mediation and Divorce in South Africa" (1990) 107 *South African Law Journal* 251-278

This article examines the proposed introduction of mediation in the divorce process in South Africa. The authors argue that if implemented, the proposal would reproduce the defects experienced in other countries which have experimented with mediation. They also claim that the scheme would further disadvantage the large section of the South African population who already have problems obtaining legal protection.

Monique Charlebois, "Book Review: Lenore J. Weitzman, THE DIVORCE REVOLUTION: THE UNEXPECTED CONSEQUENCES FOR WOMEN AND CHILDREN IN AMERICA (1985)" (1989) 3 *Canadian Journal of Women and the Law* 287-315

For annotation, see Chapter 16: BOOK REVIEWS.

Mary Irene Coombs, "Agency and Partnership: A Study of Breach of Promise Plaintiffs" (1989) 2 *Yale Journal of Law and Feminism* 1-23

The author reviews the history for suits of breach of promise to marry, identifying the real economic injury suffered by women in the nineteenth and early twentieth century by the loss of prospect of marriage. She explores the goals and needs of the plaintiffs, and criticisms of both the women and the cause of action. She argues that the commencement of a lawsuit is an act of empowerment, and that suits for breach of promise to marry contradict the image of passivity and victimization on which the action is founded. Although the action was at variance with feminists' perception of women's long-term interests, she claims it should not have been rejected. She draws an analogy between the foundation of the breach of promise action and claims by right wing women to the benefits of traditional gender roles.

Rosalind Currie, "The New Family Law Act: A Legal Revolution?"

(1987) *Breaking the Silence* 23-25

This article outlines the main changes to matrimonial property law occasioned by the 1986 ONTARIO FAMILY LAW ACT. Upon marriage breakdown, all assets acquired during the marriage must be divided equally between the spouses, except in "unconscionable circumstances" specifically set out in the statute. The author explains the equal division of the matrimonial home, and considerations in granting an order for exclusive possession, including violence toward a spouse or child. Common law spouses may now seek support after three years of cohabitation, but property provisions only apply to married couples. The author is optimistic the ACT will result in greater women's equality.

Laura Ann Davis, "A Feminist Justification for the Adoption of an Individual Filing System" (1988) 62 *Southern California Law Review* 197-252

The author discusses the historical development of joint filing, the legislative attempts to deal with the "single penalty" and the "marriage penalty", and the legislative attempts to deal with the tax discrepancies that occur between common law states and community property states. The article proposes an eclectic approach to a feminist position, borrowing from both liberal and radical feminism, to justify working for change within the present tax system as a means eventually to change the entire patriarchal social structure.

Marc Feldman, "Jewish Women and Secular Courts: Helping a Jewish Woman Obtain a Get" (1989-90) 5 *Berkeley Women's Law Journal* 139-169

A Jewish husband holds unequal power over his wife in a divorce situation, because he can use as a bargaining tool over divorce settlement issues, the religious requirement that he deliver a "get" to his wife before she can remarry. The author analyzes case law, and the New York "get statute" and its constitutional implications, and recommends a solution to the inequality arising from Jewish law.

Emily Joselson and Judy Kaye, "Pro Se Divorce: A Strategy for Empowering Women" (1983) 1 *Law and Inequality* 239-275

As law students active in a community legal clinic, the authors embarked upon "an experiment in feminist legal practice". Focusing on a "self-help" divorce project designed to teach women how to do their own uncontested divorces, they sought to see if such a project could "empower" women and "demystify" the legal system. In defining their terms, four "levels" of empowerment are offered: Control and Confidence; Legal Demystification; Connecting with Other Women; and Feminist Consciousness-Raising. The students discuss the degree to which women participants reached each level, and the problems some encountered. They conclude that clinics can lend themselves to consciousness raising, if there is the structure and staff to promote talking, sharing, and the examination of women's feelings and experiences.

Herma Hill Kay, "An Appraisal of California's No-Fault Divorce Law" (1987) 75 _California Law Review_ 291-319
The author claims that the California no-fault divorce law of 1970 failed to account for the unequal position of women in the traditional family, although subsequent amendments ensure more substantive equality and encourage experimentation with a variety of family forms. She concludes with proposals for further reform.

Elizabeth Kingdom, "Cohabitation Contracts and Equality" (1990) 18 _International Journal of the Sociology of Law_ 287-298
This article examines two different views on the relationship between the use of cohabitation contracts and equality between domestic and sexual partners both married and not married -- the view that they are inappropriate market devices that cannot promote genuine equality between partners, and the contrary view that marketplace ethics are not inimical to the ethics of personal relations and may instead promote equality. The author concludes that neither view holds because there is no necessary relationship between the use of cohabitation contracts and the promotion of equality or inequality in cohabitation relationships.

Marjorie E. Kornhauser, "The Rhetoric of the Anti-Progressive Income Tax Movement: A Typical Male Reaction" (1987) 86 _Michigan Law Review_ 465-523
This article discredits neoconservative economic policies and the concept of a flat tax system, and notes that political rhetoric has inappropriately linked economic, social, philosophical, and political

principles which at all are not related. The author defends the progressive tax system from several perspectives, but particularly from Carol Gilligan's feminist perspective of inter-relatedness and inter-dependence. She argues that a progressive tax system, based on ability to pay, meets the need to connect with others, without sacrificing too much of the self.

Nora Jane Lauerman, "Book Review: Lenore J. Weitzman, THE DIVORCE REVOLUTION: THE UNEXPECTED SOCIAL AND ECONOMIC CONSEQUENCES FOR WOMEN AND CHILDREN (1985)" (1986) 2 _Berkeley Women's Law Journal_ 246-257
For annotation, see Chapter 16: **BOOK REVIEWS.**

Nora Jane Lauerman, "A Step Toward Enhancing Equality, Choice, and Opportunity to Develop in Marriage and at Divorce" (1987) 56 _University of Cincinnati Law Review_ 493-519
Part of a Symposium on Feminist Moral, Social, and Legal Theory, this article examines the law with respect to family dissolution in an effort to ascertain whether modern family law concepts are more conducive to equal relationships between men and women than were traditional family law concepts. The author claims that while legislation which shifted from fault-based to no-fault on its face fostered equality between the sexes, its actual impact was mixed. She discusses the findings of Lenore Weitzman's ten-year study (see: Weitzman, THE DIVORCE REVOLUTION: THE UNEXPECTED SOCIAL AND ECONOMIC CONSEQUENCES FOR WOMEN AND CHILDREN (1985)), specifically the data with respect to spousal support and marital property division, and reports that judicial decisions have been especially harsh for former full-time homemakers and custodial mothers of children, because they assume an equality between the spouses' potential earning circumstances which does not exist. She concludes with the recommendation that pre-marital agreements dealing with maintenance and property division may either avoid these results, or mitigate the harshness of such results.

Thomas Lyon, "Sexual Exploitation of Divorce Clients: The Lawyer's Prerogative" (1987) 10 _Harvard Women's Law Journal_ 159-201
This article explores sexual relations between divorce clients and their lawyers in light of the similarity to the therapist-patient relationship.

The author discusses the power imbalance, the harm of sexual exploitation, and the possibility of redress through tort suits and disciplinary
actions. He proposes improvements to divorce representation through
an understanding of the emotions which pervade the divorce process.

**Maureen Maloney, "Women and the Income Tax Act: Marriage,
Motherhood and Divorce" (1989) 3 _Canadian Journal of Women and the
Law_ 182-210**
The author argues that the Canadian INCOME TAX ACT
discriminates against women on the basis of sex, and that the extent of
the discrimination is illustrated by its provisions with respect to marriage,
motherhood, and divorce. Her primary focus is on the treatment of
marriage, particularly the problem of reconciling individual taxation with
ability to pay objectives. She proposes and evaluates alternate forms of
taxation, and discusses the subject of household income, outlining
possible approaches and selecting the one most likely to achieve equality
between the sexes and equity between classes. Existing provisions of the
ACT are unacceptable in an era of mandated equality under the
CHARTER OF RIGHTS AND FREEDOMS. She concludes that radical reforms which reflect feminist concern for the economic disadvantages of women are required.

**Isabel Marcus, "Locked In and Locked Out: Reflections on the History
of Divorce Law Reform in New York State" (1988/89) 37 _Buffalo Law
Review_ 375-483**
This article seeks to provide both an account of New York State
divorce law reform and an analysis of law reform as a symbolic activity
for society generally and for the specific constituencies said to be the
beneficiaries of any specific reform. The author pursues both objectives
on the basis of five historical narratives which document the ideological
substance and meaning of divorce law reform. The narratives relate to
specific themes in the debate -- namely, the legal identity of married
women, the expansion of the grounds for divorce, and post divorce
maintenance for women -- and to legal reform process and outcome.
She concludes that divorce law reform in the name of gender neutrality
will fail if it either ignores or denies the ideological, economic, and
power significance of gendered identity in American culture and history.

Isabel Marcus, "Reflections on the Significance of the Sex/Gender System: Divorce Law Reform in New York" (1987) 42 *University of Miami Law Review* 55-73
    This paper was originally presented at a symposium entitled Excluded Voices: Realities in Law and Law Reform. Through an examination of the changes in divorce law in New York, the author shows that although the "separate spheres" doctrine is no longer strictly enforced, sex and gender are still determining factors. She argues that whether or not the rules governing a sex-based institution like marriage are sex- or gender-specific, the context in which they operate is genderized, and therefore gender plays a key role. She concludes that the question of whether or not law reform should be gendered must acknowledge the centrality and the complexity of the concepts of sex and gender.

Lorna R. Marsden and Joan E. Busby, "Feminist Influence Through the Senate: The Case of Divorce, 1967" (1989) 14:2 *Atlantis* 72-80
    For annotation, see Chapter 10: **LEGAL HISTORY.**

Martha Minow, "Consider the Consequences -- Book Review: Lenore Weitzman, THE DIVORCE REVOLUTION: THE UNEXPECTED SOCIAL AND ECONOMIC CONSEQUENCES FOR WOMEN AND CHILDREN IN AMERICA (1985)" (1986) 84 *Michigan Law Review* 900-916
    For annotation, see Chapter 16: **BOOK REVIEWS.**

L. J. Moran, "A Study in the History of Male Sexuality in Law: Non-Consummation" (1990) 1:2 *Law and Critique* 155-171
    For annotation, see Chapter 10: **LEGAL HISTORY.**

Mary Jane Mossman, "Book Review: John Eekelaar and Mavis Maclean, MAINTENANCE AFTER DIVORCE (1986)" (1989) 3 *Canadian Journal of Women and the Law* 293-302
    For annotation, see Chapter 16: **BOOK REVIEWS.**

A. Orlando, "Exclusive Possession of the Family Home: The Plight of

Battered Cohabitees" (1987) 45 *University of Toronto Faculty of Law Review* 152-178
   For annotation, see Chapter 3: **CRIMINAL LAW – BATTERING.**

Carol J. Rogerson, "The Causal Connection Test in Spousal Support Law" (1989) 8 *Canadian Journal of Family Law* 95-132
   Family law has moved from the traditional model of spousal support to the causal connection model, which, the author argues, is ultimately a statement about the institution of marriage. She examines the application of the causal connection test in case law, and concludes that the test is best used as an interpretive device rather than a threshold test, because, by definition, every marriage involves enough causal connection to satisfy the threshold test.

Barbara R. Rowe and Jean M. Lown, "The Economics of Divorce and Remarriage for Rural Utah Families" (1990) 16 *Journal of Contemporary Law* 301-332
   The authors examine research with respect to economic consequences of divorce for urban families, and then report the findings of a study of similar consequences for rural families in Utah. They conclude that women's role as the caretaker for children, limited earning potential because of wage discrimination, inadequate divorce settlements, and gender-specific roles assumed within traditional marriages all result in negative financial consequences for divorced women. They conclude that, because of these financial realities, equal sharing of marital assets may not be a just and equitable settlement.

Martha Shaffer, "Divorce Mediation: A Feminist Perspective" (1988) 46 *University of Toronto Faculty Law Review* 162-200
   This article discusses divorce mediation as an instance of the current trend toward all forms of Alternative Dispute Resolution. The author acknowledges the appeal of the idea of mediation, but argues that as currently conceived and practised, mediation has a detrimental impact on women due both to the impact of power inequality, and to the ideal of mediator neutrality. She concludes that a more sophisticated understanding of the power dynamic is essential before mediation can be designed to serve the interests of women.

M. Dwayne Smith and Nathan Bennett, "Poverty, Inequality, and Theories of Forcible Rape" (1985) 31 _Crime and Delinquency_ 295-305
For annotation, see Chapter 3: CRIMINAL LAW -- RAPE.

Faith H. Spencer, "Expanding Marital Options: Enforcement of Premarital Contracts During Marriage" [1989] _University of Chicago Legal Forum_ 281-308
This paper identifies the beginning and the end of marriage as the only time the law will presently become involved. The author argues for legal enforcement of premarital contracts at any time throughout the marriage. She concludes that not to enforce contracts during marriage is to place an unnecessary limitation on freedom to contract, and that enforcement could enhance marriage by providing for dispute resolution, rather than divorce.

Nadine Taub, "Book Review: Lenore J. Weitzman, THE DIVORCE REVOLUTION: THE UNEXPECTED SOCIAL AND ECONOMIC CONSEQUENCES FOR WOMEN AND CHILDREN IN AMERICA (1987)" (1988) 13 Signs: _Journal of Women in Culture and Society_ 578-583
For annotation, see Chapter 16: BOOK REVIEWS.

Poverty

Jennifer Aitken, "A Stranger in the Family: The Legal Status of Domestic Workers in Ontario" (1987) 45 _University of Toronto Faculty of Law Review_ 394-414
This article discusses the exclusion of domestic workers from Canadian labour legislation's protection, specifically the protection regarding maximum hours of work and overtime pay. The author claims this exclusion, and the general social, economic, and legal disadvantages suffered by domestic workers, is indicative of society's continuing to equate "women" with "free housework." She claims that the domestic worker, viewed as part of the "family unit," is not protected because of notions of family privacy. She concludes that real equality for both

domestic workers and for women in general requires radical restructuring of the organization of work, child care, and home life.

Penny Andrews, "The Legal Underpinnings of Gender Oppression in Apartheid South Africa" (1986) 3 *Australian Journal of Law and Society* **92-107**
For annotation, see Chapter 6: FIRST NATIONS AND RACE.

Marie Ashe, "Book Review: Barbara C. Gilpi, Nancy Hartsock, Clare Novak, and Myra Strober, (eds.), WOMEN AND POVERTY (1986)" (1987) 89 *West Virginia Law Review* **1183-1189**
For annotation, see Chapter 16: BOOK REVIEWS.

M. Avery, "Legal Action for Women: Streets and Statutes" (1987) 17:11 *Off Our Backs* **24-25**
This article provides a brief history of Legal Action for Women (LAW) which provides free legal services to women in San Francisco's Tenderloin and Miasian districts on battering, rape, child custody, and prostitution charges, and immigration and juvenile arrests. LAW is coordinated by the U.S. Prostitutes Collective, and is modeled on a similar service in London organized by the English Collective of Prostitutes. Like the English service, the American service grew out of the insensitivity of social service bureaucracies and the law to poor women.

Mary E. Becker, "Politics, Differences and Economic Rights" [1989] *University of Chicago Legal Forum* **169-189**
The author argues that placing emphasis on the "differences" between men and women is dangerous as differences are used to justify separate, unequal spheres for women. She examines the political and economic cost to women of being different by assessing the economic status of women in employment, divorce, social assistance, and welfare. Despite the presence of an equality norm, women are far from economic parity with men and she suggests legislative improvements. The differences between men and women weaken women's economic and political power through socialization, unconscious discrimination, and the design of jobs for workers with wives. She explains why there is a tendency to suppress the existence of the struggle between the sexes, and

how relationships with men and divisions between women hinder effective political participation by women.

**Johanna Brenner, "Towards a Feminist Perspective on Welfare
Reform" (1989) 2 *Yale Journal of Law and Feminism* 99-129**
The author claims that the feminist debate on welfare reform
illustrates the tension between the difference and equal treatment strategies. She engages in the theoretical debate around welfare as a
reflection of gender inequality by examining the "reforms" in the United
States FAMILY SUPPORT ACT of 1988. She offers a strategy toward
a welfare policy which promotes the independence of women as
individuals, and also supports them as mothers.

**Diane Chalmessin, "The End of the 'Man in the House' Rule: A
Victory for Women?" (1987) *Breaking the Silence* 16-17**
In 1987 the Ontario government ended the "spouse in the house"
rule which disentitled a single welfare mother from social assistance
benefits if she lived with someone who even partially supported her or
accepted responsibility for her children. The rule was part of a "witch
hunt" for women who get money from their lovers, and the author hopes
its removal is one step toward the elimination of discrimination against
poor women. A welfare mother should be considered single until she
has lived with a man long enough that he is legally obligated to support
her and her children.

**Christine Davies, "Divorce and the Older Woman in Canada" (1988)
29 *Cambrian Law Review* 17-25**
The majority of elderly women in Canada live in poverty. The
author describes the reasons for this phenomenon, examines the situation
of the elderly divorced, and suggests resolutions in the areas of spousal
maintenance and pensions.

**Susanna Downie, "Women's Agenda Spurs Legislators to Pass Bucks"
(1986) 3 *New Directions for Women* 11**
The author describes lobbying efforts of the Women's Agenda in
Pennsylvania, which "seeks to make the American dream of equal
opportunity a reality for all Americans." This lobby includes the

controversial "Our Piece of Pie" campaign, in which women bake pies for state legislators to create goodwill before presenting their proposed Women's and Children's Budget. She claims that these efforts will benefit women and children in forthcoming budgets, which is especially important because of governmental budget cuts.

Nitya Duclos, "Breaking the Dependency Circle: The Family Law Act Reconsidered" (1987) 45 *University of Toronto Faculty of Law Review* 1-35
The author examines the legislation in Ontario dealing with the economic consequences of marital dissolution for the family. She argues that the alleviation of economic disaster for women is an appropriate goal for law, and that current legislation is not adequate. What is required is an underlying concern for the reality of the economic oppression experienced by women, and she concludes with a recommendation that a "lost opportunity cost" approach be utilized to attain a new form of economic equality for women.

Siegrun F. Fox, "Rights and Obligations: Critical Feminist Theory, the Public Bureaucracy, and Policies for Mother-Only Families -- Book Review: Kathy E. Ferguson, THE FEMINIST CASE AGAINST BUREAUCRACY (1984); Wendy McElroy, FREEDOM, FEMINISM AND THE STATE (1986); Lenore J. Weitzman, THE DIVORCE REVOLUTION (1985); Ruth Sidel, WOMEN AND CHILDREN LAST (1986); Irwim Garfinkel and Sara McLanahan, SINGLE MOTHERS AND THEIR CHILDREN (1986)" (1987) 47 *Public Administration Review* 436-440
For annotation, see Chapter 16: BOOK REVIEWS.

J. Francis, "Disabled Native Women" (1985) 3 *Just Cause* 14-16
For annotation, see Chapter 6: FIRST NATIONS AND RACE.

Nancy Fraser, "Women, Welfare and the Politics of Need Interpretation" (1987) 2 *Hypatia: A Journal of Feminist Philosophy* 103-121
This article provides an analysis of the United States welfare system which exposes the system's underlying gender norms, and demonstrates how its administrative practices preemptively define women's needs. The

author then situates these practices in the struggle over the interpretation of social needs where, she thinks, feminists can intervene.

Jacques Frémont, "Droit Public Assurance-chômage, maternité et adoption: les récents modifications et leur validité" (1982-1983) 17 _Chroniques Sectorielles_ 497-506
  For annotation, see Chapter 2: CONSTITUTIONAL LAW.

Margaret Leighton, "Handmaids' Tales: Family Benefits Assistance and the Single-Mother-Led Family" (1987) 45 _University of Toronto Faculty of Law Review_ 324-354
  The author discusses the impact of social assistance programs on single mother families. She argues that despite sympathy for single woman parents because of low wages, cost of child care, and forced reliance on a former spouse for economic support, the ideology of the welfare system perpetuates the same conditions with such policies as the "man in the house" rule. She recommends reform of the program to allow benefit payments on the basis of need, rather than relationship status.

Sheryl Gordon McCloud, "Feminism's Idealist Error" (1986) 14 _Review of Law & Social Change_ 277-320
  The author claims that much feminist jurisprudence treats sexual equality as an ideal value of either the "equal treatment" or "positive action" type; and she argues that both fail to appreciate the economic consequences of equality for the majority of working-class women. The majority of working women are confronted by diminishing substantive legal protections and a condition of relative scarcity of economic benefits in a class-divided society. For the minority of women who have gained access to professional, entrepreneurial, and skilled positions, privilege and access grow. Feminist theory, by either ignoring class or treating all women as a single class, obscures this dual impact of sexual equality jurisprudence on women's employment rights. The author proposes the "materialist" appreciation of freedom and necessity as a more accurate way to evaluate employment law.

Sara S. McLanahan, Annemette Sorensen, and Dorothy Watson, "Sex

Differences in Poverty, 1950-1980" (1989) 15 *Signs: Journal of Women in Culture and Society* **102-122**

The feminization of poverty is a demonstrable fact. However, absolute poverty rates (poor women/total women or poor men/total men) do not give a true picture. The authors use a sex/poverty ratio (women's poverty rate/men's poverty rate), which compensates for overall shifts in the poor population, and examine the contribution made to the feminization of poverty by the changes which have occurred in family structure and household organisation. They discuss three possible methods for reducing the poverty of women.

Mary Jane Mossman and Morag MacLean, "Family Law and Social Welfare: Toward a New Equality" (1985) 5 *Canadian Journal of Family Law* **79-110**

This article discusses the liberalization of divorce law, which, the authors argue, has been a major contributing factor to the feminization of poverty. They suggest that any reforms must deal with the differential financial impact divorce has on men and women, in order to ensure that the principles of equality and independence espoused in the divorce legislation apply equally to men and women. They also discuss the need to merge the goals of family law and those of social welfare programs in order to achieve just results for women.

Laurie Nsiah-Jefferson, "Reproductive Laws, Women of Color, and Low-Income Women" (1989) 11 *Women's Rights Law Reporter* **15-38**

For annotation, see Chapter 6: **FIRST NATIONS AND RACE.**

Suzanne E. Osterbusch, Sharon M. Keigher, Baila Miller, and Nathan L. Linsk, "Community Care Policies and Gender Justice" (1987) 17 *International Journal of Health Services* **217-231**

The authors argue that social policies which emphasize home-based care of the elderly are premised on saving the state money, and do not take into consideration the gender issues which arise because the caregiver is usually female and unpaid. They "examine community care policies from a perspective of gender justice, ... the needs of carers and ... the social costs of neglecting these needs." After surveying the personal costs to the female caregiver, they recommend policies to maximize gender justice.

Diana M. Pearce and Kelley Ellsworth, "Welfare and Women's Poverty: Reform or Reinforcement?" (1990) 16 _Journal of Legislation_ 141-150

Over the last two decades, poverty has increased among single parent, women-maintained families. According to the authors, this -- combined with decreased poverty among the elderly and two-parent families -- has resulted in the feminization of poverty. They argue that female poverty is unique due both to the economic burdens associated with women having primary responsibility for child care, and to the sexist nature of the labour market where women experience discrimination, harassment, and confinement to pink collar jobs. They argue as well that subjecting poor women to programs designed for poor men will not work, and will, instead, consign the women to a life of poverty. They conclude that women's poverty can only be alleviated by initiatives which address directly the foundations of the feminization of poverty, among which they would include pay equity, an end to gender segregation in the labour force, flexible work hours, universal affordable day care, a more egalitarian unemployment insurance program, and increased minimum wage for all workers. This article is part of a Symposium on Poverty, Legislation, and Law.

Susannah Worth Rowley, "Women, Pensions and Equality" (1986) 10 _Dalhousie Law Journal_ 283-356

The author claims that society reveals the value it places on the contribution of women in the high proportion of elderly women who are poor. The manner in which the pension system in Canada denies equal protection to women is explained in detail. She discusses concepts of equality, including the American "disparate impact" theory, and reviews proposed reform measures. She argues that the Canadian pension system will never be constitutional as long as benefits to women are based on income derived from discriminatory wage scales and until pension plans recognize the value of unpaid women's labour. Statistical tables are included as evidence of gender inequality within the system.

Elisabeth Sachs, "Support and Custody Enforcement Programme: the Experience of Two Years" (1989) 11 _Advocates' Quarterly_ 31-42

The author describes the workings of the Ontario SUPPORT AND CUSTODY ORDERS ENFORCEMENT ACT, 1985, under which 61,000 orders had been filed by the end of August 1989. She reports that the legislation, which aims to "change societal attitudes in order that the honouring of support obligations becomes a matter of course," has reduced default rates.

Barbara Stark, "Spousal Support Since the Enactment of No-Fault Divorce: Small Change for Women" (1989) 27 *Family and Conciliation Courts Review* 59-70

The author argues that traditional spousal support has never been a cure for women's dependency and poverty at divorce, because spousal support does not address the real causes of the feminization of poverty, which she identifies as the lack of equal opportunity in the marketplace, and the uncompensated child care responsibilities assumed by women. She concludes that women's best and perhaps only chance for escaping dependency and poverty is work-force participation, and recommends that approaches to spousal support be predicated upon providing women whatever is required to gain access to the public sphere.

V. Sterling, "Pension Plans and Sex Discrimination" (1985) 3 *Canadian Journal of Insurance Law* 66-78

For annotation, see Chapter 2: **CONSTITUTIONAL LAW.**

Property

"A Much Needed Change: Land Rights For Women in Andhra Pradesh" (1983) 3:5 *Manuski* 7-9

The article discusses the 1983 proposed changes to the HINDU SUCCESSION ACT, 1956, which made daughters equal to sons as inheritors of property acquired by the parents in their lifetime. However, ancestral property, governed by customary law, only recognizes males as members of joint families. The author explains family structure, how property is devised, and how the Andhra Pradesh Amendment bill seeks to include daughters into Hindu joint families. While the bill is a positive step towards equality, restrictions on a woman's rights as a joint family member remain.

Constance B. Backhouse, "Married Women's Property Law in Nineteenth-Century Canada" (1988) 6 _Law and History Review_ 211-257
This is an historic account of the evolution of married women's property rights in Canada from 1800-1900. The author describes the three "waves" of change which began with emergency relief allowing women to hold property after marriage breakdown to the development of "separate estates," and finally statutes granting women control over their earnings and giving them dispositive powers. She comments on the motivations and goals of legislators in their enactment, and describes the judiciary's deliberate campaign to nullify the statutory reforms of the second and third waves. She questions whether feminists of the 19th century would be satisfied today with egalitarian property laws when actual access to wealth and property is still so skewed in favour of men.

Norma Basch, "The Emerging Legal History of Women in the United States: Property, Divorce, and the Constitution" (1986) 12 _Signs: Journal of Women in Culture and Society_ 97-117
The author argues that women's legal history is emerging and that it is important that continuing work be done linking the purely historical and the purely legal. The history of three areas of law -- married women's property rights, divorce, and constitutional law -- are reviewed.

Norma Basch, "Marriage and Property in Nineteenth-Century New York" (1983) 2:3 _American Historical Review_ 374-393
The article explores numerous literary works on the history of women from the American Revolution to the Progressive Era in three "pivotal" areas of law: married women's property rights, divorce, and constitutional developments. The literature underscores the changing relationship between women, the family, and the state.

Clare F. Beckton, "The Impact on Women of Entrenchment of Property Rights in the Canadian Charter of Rights and Freedoms" (1985) 9 _Dalhousie Law Journal_ 288-312
For annotation, see Chapter 2: CONSTITUTIONAL LAW.

Lucie Cheng, "Women and Class Analysis in the Chinese Land Revolution" (1988-89) 4 _Berkeley Women's Law Journal_ 62-93

The Chinese Communist Party established a short-lived Soviet Republic at Jiangxi during the early 1930's. A system of land reform, using three distinct approaches of distributing land to women, presented issues that, the author claims, continue to challenge those who seek radical change for women. The "proto-feminist" approach saw women as an oppressed class within a system of patriarchy. The "familistic" approach largely ignored sexual inequality, focusing instead on class status. The "synthetic" approach considered both gender inequality and class exploitation, "focusing on the individual woman's specific role in the social structure". Proponents of synthesis, the author reports, would not believe Marxism or feminism alone could adequately deal with the gender-class dilemma. Method of distribution is, she suggests, a significant indicator of priorities with regard to gender equality. The author concludes that "women cannot have an independent class status within a household-based economy under patriarchy, and any artificial manipulation of class criterion by formalistic legal definitions will be unlikely to succeed."

Richard H. Chused, "Married Women's Property and Inheritance by Widows in Massachusetts: A Study of Wills Probated Between 1800 and 1850" (1986) 2 *Berkeley Women's Law Journal* 42-88

The author investigates private property dispositions in Massachusetts wills during the first half of the 19th Century to discover whether equitable rules were followed for married women. He also tries to discover why the state adopted married women's acts.

Joan Heifetz Hollinger, "Blest Be the Tie That Binds -- Book Review: Mary Ann Glendon, THE NEW FAMILY AND THE NEW PROPERTY (1981)" (1983) 81 *Michigan Law Review* 1065-1082

For annotation, see Chapter 16: BOOK REVIEWS.

G. Ireland, "The Family Law Reform Act and Its Effect on Farm Women" (1984) 7 *Canadian Community Law Journal* 72-74

The author examines the impact of matrimonial property legislation on farm women in Ontario. She argues that there are still many open questions with respect to the division of farm property upon marriage dissolution, a circumstance which is exacerbated by frequent heavy financing of farming operations, as well as by the view that the farm woman's role is merely a housewife and not farming partner. She concludes that farm women are still in a very vulnerable position post-divorce.

Elizabeth Kingdom, "Cohabitation Contracts: A Socialist-Feminist Issue" (1988) 15 _Journal of Law and Society_ 77-89
This article analyzes cohabitation contracts, specifically those with respect to property rights, from a socialist feminist perspective. The author examines both historical and current legal documents and data, and concludes in favour of legal recognition of cohabitation contracts in order to increase the range of options available to people. She includes, however, a disclaimer, namely that such recognition is troublesome because the ideology of equality which pervades most contracts frequently disfavours women.

Mary Lyndon Shanley, "Suffrage, Protective Labour Legislation, and Married Women's Property Laws in England" (1986) 12 _Signs: Journal of Women in Culture and Society_ 62-77
For annotation, see Chapter 10: **LEGAL HISTORY.**

Sally Burnett Sharp, "The Partnership Ideal: The Development of Equitable Distribution in North Carolina" (1987) 65 _North Carolina Law Review_ 195-255
This article discusses the North Carolina marital property legislation, which is based on a partnership model of marriage, and which has produced significant changes in family law since enactment. The author examines judicial interpretation of the statute, and suggests interpretations in difficult areas which have yet to be adjudicated. She concludes that divisions of property need to be equitable as opposed to equal, and that they must legitimize the contributions of homemaker spouses.

June Miller Weisberger, "The Wisconsin Marital Property Act: Highlights of the Wisconsin Experience in Developing a Model for Comprehensive Common Law Property Reform" (1985) 1 _Wisconsin Women's Law Journal_ 5-68
This article examines matrimonial property legislation passed in Wisconsin in 1984, which introduced a community property regime. The

author discusses the goals of the reform, which are to have the legislation reflect the concept of marriage as a partnership, and then examines alternatives to the common law property regime. These alternatives include community property, in which the presumption of co-ownership begins at one of either marriage or the dissolution of that marriage through divorce or death; and the UNIFORM PROPERTY ACT, which provides equitable grounds for governing property division. She concludes that the Wisconsin MPA, which identifies areas of key concern -- property classification, management and control of property, and marital property agreements -- can provide significant guidance to any state enacting similar legislation.

CHAPTER 5
FEMINIST THEORY

General

Rosalie Silberman Abella, "The Social and Legal Paradigms of Equality" (1989) 1 *Windsor Review of Legal and Social Issues* 5-16
For annotation, see Chapter 2: CONSTITUTIONAL LAW.

Kathryn Abrams, "Kitsch and Community -- Book Review: Robert Bellah, HABITS OF THE HEART (1985); Benjamin Barber, STRONG DEMOCRACY (1984); and Michael Walzer, EXODUS AND REVO-LUTION (1985)" (1986) 84 *Michigan Law Review* 941-962
For annotation, see Chapter 16: BOOK REVIEWS.

Joan Acker, "Class, Gender, and the Relations of Distribution" (1988) 13 *Signs: Journal of Women in Culture and Society* 473-497
This article reconsiders and criticizes Marxist analysis of women's labour. The author argues that the relations which produce class are themselves a gendered process that reinforces women's place in the wage labour and domestic spheres, and concludes that both gender and class are equally integral to understanding exploitation.

Anita L. Allen, "Taking Liberties: Privacy, Private Choice, and Social Contract Theory" (1987) 56 *University of Cincinnati Law Review* 461-490
For annotation, see Chapter 1: ABORTION AND REPRODUC-TION.

Elizabeth S. Anderson, "Women and Contracts: No New Deal -- Book Review: Carole Pateman, THE SEXUAL CONTRACT (1988)" (1990) 88 *Michigan Law Review* 1792-1810

For annotation, see Chapter 16: **BOOK REVIEWS.**

Caroline Andrew, "Women and the Welfare State" (1984) 17 *Canadian Journal of Political Science* 667-683
The author examines the role women play in various aspects of the welfare state: organizing and lobbying for the programs; as workers for the welfare state; and as clients of the welfare state. She concludes that gender is an important part of the politics of the welfare state, and that alliances between women as workers and as clients, and the general population are crucial in developing a feminist strategy for change.

Marie Ashe, "Mind's Opportunity: Birthing a Poststructuralist Feminist Jurisprudence" (1987) 38 *Syracuse Law Review* 1129-1173
The author identifies the salient features of feminist jurisprudence as the central concern with the universal cultural reality of female subordination, and the refusal to accept subordination as accidental or necessary. She suggests that new avenues of exploration are available at the intersection of feminist jurisprudence and poststructuralist thought. The failure of liberal feminist jurisprudence has, she claims, become obvious with the significant change in gender relations. This has been paralleled by the failure of non-jurisprudential feminist thought with its confusions of liberal theory and uncertainty over divisions. She argues that leftist feminist legal theorists, with the contributions of poststructuralist methodology and epistemological inquiry, the philosophical and literary process, have included different and varying voices claiming identity as 'female,' and that a change in thinking on gender differentiation is now possible, with inquiry at a depth not reached by liberal investigation.

Katherine T. Bartlett, "Feminist Legal Methods" (1990) 103 *Harvard Law Review* 829-887
This article identifies and critically examines three feminist methods which reflect the status of women as "outsiders," including asking the 'woman question,' feminist practical reasoning, and consciousness raising. The author claims that articulating methods is important for increased awareness of the nature of what feminists do and how to do it better. She examines the relationship between feminist methods and substantive legal rules arguing that these methods "provide an appropri-

ate constraint upon the application of substantive rules". She explores the nature of the claims to truth that those using these methods can make, and then analyzes three theories of knowledge reflected in feminist legal literature, namely, rational empiricism, standpoint epistemology, and postmodernism. She offers a fourth approach, "positionality," as the best explanation what being "right" in law means. Positionality acknowledges the existence of "empirical truths, values and knowledge," but also their contingent and provisional nature. Positionality, in consequence, makes truth subject to continuing revision through feminist methods.

Mary E. Becker, "Politics, Differences and Economic Rights" [1989] _University of Chicago Legal Forum_ 169-189
     For annotation, see Chapter 4: **FAMILY LAW -- POVERTY.**

Leslie Bender, "Changing the Values in Tort Law" (1990) 25 _Tulsa Law Review_ 759-773
     In this article, which is part of a Symposium on Feminist Jurisprudence, the author proposes that the language of economics be rejected in favour of a language of care in the resolution of torts cases. She emphasizes that the power between the parties must be balanced.

Leslie Bender, "A Lawyer's Primer on Feminist Theory and Tort" (1988) 38 _Journal of Legal Education_ 3-37
     The author examines the word "feminism" and stereotypes of feminism, and discusses the integration of practice and theory. In a critical examination of the ideological premises of different feminisms, she examines the role of patriarchy in the construction of substantive law, and the implicit male norm in a historical, theoretical, and scientific context. She then looks at the implicit male norm in negligence law, particularly the use of reasonable person, rather than the reasonable man, and the concept of standard of care. She claims that the sex/gender duality is a reflection of the self/other opposition in a culture designed from the masculine perspective, and that it would be better to focus on responsibilities, rather than rights. In an ethic based on care and responsibility, she argues, the understanding of "reasonableness" would be "responsibility," and "standard of care" would be "standard of caring" or "consideration of another's safety and interests". The premise of negligence law would then be that no one should be hurt; and its

focus would then become responsibility rather than rights, interconnectedness rather than separation, and priority of safety rather than profit and efficiency.

Agnete Weis Bentzon, "Comments on Women's Law in Scandinavia" (1986) 14 *International Journal of the Sociology of Law* 249-253
   With the aim of improving the status of women in law and society, the author focuses on the need to develop "action oriented" theories centred around the status of women. She notes the strong link between the feminist movement and women's law, particularly on notions of justice and freedom. She examines the triangular connection between women, law, and society, and explores their relationship from the standpoint of "women's reality." She emphasizes that "law is a human construct," and that it is important to incorporate into its methodology and practice, more connections with women's experience in society as identified in social science studies.

Lawrence A. Blum, "Gilligan and Kohlberg: Implications for Moral Theory" (1988) 98 *Ethics* 472-491
   The author claims that Gilligan's work in moral developmental psychology is important for moral philosophy. Kohlberg's view has been the dominant conception of morality in contemporary philosophy, and has recently been under attack for insufficiently considering personal integrity and the legitimacy of personal concerns. He suggests that Gilligan's criticism is distinct, because for her, care and responsibility are an element of morality itself, and genuinely distinct from impartiality. He discusses the major differences between Kohlberg and Gilligan, and recommends pursuing implications of Gilligan's work for an adequate moral theory which takes into account territory not readily encompassed within existing categories of contemporary ethics.

Eileen Boris, "Looking at Women's Historians Looking At 'Difference'" (1985) 3 *Wisconsin Women's Law Journal* 213-238
   Part of the 1986 Feminism and Legal Theory Conference, this article traces the historical progress of the difference debate, and discusses the advantages and disadvantages for women of both the "sameness" and "difference" paradigms. Ideas of female difference become politicized in the public realm, and the author cites the debate

over comparable worth and affirmative action as an instance of this. She
concludes that neither the structure of politics, the economy, nor the
family allow sufficient opportunities for women to change their material
circumstances in a freely chosen fashion.

**Eileen Boris, "The Power of Motherhood: Black and White Activist
Women Redefine the 'Political'" (1989) 2 *Yale Journal of Law and
Feminism* 25-49**
    For annotation, see Chapter 6: FIRST NATIONS AND RACE.

**Anne Bottomley, "Critical Legal Studies: Becoming Feminists" (1986)
166 *Spare Rib* 12**
    The author reports on a meeting of the women's caucus of critical
legal studies (CLS), which demonstrated some of the difficulties within
feminism, including the absence of a structure for discussing issues of
women of colour, the lack of inter-disciplinary study, the question of
attendance by males, the varying financial resources of attendees, and the
movement's Anglo-Saxon bias. However, she concludes, the search for
solutions to patriarchy must be carried out on an international level, and
women must give support and gain solidarity through such interactions.

**Anne Bottomley, Susie Gibson, and Belinda Meteyard, "Dworkin;
Which Dworkin? Taking Feminism Seriously" (1987) 14 *Journal of Law
and Society* 47-60**
    The authors claim that feminist acceptance of the subordination of
women must change, and that feminists are divided over major issues.
Feminist work within CLS is problematic, because it is usually concerned
with family law or sex discrimination. Work must also be done in areas
fundamentally pertaining to women, such as capitalist social formation,
the appearance of separation, the public/private dichotomy, and market
and family. They conclude that unlike Marxism, in which the revolution
is in public sphere alone, feminism is the imperative link between theory
and practice -- in feminist legal practice, the constant question is theory
in praxis.

**Susan B. Boyd and Elizabeth A. Sheehy, "Feminist Perspectives on
Law: Canadian Theory and Practice (Alternate Title: Canadian**

Feminist Perspectives on Law)" (1986-1988) 2 *Canadian Journal of Women and the Law* 1-40 (Alternate Cite: (1986) 13 *Journal of Law and Society* 283)

The authors survey Canadian feminist legal literature, and conclude that much work leaves theoretical positions unstated, although the majority is implicitly within the liberal human rights paradigm. They further argue that unstated and untested assumptions or political theories constrain creative feminist critique.

David Bradley, "Perspectives on Sexual Equality in Sweden" (1990) 53 *Modern Law Review* 283-303

Using Sweden as a case study, this article attempts to illustrate the difficulties in breaking through economic and social structures in a political system with a relatively high commitment to egalitarianism. The author argues that women remain disadvantaged in Sweden, and points to the tension between the promotion of sexual equality and inequality of wealth and class as the cause. He concludes that mobilization on a single issue such as sexual equality may always fall short and, citing the parallels between Marxism and some strands of feminism, suggests that more theory and ideology is required.

Sarah E. Burns, "Apologia for the Status Quo -- Book Review: David L. Kirp, Mark G. Yudolf, and Marlene Strong Franks, GENDER JUSTICE (1986)" (1986) 74 *Georgetown Law Journal* 1769-1797

For annotation, see Chapter 16: **BOOK REVIEWS**.

Karen Busby, "The Maleness of Legal Language" (1989) 18 *Manitoba Law Journal* 191-212

The elimination of sexist language, the author thinks, is the key to the elimination of sexism, and she asks whether legal language has a male bias and, if it does, whether its intrinsic message is one which reinforces "the superiority of the male and its politics, patriarchy"? By examining the various components of legal language, she links "language, gender and oppression in the context of the legal resister," and concludes that legal discourse "systematically excludes, devalues, trivializes and ignores women".

Maureen Cain, "Realism, Feminism, Methodology, and Law" (1986) 14 _International Journal of the Sociology of Law_ 255-267
The author claims that the issues in feminist methodology are related to who does the research, and for whom and about whom it is done. The epistemological question is how to know and find out about the social world. She argues that the historical nature of knowledge, in which observations are historical and observers are engaged in the historical process, entitles some subjects to formulate how to be theorized, while others require essential conjunction with respective theoretical standpoints. She claims that there is language available to think of the intransitive relationship abutting female experience, and that is possible for feminine understanding to develop through recognition of women's experience.

Maureen Cain, "Towards Transgression: New Directions in Feminist Criminology" (1990) 18 _International Journal of the Sociology of Law_ 1-17
For annotation, see Chapter 3: CRIMINAL LAW -- GENERAL.

Patricia A. Cain, "Feminist Jurisprudence: Grounding the Theories" (1989) 4 _Berkeley Women's Law Journal_ 191-214
For annotation, see Chapter 12: LESBIANISM AND SEXUAL ORIENTATION.

Clare Calhoun, "Justice, Care, Gender Bias" (1988) 135 _Journal of Philosophy_ 451-463
This article discusses Gilligan's challenge to moral theory (see: Gilligan, "Moral Orientation and Moral Development" in Kittay and Meyers, (eds.), WOMEN AND MORAL THEORY (1987); Gilligan, IN A DIFFERENT VOICE (1982)), which is a challenge to both the dominance of the ethic of justice, and the presumption that moral theory is gender neutral. The author questions the need to eliminate gender bias as against eliminating all bias, and concludes that because some moral issues are more critical for women, and because any achievement of gender neutrality involves setting priorities for these and other issues, specific gender analysis is required. She recommends inclusion of gender-sensitivity to the existing tools of philosophical analysis in order to create an ideology of the moral life.

Cheshire Calhoun, "Responsibility and Reproach" (1989) 99 *Ethics* 389-406
In this article, which is part of a Symposium on Feminism and Political Theory, Calhoun discusses the confusion women experience over moral responsibility.

Claudia Card, "Women's Voices and Ethical Ideals: Must We Mean What We Say? -- Book Review: Eva Feder Kittay and Diana T. Meyers (eds.), WOMEN AND MORAL THEORY (1987)" (1988) 99 *Ethics* 125-135
For annotation, see Chapter 16: **BOOK REVIEWS**.

Ruth E. Chang, "Book Review: Christine Delphy, CLOSE TO HOME: A MATERIALIST ANALYSIS OF WOMEN'S OPPRESSION (1984)" (1988) 11 *Harvard Women's Law Journal* 269-278
For annotation, see Chapter 16: **BOOK REVIEWS**.

Elizabeth B. Clark, "Book Review: Michael Grossberg, GOVERNING THE HEARTH (1985)" (1985) 2 *Wisconsin Women's Law Journal* 159-167
For annotation, see Chapter 16: **BOOK REVIEWS**.

Elizabeth B. Clark, "Religion, Rights, and Difference in the Early Woman's Rights Movement" (1985) 3 *Wisconsin Women's Law Journal* 29-57
Part of the 1986 Feminism and Legal Theory Conference, this article discusses the historical inter-relationship between the concept of equality and "liberal Protestantism," which, the author claims, strongly influenced early feminist theory. She argues that nineteenth century feminism was governed not by a goal of majoritarian democracy, but rather by an appeal to communal moral consensus. This stance, she argues, arose from a view of woman as different, and from an identification of the female with morality and spirituality. She concludes with the observation that this theoretical perspective is the basis of feminism's present notion of "rights," which ultimately limits the possibilities of transformative change.

Lorraine Code, "Book Review: Katherine O'Donovan, SEXUAL DIVISIONS IN LAW (1985)" (1986) 2 *Canadian Journal of Women and the Law* 190-198
For annotation, see Chapter 16: **BOOK REVIEWS.**

David Cole, "Getting There: Reflections on Trashing from Feminist Jurisprudence and Critical Theory" (1985) 8 *Harvard Women's Law Journal* 59-91
This article discusses the Critical Legal Studies (CLS) methodology of 'trashing,' which seeks to expose and undermine the ideological function of law. Law, CLSers claim, treats as objective, natural, and unalterable that which is actually subjective, contingent, and mutable. The author suggests that if CLS lacks transformative power, it is because it can't self-reflect and represents an insular idealism. Feminism, he argues, demonstrates the ability simultaneously to self-reflect and search for intersubjectivity because it links both theory and practice, and reaches consensus about meaning through discourse. It leaves the development of substantive values and norms to participants, the only requirement being that the values are not imposed. He is concerned that as feminism becomes more established and feminist critiques attain the status of dogmas unquestioningly accepted, it may lose its self-reflective force.

David Cole, "Strategies of Difference: Litigating for Women's Rights in a Man's World" (1984) 2 *Law and Inequality* 33-95
Although the United States Supreme Court may have a conceptual difficulty dealing with "different" women seeking "similar" treatment in sex discrimination cases, when the contested treatment has an impact upon men, the author argues, the Court seems more capable of perceiving the injustice. It is, therefore, not surprising that male plaintiffs have dominated sex discrimination cases. In most of these, he notes, women have participated as counsel, which has been a useful strategy when women's perspectives have guided the litigation. He examines the effects of gender perspectives by analyzing several leading sex discrimination cases brought by male plaintiffs, and argues for a judicial neutrality that takes a woman's difference into account without subordinating her. He concludes that the history and theory of U.S. and French feminism shows that gender difference can be recognized without disparagement only when women are full participants in the act of recognition.

Ruth Colker, "The Anti-Subordination Principle: Applications" (1985) 3 *Wisconsin Women's Law Journal* 59-80
    For annotation, see Chapter 6: FIRST NATIONS AND RACE.

Joanne Conaghan, "The Invisibility of Women in Labour Law: Gender-Neutrality in Model-building" (1986) 14 *International Journal of the Sociology of Law* 377-392
    This is a feminist critique of the two dominant models used in labour law analysis. The author argues that each is gender-blind in that each fails to recognize that work experiences are different for men and women. She examines the "traditional pluralist model" and the "radical pluralist critique," and compares them with the reality of women in the labour market. Gender-neutrality assumes that gender is not a relevant factor in determining power relationships, and neither framework has a conception of patriarchal power. Any feminist perspective, she claims, must recognize that labour relations is not merely a power conflict between capital and labour, and she commends the Marxist-Feminist approach for specifically addressing gender hierarchy in the labour market.

Drucilla Cornell, "Beyond Tragedy and Complacency; Book Review: Roberto Unger, POLITICS (1987)" (1987) 81 *Northwestern University Law Review* 693-717
    For annotation, see Chapter 16: BOOK REVIEWS.

Brenda Cossman, "The Precarious Unity of Feminist Theory and Practice: The Praxis of Abortion" (1986) 44 *University of Toronto Faculty of Law Review* 85-108
    For annotation, see Chapter 1: ABORTION AND REPRODUCTION.

Cherise Cox, "Anything Less is Not Feminism: Racial Difference and the W.M.W.M." (1990) 1:2 *Law and Critique* 237-248
    For annotation, see Chapter 6: FIRST NATIONS AND RACE.

Kimberle Crenshaw, "Demarginalizing the Intersection of Race and

Sex: A Black Feminist Critique of Antidiscrimination Doctrine, Feminist Theory and Antiracist Politics" [1989] _University of Chicago Legal Forum_ 139-167
    For annotation, see Chapter 6: FIRST NATIONS AND RACE.

Dawn H. Currie, "Battered Women and The State: From the Failure of Theory to a Theory of Failure" (1990) 1:2 _Journal of Human Justice_ 77-96
    For annotation, see Chapter 3: CRIMINAL LAW -- BATTERING.

Clare Dalton, "An Essay in the Deconstruction of Contract Doctrine" (1985) 94 _Yale Law Journal_ 997-1113
    The author examines contract law as applied by judges and elaborated by commentators, and identifies three dominating themes -- namely, dependence on the dualities of public/private, objective/subjective, and form/substance. In favouring one pole of each duality, hierarchy avoids its underlying structure of power and knowledge. She criticizes legal liberalism, draws on poststructuralism and deconstructive strategies, and finds that traditional doctrinal analysis is not reflective of reality.

Clare Dalton, "The Faithful Liberal and the Question of Diversity" (1989) 12 _Harvard Women's Law Journal_ 1-10
    The author identifies two conditions as necessary for diversity in legal scholarship -- journals willing to publish works alien to traditional canons of legal thought, and an audience capable of sharing the author's experiences and perspective. Through an analysis of Owen Fiss's "The Death of Law?" ((1986) 72 _Cornell Law Review_ 1), she explores these themes. She argues that critical legal theory, not mainstream liberal theory, provides a nurturing medium for feminist and minority scholarship. She concludes that if Fiss is representative, it is clear that the mainstream has not yet learned to "yield its place at the centre of the universe."

Katherine de Jong, "On Equality and Language" (1985) 1 _Canadian Journal of Women and the Law_ 119-133
    For annotation, see Chapter 2: CONSTITUTIONAL LAW.

Maeve E. Doggett, "Greenham Common and Civil Disobedience: Making New Meanings for Women" (1989-1990) 3 *Canadian Journal of Women and the Law* 395-418

This article begins with a chronology of the all-female civil disobedience at Greenham Common, protesting the installation of long-range nuclear weapons, of the charges laid and not laid, and of the media attention to the protest. The author identifies differentiating features of this women's peace-camp protest: (1) the exclusion of men in the woman-only camp, although support by men was officially welcomed, their presence was not; (2) the position of non-violence, despite provocation from the public and police; and (3) the consensus decision-making. The group made extensive use of songs, chanting, symbols of life, of the chain or web of connectedness, and their action thus assumed a particular quality. She claims that the form of civil disobedience chosen by this peace group raises serious questions about women's obligation to obey laws in a liberal democratic state, because women are neither in receipt of the benefits of liberal democratic citizenship, nor have they consented to the liberal democratic decision-making process.

Ellen C. DuBois, Mary C. Dunlap, Carol Gilligan, Catharine Mac-Kinnon, and Carrie Menkel-Meadow, Conversants, "Feminist Discourse, Moral Values, and the Law -- A Conversation" (1985) 34 *Buffalo Law Review* 11-87

This is a discourse on women, feminism, and the overlay of law by the five women on the panel. They discuss the importance of law to feminist theory, including all the clusters of theory -- physical health, money, violence/empowerment, and creativity. MacKinnon talks about gender neutrality and dominance; Gilligan of moral development in two voices, care and justice; Menkel-Meadow about the intrinsic importance of the value of care for reconstruction; and DuBois about the creation of history, and women's responsibility for their own oppression, and their potential for liberation.

Nitya Duclos, "Lessons of Difference: Feminist Theory on Cultural Diversity" (1990) 38 *Buffalo Law Review* 325-381

For annotation, see Chapter 6: **FIRST NATIONS AND RACE.**

Murray Edelman, "The Construction of Social Problems as Buttresses of Inequities" (1987) 42 _University of Miami Law Review_ 7-28

Part of a symposium entitled Excluded Voices: Realities in Law and Law Reform, this paper examines how and why some social conditions come to be seen as problems, while others do not. The author argues that the recognition of social problems reinforces ideology by signifying who and what is of concern, and that the definition of a social problem rationalizes existing inequities, reinforcing the power of those in control.

Jean Bethke Elshtain, "Ordinary Scholarship -- Book Review: Judith N. Shklar, ORDINARY VICES (1984)" (1985) 94 _Yale Law Journal_ 1270-1284

For annotation, see Chapter 16: BOOK REVIEWS.

Susan Erickson, "Book Review: Josephine Donovan, FEMINIST THEORY: THE INTELLECTUAL TRADITIONS OF AMERICAN FEMINISM (1985); Claire Duchen, FEMINISM IN FRANCE: FROM MAY '68 TO MITTERAND (1986)" (1985) 4 _Wisconsin Women's Law Journal_ 117-128

For annotation, see Chapter 16: BOOK REVIEWS.

Sabine Erika, "Patriarchy and the State" (1986) 3 _Australian Journal of Law and Society_ 53

The author defines patriarchy as a system in which women are invisible and powerless, and argues that the overwhelming power of aging white males is enforced in a myriad of ways, including: (1) the fictitious dichotomy between the private and public spheres; (2) conflicts between the needs of the capitalist system (i.e. increased workforce) and the patriarchal system (i.e. maintenance of traditional family, and woman's place within it); and (3) the construction of masculinity and femininity.

Karlene Faith, "Justice Where Art Thou? and Do We Care?: Feminist Perspectives on Justice for Women in Canada" (1989) 1:1 _Journal of Human Justice_ 77-98

For annotation, see Chapter 6: FIRST NATIONS AND RACE.

Martha L. Fineman, "Challenging Law, Establishing Differences: The Future of Feminist Legal Scholarship" (1990) 42 *Florida Law Review* **25-43**

Part of a Symposium on Women and the Law, this article discusses feminist legal theory. The author questions both the statedly universal ideal of equality in dominant legal thought, as well as the structure and nature of the law which, she claims, maintains the existing distribution of power and economic benefits. Her feminist theory is "decidedly anti-assimilationist," and she laments that to succeed in law, women have often "adopted assimilation as their intellectual strategy and equal treatment as their substantive principle." She discusses the relative theoretical and strategic merits of abstract grand-theory, and more specific middle-level theory, and asserts that all feminist methodology must be critical, (i.e. politically rather than legally focused), seek to present alternatives to the existing order, and recognize no division between law and power. The author discusses essentialism, and concludes that an individualized mode of representation is inappropriate, because it only empowers individual women and encourages tokenism.

Martha L. Fineman, "Introduction to the Papers: The Origins and Purpose of the Feminism and Legal Theory Conference" (1985) 3 *Wisconsin Women's Law Journal* **1-3**

In her Introduction to the 1986 Feminism and Legal Theory Conference, the author outlines the background leading to the choice of the topic for the Conference, the difference debate. She claims that differences between men and women are both a source of oppression and a source of energy and strength for women, and must be addressed in any theory of equality.

Lucinda M. Finley, "Breaking Women's Silence in Law: The Dilemma of the Gendered Nature of Legal Reasoning" (1989) 64 *Notre Dame Law Review* **886-910**

This article examines the ways in which legal language reinforces certain ideologies, while silencing alternatives. The author argues that because privileged white men have controlled legal discourse, they are considered the norm under the law, and the law reflects their reality. Because women's realities do not fit into the legal language, women, she claims, are silenced. The author thinks that to break their legal silence, women must bring their own experiences and perspectives into the law.

She concludes that although legal language can help women if it validates their concerns, it can also discredit them, if they do not speak within its confines.

Owen M. Fiss, "Coda" (1988) 38 _University of Toronto Law Journal_ 229-244
    For annotation, see Chapter 2: **CONSTITUTIONAL LAW.**

Owen Flanagan and Kathryn Jackson, "Justice, Care, and Gender: The Kohlberg-Gilligan Debate Revisited" (1987) 97 _Ethics_ 622-637
    Lawrence Kohlberg's theory of justice as fairness has dominated moral psychology for the last twenty years. Carol Gilligan's IN A DIFFERENT VOICE (1982) is, the authors claim, both a challenge to the comprehensiveness of Kohlberg's theory and a revealing look at the way liberal society distributes various psychological competencies between the sexes. According to Gilligan, men, more often than women, conceive of morality as consisting substantively of obligations and rights, and procedurally of demands of fairness and neutrality, while women, more often than men, see morality as emerging from the needs of others in the context of particular relationships; and Gilligan claims Kohlberg's exclusive focus on justice has obscured the ethic of care she associates with women and denied its normative significance. The authors provide a critical evaluation of Gilligan's theory through an exhaustive survey of her writing and of Kohlberg's responses. They conclude, in opposition to Kohlberg, that there is no one ideal type of moral personality, because moral personality occurs at a level too open to both social and self-determination.

Jane Flax, "Postmodernism and Gender Relations in Feminist Theory" (1987) 12 _Signs: Journal of Women in Culture and Society_ 621-643
    The author claims that Western culture is in the middle of a transformation as radical as that from medieval to modern society. She identifies three kinds of theory that best represent our time "apprehended in thought:" psychoanalysis, feminist theory, and postmodern philosophy. The article focuses on feminist theory as both a part of and a critique of the transformation's social and philosophical content. She contends that feminist theory must explore knowledge and viewpoints suppressed by the dominant male ethos, and that feminist theory should

be critical, compensatory, and necessarily partial.

David Fraser, "And Now for Something Completely Different: Judging Interpretation and the Canadian Charter of Rights and Freedoms" (1987) 7 _Windsor Yearbook of Access to Justice_ 66-78
For annotation, see Chapter 2: **CONSTITUTIONAL LAW.**

David Fraser, "What's love got to do with it? Critical legal studies, feminist discourse, and the ethic of solidarity" (1988) 11 _Harvard Women's Law Journal_ 53-81
The author examines the inherent contradictions in feminist legal theory and legal practice, and searches for an adequate praxis within the patriarchal and oppressive legal education system for himself as a white, male, heterosexual professor. He concludes that feminism and critical legal studies are both movements for political change, and argues that neither should maintain "instrumental silence" toward the other. He claims critical legal scholars should recognize the different cultural experiences of women, and discuss the roadblocks to, as well as enabling moments of, the creation of an ethic of solidarity.

Nancy Fraser, "Talking about Needs: Interpretive Contests as Political Conflicts in Welfare-State Societies" (1989) 99 _Ethics_ 291-313
Part of a Symposium on Feminism and Political Theory, this article attempts to "sort out the emancipatory from the repressive possibilities of needs-talk." The author focuses on discourses about needs, and the politics of need interpretation.

Marilyn Friedman, "Feminism and Modern Friendship: Dislocating the Community" (1989) 99 _Ethics_ 275-290
This article is part of a Symposium on Feminism and Political Theory. Although communitarians and feminists may appear to have a lot in common in their opposition to the abstract individualist view of liberal ideology, the author shows how the communitarian vision incorporates models which have been oppressive to women. She develops the concept of friendship as a different type of community and social relationship.

Judy Fudge, "The Public/Private Distinction: The Possibilities of and the Limits to the Use of Charter Litigation to Further Feminist Struggles" (1988) 25 *Osgoode Hall Law Journal* 485-554
For annotation, see Chapter 2: CONSTITUTIONAL LAW.

Shelley Gavigan, "Marxist Theories of Law" (1981) 4 *Canadian Criminology Forum* 1-12
The author examines some of the more recent Marxist theories of law in relation to civil liberties and equal rights laws. Beginning with the work of Eugene Pashukanis, she analyzes the responses of such authors as Colin Sumner, E.P. Thompson, and Juliet Mitchell. A parallel is drawn between the women's movement and the movements of other oppressed groups fighting for equal rights, with particular attention paid to the difference between formal legal rights and the possibility of real, substantive change in the patriarchal and oppressive social structure of capitalism.

John D. Gibson, "Childbearing and Childrearing: Feminists and Reform" (1987) 73 *Virginia Law Review* 1145-1182
The author questions the use of the equality paradigm in analyzing women's position, especially as it relates to workplace policies dealing with childbearing and rearing. He examines the sameness/difference debate, and concludes that the radical feminist approach provides important insights on legal reform in this area. Reforms such as childrearing and nurturing leave, he suggests, could result in eventual radical justification for preferential treatment policies which are currently held as discriminatory by United States courts. He concludes that there is a great danger of misunderstanding such reform within the existing liberal legal order.

Susie Gibson, "Book Review: Susan Edwards (ed.), GENDER, SEX AND THE LAW (1985)" (1986) 14 *International Journal of the Sociology of Law* 423-428
For annotation, see Chapter 16: BOOK REVIEWS.

Susie Gibson, "Continental Drift: The Question of Context in Feminist Jurisprudence" (1990) 1:2 *Law and Critique* 173-200

Part of a Symposium on Sex and Difference, this article examines the extent to which feminist jurisprudence is applicable in differing jurisdictions, specifically the United States and Britain, where there is significant difference in background and approach to law. According to the author, feminist jurisprudence is a "radical engagement with the law," which examines the interface of social, political, and legal discourse, and which therefore claims that the legal and political presences in scholarship emanating from different and distinctive jurisdictions is also distinctive. She concludes that feminist jurisprudence should not pursue a singular women's interest in law, but instead examine the effects which emerge at the "intersection of different discourses."

Carol Gilligan, "Reply (to MacKinnon)" (1986) 11 *Signs: Journal of Women in Culture and Society* 324-333

The author asserts that the different voice -- see her, IN A DIFFERENT VOICE (1982) -- is characterized by theme, not gender, and that the association with gender is purely empirical. Male and female voices highlight the distinction between two modes of thought, and are not a generalization about either sex. The fact that educated women are capable of high levels of justice reasoning has no bearing, she concludes, on the question of how they frame moral problems.

Ruth Bader Ginsburg and Barbara Flagg, "Some Reflections on the Feminist Legal Thought of the 1970s" [1989] *University of Chicago Legal Forum* 9-21

This article discusses feminist litigation during the 1970's. The authors illustrate the then-prevailing judicial attitudes with respect to gender-based distinctions through a review of cases brought forward by the ACLU Women's Rights Projects, and the changes achieved by them. The authors think unfair the criticism of 1970's litigation as assimilationist in outlook, and as opening doors only for elite women willing to be treated as men. The litigation, they claim, unsettled accepted conceptions of women's and men's separate spheres, and provided impetus for ongoing advancement. Litigation at that time could not have done more. They conclude that the tendency to regard one's own feminism as the only truth is fatal; if that tendency is controlled, feminist legal theory will, they think, be something to celebrate.

Mary Ellen Griffith, "Sexism, Language, and the Law" (1989) 91 _West Virginia Law Review_ 125-151

This article seeks to explain the absence of women in the language of law, and to investigate the resources available to facilitate the inclusion of women in law language. The author first provides a history of the absence of women in legal language, by reporting the results of a computer assisted search for the 'reasonable women' in judicial decisions. She then discusses the importance of language in social organization, and characterizes the impact of women on sex differentiation and sexism in language. The article concludes with a discussion of the deeper concerns of feminist theorists, regarding women's silence, alienation, and oppression, and with the suggestion that the language of law will change as women become the speakers of the law.

Marjet Gunning, "Women, Rights and Difference" (1987) 9 _Liverpool Law Review_ 133-155

The author thinks that in the dominant cultural image, law reflects the masculine, and that there is a tendency to an essentialist view in contemplating a different feminine culture. This is so because it is difficult to express positive difference without creating a new normative system. For this reason, she concludes, feminist legal theory is at a cross-roads of theoretical problems.

Catharine W. Hantzis, "Is Gender Justice a Completed Agenda? The Feminization of America: How Women's Values are Changing Our Public and Private Lives -- Book Review: Elinor Lenz and Barbara Myerhoff, THE FEMINIZATION OF AMERICA (1985)" (1987) 100 _Harvard Law Review_ 690-713

For annotation, see Chapter 16: **BOOK REVIEWS.**

John Hardwig, "Should Women Think in Terms of Rights?" (1984) 94 _Ethics_ 441-455

This article canvasses the claim made by some feminists that the rights talk used in other forms of liberationist thought ought to be used in the context of personal relationships -- marriage, love, and friendship -- which women's liberation alone addresses, and demands be changed. The author argues that while rights are necessary to produce an ethic of impersonal public relationships, and ought, therefore, be deployed by women when addressing public, social justice issues, they are inappropriate in the context of close personal relationships, because they fail adequately to describe what is going on in such relationships, and because rights fit neither as an ethical category nor ideal for personal relationships.

Angela P. Harris, "Race and Essentialism in Feminist Legal Theory" (1990) 42 *Stanford Law Review* 581-615
    For annotation, see Chapter 6: FIRST NATIONS AND RACE.

Mark Harris, "Book Review: Catharine A. MacKinnon, TOWARD A FEMINIST THEORY OF THE STATE (1989)" (1990) 27 *Harvard Journal on Legislation* 294-302
    For annotation, see Chapter 16: BOOK REVIEWS.

Frances Heidensohn, "Models of Justice: Portia or Persephone? Some Thoughts on Equality, Fairness, and Gender in the Field of Criminal Justice" (1986) 14 *International Journal of the Sociology of Law* 287-297
    For annotation, see Chapter 3: CRIMINAL LAW -- GENERAL.

Virginia Held, "Birth and Death" (1989) 99 *Ethics* 362-368
    For annotation, see Chapter 1: ABORTION AND REPRODUC-TION.

Virginia Held, "Feminism and Epistemology: Recent Work on the Connection Between Gender and Knowledge" (1985) 14 *Philosophy and Public Affairs* 296
    The author argues that gender is more pervasive and fundamental than class, and affects most social interactions between humans. She inquires why the male control of women's productive and reproductive labour, which includes sexuality, family life, kinship formations, and birthing, has only been discovered in the last decade, and suggests that a new epistemology, which will provide a less biased, more comprehensive view of reality, is required.

Lynne N. Henderson, "Legality and Empathy" (1987) 85 _Michigan Law Review_ 1574-1653

The author claims that the phenomenon of empathic knowledge, where the situation of the other is understood with compassion, is not excluded from legality, and that it can aid the processes of discovery and justification. She discusses the myths about empathy and legality, and examines cases with empathic narrative, and others where discrimination is predominant. She concludes that empathy is not the full answer, but that moral choice and responsibility are an important part of the legal process.

Jacinth Herbert, "'Otherness' and the Black Woman" (1989) 3 _Canadian Journal of Women and the Law_ 269-278

For annotation, see Chapter 6: FIRST NATIONS AND RACE.

Nancy Holmstrom, "A Marxist Theory of Women's Nature" (1983-84) 94 _Ethics_ 456-473

This article provides a Marxist contribution to the sameness/difference debate, and claims that under the Marxist view of the social production of human nature, men and women do have distinctive natures. The author submits, however, that nothing follows from this with respect to how women ought or ought not to live, and more generally, that it does not mean that the sexual/social roles of men and women cannot, or should not, be radically changed.

Adrian Howe, "'Social Injury' Revisited: Towards a Feminist Theory of Social Justice" (1987) 15 _International Journal of the Sociology of Law_ 423-435

In the 1940's, "social injury" became part of the "criminological repertoire" as the definition of crime was broadened to encompass white-collar crime. The author discusses the debates over the interpretation and characterization of social injury crime since that time, and notes that the concept of injury is resurfacing in feminist analysis of anti-discrimination and affirmative action legislation. He recommends that feminist legal theory "analytically privilege the concept of social injury" and gender-specific injury, because unlike discrimination or oppression, it has actionable status.

Allen Hunter, "The Role of Liberal Political Culture in the Construction of Middle America" (1987) 42 *University of Miami Law Review* 93-126

This paper was originally presented at a symposium entitled Excluded Voices: Realities in Law and Law Reform. The paper's central theme is an analysis of the role played by liberals in creating the "unanchored" political identity of Middle Americans. The author argues that when Middle America was "created" in about 1970, Middle Americans had no strong political allies to speak for their interests. They were attracted to the interest groups and causes supported by the liberals, but they felt betrayed when blacks, women, and youth benefitted from the movement, while the cost was put partly onto them. As a result, the populist rhetoric of the traditionalists appealed to them: they could both attack the less powerful and, by attacking "liberal, statist elites," represent themselves as the betrayed and excluded "silent majority." The author concludes that it is as a result of the interaction of liberal policies and conservative rhetoric that today Middle Americans feel excluded and dispossessed, while at the same time opposing any benefits for the excluded and dispossessed.

Ellen Jacobs, "Book Review -- Ann Ferguson, BLOOD AT THE ROOT: MOTHERHOOD, SEXUALITY AND MALE DOMINANCE (1989)" (1990) 19:1 *Resources for Feminist Research/ Documentation sur la Recherche Féministe* 5-6

For annotation, see Chapter 16: **BOOK REVIEWS**.

Kathleen B. Jones, "Citizenship in a Woman-Friendly Polity" (1990) 15 *Signs: Journal of Women in Culture and Society* 781-812

Citizenship in a Western liberal democracy involves the subordination of one's gender, race, and class to a national identity, and loyalty to the state. The author describes this as exchanging the private self for a public one, and claims that women do not achieve citizenship as women, but rather as people who happen to be female. This paper develops a feminist theory of citizenship which integrates the personal and the political. Women's experiences embody interaction with a vast number of cultures - male, female, ethnic, religious, and so on. If the traditional oppositional ways of thinking are abandoned, the author concludes, this body of experience becomes accessible, and citizenship as a gendered being is possible.

Jean E. Keet, "Women and the Law: the Charter of Rights and Freedoms" (1985) 7 *Canadian Criminology Forum* 103-115
    For annotation, see Chapter 2: CONSTITUTIONAL LAW.

P. Kirby, "Marrying Out and Loss of Status: the Charter and New Indian Act Legislation" (1985) 1 *Journal of Law and Social Policy* 77-95
    For annotation, see Chapter 6: FIRST NATIONS AND RACE.

Marlee Kline, "Race, Racism, and Feminist Theory" (1989) 12 *Harvard Women's Law Journal* 115-139
    For annotation, see Chapter 6: FIRST NATIONS AND RACE.

Linda J. Krieger, "Through A Glass Darkly: Paradigms of Equality and The Search for a Woman's Jurisprudence" (1987) 2:1 *Hypatia: A Journal of Feminist Philosophy* 45-61
    This article claims that legal theory is dependent upon paradigms which determine how we look at particular issues and what we will see. Paradigms, the author argues, go through two repeating stages. The first is acceptance by a "community," until such time as anomalies or "counter-instances" are discovered which challenge the paradigm. If the anomalies are significant and resist reconciliation, a stage of "crisis" or transformation develops, and a new paradigm may be accepted. She claims that the liberal equal treatment paradigm has been confronted with problems relating to pregnancy and childbirth, and is now in a state of paradigm change, and she reviews the competing alternatives presented by Carol Gilligan's IN A DIFFERENT VOICE (1982).

Linda J. Lacey, "Introducing Feminist Jurisprudence: An Analysis of Oklahoma's Seduction Statute" (1990) 25 *Tulsa Law Journal* 775 - 798
    After surveying the three main feminist schools of thought -- cultural, liberal, and radical -- the author analyzes the Oklahoma Seduction Statute from each of these perspectives. This article is part of a Symposium on Feminist Jurisprudence.

Kathleen A. Lahey, "Civil Remedies for Women: Catching the Critical Edge" (1988) 17:3 *Resources for Feminist Research/ Documentation sur la Recherche Féministe* 92-95

This article inquires whether civil remedies are an appropriate means for feminists to achieve societal reconstruction and, more particularly, whether the criminal law, as an instrument of the patriarchal state, or civil law, which de-politicizes and individualizes harm, is the better remedy. The author suggests looking beyond this dichotomy, to the best means to bring about substantive change to the law, and how to make those changes effective. She suggests further areas of study and research, including problems of individuation and personalization, the possibility of funding administrative and common law procedures, more creative remedies, and the means to narrow the division between the criminal and civil law.

Kathleen A. Lahey, "Feminist Theories of (In)Equality" (1985) 3 *Wisconsin Women's Law Journal* 5-27

For annotation, see Chapter 2: **CONSTITUTIONAL LAW.**

Kathleen A. Lahey, "'...Until Women Themselves Have Told All That They Have To Tell...'" (1985) 23 *Osgoode Hall Law Journal* 519-541

Part of a Symposium on Canadian Legal Scholarship, this article discusses the hostility to political content in feminist scholarship, which critics allege is apt to distort reality by its biased emphasis. The author argues that the male paradigm of knowledge promotes idealization of types, and leads to dichotomies and to hierarchy. In the feminist paradigm, female social and biological experience is the basis for formation of knowledge, and feminist method is consciousness-raising which increases personal vulnerability and rejects linearity, inevitability, and laws. However, she cautions that feminist scholarship is, by definition, ambiguous, and that without care new paradigms can model old ones with scholars practising scholarship for the sake of power, rather than for the sake of a loving world.

Kathleen A. Lahey and Sarah W. Salter, "Corporate Law in Legal Theory and Legal Scholarship: From Classicism to Feminism" (1985) 23 *Osgoode Hall Law Journal* 543-572

Part of a Symposium on Canadian Legal Scholarship, this article reviews feminist literature on corporate law from liberal, socialist, and radical perspectives. Radical feminist literature offers the most powerful critique of corporatism, the development of the corporate form, and its role in serving liberal and capitalist patriarchy. The authors also examine mainstream, classical, and realist legal scholarship to see if "masculinist" scholarship relates at all to feminist analysis. Feminist lawyers, they claim, must reveal how the processes and ethics of corporate law directly and indirectly contribute to the worldwide domination of women.

Legal Theory Students, University of Victoria, "Understanding Equality: A Reply to Dale Gibson" (1990) 1:3 _Constitutional Forum: Forum Constitutionnel_ 18-19
For annotation, see Chapter 2: CONSTITUTIONAL LAW.

Christine A. Littleton, "Equality Across Difference: A Place for Rights Discourse" (1985) 3 _Wisconsin Women's Law Journal_ 189-212
Part of the 1986 Feminism and Legal Theory Conference, this article discusses the usefulness of "equality" and "rights" within legal discourse, and argues that the issue is less whether to use this form of argument, and more how to argue within rights discourse. The author claims that it is crucial not to accept uncritically a particular "brand" of equality, but to formulate new concepts of equality. She examines American litigation, especially with respect to pregnancy claims, and concludes with a recommendation that feminists employ a comparative rights analysis in an attempt to "place women's experience alongside men's."

Christine A. Littleton, "Equality and Feminist Legal Theory" (1987) 48 _University of Pittsburgh Law Review_ 1043-1059
The author argues that feminist legal theory has three interrelated theories with respect to equality: sex discrimination, the unjustified stereotyping of women; gender oppression, the restriction of women to particular social roles; and sexual subordination, the devaluation and disaffirming of anything female. Implicated in all three strands is the question of difference, and its relationship to the construction of inequality. Since equality can also be created, and legal meaning re-created, determinations of value are not made in an unbiased manner, until the "male is important, female is trivial" links are shed. She suggests that this understanding will provide the way for advocates of women to challenge structures which create inequality.

Christine A. Littleton, "In Search of a Feminist Jurisprudence" (1987) 10 *Harvard Women's Law Journal* 1-7

This short article is in celebration of the tenth anniversary of the JOURNAL. The author discusses the paradox of feminist jurisprudence, and the commonality in diversity of women's experience. She criticizes law's omission of bias against women's concerns; examines the role of law in social order; confirms that scholarship is inclusive of sociology, legal reform, and tactics; and criticizes the form and categories of current legal concepts. Feminist jurisprudence is pragmatic, with methodology and theory intermeshed. She concludes that feminists have discovered an endless variety of women's experience which the law affects.

Kathleen E. Mahoney, "Book Review: A. Alan Borovoy, WHEN FREEDOMS COLLIDE: THE CHASE FOR OUR CIVIL LIBER-TIES" (1990) 28 *Alberta Law Review* 715-729

For annotation, see Chapter 16: BOOK REVIEWS.

Diana Majury, "Strategizing in Equality" (1985) 3 *Wisconsin Women's Law Journal* 169-187

Part of the 1986 Feminism and Legal Theory Conference, this article discusses the debate with respect to the efficacy of equality-based arguments for feminism, and the theory of equality which is more useful within such an argument. The author argues that women's exposing of their oppression, their questioning their involvement in -- and possible co-optation by -- the legal profession, and their making equality-based legal arguments, are not mutually exclusive; on the contrary, she claims that they are, in fact, mutually supportive positions.

Isabel Marcus, "Reflections on the Significance of the Sex/Gender System: Divorce Law Reform in New York" (1987) 42 *University of Miami Law Review* 55 - 73

For annotation, see Chapter 4: FAMILY LAW -- MARRIAGE AND DIVORCE.

Mari J. Matsuda, "Liberal Jurisprudence and Abstracted Visions of Human Nature: A Feminist Critique of Rawls' Theory of Justice" (1986) 16 *New Mexico Law Review* 613-629

The author argues that clarity of vision is not achieved by Rawlsian abstraction, and that instead abstraction is the first step to androcentric ignorance. Experience is a more valuable truth-seeking tool than abstraction. Instead of valuing self-interest and assuming that mutual concern is an extension of self-interest, as does Rawls, collectivists value care for others, and assume that the world may not be an endless grab for goods.

Mari J. Matsuda, "When the First Quail Calls: Multiple Consciousness as Jurisprudential Method" (1988) 11 _Women's Rights Law Reporter_ **7-10**
For annotation, see Chapter 6: **FIRST NATIONS AND RACE.**

Sheryl Gordon McCloud, "Feminism's Idealist Error" (1986) 14 _Review of Law & Social Change_ **277-320**
For annotation, see Chapter 4: **FAMILY LAW -- POVERTY.**

Sally Engle Merry, "The Discourses of Mediation and the Power of Naming" (1990) 2 _Yale Journal of Law and the Humanities_ **1-36**
This article examines and criticizes the power of the law to construct authoritative visions of our social world. The author conducts an ethnographic study of the ways and the process of naming in lower courts and mediation, and claims that this is a form of cultural domination over those who bring their interpersonal problems to court. Legal interpretation, she concludes, often conflicts with moral and community interpretations.

Martha Minow, "Beyond Universality" [1989] _University of Chicago Legal Forum_ **115-138**
The author begins by defining feminism as the effort to take all women seriously by challenging power structures that have either degraded or excluded some or all women. She notes that to date there has been little serious criticism of feminist legal scholarship. When it comes (which she welcomes as the hallmark of respect it deserves), she predicts that it will centre around the following points: that legal feminism is unresponsive to the central issues of jurisprudence; that it is without its own distinctive legal theories; and that it is inconsistent and incoherent. She forcefully and succinctly details her response to these

anticipated criticisms, focusing on feminism's varied perspectives which challenge traditional assumptions about the nature of truth and knowledge.

Martha Minow, "Interpreting Rights: An Essay for Robert Cover" (1986) 96 *Yale Law Journal* 1860-1915

This article defends rights and rights talk against right-wing and left-wing criticisms, by providing a version of legal interpretation which permits struggle with and against established patterns of power and authority, and the creation of norms, in the language of rights, both within and outside of legal institutions. The author claims that interpretive activity is pluralistic, and that through it, people gain a sense of potential community membership without relinquishing struggles over meaning and power. She illustrates this claim through a discussion of children's rights, and defends her approach against both the critics of rights and the charge that interpretation, at least in law, is violence. She concludes that rights are a kind of communal discourse that reconfirms the difficult commitment to live together, even while engaging in conflicts and struggles over meaning.

Martha Minow, "Introduction: Finding Our Paradoxes, Affirming Our Beyond" (1989) 24 *Harvard Civil Rights-Civil Liberties Law Review* 1-7

In her introduction to the three essays which comprise the major part of this issue, the author claims they are "third stage feminist scholarship" works in that they "reject the preoccupation with similarities and differences between men and women." Instead, they offer the "rich and compelling depictions of realities ignored by ... conceptual fights," because they examine "the actual consequences of legal rules in people's lives."

Martha Minow, "Law Turning Outward" (1987) 20 *Telos* 79

There is a trend in legal theory to use non-legal methodologies and insights. The author describes three such movements -- law and economics, critical legal studies, and literary theory -- and her disillusionment with each project. She questions why theorists are looking outside the law, and calls for dialogue instead of competition, and for comprehensible legal discourse.

Martha Minow, "Making All the Difference: Three Lessons in Equality, Neutrality, and Tolerance" (1990) 39 _DePaul Law Review_ 1-13

This article is the text of a speech delivered by the author as distinguished Scholar-In-Residence, DePaul University College of Law, 1989. In it, the author discusses the obstacles to reform embedded in the very concepts -- equality, neutrality, and tolerance -- used by civil rights and women's rights reformers. These obstacles arise, she claims, because our conceptions of equality, neutrality, and tolerance rely too much upon distinction-drawing in terms of racial, sexual, or religious difference as problem-solving devices. She urges a reinterpretation of equality, neutrality, and tolerance, which would de-emphasize differences.

Martha Minow, "The Supreme Court 1986 Term, Foreword: Justice Engendered" (1987) 101 _Harvard Law Review_ 10-45

For annotation, see Chapter 2: **CONSTITUTIONAL LAW.**

J. Moon, "An Essay on Local Critique" (1986) 16 _New Mexico Law Review_ 513-534

The author takes the opportunity presented by the Johnson and Scales article (K. Johnson and A. Scales, An Absolutely, Positively True Story: Seven Reasons Why We Sing (1986) 16 _New Mexico Law Review_ 433) to discuss what happens when we attempt what he calls local critique. In a complex, philosophical discussion, he tries to describe what "local critique" can be, without limiting it by definition. His description includes activity which takes place on the fringe of an institutional mechanism and practice, which emphasizes individual experience, and which takes place in relation to, and in critique of, the dominant medium. He then compares four philosophical approaches - phenomenological, existential, Wiggenstein's and Gramsci's - to local critique, concluding that the four theories may intersect despite their apparent inconsistencies with each other, and that they may be useful in liberating us "from illusions about [our] conceptual system." This article is part of a Symposium on Legal Education.

Jenny Morgan, "Feminist Theory as Legal Theory" (1988) 10 _Melbourne University Law Review_ 743-759

This article focuses on the two major theoretical areas in American feminist legal scholarship: the sameness/difference debate, and the

distinction between public and private life. The author reviews Carol
Gilligan's work on the sameness/difference debate, and identifies its centrality to the concept of constitutional equality. The review also contains
an analysis of Fran Olson's work on the public/private dichotomy, and
feminist perspectives on black-letter law.

**Elizabeth R. Morrissey, "Contradictions Inhering in Liberal Feminist
Ideology: Promotion and Control of Women's Drinking" (1986) 13
Contemporary Drug Problems 65-87**
     The liberal feminist agenda does not challenge the hierarchical
structure of society, but seeks only for women to have the same choices
available as do men. In the politics of alcohol, the author argues, liberal
feminists have accepted male symbolic functions of alcohol. This has
resulted, she claims, in decreased public attention to the drinking
practices and problems of women, and political conflict between women
within and outside the alcoholism and women's health movements. The
author questions acceptance of typically male drinking behaviour within
a male dominated social structure which includes the subordination of
women. The article includes a bibliography.

**Mary Jane Mossman, "Book Review: Katherine O'Donovan, SEXUAL
DIVISIONS IN LAW (1985)" (1986) 36 *University of New Brunswick Law
Journal* 221-225**
     For annotation, see Chapter 16: **BOOK REVIEWS**.

**Mary Jane Mossman, "Feminism and Legal Method: The Difference
It Makes" (1985) 3 *Wisconsin Women's Law Journal* 147-168**
     This is an updated version of an earlier paper presented at the
Feminist Legal Issues Conference (see: Mossman, (1986) 3 *Australian
Journal of Law and Society* 30-51), in which the author examines judicial
interpretation of anti-discrimination litigation. The author also discusses
the question of difference, and urges lawyers to ensure that the voice of
care is not ignored in law.

**Mary Jane Mossman, "Feminism and Legal Method: The Difference
It Makes" (1986) 3 *Australian Journal of Law and Society* 30-51**
     The author uses two early twentieth century cases to illustrate how

legal method maintains gender relations. She suggests that gender and power are inextricably linked in legal method, and that what drives results is not legal methodology, but judicial attitudes towards gender difference. She doubts that legal method can be transformed by feminism, and illustrates how legal method resists feminist inquiry.

Jennifer Nedelsky, "Reconceiving Autonomy: Sources, Thoughts and Possibilities" (1989) 1 _Yale Journal of Law and Feminism_ 7-36
This article rejects liberal individualism, and seeks to reconstruct autonomy from a feminist perspective which simultaneously asserts a woman's "self-hood," and the social nature of human beings. The author combines this feminist insight with an analysis of administrative law, examining how bureaucracy destroys autonomy, and how liberal rights, when tied closely to property rights, may also undercut autonomy. She concludes by arguing for more collective power and responsibility, which, in her view, will lead to a new conception of autonomy.

Katherine O'Donovan, "Engendering Justice: Women's Perspectives and the Rule of Law" (1989) 39 _University of Toronto Law Journal_ 127-148
The author argues that the rule of law has not fulfilled the promise of equality for women, because the form and process of law denies women's claims to equality in the name of judicial neutrality, and because anti-discrimination legislation requires a comparison to a similarly situated male. Feminists argue that the view of an autonomous, individuated self which is embedded in liberal political theory is a male view, and not universal. Women's values are not recognized in legal or political discourse, and to effect change in that discourse will require analysis of language as constructive of reality.

Onora O'Neill, "Justice and the Virtues" (1989) 34 _American Journal of Jurisprudence_ 1-18
The author argues that "recurrent confrontation between the advocates of justice and the friends of the virtues ... are both unnecessary and unconvincing." Liberal philosophy holds that the "good life" is not settable, while its critics "conclude that liberal justice is illusory." She argues that "certain universal principles of justice and of virtue can both be constructed."

Susan Moller Okin, "Justice and Gender" (1987) 16 *Philosophy and Public Affairs* 42-72
   For annotation, see Chapter 4: FAMILY LAW -- GENERAL.

Susan Moller Okin, "Reason and Feeling in Thinking about Justice" (1989) 99 *Ethics* 229-249
   For annotation, see Chapter 4: FAMILY LAW -- GENERAL.

Susan Moller Okin, "Women and the Making of the Sentimental Family" (1981) 2:1 *Philosophy & Public Affairs* 65-88
   This article outlines the philosophies of Locke and Hobbes, and claims that the idea of natural equality poses serious problems for each, as regards the position of women, because neither provides any solution. The author claims that in order to circumvent these problems, society developed the idealized notion of the sentimental family in the late eighteenth century, and that this notion provided a further rationale for the subordination of women.

Frances Olsen, "The Family and the Market: A Study of Ideology and Legal Reform" (1983) 96 *Harvard Law Review* 1497-1578
   For annotation, see Chapter 4: FAMILY LAW -- GENERAL.

Frances Olsen, "From False Paternalism to False Equality: Judicial Assaults on Feminist Community, Illinois: 1869-1895" (1986) 84 *Michigan Law Review* 1518-1541
   For annotation, see Chapter 10: LEGAL HISTORY.

Frances Olsen, "The Politics of Family Law" (1984) 2 *Law and Inequality* 1
   For annotation, see Chapter 4: FAMILY LAW -- CUSTODY.

Barbara Omolade, "The Unbroken Circle: A Historical and Contemporary Study of Black Single Mothers and Their Families" (1985) 3 *Wisconsin Women's Law Journal* 239-274
   For annotation, see Chapter 6: FIRST NATIONS AND RACE.

Christine A. Pagac, "Book Review: Susan Moller Okin, JUSTICE, GENDER AND THE FAMILY (1989)" (1990) 88 _Michigan Law Review_ 1822-1827

For annotation, see Chapter 16: BOOK REVIEWS.

Julia Penelope, "Language and the Transformation of Consciousness" (1986) 4 _Law and Inequality_ 379-391

The author examines feminist views of conflict, and argues that feminists must acknowledge the "war" or "battle of the sexes," and admit a chosen side because feminist values contradict values of heteropatriarchy. She argues that feminists perceive argument as bad, and that women and feminists avoid arguing with other women and feminists; she then proposes a model of "argument as dance," in which participants are willing, working together, artistic, and pleasant. She concludes that new metaphors are necessary to conceptualize or frame new ideas, and she challenges feminists to learn cooperatively and to talk and think differently.

Deborah C. Poff, "Feminism and Canadian Justice: How Far Have We Come?" (1990) 2:1 _Journal of Human Justice_ 93-104

For annotation, see Chapter 2: CONSTITUTIONAL LAW.

Rosemary Pringle, "Book Review: Carol Smart, FEMINISM AND THE POWER OF LAW (1989)" (1990) 18 _International Journal of the Sociology of Law_ 229-232

For annotation, see Chapter 16: BOOK REVIEWS.

Margaret Jane Radin, "Market-Inalienability" (1987) 100 _Harvard Law Review_ 1849-1936

For annotation, see Chapter 14: PROSTITUTION.

Nicole Hahn Rafter and Elena M. Natalizia, "Marxist Feminism: Implications for Criminal Justice" (1981) 27 _Crime and Delinquency_ 81-98

For annotation, see Chapter 3: CRIMINAL LAW -- GENERAL.

Benita Ramsey, "Introduction -- Excluded Voices: Realities in Law and Law Reform" (1987) 42 _University of Miami Law Review_ 1-5

This paper was originally presented as an introduction to a symposium entitled Excluded Voices: Realities in Law and Law Reform. The author focuses on the importance of language in creating and maintaining power. Those who are in power are, she claims, able to define their own language as dominant, and to exclude the language of all others. The purpose of the symposium was therefore to allow those whose voices have been marginalized to speak out. The author concludes that for social change to occur, those who are disempowered must speak out to redefine the dominant language, and to demand a response.

Judith Resnik, "Feminism and the Language of Judging" (1990) 22 _Arizona State Law Journal_ 31-38

This paper was originally presented as part of the Panel on Compassion and Judging at the Conference of the Association of American Law Schools. The author explores the impact of the language of feminism on a conversation about judging. Because feminist language focuses on interconnections, it points out the gap between the theory of impartial judges and the reality of judges who are connected with their communities. Hierarchy is challenged -- judges can be judged, and judging is seen as a difficult and complex, but daily activity -- as is the adversarial system. She submits that the result of this challenge will be compassion.

Deborah L. Rhode, "Feminist Critical Theories" (1990) 42 _Stanford Law Review_ 617-638

The author describes the underlying philosophy of critical feminists, and draws distinctions between them and critical legal theorists and other feminist legal theorists. The critical feminist project "seeks to promote equality between men and women, ... to make gender a focus of analysis ... and aspires to describe the world in ways that correspond to women's experience." She grapples with the problems of grounding a theory in experiential analysis, confronts the ideology that underpins liberal legal thought, and surveys critical feminism's alternate visions of society.

Deborah L. Rhode, "Gender and Jurisprudence: An Agenda For

Research" (1987) 56 *University of Cincinnati Law Review* 521-534
    Part of a Symposium on Feminist Moral, Social, and Legal Theory,
this article discusses feminist research and feminist jurisprudence, and
claims that both demonstrate a critique of existing analytical frameworks
which goes beyond accumulation of knowledge on women's issues, and
instead challenges the very notion of what constitutes knowledge. The
author demonstrates her claim with reference to research on occupational status disparities which has attributed only a small part of
status/pay differential between men and women to objective factors, such
as education, experience, or hours of work. Present research regarding
comparable worth remedies and strategies for pay equity, she argues, is
necessarily examining less superficial factors. She carries out a similar
analysis of family law, and claims the need for systematic study is
especially critical in this area, because of the "troubled history of prior
reform efforts." She concludes with a recommendation for systemic
research which will allow for more than rhetorical commitment to gender
equality.

    Janet Rifkin, "Mediation From a Feminist Perspective: Promise and
Problems" (1984) 2 *Law and Inequality* 21-31
    The author argues that interest in alternative dispute resolution,
especially mediation, may be detrimental to the interests of women,
because they are less empowered, and may need the formal legal system
to protect existing rights. The author examines the traditional male legal
pedagogy from which interest in mediation arises, and notes that
mediation challenges the structure and authority of this hierarchical
paradigm. She claims that this points to the need to develop a feminist
pedagogy, for if the "neutrality" of the mediator masks the same
"objectivist" paradigm of law, then mediation will reinforce this ideology,
further institutionalizing male power. She examines two case studies of
mediation -- a divorce matter and a sexual harassment complaint -- and
argues that the pattern of dominance and the hierarchy of the relationships had been altered.

    Janet Rifkin, "Toward a Theory of Law and Patriarchy" (1980) 3
Harvard Women's Law Journal 83-95
    Patriarchy is a form of group organization in which males are the
dominant power, and determine the part women shall play, and the capa-
bilities assigned to them. The author argues that law is a paradigm of

male-ness which functions as a hegemonic ideology. In her view, this explains why legal change does not lead to social reordering. Capitalism, she claims, preserves, transforms, and updates existing patriarchal forms, and the conception of women as the property of men. She concludes that the struggle for sexual equality must challenge, not reify, the male paradigm of law.

Carol M. Rose, "Property as Storytelling: Perspectives from Game Theory, Narrative Theory, Feminist Theory" (1990) 2 *Yale Journal of Law and the Humanities* 37-56

Theorists such as Locke, Blackstone, and Demsetz resort to story-telling to explain the classic theory of property, by proposing that people desiring more property for themselves, rather than less (preference ordering), is "simply natural" or "just there" as a part of human nature. In a series of "thought experiments" on preference ordering, the author reveals personalities, such as "Mom" or "the Good Citizen," who have more cooperative preferences, seeking joint utility before self-interest. The Good Citizen and Mom, she claims, are constantly visible in society and law, yet are unaccounted for in classic theory. She argues that private property is dependent on cooperation and not self-interest to create and sustain the system, and that classic theorists, who were not counting on cooperation but can't do without it, are forced to explain post hoc through stories. While feminist literature recognizes caring co-operation, it is the dominant story-teller, she claims, who can make his position seem like the natural one. She concludes that if Mom can tell her story, perhaps a community can be created where cooperation is possible, and all will be better off for it.

Nikolas Rose, "Beyond the Public-Private Division: Law, Power and the Family" (1987) 14 *Journal of Law and Society* 61-76

For annotation, see Chapter 4: **FAMILY LAW -- GENERAL.**

J. Saint-Arnaud, "L'argument de la différence et le partage des rôles sociaux" (1985) 1 *Canadian Journal of Women and the Law* 69-78

This article responds to Lucas' thesis (see: J. R. Lucas, "Vive la différence" (1978) 53 *Philosophy* 363) that equality is not a solution to the injustices suffered by women. The author claims that to retain the dichotomy of masculine and feminine is to refuse women access to institutional power. She argues that only differences connected to reproductive activity should be institutionalized; others should be dealt with by the revision of sexist stereotypes connected to traditional roles.

Ann C. Scales, "The Emergence of Feminist Jurisprudence: An Essay" (1986) 95 _Yale Law Journal_ 1373-1403

The author argues that feminist legal theory on the difference debate and special rights represents the circularity of abstract liberal legal thinking, the male norm in the name of neutrality and universalism as ideology. Feminist jurisprudence must be radical and go to the root of inequality. She contends that 'rights-based' and 'care-based' theories are incompatible and that a choice is required. Feminism must bring law to purpose, to decide the moral crux of real human situations, and to create a concrete universality. Differences are constitutive of the universal itself and are systemically related to each other. She claims feminism is emergent and always changing, and is beyond liberalism and Marxism. The social experiences of males and females are not the same. It is impossible to remedy gender inequality, so feminists must focus on real issues of equality like domination, disadvantage and disempowerment, not on differences.

Ann C. Scales, "Feminists in the Field of Time" (1990) 42 _Florida Law Review_ 95-123

Part of a Symposium on Women and the Law, this article analyzes common law from a feminist perspective, examining tort law in particular. The author discusses the change in terminology from "reasonable man" to "reasonable person," and the fact that this semantic change has done little to change the underlying male norm which systematically excludes issues crucial to women -- reproductive harm, women battering and sexual harassment. She claims, however, that this exclusion must be examined more deeply; it results from neither a mere failure to include feminist study nor a massive failure in empathy, but is a problem of differing realities. She discusses male and female understandings of space, time and causality, and claims that legal concepts are understood differently by men and women because of differences in these underlying notions of truth. A recognition of these alternative conceptions is essential to the struggle for human dignity; to fail in this understanding will leave women again silent, worthless, and non-existent.

Ann C. Scales, "Militarism, Male Dominance and Law: Feminist Jurisprudence as Oxymoron?" (1989) 12 _Harvard Women's Law Journal_ 25-73

The author defines militarism as the "pervasive cluster of forces that keeps history insane: hierarchy, conformity, waste, false glory, force as the resolution of all issues, death as the meaning of life, and a claim to the necessity of all that." Militarism should not only be on the feminist agenda, but ought be viewed as being "in fundamental symbiosis with gender oppression." Inasmuch as law is more an obstacle than a help to change, feminist jurisprudence may seem oxymoronic. However, using the example of the Greenham Common Women's Peace Camp in England, she illustrates that feminism can be a tool for change. She provides a feminist analysis of the "political question" doctrine and other rationales used by courts to avoid ruling on peace issues brought forward by civil disobedience. Additionally, she argues in support of the defence of necessity which has been unsuccessfully argued by activists who have been charged.

Ann C. Scales, "Towards a Feminist Jurisprudence" (1981) 56 _Indiana Law Journal_ 375-444

For annotation, see Chapter 8: **LABOUR AND EMPLOYMENT - - GENERAL.**

Elizabeth M. Schneider, "The Dialectic of Rights and Politics: Perspectives from the Women's Movement" (1986) 61 _New York University Law Review_ 589-652

This article examines the nature of legal rights and reviews Critical Legal Studies (CLS) and feminist critiques of rights analysis. The author argues that women's self and other are inter-connected in the care/justice paradigm and argues for a reconstruction of the rights of the individual within a social network. She concludes that rights claims shape public discourse and that the struggle for rights is an affirmation of who women are and what women seek as feminists.

Vicki Schultz, "Room to Manoeuver (f)or a Room of One's Own? Practice Theory and Feminist Practice" (1989) 14 _Law and Social Inquiry_ 123-164

This is a comment on Rosemary J. Coombe's "Room for Manoeuver: Toward a Theory of Practice in Critical Legal Studies," both of which are part of a Symposium on Critical Empiricism and Sociological Studies. The comment claims that Coombe's practice theory is useful to feminists because it lends support to the feminist claim that current gender relations are contingent, but that since it has no theory of women's oppression, and in consequence no inherent feminist politics, it is no more than that -- a useful resource. The author concludes that what is central to feminist practice is not the insight that gender relations can change, but the process of persuading people that they should wish to change them, and she suggests that to do this, feminists have to tell powerful stories -- "stories of power and pain, of passion and possibility; stories of need and neglect, of creativity and connection" -- which instantiate oppression and provide counter-visions.

Martin D. Schwartz and Gerald T. Slatin, "The Law on Marital Rape: How do Marxism and Feminism Explain its Persistence" (1984) 8 _ALSA Forum_ 244-264
>   For annotation, see Chapter 3: **CRIMINAL LAW -- RAPE.**

Selma Sevenhuijsen, "Fatherhood and the Political Theory of Rights: Theoretical Perspectives of Feminism" (1986) 14 _International Journal of the Sociology of Law_ 329-340
>   For annotation, see Chapter 4: **FAMILY LAW -- GENERAL.**

Mary Lyndon Shanley, "Book Review: Josephine Donovan, FEMIN-IST THEORY: THE INTELLECTUAL TRADITIONS OF AMERI-CAN FEMINISM (1985); David L. Kirp, Mark G. Yudof, and Marlene Strong Franks, GENDER JUSTICE (1986)" (1987) 13 _Signs: Journal of Women in Culture and Society_ 175-178
>   For annotation, see Chapter 16: **BOOK REVIEWS.**

Suzanna Sherry, "Civic Virtue and the Feminine Voice in Constitutional Adjudication" (1986) 72 _Virginia Law Review_ 543-616
>   For annotation, see Chapter 2: **CONSTITUTIONAL LAW.**

Suzanna Sherry, "An Essay Concerning Toleration" (1987) 71

Minnesota Law Review 963-989

This article compares Lee C. Bollinger's THE TOLERANT
SOCIETY: FREEDOM OF SPEECH AND EXTREMIST SPEECH IN
AMERICA (1986) and David A. J. Richard's TOLERATION AND
THE CONSTITUTION (1986) to illustrate ways of dealing with issues
of tolerance. Ultimately, we must develop entirely new methods of
discourse, and not rely on a reformulation of the traditional liberal rights
model.

Carol Smart, "Feminism and Law: Some Problems of Analysis and
Strategy" (1986) 14 *International Journal of the Sociology of Law* 109-123

The author argues that a body of theoretical analysis is developing
from feminist work on law. She attributes this development to two
factors: to disappointment experienced by feminists regarding the
outcome of successful law reform campaigns and the resulting impulse
to develop analysis of the role of law in creating, reproducing or
mitigating forms of oppression; and to wider developments in feminism
and especially to the growth of the view that gender inequality is part of
a system of oppression in which the state and law are fully implicated.
She identifies the problem facing feminism in terms of its traditional
engagement with law reform and its recognition of the central role of law
in reproducing women's oppression and explores the contradictions and
problems facing feminists who continue to engage in law as part of a
political struggle. She concludes that the goal of engaging with law as
part of the feminist political struggle is a strategy which integrates
feminist theory and practice.

Carol Smart, "Regulating Families or Legitimating Patriarchy? Family
Law in Britain" (1982) 10 *International Journal of the Sociology of Law*
129-147

For annotation, see Chapter 4: FAMILY LAW -- GENERAL.

Margot Stubbs, "Feminism and Legal Positivism" (1986) 3 *Australian
Journal of Law and Society* 63-91

The author argues that feminist theory must necessarily transcend
positivism's claim to trans-historicity and universality, and that the
functional, ideological role of positivism in the reproduction of gender
and class relations of capitalist society must be recognized as a self-

-contained system. She claims that much current feminist literature is expressed within positivism, especially works with respect to points where law directly intersects with experience -- namely, rape, abortion, criminal, and family law. She finds that there is little questioning of the structure of the legal order -- its supposed formality, generality, and autonomy -- and she concludes that positivism must be subjected to criticisms similar to those currently being directed at liberalism.

Cass R. Sunstein, "Introduction: Notes on Feminist Political Thought" (1989) 99 _Ethics_ 219-228
This article, which introduces a Symposium on Feminism and Political Theory, outlines the themes of feminist political thought -- different voice, equality, reproduction, universality and partiality, and sexuality -- and relates them to the essays in the symposium.

Esmeralda Thornhill, "Focus on Black Women!" (1985-86) 1 _Canadian Journal of Women and the Law_ 153-162
For annotation, see Chapter 6: FIRST NATIONS AND RACE.

Margaret Thornton, "Affirmative Action, Merit and the Liberal State" (1985) 2 _Australian Journal of Law and Society_ 28-40
For annotation, see Chapter 8: LABOUR AND EMPLOYMENT -- AFFIRMATIVE ACTION.

Margaret Thornton, "Feminist Jurisprudence: Illusion or Reality?" (1986) 3 _Australian Journal of Law and Society_ 5-29
The author describes law as a mechanism of social control, which reproduces the dominant ideology. Mainstream (malestream) thought, she claims, is characterized by the exclusion of women from the society of equals and the elevation of the public above the private sphere. Its intellectual tradition emphasizes the marginality of women in the public sphere. This ideology is resistant to change and is functionally necessary to capitalism. The liberal state in consequence responds with ambivalence to the feminist movement because of epistemological constraints and liberal thought structures which are sexualized and hierarchized dualisms. She argues that in the feminist model of law reform and the search for equality, formal equality is demonstrated to create and

entrench substantive inequality. The author submits that the academic challenge is to reveal that traditional scholarship is quintessentially male masquerading as neutrality. Most significant feminist scholarship is interdisciplinary and eschews positivism. The critique is informed and reflective and constitutes a search for intersubjectivity. Feminist scholarship, she concludes, validates norms through consensus and discussion rather than through a search for objective truth. The experiential dimension is all important, and high levels of abstraction are rejected.

Peter Tumulty, "Aristotle, Feminism and Natural Law Theory" (1981) 55 _New Scholasticism_ 450-464
    The author raises "serious misgivings about the adequacy of popular, contemporary moral theories which are rooted in subjectivism to provide an adequate understanding of the struggle to secure justice for women, or any other minority." He argues for a return to natural law as espoused by Aristotle, and attempts to refute empiricism and materialism.

Shauna Van Praagh and Barbara Austin, "Book Review -- Lorraine Code and Christine Overall, eds., FEMINIST PERSPECTIVES: PHILOSOPHICAL ESSAYS ON METHOD AND MORALS (1988)" (1989) 47 _University of Toronto Faculty Law Review_ 1016-1019
    For annotation, see Chapter 16: BOOK REVIEWS.

Judith Vega, "Coercion and Consent: Classic Liberal Concepts in Texts on Sexual Violence" (1988) 16 _International Journal of the Sociology of Law_ 75-87
    For annotation, see Chapter 3: CRIMINAL LAW -- BATTERING.

Virginia L. Warren, "How Radical is Liberalism? -- Book Review: James S. Fishkin, JUSTICE, EQUAL OPPORTUNITY, AND THE FAMILY (1983)" (1984) 82 _Michigan Law Review_ 761-780
    For annotation, see Chapter 16: BOOK REVIEWS.

Robin West, "Deconstructing the CLS-FEM Split" (1985) 2 _Wisconsin Women's Law Journal_ 85-92

The author examines the role of deconstruction as a tool of analysis, and applauds its use for the disempowered within any hierarchical organization. She relates the use of deconstruction by the Critical Legal Studies (CLS) school, and the value of analysis of the law from within this perspective, in unmasking legal power and the working of legal institutions. She claims, however, that feminists must use the analysis of deconstruction on the work of the white, middle class, male, tenured professors who are members of CLS. She specifically examines a work by Duncan Kennedy [see: Kennedy, "Psycho-Social CLS: A Comment on the Cardozo Symposium" (1985) 6 _Cardozo Law Review_ 1013], and claims that CLS claims about women in CLS emanate from both the heterosexual culture and the CLS sub-culture, and have to do with the nature of desire, and sexual desire, as immutable. She concludes that feminists must challenge the eroticization of relationships of dominance by male CLSers, and that absent such deconstruction, must recognize that the CLS movement is not an acceptable sphere for feminist work. She further concludes, however, that the members of CLS, if following their own dictates, should be "willing listeners" to feminist claims, and recommends that feminists continue to cultivate the CLS audience.

Robin West, "The Difference in Women's Hedonic Lives: A Phenomenological Critique of Feminist Legal Theory" (1985) 3 _Wisconsin Women's Law Journal_ 81-145

Part of the 1986 Feminism and Legal Theory Conference, this article discusses the difference in the ways men and women experience the world, and the author claims that not only do women suffer more than do men, but that this gender-based suffering is largely ignored by the male legal culture. She states her belief that most people resist their own pain, but also that most people sympathetically resist pain suffered by others, when it is meaningfully communicated to them. She concludes with an urging to feminists to articulate the pain in their lives, so that women can understand the truth about their inner lives and human nature.

Robin West, "Equality Theory, Marital Rape, and the Promise of the Fourteenth Amendment" (1990) 42 _Florida Law Review_ 45-79

For annotation, see Chapter 2: **CONSTITUTIONAL LAW.**

Robin West, "Feminism, Critical Social Theory and the Law" [1989] *University of Chicago Legal Forum* 59-96

The author claims that the critical social theory of writers such as Michel Foucault and Roberto Unger, is a grave hindrance to any understanding of patriarchy. Critical social theorists discuss four central ideas -- the nature of power, of knowledge, of morality, and of the self. Foucault's appeal to speak of power in positive terms is of little assistance to feminism, because modern patriarchal power is different from other forms of modern social power. Women's silence is of more significance than women's discourse, which makes the focus on knowledge and discourse of little relevance to feminism. This is so, the author claims, because the retreat by modern women into numbing silence is an epistemic "way of knowing." Unger's notion of political morality, based on denaturalization of society, is simply not true for women. The feminist critique of the liberal self is more extensive than the critique of critical theory because the feminist critique has shown the self to be an invention of a general power matrix of patriarchy. The author concludes that concentration on the prevailing ideas of critical social theory will frustrate feminist attempts to end patriarchy.

Robin West, "Jurisprudence and Gender" (1988) 55 *University of Chicago Law Review* 1-72

The author argues that modern jurisprudence is masculine, and fails to reflect the values, dangers, and fundamental contradictions of women's lives. The task of feminist jurisprudence, she concludes, is twofold -- unmasking the patriarchy behind "ungendered" law and theory; and reconstructing jurisprudence so as to reveal women's distinctive state of being.

Robin West, "Law, Rights, and Other Totemic Illusions: Legal Liberalism and Freud's Theory of the Rule of Law" (1986) 134 *University of Pennsylvania Law Review* 817-882

This article examines Freud's legal theory which consists of a defence of the Rule-of-Law. According to the author, Freud makes two essential claims about human nature: firstly, that the uninhibited individual possesses dangerously antisocial instinctual desires, which are at war with civilization; and second, that this threat is not neutralized by the individual's empathy or communitarian altruism. On the basis of these, Freud concluded that only an appeal to a higher authority will assure obedience. The author discusses Freud's possible responses to modern critics of legal liberalism -- including law and economics, critical legal studies (CLS), feminism, and deconstructionism. Feminism, she argues, rejects Freud's second claim, and thus provides a radically different solution to the problem of power.

Robin West, "Love, Rage and Legal Theory" (1989) 1 _Yale Journal of Law and Feminism_ 101-110
    The author claims that both love and rage are motivating factors and integral aspects of feminist jurisprudence and legal practice. Love, which creates feminist morality and recognizes our "connectedness" to others, and rage, which creates our sense of justice, are part of a whole, which West argues has led to an ambiguity in recent feminist scholarship. This ambiguity results in an almost schizophrenic rejection of the dominant ethic motivated by that rage, combined with an acceptance of that ethic, due to the repression of that rage. She concludes that it is important for feminists to recognize this ambiguity, and then to trust the rage a little more and the repression a little less, in order to develop a truly feminist theory of justice.

Lucie E. White, "Subordination, Rhetorical Survival Skills, and Sunday Shoes: Notes on the Hearing of Mrs. G." (1990) 38 _Buffalo Law Review_ 1-58
    The author argues that procedural justice requires more than formal access to the legal system, and that political and legal institutions must recognise the way speech norms and practices reflect gender, race and class subordination. She claims that the voices of subordinated groups are often perceived negatively by dominant groups, and therefore the information presented is devalued or ignored. The story of an administrative hearing concerning a welfare overpayment to a poor black woman provides the framework for the author's analysis.

Joan C. Williams, "Deconstructing Gender" (1989) 87 _Michigan Law Review_ 797-845
    This article deals with the split within feminism on gender sameness and gender difference, and the assimilationist's focus on gender sameness. The author replies with a challenge to assimilationists: (1) that Gilligan's (see: IN A DIFFERENT VOICE (1982)) 'woman's voice'

is not a description of women's psychology, but instead is a new epistemology which rehabilitates traditional stereotypes; and (2) that the challenge to male norms can be made without resort to domesticity, which argument perpetuates existing power relations within a deeply gendered system where men and women face different choices. She concludes with an alternative vision of gender, a rejection of gender neutrality, and with the claim that the position of women will remain fundamentally unchanged until labour is restructured.

Patricia Williams, "Alchemical Notes: Reconstructing Ideals from Deconstructed Rights" (1987) 22 *Harvard Civil Rights-Civil Liberties Law Review* 401-433
     For annotation, see Chapter 6: FIRST NATIONS AND RACE.

Patricia Williams, "Fetal Fictions: An Exploration of Property Archetypes in Racial and Gendered Contexts" (1990) 42 *Florida Law Review* 81-94
     For annotation, see Chapter 6: FIRST NATIONS AND RACE.

Patricia Williams, "Response to Mari Matsuda – 1988 Women of Colour and the Law Conference at Yale University" (1989) 11 *Women's Rights Law Reporter* 11-13
     For annotation, see Chapter 6: FIRST NATIONS AND RACE.

Patricia Williams, "Spirit-Murdering the Messenger: The Discourse of Fingerpointing as the Law's Response to Racism" (1987) 42 *University of Miami Law Review* 127-157
     For annotation, see Chapter 6: FIRST NATIONS AND RACE.

Wendy Williams, "Notes From a First Generation" [1989] *University of Chicago Legal Forum* 99-113
     The author identifies two approaches to legal feminism: symmetry, which advocates formal equality; and asymmetry, which advocates a legal response that recognizes gender difference. She illustrates how these approaches were played out in CALIFORNIA FEDERAL SAVINGS AND LOAN ASSOC. v. GUERRA 479 U.S. 272 (1987), a case which

deals with maternity benefits and leave. As a symmetrist herself, she defends formal equality, claiming that it does not ignore the differences between men and women, and that it rejects instead sex-based laws which limit our ability to define ourselves. She suggests that the differences between the two positions may be generational because the first generation of feminists began by opposing existing gender-based laws.

Heather Ruth Wishik, "To Question Everything: The Inquiries of Feminist Jurisprudence" (1985) 1 _Berkeley Women's Law Journal_ 64-77
This article explores the questions feminists are asking, how recent ones differ from conventional questions asked about women and the law, and what methods are needed in the future to formulate questions well. The development of feminist legal scholarship stretches from "compensatory scholarship," the 'add women and stir' approach, to the "conceptualization of a feminist method with which to understand and examine the law." The author discusses seven questions posed by feminist inquiry with respect to the relationship between law and society. Four questions are universal in feminist jurisprudence, and help identify how law and existence is gendered by patriarchy. The last three are inventive, imagining a world without patriarchy.

Iris Marion Young, "Difference and Policy: Some Reflections in the Context of New Social Movements" (1987) 56 _University of Cincinnati Law Review_ 535-550
Part of a Symposium on Feminist Moral, Social, and Legal Theory, this article examines the theoretical and political debate about sameness and difference, and acknowledges that risks emanate from either. She argues that while the liberal humanist ideals have inspired movements against oppression and domination, the supposedly neutral standards claimed within liberalism are biased in favour of privileged groups, and consequently force disadvantaged persons to deny identity or culture to properly measure up to the "neutral" standards. The politics of difference, however, is more liberating because asserting the value and specificity of the culture and attributes of groups revitalizes even dominant culture, promotes group solidarity, and provides a standpoint from which to criticize prevailing institutions and norms. She concludes with the assertion that the contradiction in asserting individual's right to inclusion (i.e. sameness argument) and the group's right to different

treatment (i.e. difference argument) is more perceived than real, and only requires de-normalizing of the ways institutions formulate rules for inclusion.

Iris Marion Young, "Polity and Group Difference: A Critique of the Ideal of Universal Citizenship" (1989) 99 *Ethics* 250-274
   The author argues that the extension of equal citizenship rights does not create social justice and equality because the oppressed, excluded groups remain second class citizens. The challenge to equal treatment is differentiated citizenship, which she sees as the best way to inclusion and participation of everyone in social and political institutions. She criticizes citizenship as a generality because it suppresses differences and excludes different perspectives from public discourse. She claims that under a regime of differentiated citizenship, there would be group representation, fairness would be institutionalized, and differences would be acknowledged. Differentiated citizenship, she concludes, is problematic only if difference means deviance or deficiency.

Ecology

Jim Cheney, "Eco-feminism and Deep Ecology" (1987) 9 *Environmental Ethics* 115-145
   This article analyzes deep ecology theory from the eco-feminist perspective. Deep ecology is atomistically conceived, rights-based theorizing, whereas eco-feminism demands some change. The author presents Gilligan's (Carol Gilligan, IN A DIFFERENT VOICE (1982)) analysis of gender differences in moral reasoning, and argues for a shift from a focus on the rights of actors to a view that makes the good of the whole the standard for adjudicating claims of the parts. This shift from an atomistic conception of self in ethical relationships, to that of sustaining connection, the author concludes, is a shift from abstract moral reasoning to an emphasis on context within relations of care and responsibility.

Patrick D. Murphy, "Sex-Typing the Planet" (1988) 10 *Environmental Ethics* 155-168

This is a critique of the attempt by the ecology movement to reinvigorate the 'Gaia hypothesis' in an attempt to resanctify nature. The hypothesis holds that man functions as intellect and the protector of Gaia, and this, in the author's view, inadvertently reinforces androcentrism. He argues that writings of ecologists reflect sex stereotyping. A heterarchical viewpoint, he concludes, can recognize bio-gender differences without falling prey to the socio-gender hierarchical sex-typing rampant in our culture.

Ariel Kay Salleh, "Deeper than Deep Ecology: The Eco-Feminist Connection" (1984) 6 *Environmental Ethics* 339-346

This is a feminist critique of deep ecology, which claims that its tacit methodological approach is inconsistent with the deep ecologist's own substantive commitments. The author discusses the shortcomings of deep ecology in terms of the broader feminist critique of patriarchal culture, and points out some practical and theoretical contributions which eco-feminism can make to a genuinely deep ecology theory.

Karen J. Warren, "Feminism and Ecology: Making Connections" (1987) 9 *Environmental Ethics* 3-20

The author criticizes four leading versions of feminism from an eco-feminist perspective. Liberal feminism, traditional Marxist feminism, radical feminism, and socialist feminism, she argues, each provide important insights into the oppression of women and nature, but none taken by themselves is adequate as a theoretical grounding for eco-feminism. What is needed is an integrative, transformative feminism which moves beyond the current debate, and makes a responsible ecological perspective central to feminist theory and practice. She claims the need to recognize, and to make explicit, the interconnections between all systems of oppression.

Michael E. Zimmerman, "Feminism, Deep Ecology, and Environmental Ethics" (1987) 9 *Environmental Ethics* 21-44

This article defends the deep ecology movement from eco-feminist criticisms, which are that deep ecology continues the androcentric, hierarchical, dualistic, atomistic, and abstract underpinnings of rights based theory. The author argues that it may be dangerous entirely to reject the morality of rights and that over-emphasizing internal relatedness might lead to environmental totalitarianism, which sacrifices the individual for the good of the whole. He suggests that the doctrine of rights may be useful if applied in a non-patriarchal, non-atomistic view of humanity and nature, and argues that society must use available moral doctrines, science, and technology to protect people while in the process of developing non-patriarchal categories. He concludes that we may take hope from the global awakening of the quest for the feminine voice that can temper the one-sidedness of the masculine voice.

Law and Literature

Jane Maslow Cohen, "Feminism and Adaptive Heroinism: The Paradigm of Portia as a Means of Introduction" (1990) 25 *Tulsa Law Journal* 657-734
   Part of a Symposium on Feminist Jurisprudence, the author suggests that legal feminists need to look at lawyering, and how a feminist lawyer would behave. After describing the "Portia Paradigm," she analyzes Portia's role in THE MERCHANT OF VENICE, and concludes that feminists must give up the notion that mercy is feminine.

Carolyn Heilbrun and Judith Resnik, "Convergences: Law, Literature and Feminism" (1990) 99 *Yale Law Journal* 1913-1956
   This essay dissents from the creation of law and literature studies that exclude feminist perspectives. The study of the two fields together provides an opportunity to analyze the common assumption of women as "other," the object of the discussion and not the speaker. The authors adopt the format of dialogue and discuss their experiences writing and teaching about women and gender theory.

Linda R. Hirshman, "Brontë, Bloom, and Bork: An Essay on the Moral Education of Judges" (1988) 137 *University of Pennsylvania Law Review* 177-230

The author examines the "hollowness of value-free positivism," the rejection of morally neutral relativism in civic culture, and the law and literature movement's success. She specifically examines the legal status of abortion from within the perspective of a developed framework for moral thought, and adds to the debate a selection from fiction on women and on women and babies. She concludes that the feminist critique of literature may equally serve to allow for an enriched legal, juridical, and public life.

Judith Schenck Koffler, "The Feminine Presence in Billy Budd" (1989) 1 *Cardozo Studies in Law and Literature* 1-14
The story of Billy Budd, his trial and execution aboard a man of war, has been a favourite text in law and literature, raising old jurisprudential questions about guilt and responsibility, power and its abuse, and justice and mercy. The author notes that the story is also about love, homosexual love, the unsettling of gender categories, and conflicts between soft and hard, heart and intellect and "Capt. Vere's dismissal of 'the feminine in man' and Billy's physical loveliness." The "feminine absence" in the story is created by the expulsion, and then pathologization, of the feminine. She explores how the themes of mutiny and repression have as much to do with the "feminine in man" as with law and war. Responses by Robin West and James Warren follow.

David Farrell Krell, "Lucinde's Shame: Hegel, Sensuous Woman, and the Law" (1989) 10 *Cardozo Law Review* 1673-1693
The author discusses the predicament of women in Hegel -- namely that if woman is purged from the system, the spirit will die, but if she remains within the system, woman condemns the spirit to a fate worse than death. He suggests that in his references to Lucinde, Hegel talks of two kinds of appropriation: the girl, woman or wife as tokens of masculine desire; and love as non-mediated substantiality of spirit. Hegel, he claims, describes the family as a unit of sensibility surrendered to the maid, and natural love receiving its spiritual bond through the solemnization of marriage. He says that love can make demands different from marriage through the substantial unity of spirit in sensibility.

Anita L. Morse, "Pandora's Box: An Essay Review of American Law

and Literature on Prostitution" (1985) 4 *Wisconsin Women's Law Journal*
21-62
For annotation, see Chapter 14: **PROSTITUTION.**

**Frances Olsen, "Comments on David Krell's 'Lucinde's Shame: Hegel,
Sensuous Women, and the Law'"** (1989) 10 *Cardozo Law Review*
1687-1693
The article discusses whether men and women can relate to each
other as equals, or not at all. In discussing the problem that gender
hierarchy presents for ethical men, the author proposes three scenarios:
following Hegel, to acknowledge inequality, apparently accepting
inequality, and possibly encouraging non-ideal policies; following
Lucinde, to pretend equality already exists, and build on exceptional
women; following Austen's Elizabeth, to reject all choices offered by
men, and choose to recognize the radical subordination of women and
make the best of it. She discusses other literary situations which show
the pervasive subordination of women to men which causes intolerable
lives and the pathetic outcome of the male-dominated household.

**Susan Staves, "'The Liberty of a She-Subject of England': Rights
Rhetoric and the Female Thucydides"** (1989) 1 *Cardozo Studies in Law
and Literature* **161-184**
For annotation, see Chapter 10: **LEGAL HISTORY.**

James Warren, "Bristol Molly: Sexuality, Power, Silence" (1989) 1
Cardozo Studies in Law and Literature 21-26
This is a response to Judith Koffler's article, "The Feminine
Presence in BILLY BUDD," published in the same volume. The author
questions whether BILLY BUDD succeeds in provoking thought about
sexual repression or whether it merely becomes part of "the historical
network of sexuality and power," and he suggests that Koffler's article
falls into this same trap. He then argues that the character of Bristol
Molly provides a feminine presence in the novel, but in the role of a
subject for victimization. In this fashion, he concludes, the novel
maintains the conventional images of masculinity and femininity,
although this is done to provoke discussion.

Robin West, "Economic Man and Literary Woman: One Contrast"
(1988) 39 *Mercer Law Review* 867-878
The author argues that in a literary analysis of law, the literary woman represents a vision of human nature which holds moral promise in contrast with the economic man who is a rational maximizer of his own utility and impotence, unable to recognize the subjective well-being of others. She argues that the economic view is invalid because we do not know ourselves as economic man would suggest. She claims that literature is a means by which we glimpse the truth. Because literary states are multi-motivational, complex and educable, and because literary woman's empathic competence constitutes moral promise, it is possible, she concludes, to teach empathy in the hard case. Consequently, literature gives a vital interdisciplinary and critical perspective to law.

Robin West, "The Feminine Silence: A Response to Koffler" (1989)
1 *Cardozo Studies in Law and Literature* 15-20
This article is a response to Judith Koffler's article, "The Feminine Presence in BILLY BUDD," published in the same volume. The author argues that BILLY BUDD is a story of patriarchy, not of law. She accepts Koffler's assertion that Melville intended to subvert our notions of the masculine and the feminine by his portrayal of Billy's femininity. However, she argues that Billy is feminine in other ways as well: his virtue, his silence, and his victimization. She claims that the obstacle to the love of men for men is the violent attitudes exemplified by war. If women are to help men in overcoming this, she concludes, they must break their silence and participate in the legal, social and political arenas.

Sexuality

Joan Acker and Kate Barry, "Comments on MacKinnon's 'Feminism, Marxism, Method, and the State'" (1984) 10 *Signs: Journal of Women in Culture and Society* 175-179
This is a response to Catharine MacKinnon's "Feminism, Marxism, Method, and the State: An Agenda for Theory" [(1982) 7 *Signs: Journal of Women in Culture and Society* 515] and her "Feminism, Marxism,

Method, and the State: Toward Feminist Jurisprudence" [(1983) 8 *Signs: Journal of Women in Culture and Society* 635]. The authors applaud the challenge MacKinnon presents, but claim the underlying incompatibility between her theory and method leaves her with brilliant insights without theoretical ground for accomplishing new synthesis. They also criticize her work for failing to deal with women in developing countries and for dealing only partially with minorities and poor and working class women in industrialized countries. Nevertheless, the reviewers conclude, MacKinnon has much of interest to say about rape and the legal system.

   Christine Ball, "Female Sexual Ideologies in Mid to Late Nineteenth - Century Canada" (1985-1986) 1 *Canadian Journal of Women and the Law* 324-337
   The author examines the ideologies of female sexuality in the latter half of the nineteenth century by studying both medical and non-medical literature in Canada, the United States and Britain. She discusses the historical/cultural context, female sexuality in the Victorian era, and the "vital point" that female sexuality was never viewed as existing separately from male sexuality. Because of the Victorian view of social order as connected to the moral or sexual order, women could not be seen to have strong sexual urges, else social chaos would occur.

   Katherine T. Bartlett, "MacKinnon's Feminism: Power on Whose Terms? -- Book Review: Catharine MacKinnon, FEMINISM UN-MODIFIED (1987)" (1987) 75 *California Law Review* 1559-1570
   For annotation, see Chapter 16: BOOK REVIEWS.

   Beth Bernstein, "Difference, Dominance, Differences: Feminist Theory, Equality, and the Law -- Book Review: Zillah Eisenstein, THE FEMALE BODY AND THE LAW (1989)" (1989-90) 5 *Berkeley Women's Law Journal* 214 - 226
   For annotation, see Chapter 16: BOOK REVIEWS.

   Kay Boulware-Miller, "Female Circumcision: Challenges to the Practice as a Human Rights Violation" (1985) 8 *Harvard Women's Law Journal* 155-177
   For annotation, see Chapter 2: CONSTITUTIONAL LAW.

Neil T. Boyd, "Sexuality and the State: A Comment on Moral Boundaries in the Physical Realm" (1989) 7 _Canadian Journal of Family Law_ 353-366

The author claims that there are two major themes in the discourse about the moral boundaries of sexuality: (1) the dynamic of coercion and consent; and (2) the dynamic of monogamy and polygamy. Sexual behaviour is defined by male sexuality, while the victims of prostitution and pornography are almost always female. He argues that tougher criminal laws, which would have a large impact on prostitutes, young lovers, and adolescent homosexuals are not supportable merely to provide state support for a particular form of sexual relationship, that is legally sanctioned marriage.

Susan J. Brown, "Book Review: Catherine A. MacKinnon, TOWARD A FEMINIST THEORY OF THE STATE (1989)" (1990) 24 _University of British Columbia Law Review_ 146-149

For annotation, see Chapter 16: **BOOK REVIEWS.**

Martha Chamallas, "Consent, Equality, and the Legal Control of Sexual Conduct" (1988) 61 _Southern California Law Review_ 777-862

The author argues that sexual conduct is highly regulated, but not within a context of any unifying conception or vision. On the contrary, there are three views of sexual conduct, which she identifies as follows: (a) traditional, which is moralistic, and locates sex only in marriage, for procreation; (b) liberal, which draws a distinction between morality and legality; and (c) egalitarian, which fosters equality between the sexes, encouraging non-coerced decisions.

Ruth Colker, "Feminism, Sexuality, and Self: A Preliminary Inquiry Into the Politics of Authenticity; Book Review: Catherine MacKinnon, FEMINISM UNMODIFIED (1987)" (1988) 68 _Boston University Law Review_ 217-264

For annotation, see Chapter 16: **BOOK REVIEWS.**

T. Brettel Dawson, "Book Review: Catharine MacKinnon, FEMINISM UNMODIFIED (1987)" (1988) 20 _Ottawa Law Review_ 241-249

For annotation, see Chapter 16: **BOOK REVIEWS.**

H. F. Ellenberger, "Mutilation corporelles infligées aux femmes; étude victimologique" (1980) 13:1 *Criminologie* 80-93

This article describes ritual female circumcision in North Africa, its physical and psychological ramifications, and the author notes that the practice has been upheld by anthropologists and African heads of state as an essential element of tribal culture. The author discusses different theories about the origins and purpose of the practice, and concludes that it represents an extreme form of aggression against women. The Chinese practice of foot-binding is described as a method of maintaining women in a state of physical inferiority for the erotic pleasure of men.

Lucinda M. Finley, "The Nature of Domination and the Nature of Women: Reflections on Feminism Unmodified -- Book Review: Catharine MacKinnon, FEMINISM UNMODIFIED (1987)" (1988) 82 *Northwestern University Law Review* 352-386

For annotation, see Chapter 16: **BOOK REVIEWS.**

Angela P. Harris, "Categorical Discourse and Dominance Theory -- Book Review: Catharine A. MacKinnon, TOWARD A FEMINIST THEORY OF THE STATE (1989)" (1989-90) 5 *Berkeley Women's Law Journal* 181-196

For annotation, see Chapter 16: **BOOK REVIEWS.**

Miriam M. Johnson, "Comments on MacKinnon's 'Feminism, Marxism, Method, and the State'" (1984) 10 *Signs: Journal of Women in Culture and Society* 180-182

This is a response to Catharine MacKinnon's "Feminism, Marxism, Method, and the State: An Agenda for Theory" [(1982) 7 *Signs: Journal of Women in Culture and Society* 515] and her "Feminism, Marxism, Method, and the State: Toward Feminist Jurisprudence" [(1983) 8 *Signs: Journal of Women in Culture and Society* 635]. The author agrees with MacKinnon that "sexuality defines gender," which she proceeds to discuss in terms of psychoanalytic theory. She concludes that MacKinnon has documented well the connection between sexuality and gender, and that the next step is to end that connection.

Kenneth L. Karst, "Women's Constitution" (1984) 3 *Duke Law Journal*

447-508
> For annotation, see Chapter 2: CONSTITUTIONAL LAW.

Nannerl O. Keohane, "Feminist Scholarship and Human Nature --
Book Review" (1982) 93 _Ethics_ 102-113
> For annotation, see Chapter 16: BOOK REVIEWS.

Gary D. La Free, "Male Power and Female Victimization: Toward a
Theory of Interracial Rape" (1982) 88 _American Journal of Sociology_
311-327
> For annotation, see Chapter 6: FIRST NATIONS AND RACE.

Sylvia A. Law, "Equality: The Power and Limits of the Law -- Book
Review: Zillah R. Eisenstein, FEMINISM AND SEXUAL EQUALITY
(1984)" (1986) 95 _Yale Law Journal_ 1769-1788
> For annotation, see Chapter 16: BOOK REVIEWS.

Sylvia A. Law, "Homosexuality and the Social Meaning of Gender"
[1988] _Wisconsin Law Review_ 187-235
> For annotation, see Chapter 12: LESBIANISM AND SEXUAL
ORIENTATION.

Sylvia A. Law, "Rethinking Sex and the Constitution" (1984) 132
University of Pennsylvania Law Review 955-1039
> For annotation, see Chapter 2: CONSTITUTIONAL LAW.

Leigh Morgan Leonard, "A Missing Voice in Feminist Legal Theory:
The Heterosexual Presumption" (1990) 12 _Women's Rights Law Reporter_
39-49
> For annotation, see Chapter 12: LESBIANISM AND SEXUAL
ORIENTATION.

Christine A. Littleton, "Book Review: C. A. MacKinnon, FEMINISM
UNMODIFIED (1987)" (1989) 41 _Stanford Law Review_ 751-788

For annotation, see Chapter 16: **BOOK REVIEWS.**

Christine A. Littleton, "Reconstructing Sexual Equality" (1987) 75 *California Law Review* 1279-1337
 This is a feminist critique of equality as a social construct which can be deconstructed and re-constructed. The author contrasts two models of equality -- equality as acceptance and equality as empowerment. In the first model, difference, real or perceived, is not permitted to make a difference in lived-out equality of persons. The legal system's response to the civil rights movement was an instance of equality as acceptance, which presumes symmetricality and which requires of women either assimilation or androgyny. She claims that the special rights or empowerment model is asymmetrical. In conclusion, she suggests the ramifications of equality as acceptance must be researched and that empirical data is needed on what differences exist and how they are created and maintained.

Scott Lyall and Anita Szigeti, "Book Review: Catharine A. MacKinnon, TOWARD A FEMINIST THEORY OF THE STATE (1989)" (1990) 48 *University of Toronto Faculty of Law Review* 185-190
 For annotation, see Chapter 16: **BOOK REVIEWS.**

Catharine MacKinnon, "Feminism, Marxism, Method, and the State: An Agenda for Theory" (1982) 7 *Signs: Journal of Women in Culture and Society* 515
 The author claims that sexuality is to feminism what work is to Marxism, and that the expression of sexuality organizes society into two sexes, men and women, a division which underlies the totality of social relations. Sexuality is central to feminist theory because the male point of view is so pervasive that women are the walking embodiment of men's needs. Feminist method, she concludes, holds that the relationship between method and truth is the ultimate critique.

Catharine MacKinnon, "Feminism, Marxism, Method, and the State: Toward Feminist Jurisprudence" (1983) 8 *Signs: Journal of Women in Culture and Society* 635-658
 The author presents a feminist theory of power, namely, that power

is the male/female eroticization of male dominance. No woman escapes the meaning of being woman within a gendered social system because sex inequalities are universal and because the state is male and is constituted in the interest of men. She thinks the issue of rape central to feminism, because it raises the question of whether under male dominance, all intercourse is coercive. A feminist theory of the state, she concludes, requires new understandings, new normative experiences and a new relation between life and law.

Catharine MacKinnon, "Reply to Miller, Acker and Barry, Johnson, West, and Gardiner" (1984) 10 _Signs: Journal of Women in Culture and Society_ **184-188**
The author replies to these reviewers of her earlier articles (Catharine MacKinnon, "Feminism, Marxism, Method, and the State: An Agenda for Theory" (1982) 7 _Signs: Journal of Women in Culture and Society_ 515 and "Feminism, Marxism, Method, and the State: Toward Feminist Jurisprudence" (1983) 8 _Signs: Journal of Women in Culture and Society_ 635), dealing specifically with issues raised by each, including the role of Marxist theory in her feminist theory, the construction of sexuality, and the interrelationship between theory and the "world the way it is."

Catharine MacKinnon, "Sexuality, Pornography, and Method: 'Pleasure under Patriarchy'" (1989) 99 _Ethics_ **314-346**
Part of a Symposium on Feminism and Political Theory, this article describes women's experience of sex as male dominance, and looks at pornography, rape, sexual abuse, and other violence against women in this context. The author concludes that "to seek sexual equality without political transformation is to seek equality under conditions of inequality."

John A. Miller, "Comments on MacKinnon's 'Feminism, Marxism, Method, and the State'" (1984) 10 _Signs: Journal of Women in Culture and Society_ **168-175**
This is a response to Catharine MacKinnon's "Feminism, Marxism, Method, and the State: An Agenda for Theory" [(1982) 7 _Signs: Journal of Women in Culture and Society_ 515] and her "Feminism, Marxism, Method, and the State: Toward Feminist Jurisprudence" [(1983) 8 _Signs:_

Journal of Women in Culture and Society 635]. The author claims that
her work is extremely narrow and fails to acknowledge the extent to
which she relies on historical materialist analysis. This method of
analysis forms the basis for MacKinnon's two central arguments -- the
sexual objectification of women, and the social manufacturing of women's
consent to traditional sexuality -- because historical materialism brings
to light the inequality in each. He concludes that MacKinnon has failed
to resolve the methodological problem inherent in this approach and that
these problems remain to be faced by radical feminists.

Susan Moller Okin, "Feminism, the Individual and Contract Theory --
Book Review: Carole Pateman, THE SEXUAL CONTRACT (1988)."
(1990) 100 *Ethics* 658-669
     For annotation, see Chapter 16: **BOOK REVIEWS**.

Frances Olsen, "Statutory Rape: A Feminist Critique of Rights
Analysis" (1984) 63 *Texas Law Review* 387-432
     For annotation, see Chapter 3: **CRIMINAL LAW -- RAPE**.

G. Parker, "The Legal Regulation of Sexual Activity and the Protection
of Females" (1983) 21 *Osgoode Hall Law Journal* 187-244
     For annotation, see Chapter 10: **LEGAL HISTORY**.

Carole Pateman, "Sex and Power -- Book Review: Catherine A.
MacKinnon, FEMINISM UNMODIFIED: DISCOURSES ON LIFE
AND LAW (1987)" (1990) 100 *Ethics* 398-407
     For annotation, see Chapter 16: **BOOK REVIEWS**.

Helen Patey, "Book Review: Marcia Westkott, THE FEMINIST
LEGACY OF KAREN HORNEY (1986)" (1986/1988) 2 *Canadian
Journal of Women and the Law* 455-459
     For annotation, see Chapter 16: **BOOK REVIEWS**.

Andrew Ross, "Politics Without Pleasure -- Book Review: Catharine
A. MacKinnon, FEMINISM UNMODIFIED (1987)" (1988) 1 *Yale*

Journal of Law and the Humanities 193-201
    For annotation, see Chapter 16: BOOK REVIEWS.

Carol Smart, "Law's Power, the Sexed Body, and Feminist Discourse"
(1990) 17 _Journal of Law and Society_ 194-210
    For annotation, see Chapter 3: CRIMINAL LAW – RAPE.

J. C. Smith, "Book Review: Catharine A. MacKinnon, TOWARDS A
FEMINIST THEORY OF THE STATE (1989)" (1990) 69 _Canadian Bar
Review_ 597-601
    For annotation, see Chapter 16: BOOK REVIEWS.

Cass R. Sunstein, "Feminism and Legal Theory – Book Review:
Catharine MacKinnon, FEMINISM UNMODIFIED (1987)" (1988) 101
Harvard Law Review 826-848
    For annotation, see Chapter 16: BOOK REVIEWS.

Nancy W. Waring, "Coming to Terms With Pornography: Toward a
Feminist Perspective on Sex, Censorship, and Hysteria" (1986) 8 _Research
in Law, Deviance & Social Control_ 85-112
    The author argues that pornography is an agent of the larger
representational system of patriarchal heterosexuality, and that Holly-
wood film underlines the embeddedness of pornographic representations
in patriarchy. A psychoanalytic analysis of film suggests, she claims, that
it expresses men's residual unconscious anxiety about the female body.
She criticizes the Minneapolis Ordinance drafted by MacKinnon and
Dworkin for intending to police the borders around dominant pornography rather than discovering constructive ways to cross them. She
concludes that it is essential to investigate the workings of sexual fantasy,
pornography and the social construction of sexuality.

Lois A. West, "Comments on MacKinnon's 'Feminism, Marxism,
Method, and the State'" (1984) 10 _Signs: Journal of Women in Culture
and Society_ 183-184
    This is a response to Catharine MacKinnon's "Feminism, Marxism,
Method, and the State: An Agenda for Theory" [(1982) 7 _Signs: Journal_

of Women in Culture and Society 515] and her "Feminism, Marxism, Method, and the State: Toward Feminist Jurisprudence" [(1983) 8 *Signs: Journal of Women in Culture and Society* 635]. The author agrees with MacKinnon's submission that rape laws reflect male thinking and mystify consciousness as ideology, and with her analysis of sex/gender oppression as oppression of sexuality. She criticizes MacKinnon's project, however, for failing to provide a practical feminist strategy.

Christina B. Whitman, "Law and Sex — Book Review: Catharine MacKinnon, FEMINISM UNMODIFIED (1987)" (1988) 86 *Michigan Law Review* **1388-1403**
For annotation, see Chapter 16: BOOK REVIEWS.

Joan C. Williams, "Feminism and Post-Structuralism — Book Review: Zillah R. Eisenstein, THE FEMALE BODY AND THE LAW (1988)" (1990) 88 *Michigan Law Review* **1776-1791**
For annotation, see Chapter 16: BOOK REVIEWS.

Jennifer Wriggins, "Book Review: Catharine MacKinnon, FEMINISM UNMODIFIED (1987)" (1987) 10 *Harvard Women's Law Journal* **353-356**
For annotation, see Chapter 16: BOOK REVIEWS.

Alison Young, "Of The Essential in Criticism: Some Intersections in Writing, Political Protest and Law" (1990) 1:2 *Law and Critique* **201-218**
Part of a Symposium on Sex and Difference, this article examines sexual essentialism with reference to the academic study of women's law, the structure of the Greenham Common peace camp in Britain, and French feminism. According to the author, essentialism is "an elevation and celebration of Woman" which involves notions of woman's voice and of biological womanhood as axiomatically linked to social problems. She concludes that essentialist analysis should be conducted in legal theory, and that critique of law with respect to sex must be essentialist.

CHAPTER 6
JUDGES AND COURTS

Shirley S. Abrahamson, "The Woman Has Robes: Four Questions" (1984) 14 *Golden Gate University Law Review* 489-503
A member of the Wisconsin Supreme Court, the author faced four questions at her first news conference and continues to face them: Were you appointed because you are a woman? Do you think you were appointed as the token woman on the bench? Do you view yourself as representing women in the courts? Do you think women will make a difference in the administration of justice? She describes her career in the law and comments on what women as human beings can bring to the law, and the administration of justice. This is part of the Symposium Issue: National Association of Women Judges.

Doris Anderson, "The Canada Act 1982 -- Aftermath and Consequences for Women's Rights" [1983] *Canadian Community Law Journal* 128-135
For annotation, see Chapter 2: CONSTITUTIONAL LAW.

Doris Anderson, "The Supreme Court and Women's Rights" (1980) 1 *Supreme Court Law Review* 457-460
For annotation, see Chapter 2: CONSTITUTIONAL LAW.

Micheline Baril, Marie-Marthe Cousineau, and Sylvie Gravel, "Quand Les Femmes Sont Victimes...Quand Les Hommes Appliquent La Loi" (1983) 16:2 *Criminologie* 89-100
For annotation, see Chapter 3: CRIMINAL LAW -- BATTERING.

R. Beaudry, "Survol Bibliographique de la Littérature Criminologique Féminine" (1983) 16:2 *Criminologie* 121-125
For annotation, see Chapter 3: CRIMINAL LAW -- GENERAL.

Rose Elizabeth Bird, "Remarks by Rose Elizabeth Bird, Chief Justice of the Supreme Court of California, to the National Association of Women Judges, San Francisco, California, October 8, 1983" (1984) 14 *Golden Gate University Law Review* 481 - 487

The author traces the history of women on the bench and in the practice of law in California, and comments on the fate of women in the labour force generally.

Christine Boyle, "Sexual Assault and the Feminist Judge" (1985) 1 *Canadian Journal of Women and the Law* 93-107

For annotation, see Chapter 3: **CRIMINAL LAW -- RAPE.**

Kristin Bumiller, "Fallen Angels: the Representation of Violence Against Women in Legal Culture" (1990) 18 *International Journal of the Sociology of Law* 125-141

For annotation, see Chapter 3: **CRIMINAL LAW -- RAPE.**

Patricia A. Cain, "Good and Bad Bias: A Comment on Feminist Theory and Judging" (1988) 61 *Southern California Law Review* 1945-1955

This is a response to Resnik's proposal for a dialogue on the aspirations we hold for judges (Judith Resnik, "On The Bias: Feminist Reconsiderations of the Aspirations for our Judges" (1988) 61 *Southern California Law Review* 1877). The author welcomes this dialogue and contributes from her own experiences as a feminist, lawyer and educator. Judicial bias, based upon a judge's personal experience, can be good or bad bias, and she comments on the difficulty of making such distinctions and maintaining the good bias in judging. We should value judges with varied life experiences, who seek to broaden their perspectives and who "transcend self" to "really listen" to the story being told. Through "stories", the author personalizes several court cases, placing the law in human context. Storytelling means advocating the client's story, and helps remove the separation between the bench and litigant.

Anita Cava, "Taking Judicial Notice of Sexual Stereotyping" (1990) 43 *Arkansas Law Review* 27-56

This article examines the issue of employment decisions based on sexual stereotyping. The author identifies three justifications for sexual stereotyping in the case law, concludes that the courts have not adequately recognised the complexity of this issue, and calls for legislation which is informed by a fuller understanding of stereotyping.

Dorothy E. Chunn and Robert J. Menzies, "Gender Madness and Crime: The Reproduction of Patriarchal and Class Relations in a Psychiatric Court Clinic" (1990) 1:2 _Journal of Human Justice_ 33-54
For annotation, see Chapter 3: CRIMINAL LAW – GENERAL.

B.J. Cling, "Rape Trauma Syndrome: Medical Evidence of Non-Consent" (1988) 10 _Women's Rights Law Reporter_ 243-259
For annotation, see Chapter 3: CRIMINAL LAW – RAPE.

Beverly B. Cook, "Women Judges: A Preface to Their History" (1984) 14 _Golden Gate University Law Review_ 573-610
Part of the Symposium Issue: National Association of Women Judges, this article claims that three conditions must be met for the number of women on the bench to move beyond tokenism. The author presents information on the numbers of women on the bench throughout the United States, and concludes that any female participation on the bench beyond tokenism will be resisted if it "means a real rather than a symbolic shift in the balance of power between the sexes."

Mary C. Dunlap, "The 'F' Word: Mainstreaming and Marginalizing Feminism" (1989/90) 4 _Berkeley Women's Law Journal_ 251-258
Feminism is still perceived as a "dirty" word and calling oneself a feminist continues to be a brave act. But feminism is a good word, and in discussing the importance of language, the author identifies real "F" words for the Twentieth National Conference on Women and the Law. Included in her list are the "five-four" Supreme Court decisions which have put women further away from constitutional equality and have "frittered" away rights of choice especially for poor women, sick women and women of colour. The "fanatical right", "fascists" and "fundamentalists" draw her attention as do legal "fictions" like the "reasonable man" and "Equal Justice Under the Law." The greatest enemy of all the "F" words, she concludes, is "fear," and to overcome fear is to have it all.

David Fraser, "And Now for Something Completely Different: Judging Interpretation and the Canadian Charter of Rights and Freedoms" (1987) 7 *Windsor Yearbook of Access to Justice* 66-78
   For annotation, see Chapter 2: CONSTITUTIONAL LAW.

Gender Bias Study Committee of the Court System in Massachusetts, "Gender Bias Study of the Court System in Massachusetts" (1990) 24 *New England Law Review* 745-856
   This is a reprint of the official report of the Gender Bias Study Committee appointed by the Massachusetts Supreme Court to determine the extent and nature of gender bias in the Massachusetts judiciary and to make recommendations to promote equal treatment of men and women. The Committee found bias against women in various aspects of family law, including alimony and child care. It also found gender bias in the treatment of crimes of violence against women, in the juvenile justice system, in the award of civil damages, in courthouse interactions involving women, and among court personnel. The report includes recommendations for the elimination of gender bias with respect to each topic canvassed.

Ruth Bader Ginsburg, "Remarks on Women Becoming Part of the Constitution" (1988) 2 *Law and Inequality* 19-25
   For annotation, see Chapter 2: CONSTITUTIONAL LAW.

Jill Laurie Goodman, "Sexual Harassment: Some Observations on the Distance Travelled and the Distance Yet to Go" (1981) 10 *Capital University Law Review* 445-468
   For annotation, see Chapter 8: LABOUR AND EMPLOYMENT -- SEXUAL HARASSMENT.

Gerard S. Gryski, Eleanor C. Main, and William J. Dixon, "Models of State High Court Decision Making in Sex Discrimination Cases" (1986) 48 *Journal of Politics* 143-155
   The authors examine the practices of the high courts in states to identify prediction indicators of a court's vote on sex discrimination appeals. Their final model "predicts that a state high court is most likely to find sex discrimination in a non-criminal case brought by a female

before an appointed court with at least one female member and a high reputation."

Winifred L. Hepperle, "Book Review: Betty Medsger, FRAMED: THE NEW RIGHT ATTACK ON CHIEF JUSTICE ROSE BIRD AND THE COURTS (1983)" (1984) 14 _Golden Gate University Law Review_ 505-517
    For annotation, see Chapter 16: BOOK REVIEWS.

S. V. N. Hodgson and Burt Pryor, "Sex Discrimination in the Courtroom: Attorney Gender and Credibility" (1985) 71:2 _Women Lawyers Journal_ 7-8
    This is a report of a study of university undergraduate students' attitudes to female attorneys. It explores the relationship of gender and credibility, verdict differences and gender and retaining a lawyer. Female lawyers were perceived as less credible, on the basis of trustworthiness and competence. The authors suggest that female attorneys develop communications strategies to build credibility.

Pamela Jenkins and Barbara Davidson, "Battered Women in the Criminal Justice System: An Analysis of Gender Stereotypes" (1990) 8 _Behavioral Sciences and the Law_ 161-170
    For annotation, see Chapter 3: CRIMINAL LAW -- BATTERING.

Gladys Kessler, "Foreword" (1984) 14 _Golden Gate University Law Review_ 473-480
    This is the foreword to the Symposium Issue: National Association of Women Judges. The author, 1982-83 President of the National Association of Women Judges, surveys the history of the Association since its inception in October 1979, describes its influence, its major projects, and future directions. She states that its concrete goals are the "elimination of gender bias in the courtroom and appointment of more women to the bench." She says it also has the purpose of conviviality for individuals who work under "stress, isolation and loneliness."

Jocelyne Legare, "La Condition Juridique Des Femmes ou L'Histo-

rique d'une 'Affaire de Famille'" (1983) 16:2 *Criminologie* 7-26
    For annotation, see Chapter 4: FAMILY LAW – GENERAL.

    Jennifer A. Levine, "Preventing Gender Bias in the Courts: A Question of Judicial Ethics" (1988) 1 *Georgetown Journal of Legal Ethics* 775-794
    The author develops a continuum of the types of gender bias and offers examples from the most blatant forms to the most subtle such as body language. Even subtle expressions of gender bias from the bench and male opponents are, she argues, extremely harmful to the female attorney, her client and the justice system. She gives statistical evidence of the breadth of the problem as well as a cause and effect analysis. She concludes with recommendations for the judiciary, changes in the Code of Judicial Conduct, the use of the Disciplinary Act in judicial discipline and the role of the bar and law schools in the fight against gender bias.

    Nancy S. Marder, "Gender Dynamics and Jury Deliberations" (1987) 96 *Yale Law Journal* 593-611
    The author examines social science studies which found lower participation by women in mock juries, and discusses the importance of full participation by women for the jury's fact-finding, interpretive, and educational roles. The gender differences she discusses include the fact that women see, hear and remember different things, and that women in a jury setting are more likely to try to accommodate different points of view. Women need to speak more and men need to listen more, if jury deliberations are to be effective in considering community values and in rendering accurate verdicts. She offers recommendations to reduce the detrimental effects of gender-related behaviour and to increase participation by women members.

    Michael Marmo, "Arbitrating Sex Harassment Cases" (1980) *Arbitration Journal* 35-40
    For annotation, see Chapter 8: LABOUR AND EMPLOYMENT – SEXUAL HARASSMENT.

    Margaret A. Miller, "Justice Sandra Day O'Connor: Token or Triumph from a Feminist Perspective" (1985) 15 *Golden Gate University Law Review* 493-524

Though feminists expected a conservative approach, they optimistically applauded Justice O'Connor's appointment as the first woman to the U.S. Supreme Court. Upon examining her voting record on issues such as affirmative action, the rights of illegitimate children, gender based discrimination and abortion, the author concludes that Justice O'Connor's record, though initially promising, was "abysmal" on abortion. In particular, she failed to realize that basic concepts of reproductive autonomy are a means of attaining equal participation in society. The author concludes that the appointment has been merely a symbolic triumph for women.

Trudy Mills, "The Use of Equal Employment Laws" (1981) 24 _Pacific Sociological Review_ 196-211
The author analyzes the use of Title VII of the U.S. Civil Rights Act 1964 which makes discrimination on the basis of sex illegal. She provides statistical analysis of sex discrimination suits filed by women in the District of Columbia between 1964 and 1975. She reports that social factors influence the decision to go to court and the process itself, and that the level of the public's awareness of the law is linked to its use.

Roma Mitchell, "Consideration of Gender in Changes in the Law" (1985) 1 _Australian Feminist Studies_ 41-53
Admitted to the bar in 1934 and now a retired judge of the Supreme Court of South Australia, the author surveys the issues relating to women and the law when she first practised and those which are paramount in the mid-1980's. She discusses the dearth of women on the bench, in senior positions in the profession and the academy, affirmative action, attitudes to women in the courtroom as witnesses and the need for education as well as equality under legislation to effect full equality within the law.

New York Task Force on Women in the Courts, "Report of the New York Task Force on Women in the Courts" (1987-88) 15 _Fordham Urban Law Journal_ 11-198
This widely ranging and very detailed report contains the Task Force's findings on the treatment of women in the New York court system, whether as litigants, attorneys, or employees, and concludes that gender bias is pervasive and has grave consequences. The findings are

based on reviews of legal and social science literature, extensive surveys, and public hearings. The report offers specific recommendations for change and concludes that change will only occur if (1) the bar and bench are prepared to undertake serious self-examination, and (2) the public demands fairness and equality in the justice system.

Lynne Pearlman and T. Brettel Dawson, "The Shaping of Equality" (1989) 10:5 _Broadside_ 8-9
    For annotation, see Chapter 2: **CONSTITUTIONAL LAW.**

Denise Reaume, "Women and the Law: Equality Claims Before Courts and Tribunals" (1980) 5 _Queen's Law Journal_ 3-45
    This pre-Charter article discusses and compares the attitudes and approaches taken by the courts and administrative tribunals to claims asserted with respect to women's rights under various Human Rights statutes as well as the Canadian Bill of Rights. Areas canvassed include women and sexuality, marriage, work, and athletics. The author reports that tribunals have consistently been more sympathetic than the courts to women's claims. To make the climate in the courts more agreeable for women, the author suggests ridding the legal profession of legal positivism, and changing the attitudes of the judiciary through exposure to women's issues, beginning with the legal education process.

Judith Resnik, "Feminism and the Language of Judging" (1990) 22 _Arizona State Law Journal_ 31-38
    For annotation, see Chapter 5: **FEMINIST THEORY -- GENERAL.**

Judith Resnik, "On The Bias: Feminist Reconsiderations of the Aspirations for our Judges" (1988) 61 _Southern California Law Review_ 1877-1943
    The author creates a dialogue between the law of judges and feminist theory, and reports that while there is an accepted view of what qualifies a person to be a judge, there is no single view in feminist theory because feminist theory on judging is in the midst of being created. Two sections of the article are devoted to explaining the legal requirements of judging, followed by examples of feminist theory and practice using

the works of Carol Gilligan, Robin West, Sara Ruddick and Rosemary Ruether. There are commentaries by women on the bench about their experiences of judging, and an exploration of feminism as a proponent of alternate dispute resolution mechanisms. She concludes that impartiality and disengagement by judges can never be achieved, and that feminism rejects the choice between "being a blank slate and imposing oneself on another, between having no interest and being corrupted by self-interest."

Janet Rifkin, "Mediation From a Feminist Perspective: Promise and Problems" (1984) 2 _Law and Inequality_ 21-31
    For annotation, see Chapter 5: FEMINIST THEORY -- GENERAL.

Deborah Ruble Round, "Gender Bias in the Judicial System" (1988) 61 _Southern California Law Review_ 2193-2220
    The often subtle nature of gender bias can make it difficult to describe and detect, yet its presence in the judicial system has serious ramifications for the client and the legal system. The author reports the findings and recommendations of two task forces, and gives examples of the manifestation of gender bias in the courtroom. She provides immediate responses for a woman faced with such discrimination, but for the long term, she calls for mandatory education in law school, mandatory continuing education for practitioners, and mandatory education for the judiciary.

Marguerite Russell, "A Feminist Analysis of the Criminal Trial Process" (1989-1990) 3 _Canadian Journal of Women and the Law_ 552-562
    For annotation, see Chapter 3: CRIMINAL LAW -- GENERAL.

Lynn Hecht Schafran, "Gender and Justice: Florida and the Nation" (1990) 42 _Florida Law Review_ 181-208
    Part of a Symposium on Women and the Law: Goals for the 1990s, this article identifies instances of gender bias in the courts, most specifically in the area of family law. The author is the director of the National Judicial Education Program to Promote Equality for Women and Men in the Courts. Women, she reports, generally lack funds to

access courts, face disastrous financial results post-divorce due to denial of meaningful alimony to long-time homemakers, must collect child support within a frequently unresponsive or hostile system, and are subject to a higher moral scrutiny in custody battles. She concludes with recommendations to educate the judiciary about the realities of women's gendered lives; but more importantly, to reconstruct legal education to ensure graduates are knowledgable about gender bias and sensitive to women's issues. She argues that women's issues are, in fact, human rights issues, and that such knowledge is essential to informed advocacy.

Lynn Hecht Schafran, "Women in the Courts Today: How Much Has Changed" (1988) 2 *Law and Inequality* 27-34
For annotation, see Chapter 2: CONSTITUTIONAL LAW.

Vicki Schultz, "Telling Stories About Women and Work: Judicial Interpretations of Sex Segregation in the Workplace in Title VII Cases Raising the Lack of Interest Argument" (1990) 103 *Harvard Law Review* 1750-1843
Sex segregation in the workplace contributes to keeping women in low paying, low status jobs. The author, who believes that what judges say and do matters, writes to show that, despite Title VII, women continue to suffer discrimination in the workplace, and that their segregation is due to "structural features of the work world" rather than to "pre-work socialization." She wrestles with the employers' "lack of interest" argument, and urges that courts broaden their interpretations and recognize the impact that they can have on the empowerment of women to claim non-traditional jobs.

Faith A. Seidenberg, "The Bifurcated Woman: Problems of Women Lawyers in the Courtroom" (1985-86) 1 *Canadian Journal of Women and the Law* 219-225
This article discusses the way men treat women in the courtroom and the strategies women lawyers have devised to respond to male attitudes. The author thinks that the lack of role models and of access to "success" jobs are subtle reminders of women's inferior status. She analyzes clothing -- the symbolism of the skirt, tie and heeled shoes -- and considers the ambivalence in dress, voice, manner of speech and body language of women in adversarial law, who are less able than

women in other professions to show their "care" voice.

Elizabeth Sheehy, "Canadian Judges and the Law of Rape: Should the Charter Insulate Bias?" (1989) 21 _Ottawa Law Review_ 151-197
    For annotation, see Chapter 3: CRIMINAL LAW -- RAPE.

N. Colleen Sheppard, "Equality, Ideology and Oppression: Women and the Canadian Charter of Rights and Freedoms" (1986) 10 _Dalhousie Law Journal_ 195-223
    For annotation, see Chapter 2: CONSTITUTIONAL LAW.

N. Colleen Sheppard, "Recognition of the Disadvantaging of Women" (1990) 35 _McGill Law Journal_ 207-234
    For annotation, see Chapter 2: CONSTITUTIONAL LAW.

Elliot E. Slotnick, "Gender, Affirmative Action, and Recruitment to the Federal Bench" (1984) 14 _Golden Gate University Law Review_ 519-571
    This article is part of the Symposium Issue: National Association of Women Judges. The author examines the records of the Carter and Reagan administrations in appointing women and non-white males to the federal bench. Using the data provided by the nominees to the Senate Judiciary Committee, he analyzes various aspects of their qualifications, and reports that Carter's affirmative action program was successful in making non-traditional appointments, and has not resulted in a reduction in quality of the bench.

Keith Soothill, Sylvia Walby and Paul Bagguley, "Judges, the Media, and Rape" (1990) 17 _Journal of Law and Society_ 211-233
    For annotation, see Chapter 3: CRIMINAL LAW -- RAPE.

Sue Stapely, "Judicial Attitudes Towards Domestic Violence" (1980) 10 _Kingston Law Review_ 156-182
    For annotation, see Chapter 3: CRIMINAL LAW -- BATTERING.

Ronald Stidman, Robert A. Carp, and C. K. Rowland, "Women's Rights Before the Federal District Courts, 1971-1977" (1983) 11 *American Politics Quarterly* 205-218

This article provides an analysis of opinions of federal district judges in women's rights and racial minority discrimination cases published between 1971 and 1977. The authors report that "the petitioner in women's rights cases was only slightly more likely to be victorious than litigants from other disadvantaged ground," that there were "no significant differences between the northern and southern judges deciding women's rights cases," and that "the judge's political party identification" was the most important variable affecting outcome.

Ricki Lewis Tannen, "Setting the Agenda for the 1990s: The Historical Foundations of Gender Bias in the Law: A Context for Reconstruction" (1990) 42 *Florida Law Review* 163-180

Part of a Symposium on Women and the Law, this article reports continued and significant influence on the legal system of a cultural ideology of male dominance and female submission, that is both publicly condemned and tacitly accepted, rationalized and promoted through gender-biased laws and discriminatory enforcement of gender-neutral laws. The author, a member of Florida's Supreme Court Gender Bias Study Commission, examines historical and anthropological writings to explain the pervasive nature of gender bias, and concludes that this exposé of the ancient premise of male dominance and female submission provides a context for reconstruction of the legal system with an egalitarian infrastructure.

Utah Task Force on Gender and Justice, "Report to the Utah Judicial Council March 1990" (1990) 16 *Journal of Contemporary Law* 135-299

This article is a reprinting of the Report by the Utah Task Force on Gender and Justice, which examined both procedural and substantive aspects of the law, to ascertain the nature, extent, and consequences of gender bias. The report defines gender bias, and then reports finding such bias in many aspects of law -- namely, domestic relations, domestic violence, child custody, adult sexual assault, judicial selection, court employment, and courtroom interaction. The report concludes with recommendations for change in each of these areas of bias.

Norma Juliet Wilker, "On the Judicial Agenda for the 80s: Equal Treatment for Men and Women in the Courts" (1980) 64 _Judicature_ 202-209
  The article's starting point is the research finding that sexism exists in the judiciary and is reflected in contemporary judicial decisions. The author describes the effect of this sexism in criminal law, family law, and the treatment of female victims. She concludes with a discussion of why these sexist attitudes exist and what can be done to change them.

Bertha Wilson, "Will Women Judges Make a Difference?" (March, 1990) _Canadian Forum_ 7-10
  The author, a justice of the Supreme Court of Canada, claims that the duality of human kind must be represented in the judiciary, and that women can offer differing perspectives, perhaps "infusing the law with an understanding of what it means to be fully human." She also claims that in some areas of the law, a distinctly male perspective is apparent. She cites as an example criminal law, some aspects of which are based upon "presuppositions about the nature of women and women's sexuality that in this day and age are little short of ludicrous."

Judith T. Younger, "The Supreme Court and the American Family -- Book Review: Eva R. Rubin, THE SUPREME COURT AND THE AMERICAN FAMILY (1986)" (1987) 4 _Constitutional Commentary_ 173-176
  For annotation, see Chapter 16: BOOK REVIEWS.

CHAPTER 7
FIRST NATIONS AND RACE

Penny Andrews, "The Legal Underpinnings of Gender Oppression in Apartheid South Africa" (1986) 3 *Australian Journal of Law and Society* 92-107

This article outlines the law and practices of apartheid South Africa, which are designed to keep black women "in their place." The author limits herself to the plight of black women because the privileges which white women enjoy in the apartheid system "renders the paternalism and sexism they are exposed to secondary." Numerous issues are covered including the codified subordination of women within the family, travel and employment restrictions, poverty, forced contraception and property and inheritance rights. The economic and political purposes behind relegating women to live in remote "homelands" or "bantustans" are revealed as well as the tenuous position of women whose right to live in a particular area is acquired through marriage.

Regina Austin, "Sapphire Bound!" [1989] *Wisconsin Law Review* 539-578

The author argues that Black female law professors must write about their problems within the legal academe, in order to challenge, and perhaps solve, those problems. She criticizes academics who conform to a purportedly racially- and gender-neutral style, and argues that both writing style and choice of topic must be confronted as biased. She concludes by urging Black female legal educators to become professional "Sapphires," whom she describes as "the stereotypical Black bitch."

Taunya Lovell Banks, "Gender Bias in the Classroom" (1990) 14 *Southern Illinois University Law Journal* 527-543

Part of a Symposium on Gender Bias in Legal Education, this article reports the results of the author's study of women law students' perceptions of the law school classroom. The study consisted of in-class surveys administered to nearly two thousand respondents at fourteen American law schools during 1987-1988 and 1988-1989; sixty per cent of the respondents were men and forty per cent were women. The author reports that more women than men perceive the law school classroom as "alienating and hostile," and her study identified lack of en- couragement -- and even actual discouragement -- by professors, hostility from male students and the law school environment in general as factors leading to this perception. She believes that students of colour share with women some of these perceptions, and she is undertaking a study of the perceptions of Hispanic-American and African-American law students. The author concludes that "while the composition of the law school classroom has changed dramatically over the last twenty years, the law school classroom is still structured to meet the needs of white up- per-middle class males." The article concludes with a response by Professors Jill E. Adams, and Leonard Lorors, as well as the author's reply to these.

Anne F. Bayefsky, "The Human Rights Committee and the Case of Sandra Lovelace" (1982) 20 *Canadian Yearbook of International Law* 244-265
      The United Nations Human Rights Committee found Canada to be in violation of its obligations, under the International Covenant on Civil and Political Rights, in the case of Sandra Lovelace, a Maliseet Indian who lost her status upon marriage to a non-Indian, according to section 12(1)(b) of the Indian Act. This note looks at the decision of the Committee, the history of this section of the Act, and Canada's response to the decision.

Julie Blackman, "Emerging Images of Severely Battered Women and the Criminal Justice System" (1990) 8 *Behavioral Sciences and the Law* 121-130
      This article discusses the psychological consequences of extraor- dinary family violence and the responses of the criminal justice system in the cases of Hedda Nussbaum, Frances McMillian and Damian Pizarro. The author argues that a woman's social class and race mediate the response of the criminal justice system. The article concludes with a discussion of society's role in idealizing the family and in silencing, ignoring, acknowledging and/or solving the problems of severely battered women.

Eileen Boris, "The Power of Motherhood: Black and White Activist Women Redefine the 'Political'" (1989) 2 _Yale Journal of Law and Feminism_ 25-49

This article explores the use of motherhood as image, experience and rhetoric in the re-definition of issues affecting women. The author contrasts the use of the concept by black and white activist women in social and political reform. Much of the article chronicles the activities and concerns of the African-American women's club movement. She observes that the "motherhood" image promoted by late nineteenth and early twentieth century feminists was based on a white, middle class model. Black women activists however remained close to the concerns of working women and strove to maintain their differences while they claimed the right to equality.

Kristin Bumiller, "Rape as a Legal Symbol: An Essay on Sexual Violence and Racism" (1987) 42 _University of Miami Law Review_ 75-91

For annotation, see Chapter 3: CRIMINAL LAW -- RAPE.

Margaret A. Burnham, "An Impossible Marriage: Slave Law and Family Law" (1987) 5 _Law and Inequality_ 187-225

This article examines the relationship between the development of family law and slave law in the 19th century. It also provides a history of slave family life, and reviews case law which evolved to regulate slave family relationships.

Kathryn A. Carver, "The 1985 Minnesota Indian Family Preservation Act: Claiming a Cultural Identity" (1986) 4 _Law and Inequality_ 327-354

This article examines the issues surrounding the adoption and foster care of First Nations children. The author reports that the 1984 Minnesota Indian Child Welfare Act was an attempt to remedy the shortcomings of the 1978 federal Indian Child Welfare Act. She attributes its defeat to legislators' lack of knowledge of the issue and to their concerns that it would transfer too much power to the Indian courts. The 1985 Minnesota Indian Family Preservation Act was successfully enacted. She attributes its success to several factors, including education about the effects on First Nations children of placement in non-First Nations environments, and emphasis on early tribal involvement in placement decisions. She concludes that this Act goes some way toward addressing the problems associated with this issue.

Ruth Colker, "Anti-Subordination Above All: Sex, Race, and Equal Protection" (1986) 61 *New York University Law Review* 1003-1063

The author argues that the equal protection doctrine needs to do better in understanding visions of equality held by blacks and women and that it requires a framework that effectively deals with affirmative action. She analyzes two principles which she claims underlie discrimination jurisprudence. The first -- the "anti-differentiation" perspective -- contends that it is inappropriate for an individual to be treated differently because of race or sex; the second -- the "anti-subordination" perspective -- thinks it inappropriate for certain groups to have subordinated status because of their lack of power within society as a whole. She claims that courts should analyze equal protection cases using the anti-subordination perspective because it rejects even facially neutral policies that perpetuate subordination of groups and accepts differentiating policies which redress subordination. She asserts that an historical review of equal protection jurisprudence and an examination of case law reveals the anti-subordination more faithful to American constitutional tradition. She concludes by suggesting a framework for its incorporation into equal protection analysis.

Ruth Colker, "The Anti-Subordination Principle: Applications" (1985) 3 *Wisconsin Women's Law Journal* 59-80

Part of the 1986 Feminism and Legal Theory Conference, this article is the second in a two-part series by the author (see: Colker, "Anti-Subordination Above All: Sex, Race, and Equal Protection" (1986) 61 *New York University Law Review* 1003). The author argues that legal recognition of the subordination of women and blacks was the impetus for modern equal protection doctrine. She makes a distinction between anti-differentiation (i.e. seeking a colour- and sex-blind society) and anti-subordination (i.e. sex- or colour-differentiations not perceived negatively unless productive of subordination). She urges an anti-subordination framework for interpretation of equal protection principles, and discusses potential legal arguments within this framework. She concludes, however, with the exhortation that, while gender-based or race-based norms are prevalent, it is important to remain cognizant that such norms do not necessarily exist without coercion.

Cherise Cox, "Anything Less is Not Feminism: Racial Difference and
the W.M.W.M." (1990) 1:2 _Law and Critique_ 237-248
Part of a Symposium on Sex and Difference, this article criticizes
feminist theory for "feminist ethnocentricity," and identifies rape, contraception and family law as areas in which the W.M.W.M. (White
Middle-class Women's Movement) has failed to question race-biased and
class-biased assumptions. The author argues that the W.M.W.M.'s focus
on sexuality as the primary source of oppression, while not irrelevant to
women of colour, does not satisfy the challenge for feminism, which is
to develop an understanding of female subjugation which is dependent
upon neither Western ethnocentricity nor the erasure of cultural
specificity. She concludes that there is a multiplicity of struggles and that
all must define the content of the struggles and the concept of sexuality.

Kimberle Crenshaw, "Demarginalizing the Intersection of Race and
Sex: A Black Feminist Critique of Antidiscrimination Doctrine, Feminist
Theory and Antiracist Politics" [1989] _University of Chicago Legal Forum_
139-167
The author argues that feminist theory and antiracist politics treat
race and gender as mutually exclusive categories of experience and
thereby marginalize Black Women. This is perpetuated by a "single-axis"
framework dominant in anti-discrimination law. The intersectional
experience is "greater than the sum of racism and sexism" and any
analysis which purports to address the subordination of Black Women
must, she claims, address this fact. In law and theory, there is an
unwillingness to recognize discrimination and sexual violence aimed
specifically against those who are Women AND Black. She argues that
the focus of feminist literature on white female sexuality ignores the
Black agenda such as addressing rape as a "weapon of racial terror"
within a legal system riddled with racist and sexist assumptions.
Feminism, she concludes, must also analyze race and facilitate the
inclusion of marginalized groups.

Richard L. Devlin, "Towards An/Other Legal Education: Some
Critical and Tentative Proposals to Confront the Racism of Modern
Legal Education" (1989) 38 _University of New Brunswick Law Journal_
89-120
The author employs a Critical Legal Studies analysis of the racism
in contemporary legal education. Liberalism is seen as the culprit as it

doesn't deal with the contradiction of freedoms founded upon domination. Addressed are such questions as law school admissions, and how
and to whom law is taught.

Nitya Duclos, "Lessons of Difference: Feminist Theory on Cultural
Diversity" (1990) 38 _Buffalo Law Review_ 325-381
    Using the cultural dilemmas facing Canada as a demonstration, this
article applies feminist difference theory to questions of cultural pluralism. The author argues that feminist theory is applicable in contexts
other than gender, that feminism must value diversity, and that it contains a version of a pluralist society which she describes as a "working
and fluid utopia."

Mary Jo Eyster, "Integrating Non-Sexist/Racial Perspectives Into
Traditional Court and Clinical Settings" (1990) 14 _Southern Illinois
University Law Journal_ 471-486
    Part of a Symposium on Gender Bias in Legal Education, this
article recounts strategies developed by the author to integrate discussion
of sexism in traditional law courses taught in a civil litigation clinic of
which she is director. The article includes a response by Professor
Howard Eisenberg.

Karlene Faith, "Justice Where Art Thou? and Do We Care?: Feminist
Perspectives on Justice for Women in Canada" (1989) 1:1 _Journal of
Human Justice_ 77-98
    This article discusses contemporary feminist perspectives on gender
and justice, with attention to selected examples of women's engagements
with Canadian courts, focusing on sexual assault, child custody, the
female offender, pornography, and the position of First Nations women.
The co-effects on women of capitalism and vestigial patriarchal hegemony, the privacy doctrine as exercised by the courts, and the question
of sex-specific versus gender-neutral legislation are emphasized. The
author considers the usefulness of Gilligan's (Carol Gilligan, IN A
DIFFERENT VOICE (1982)) theory of an ethic of justice, countering
an ethic of care in understanding the quality of women's involvements
with the legal system.

Ken Feagins, "Affirmative Action or the Same Sin?" (1990) 67 _Denver University Law Review_ 421-451

This article reviews decisions of the United States Supreme Court which scrutinize affirmative action plans established under the equal protection clause of the fourteenth amendment and Title VII of the Civil Rights Act of 1964. The author argues that the different analyses under both the equal protection clause and Title VII are unsatisfactory. Although affirmative action programmes are already subject to a presumption of unconstitutionality, he claims that courts should reject such steps towards racial equality altogether, because such programmes revive the "equal but separate" doctrine.

J. Francis, "Disabled Native Women" (1985) 3 _Just Cause_ 14-16

The author, a disabled Native woman, describes health services to Native communities across Canada as a "disgrace." Although the disabled Native person faces similar problems to other disabled Canadians, they are compounded by greater degrees of poverty, discrimination and cultural isolation. Services for the disabled are often not available, and problems of access to buildings on reserves hamper participation in community life. She portrays native women as strong--willed, hard working and independent, and as the backbone of the family unit. She concludes that although disabled Native women are not expected to fulfil the traditional role, they continue to be an integral part of the community.

Jewelle Gomez, "Repeat After Me: We Are Different. We Are the Same" (1986) 14 _New York University Review of Law and Social Change_ 935-941

For annotation, see Chapter 12: **LESBIANISM AND SEXUAL ORIENTATION.**

Katrina Grider, "Hair Salons and Racial Stereotypes: The Impermissible Use of Racially Discriminatory Pricing Schemes" (1989) 12 _Harvard Women's Law Journal_ 75-113

Some hair salons charge blacks more on the ground that their hair is "harder to style." The author argues that this perception comes from the view that white is the normal standard for beauty and black is abnormal. She urges victims of this discrimination to go to court to enforce their rights. To that end, she discusses the application of American laws to the situation.

John Gruhl, "Women as Criminal Defendants: A Test for Paternalism" (1984) 37 *Western Political Quarterly* 456-467
The author examines three theories for more lenient treatment of female felony defendants -- judicial paternalism, failure to control for charge and prior record, and failure to control for race. His research was based on Los Angeles County Superior Court records of felony cases from 1977-80. The results indicate support for the paternalism theory particularly in the pre and post trial period, but not in the decision to convict. The use of race as a variable indicates greater leniency towards black women, but virtually no differences in the prosecution rates of white women and men. He suggests that this may be the result not of paternalism, but of a response to the current social situation where more black women than white are heads of dependent households.

John Hagen, "Toward a Structural Theory of Crime, Race, and Gender: The Canadian Case" (1985) 31 *Crime and Delinquency* 129-146
On the assumption that race and gender are correlates of crime, the author provides statistics to prove three hypotheses: that the difference between racial minority and majority group crime rates are greater for women that men; that the difference between male and female crime rates are greater within racial minorities than majorities; and that the difference between racial minority and majority group crime rates increase faster for women than men with age.

Angela P. Harris, "Race and Essentialism in Feminist Legal Theory" (1990) 42 *Stanford Law Review* 581-615
The author claims that feminist legal theory needs to incorporate "multiple consciousness" and to get away from "gender essentialism" which she sees at the core of mainstream American theory. She criticizes the work of Catharine MacKinnon and Robin West and recommends storytelling as the way to begin the process towards an understanding of multiple consciousness.

Alison Hatch and Karlene Faith, "The Female Offender in Canada: A Statistical Profile" (1989-1990) 3 *Canadian Journal of Women and the*

Law 432-455

The authors review statistics from research surveys and official sources and provide a quantitative analysis of the female offender in Canada. They report that women who commit crimes are not generally within criminal stereotypes, but instead are influenced by gender-distinctive cultural, socialization, and economic factors. Female offenders are generally from disadvantaged or abusive backgrounds, and incarceration is not, the author suggests, an effective response to crimes which result from such circumstances. The authors conclude that community resources are necessary to effect positive change in these women's circumstances, and that such initiatives will be especially effective for First Nations women.

Jacinth Herbert, "'Otherness' and the Black Woman" (1989) 3 _Canadian Journal of Women and the Law_ 269-278

The author argues that a sound feminist analysis must address the relationship between race, class and gender, and that race has not been a priority in feminist theory which has tended to deny the existence of non-mainstream women. By placing Black women in a subordinate position, feminism prevents solidarity with minority women. Women of colour must not be subordinate to either Black men or white women.

Chris Hutton, Frank Pommersheim, and Steve Feimer, "'I Fought the Law and the Law Won': A Report on Women and Disparate Sentencing in South Dakota" (1989) 15 _New England Journal on Criminal and Civil Confinement_ 177-202

Part of a Women's Symposium, this article reports the findings of a study of the impact of race and sex on sentencing in South Dakota. The authors examined the files of women incarcerated in South Dakota Penitentiary between 1980 and 1988 to determine whether there was substantially significant disparity in the sentences imposed on white and First Nations women. After noting that First Nations people constitute a much higher percentage of the prison population than they do of the population generally, the authors report that the sentences of white and First Nations women are comparable for similar offenses. They caution, however, that this conclusion does not mean that the criminal justice system in South Dakota is not racially discriminatory in other of its aspects, such as arrest and plea bargaining. With respect to sex, they report that judges do discriminate in terms of sex in sentencing and that a woman will likely receive a significantly lower penalty than a man convicted of the same offence.

M. J. B. Jones, "Sexual Equality, The Constitution and Indian Status: A Comment on s. 12(1)(b) of the Indian Act" (1984) 4 *Windsor Yearbook of Access to Justice* 48-72
At the time when this article was written, section 12(1)(b) of the Canadian INDIAN ACT stipulated that marriage by a First Nations woman to a male who was non-Indian according to the terms of the ACT would result in her loss of status under the ACT. This article traces the legislative history of s. 12(1)(b), critically examines treatment of the section by Canadian courts under the Canadian BILL OF RIGHTS, reviews subsequent scrutiny by the United Nations Human Rights Committee pursuant to the International Covenant on Civil and Political Rights, and offers the author's reflections on the fate of the section under the Canadian CHARTER OF RIGHTS AND FREE-DOMS.

Mitchell Karp, "The Challenge of Symbolism" (1986) 14 *New York University Review of Law and Social Change* 943-947
For annotation, see Chapter 12: LESBIANISM AND SEXUAL ORIENTATION.

P. Kirby, "Marrying Out and Loss of Status: the Charter and New Indian Act Legislation" (1985) 1 *Journal of Law and Social Policy* 77-95
The author examines the need for a balancing of equality rights and self-determination for First Nations people, especially as it relates to the social and legal role of community legal clinics.

Marlee Kline, "Race, Racism, and Feminist Theory" (1989) 12 *Harvard Women's Law Journal* 115-139
The author responds to criticisms by women of colour that white feminist scholarship tends to assert a representative view of all women while ignoring considerations of race. She considers analytical insights about this limitation in feminist legal literature and argues that white women have to take responsibility for their work by identifying racism and helping to eliminate it.

Gary D. La Free, "Male Power and Female Victimization: Toward a Theory of Interracial Rape" (1982) 88 *American Journal of Sociology* 311-327

The article presents empirical studies that demonstrate that inter-racial rape, in particular rape of white women by black men, has increased since the 1950's. The author argues that this is the result of several factors, including white male sexual stratification which promotes white women as the standard of sexual desirability and treats women as sexual property. He sees the conflict as one between the dominant white male group and the subordinate black male group, with both groups treating women as objects and ignoring the victimization of women by this struggle.

Patricia Ladouceur and Mark Temple, "Substance Use Among Rapists: A Comparison with Other Serious Felons" (1985) 31 *Crime and Delinquency* 269-294

Part of an issue on Rape, this article uses data collected from 1979 to compare drug and alcohol use by rapists to other felons. The authors report that less than one half of rapists were found to be under the influence of any substance, and that age and race were not significant variables in determining who used drugs or alcohol.

Teresa LaFramboise and Elizabeth Anne Parent, "Book Review: Patricia Albers and Beatrice Medicine (eds.), THE HIDDEN HALF: STUDIES OF PLAINS INDIAN WOMEN (1983); Gretchen M. Bataille and Kathleen Mullen Sands, AMERICAN INDIAN WOMEN: TELLING THEIR LIVES (1984); Beth Brant (ed.), A GATHERING OF SPIRIT: WRITING AND ART BY NORTH AMERICAN INDIAN WOMEN (1984); Rayna Green, NATIVE AMERICAN WOMEN: A CONTEXTUAL BIBLIOGRAPHY (1983)" (1985) 10 *Signs: Journal of Women in Culture and Society* 782-784

For annotation, see Chapter 16: **BOOK REVIEWS**.

Carol Pitcher LaPrairie, "Selected Criminal Justice and Socio-Demographic Data on Native Women" (1984) 26 *Canadian Journal of Criminology* 161-169

This article provides an overview of research on First Nations women and the criminal justice system in Canada. Findings suggest that

First Nations women are over-represented in the federal and provincial corrections system even compared to First Nations men and that they are incarcerated for more serious offenses than non-First Nations women. The author also discusses the effects on First Nations women of loss of status for marrying a non-First Nations person, off-reserve migration and urban versus rural living. Data on employment, marital status, plus causes of death and suicide rates, suggest that First Nations women rank among the most severely disadvantaged of all groups in Canada. She concludes that more research on these influences is required and a major commitment from government and First Nations organizations is necessary to understand and address the needs of First Nations women.

Donald E. Lively, "The Supreme Court and Affirmative Action: Whose Classification is Suspect?" (1990) 17 *Hastings Constitutional Law Quarterly* 483-502

The author claims that American judicial and legislative emphasis on racial neutrality has entailed rejection of remedial measures to address the problem of racial inequality and that this approach itself discriminates against racial minorities. He reviews court objections to affirmative action, and concludes that the courts' insistence on racially neutral policies merely furthers majoritarian interests.

Thurgood Marshall, "Justice Thurgood Marshall's Remarks on the Bicentennial of the U.S. Constitution" (1987) 13 *Signs: Journal of Women in Culture and Society* 2-6

The author, a justice in the United States Supreme Court, in a commemorative speech for the bicentennial of the U.S., laments the tendency to oversimplify events during patriotic celebration, and analyzes the wording of the constitution in the context of its times. He states that the omission of Negro slaves and women from voting was intentional, and based on protection of economic interests. Moving away from such restricted notions of "liberty," "justice," and "equality" has occurred not because of the Framers of the Constitution, but instead because of those who used the constitution to better these notions. He concludes that any celebration must also include commemoration of the "suffering, struggle and sacrifice" which has allowed triumph over that which was wrong about the original document.

Mari J. Matsuda, "When the First Quail Calls: Multiple Consciousness as Jurisprudential Method" (1988) 11 _Women's Rights Law Reporter_ 7-10
This paper was originally presented at the Yale Law School Conference on Women of Colour and the Law in 1988. The author begins by explaining that "shifting of consciousness" is a daily experience for women and for people of colour. She argues that lawyers should have a similar "multiple consciousness" that will allow them to see the world from the viewpoint of others and then to apply the abstractions of legal theory to those realities. She explains that the title "When the First Quail Calls" is a reference to a signal used on the underground railroad to mark the time to set out for freedom. Her point is that legal reformers must also set out when it is still dark.

Kevin Mattson, "The Dialectic of Powerlessness: Black Identity Culture and Affirmative Action" (1990) 84 _Telos_ 177-184
The author examines the effect on young black male artists of compensatory justice and the postmodernist celebration of diversity. Looking at the rap groups Public Enemy and 2 Live Crew and at the films and public statements of Spike Lee, he asserts that their protest is style not politics. In his opinion, young black artists are using the particularist politics of victimization to claim that they are misunderstood and attacked only because they are black. At the same time postmodernism has given black voices media attention but has disarmed them by "ghettoizing" them. The result is that blacks feel that their art is part of a monolithic black culture that must be protected. He concludes that these artists view themselves as "other" and so are not able to create an autonomous identity.

Michael McDonald, "Indian Status: Colonialism or Sexism?" (1987) 9 _Canadian Community Law Journal_ 23-48
This article discusses whether (as was the case at the time the article was written) a First Nations woman who marries a non-aboriginal should be denied Indian status under THE INDIAN ACT, while a First Nations male who does so faces no such penalty. The author analyzes the issue from a socio-philosophical, rather than a socio-economic, perspective and offers an argument in favour of greater equality for First Nations women.

Patricia A. Monture, "A Vicious Circle: Child Welfare and the First Nations" (1989) 3 *Canadian Journal of Women and the Law* 1-16
    This article discusses the implications of child welfare law for aboriginal children, and documents the failure of child welfare structures and institutions in recognizing and respecting First Nations culture and traditions. It concludes that these practices are racist, and also that contemporary attempts at reform have failed.

Constance Baker Motley, "Some Recollections of My Career" (1988) 2 *Law and Inequality* 35-40
    Part of a Symposium on the American Constitution and Equality, this article is a personal history of one black woman's progression through college, law school, private practice as a civil rights lawyer, and finally to the judiciary.

Maureen Mulligan, "Obtaining Political Asylum: Classifying Rape as a Well-Founded Fear of Persecution on Account of Political Opinion" (1990) 10 *Boston College Third World Law Journal* 355-380
    This article reports that women who apply for political asylum in the United States because they "fear persecution on account of political opinion" based on experiences of brutal rapes accompanied by death threats and torture, will not necessarily be granted asylum. The author examines the conflict in the courts, the history of the applicable laws, and the treatment by the Board of Immigration Appeals and the courts. She finds sexism and racism in the BIA decisions and recommends setting basic guidelines to overcome the bias.

Laurie Nsiah-Jefferson, "Reproductive Laws, Women of Colour, and Low-Income Women" (1989) 11 *Women's Rights Law Reporter* 15-38
    The author explains that reproductive laws operate in the context of socio-economic conditions and therefore some women are left out of the decision-making process, namely black and low-income women. She concentrates on the six areas identified as particularly affecting these women by the Project on Reproductive Laws for the 1990s. These areas are concerned with the need to make new procedures accessible while guarding against abuse. She concludes by making suggestions largely based on "affirmative policy initiatives."

Karen O'Connor and Lee Epstein, "Sex and the Supreme Court: An Analysis of Judicial Support For Gender-Based Claims" (1983) 64 *Social Science Quarterly* 327-331
This article provides an analysis of the sixty-eight decisions rendered by the U.S. Supreme Court in the 1970s involving gender-based claims. The authors report that the Court has been receptive to these claims, and that most justices support gender-based claims, more than they do race-based claims.

Barbara Omolade, "The Unbroken Circle: A Historical and Contemporary Study of Black Single Mothers and Their Families" (1985) 3 *Wisconsin Women's Law Journal* 239-274
Part of the 1986 Feminism and Legal Theory Conference, this article examines the position of Black single parent mothers, who, the author claims, operate outside the traditional Black family, which is generally sexually conservative and patriarchal, with a strong sense of racial pride. She examines the historical precedents, i.e. the slave family, where single mother-led families co-existed with two-parent families. She canvasses studies regarding Black families, points to cultural biases, and states recommendations with respect to housing, health care, economic issues, public school education, and education for teens and adults. She concludes that economic instability (i.e. to be Black and poor) is the present version of the "social death of Black people," the historical version of which was to be Black and a slave.

Barbara Omolade, "Black Women, Black Men and Tawana Brawley – The Shared Condition" (1989) 12 *Harvard Women's Law Journal* 11-23
Fifteen year old Tawana Brawley remained silent throughout the trial of the six white men she said had raped her and left her covered in excrement and racial slurs. The author links this silence to the "historical conspiracy of silence surrounding all Black women's lives." Because Tawana Brawley's defenders were black male "lone warriors" who defend black women against racial violence but do not understand sexism, her voice was muted. Feminists could have helped her to speak, but for different reasons neither black nor white feminists defended her. The author concludes that to achieve liberation feminists and black nationalists must work together to challenge white male authority.

Barbara A. Owen, "Race and Gender Relations Among Prison Workers" (1985) 31 *Crime and Delinquency* 147-159
For annotation, see Chapter 8: LABOUR AND EMPLOYMENT -
- AFFIRMATIVE ACTION.

Johnny C. Parker and Linda C. Parker, "Affirmative Action: Protecting the Untenured Minority Professor During Extreme Financial Exigency" (1988) 17 *North Carolina Central Law Journal* 119-134
This article analyses affirmative action as a means for securing the continued presence of minority untenured professors in law schools, with particular reference to the affirmative action policy of the American Bar Association. In order to determine whether such policy will withstand legal challenge, the authors derive general guidelines from the case law concerning protective layoff plans. They conclude that affirmative action is essential for ensuring the retention of minority professors.

Diana M. Poole, "On Merit" (1983) 1 *Law and Inequality* 155-158
The author argues that merit is not a means of distributing opportunity, and that merit is in fact the practice of white males rewarding white males for their achievements with white male resources. She concludes that meritocracy will continue to favour white men until women and people of colour have complete access to the conditions necessary to achieve merit.

D. Sanders, "Indian Status: A Women's Issue or an Indian Issue?" (1984) 3 *Canadian Native Law Reporter* 31-40
This article discusses Canadian legislation introduced to end sexual discrimination in THE INDIAN ACT, and the implications it may have for sexual equality of Indian women as well as for aboriginal self-govern-ment. The author concludes that both goals are important, and argues for a more reasonable approach which will decrease, rather than increase controversy in passing new legislation.

Judy Scales-Trent, "Black Women and the Constitution: Finding Our Place, Asserting Our Rights" (1989) 24 *Harvard Civil Rights-Civil Liberties Law Review* 9-44
This article discusses problems black women experience in society

and in the legal system, because they are seen as a subset both of "women" and of the race "black." The author argues for the recognition of a discrete group, "black women," suggests how the group might be defined under the Equal Protection Clause of the American Constitution, and describes how this would affect other subsets, such as the black elderly and other women who are also members of minority racial groups. She appends a personal postscript on rights, in which she defends her rights analysis and describes how writing this piece has empowered her.

Sally S. Simpson, "Why Can't a Woman Be More Like A Man?" (1989) 27 *Criminology* 605-630
> For annotation, see Chapter 3: **CRIMINAL LAW -- GENERAL.**

Fran Sugar and Lana Fox, "Nistum Peyako Seht'wawin Iskwewak: Breaking Chains" (1989-1990) 3 *Canadian Journal of Women and the Law* 465-481
> This is both a report to the Canadian Task Force on Federally Sentenced Women and a personal account of First Nations women's experience of the criminal justice system. The authors document the pain inflicted upon aboriginal women because of the inherent racism and oppression in both society and the justice system. They also challenge existing research methodology as culturally irrelevant and ineffective. They conclude that racism is at the root of the violence in aboriginal women's life experiences and that reconstruction must be carried out through the aboriginal peoples' own healing processes.

Julie Taylor, "Rape and Women's Credibility: Problems of Recantations and False Accusations Echoed in the Case of Cathleen Crowell Webb and Gary Dotson" (1987) 10 *Harvard Women's Law Journal* 59-115
> For annotation, see Chapter 3: **CRIMINAL LAW -- RAPE.**

Esmeralda Thornhill, "Black Women's Studies in Teaching Related to Women: Help or Hindrance to Universal Sisterhood?" (1982) 16 *Fireweed* 77
> The author argues that women's studies is a catalyst for social change, in promoting the equality of women, based not only in sexism,

but also in racism. Black women have cultural, historical and experiential differences which need recognition, acknowledgement and sharing. She provides examples of different priorities for social change for black and white women, women from undeveloped and developed countries, which effect the question of formal equality vs. real equality.

Esmeralda Thornhill, "Focus on Black Women!" (1985-86) 1 *Canadian Journal of Women and the Law* 153-162

The author claims that black women are not included in the collage of female experience, yet their unique experience gives them a greater understanding of the oppression of women in a sexist and racist world. Within the feminist movement, she argues, Woman is synonymous with White Women while Women of Colour are seen as Others, nonpersons, dehumanized beings and sometimes are not seen at all. She claims, for example, that the feminist analogy to women and blacks would be better if referred specifically to Black female and argues that the varieties of oppression must be distinguished or the oppressed may become the oppressor. Class, race, education, privilege, political options must all be considered. Real Sisterhood, she concludes, means the willingness to eliminate racism, not by guilt but by commitment to connection.

Mary Ellen Turpel, "Aboriginal Peoples and the Canadian Charter: Interpretive Monopolies, Cultural Differences" [1989-90] *Canadian Human Rights Yearbook* 3-45

The author argues that sensitivity to cultural difference is an imperative which must inform all levels of constitutional analysis with respect to aboriginal peoples. She concludes that the Canadian CHARTER OF RIGHTS AND FREEDOMS and conception of rights in the Canadian law can be situated culturally, and that neither is universal or progressive, especially insofar as they affect First Nations peoples.

Patricia Williams, "Alchemical Notes: Reconstructing Ideals from Deconstructed Rights" (1987) 22 *Harvard Civil Rights-Civil Liberties Law Review* 401-433

The author takes issue with the Critical Legal Studies rejection of rights-based theory. The CLS argument is that the discourse should be in terms of "needs" rather than "rights". She claims that describing needs has been a failure for the blacks, and that because blacks have experienced a denial of need, the assertion of rights is empowering, a powerful motivation and source of hope. She concludes that, instead of discarding rights, CLS should redefine them so that private property rights are expanded into a concept of civil rights.

Patricia Williams, "Fetal Fictions: An Exploration of Property Archetypes in Racial and Gendered Contexts" (1990) 42 _Florida Law Review_ 81-94

Part of a Symposium on Women and the Law: Goals for the 1990s, this article examines the tension between civil liberties and private property, and argues that recent civil rights decisions of the United States Supreme Court revert law to a hierarchy where the property of some is rated as more important than the humanity of others. It uses the example of workplace restrictions because of reproductive hazards, with respect to which it claims a result occurs where employers gain a tangible property right in biological parents, and a foetus becomes a business and legal fiction. The author discusses the legacy of human ownership in black slaves, and asserts the need to challenge notions of ownership at both an institutional and personal level, and for individuals to wrest themselves from others: to self-possess in pursuit of a full self.

Patricia Williams, "Response to Mari Matsuda – 1988 Women of Colour and the Law Conference at Yale University" (1989) 11 _Women's Rights Law Reporter_ 11-13

This paper is a response to Mari Matsuda's paper "When the First Quail Calls: Multiple Consciousness as a Jurisprudential Method." The author recognizes that the quail call is a loud, alarming sound and warns that concentrating on beauty and poetry could lead to missing the signal to break for freedom. She also elaborates on multiple consciousness and the role it plays in her sense of self. Finally, she describes a personal experience and a dream to illustrate the harm in applying "neutral principles" without recognizing that members of a group are different.

Patricia Williams, "Spirit-Murdering the Messenger: The Discourse of Fingerpointing as the Law's Response to Racism" (1987) 42 _University of Miami Law Review_ 127-157

This paper was originally presented at a symposium entitled

Excluded Voices: Realities in Law and Law Reform. The author explores the damage caused to individuals and to society by the assumption that most crimes are committed by people of colour, and considers in particular two instances, the shooting of an elderly black woman, Eleanor Bumpurs, by a policeman in the course of an eviction, and the beating of three black men by white teenagers in Howard Beach. Her conclusion is that the "privatization of public space" into exclusively white and black areas is a rationalization of racism. The result is a society based on fear and hate.

Howard V. Zonana, Roxanne L. Bartel, James A. Wells, Josephine A. Buchanan, and Marjorie A. Getz, "Sex Differences in Persons Found Not Guilty by Reason of Insanity: Analysis of Data From the Connecticut NGRI Registry (Part II)" (1990) 18 *Bulletin of the American Academy of Psychiatry and the Law* **129-142**

The NGRI Registry is a comprehensive data base collected by the Law and Psychiatry Division of the Department of Psychiatry at the Yale University School of Medicine: see Zonana, et al., "Part I: The NGRI Registry: Initial Analysis of Data Collected on Connecticut Insanity Acquittees" (1990) 18 *Bulletin of the American Academy of Psychiatry and the Law* 115. In this study, thirty-one women insanity acquittees from Connecticut were matched to a group of thirty-one men NGRIs. The groups were compared with respect to demographic, criminal, and clinical characteristics. The authors report that women NGRIs were older, more likely to be married, less likely to be substances abusers, had less extensive criminal records, and were released from hospitals sooner than men. They also report differences in terms of race -- white women had less extensive criminal records and were hospitalized for shorter periods than minority women -- and that the strongest predictors of criminal recidivism were race and a diagnosis other than psychosis.

CHAPTER 8
LABOUR AND EMPLOYMENT

General

Rosalie Silberman Abella, "Employment Equity" (1987) 16 *Manitoba Law Journal* 185-201
The wage gap between women and men persists in defiance of the law and is not justified on the basis that paying women properly is too costly. The author examines provincial and federal equal pay law and concludes that such legislation has had little effect on closing the gap. The law ignores women in segregated jobs and fails to deal with the undervaluation of women's work. Obstacles to pay equity are formidable, self-perpetuating, and will not disappear on their own. The law must protect the right of every individual to have the opportunity of reaching her full potential.

H. E. Baber, "How Bad is Rape?" (1987) 2 *Hypatia: A Journal of Feminist Philosophy* 125-138
For annotation, see Chapter 3: CRIMINAL LAW -- RAPE.

Janice A. Baker and Morely H. S. Hicks, "Equal Pay for Equal Work?" (1984) 1 *Business and the Law* 38-39
The authors claim that the definition of "equal" in federal, provincial and territorial employment and human rights legislation is unequal. Canada and Quebec require equal pay for work of equal value while most jurisdictions require equal pay for similar, the same or substantially the same work. The authors compare the procedures and results of assessing job categories under these two models comparing the Human Rights Code with the Employment Standards Act of Ontario.

Mary E. Becker, "From Muller v. Oregon to Fetal Vulnerability Poli-

cies" (1986) 53 *University of Chicago Law Review* 1219-1268
For annotation, see Chapter 1: **ABORTION AND REPRODUC-
TION.**

Suzanne Bélanger, "Le Retrait Préventif de la Travailleuse Enceinte"
(1986) 1 *Canadian Journal of Women and the Law* 498-504
For annotation, see Chapter 1: **ABORTION AND REPRODUC-
TION.**

Rose Elizabeth Bird, "Remarks by Rose Elizabeth Bird, Chief Justice
of the Supreme Court of California, to the National Association of
Women Judges, San Francisco, California, October 8, 1983" (1984) 14
Golden Gate University Law Review 481 - 487
For annotation, see Chapter 7: **JUDGES AND COURTS.**

Ruth Gerber Blumrosen, "Remedies for Wage Discrimination" (1986)
20:1 *Journal of Law Reform* 99-160
The author claims that the same factors which create segregated
jobs produce discriminatorily depressed wage rates, and she offers
practical remedies for wage discrimination to encourage the Courts to
address substantive issues head on. She discusses the general requirements under Title VII of the Civil Rights Act 1964 to prove
discrimination and explains three typical patterns of wage discrimination
based on when the employer has established the extent of the injury,
when gender or race factors depress wages or when a job is undervalued
in violation of the Equal Pay Act. She concludes that the excuse of high
cost for pay equity remedies is false and should not influence the Courts.

Eileen Boris, "Homework and Women's Rights: The Case of the
Vermont Knitters, 1980-1985" (1987-88) 13 *Signs: Journal of Women in
Culture and Society* 98-120
For women requiring wage labour but also having family labour
responsibilities, homework offers needed flexibility. The author examines
the impact of home labour on wage standards for women generally, as
well as its effect on child care alternatives and other social ramifications.
The history of homework legislation offers little evidence that the state

will adequately regulate homework in the future as other industries look for a supply of cheap and flexible labour. Workplace autonomy without financial independence, the author concludes, cannot benefit working women as a group.

Eileen Boris, "The Quest for Labor Standards in the Era of Eleanor Roosevelt: The Case of Industrial Homework" (1985) 2 _Wisconsin Women's Law Journal_ 53-74

The author examines the historical development of industrial homework -- that is, production of goods, in the home, on a piece-rate basis -- and its relationship to the movement for labour standards including protective legislation for women. She specifically examines the arguments put forth by Eleanor Roosevelt for minimum wage and maximum hour legislation, and argues that such protections for women are no less important now. She demonstrates that women who do industrial homework are married women with small children, most commonly recent immigrants from Latin America or Asia, and concludes that this reality must be considered in any attempt to gain equal labour opportunities for women.

John P. Boyle, "Religious Employers and Gender Employment Discrimination" (1986) 4 _Law and Inequality_ 637-665

This article examines the extent to which the courts should defer to an employer's discriminatory religious beliefs. The author concludes that religious justification for discriminatory employment practices should not be permitted to circumvent the protection provided against such discrimination by employment law.

M. Neil Browne, "The Fundamental Tension Between Market Wages for Women and Comparable Worth" (1984) 2 _Law and Inequality_ 473-490

The author dissects the most typical response from opponents of comparable worth - that existing market forces distribute resources better than any other means, explores the assumptive underpinnings of the market defense, and analyzes the role each assumption plays in validating the market as being voluntary, efficient and fair. He argues that a wage market operates freely and fairly only in a world having these same characteristics. Because the market defense is based upon unrealistic assumptions, he concludes, it lacks credibility as opposition for comparable worth claims and functions primarily as an apology for the status quo.

Anita Cava, "Taking Judicial Notice of Sexual Stereotyping" (1990) 43 *Arkansas Law Review* 27-56
For annotation, see Chapter 7: JUDGES AND COURTS.

B.J. Cling, "On-Camera Sex Discrimination: A Disparate Impact Suit Against the Television Networks and Major Studios" (1986) 4 *Law and Inequality* 509-543
This article deals with the under-representation and negative portrayal of women on television. The author claims that the roles available for men far exceed those available for women, and that this constitutes discrimination against female actors. She also claims that the under-representation of women along with the casting of women in stereotypical roles affects the viewer's image of women. She concludes that a successful employment discrimination suit under Title VII of the Civil Rights Act of 1964, which would require networks to give women a percentage of jobs on television, would end women's under-representation on television.

Ruth Colker, "Rank-Order Physical Abilities Selection Devices for Traditionally Male Occupations as Gender-Based Employment Discrimination" (1986) 19 *University of California Davis Law Review* 761-804
Only recently have police and fire departments accepted applications from women. Some have also instituted "rank-order physical abilities tests" which perpetuate the exclusion of women in these professions. The author critically examines these tests and the assumptions about physical requirements upon which they are based. The tests overstate the importance of traditionally male physical attributes, and ignore the benefits of female physical skills. She suggests that an employer using a rank-order selection should have to demonstrate the actual link between the test and better job performance. She offers alternate selection devices and suggests a pre-test training program for candidates, noting that physical performance examinations involve skills which can readily be taught to women.

Nina L. Colwill, "Discrimination: Why Does it Work?" (1982) 47:3
Business Quarterly 20-22

This is from a series of articles entitled "Women in Business." The author suggests that sex discrimination begins with a sex-role stereotype which operates like any other belief or information gathering system. She claims that sex discrimination "works" when the people who are discriminating have the power to enforce their beliefs against a class that can be easily identified as a separate group. She concludes that because discrimination helps preserve the status quo, we accept the tradition, which we support with our sex-role stereotypes.

Nina L. Colwill, "Sex Roles; Past, Present and Future" (1982) 47:2
Business Quarterly 18-20

This article examines the gains made in the past two decades with respect to number of women in the workplace and Canadian business faculties, notwithstanding that no affirmative action programs have been in place. The author claims that the wage gap is widening rather than narrowing, and that the division of labor by sex remains rigid, but argues that the solution lies in women's demonstration of their unique skills, competence, and contribution to corporate organizations.

Joanne Conaghan, "The Invisibility of Women in Labour Law: Gender-Neutrality in Model-building" (1986) 14 *International Journal of the Sociology of Law* 377-392

For annotation, see Chapter 5: **FEMINIST THEORY -- GEN-ERAL.**

Jennifer Corcoran, "Law and the Promotion of Women" (1986) 9
Women's Studies International Forum 18-24

This article evaluates the effectiveness of United Kingdom sex discrimination legislation that has been in force since 1975. The author reports that the law is not having the impact which was expected, and that horizontal and vertical segregation by gender persists.

Christine L. Czarnecki, "Women in Poland's Workforce: Why Less Than Equal Is Good Enough" (1989) 11 *Comparative Labor Law Journal* 91-117

This article analyses the impact of the Polish attempts to reform employment laws in order to deal with increasing numbers of women in the workforce, and to ensure their equality in the workplace. The author notes that although such laws have benefitted women, the paternalism of laws which prevent women from entering hazardous occupations serve only to perpetuate stereotypical images of women. This, she concludes, constitutes discrimination against women.

Mary DeLano, "The Conflict Between State Guaranteed Pregnancy Benefits and the Pregnancy Discrimination Act: A Statutory Analysis" (1986) 74 *Georgetown Law Journal* **1743-1768**
For annotation, see Chapter 1: ABORTION AND REPRODUCTION.

Sara-Ann Determan, "Women's work" (1983) 11 *Human Rights* **30**
This is the author's June 7, 1983 acceptance speech when honoured by the Women's Legal Defense Fund for her contributions to women's and civil rights. The battles feminists face today are, in many ways, more difficult than before. Women are disproportionately poor and getting poorer. "Women's work" continues to be undervalued largely because such work is performed by women. She inquires whether the prestige and relative pay of the legal profession will fall as law becomes "women's work"? She laments that blatant gender discrimination is still a laughing matter.

Nancy E. Dowd, "Maternity Leave: Taking Sex Differences into Account" (1986) 54 *Fordham Law Review* **699-705**
For annotation, see Chapter 1: ABORTION AND REPRODUCTION.

Nancy E. Dowd, "Work and Family: The Gender Paradox and the Limitations of Discrimination Analysis in Restructuring the Workplace" (1989) 24 *Harvard Civil Rights-Civil Liberties Law Review* **79-172**
For annotation, see Chapter 4: FAMILY LAW - GENERAL.

Maxine N. Eichner, "Getting Women's Work That Isn't Women's

Work: Challenging Gender Biases in the Workplace under Title VII" (1988) 97 *Yale Law Journal* 1397-1416

Title VII of the U.S. Civil Rights Act of 1964 prohibits discrimination in employment yet the labour market remains segregated by sex. Much of the confinement of women to "pink collar" jobs is, the author claims, a result of male bias in "mischaracterizing" tasks as requiring masculine traits, or, in "misstructuring" jobs to accommodate male life-styles. The Courts, in applying either the "disparate treatment analysis" or the "disparate treatment doctrine", often fail to enforce Title VII when male-biased standards are at issue, nor do they question the legitimacy of employment requirements. Equality of opportunity, the author concludes, requires that the Courts use Title VII to challenge traditional male notions and that jobs be adapted to reflect a society composed of both men and women.

Hester Eisenstein, "Femocrats, Official Feminism, and the Use of Power: A Case Study of EEO Implementation in New South Wales, Australia" (1989) 2 *Yale Journal of Law and Feminism* 51-73

This article discusses the success of feminist interventions by "femocrats", feminist bureaucrats, in Australia. Using her own experience as a public servant from 1980-88 in New South Wales, the author describes her methodology as "writing contemporary history from within." She briefly analyzes the differences between American and Australian feminism and the acceptance of feminists within the bureaucracy. The greatest part of the article is devoted to a review of the process of implementation of the official policy of Equal Employment Opportunity. She concludes that feminist theory lags behind practice, and that the experience of femocrats so far provides grounds for reconsidering the nature of gender difference and organizational structure.

Nancy S. Erickson, "Pregnancy Discrimination: An Analytical Approach" (1981) 7 *Women's Rights Law Reporter* 11-26

This is an update to an article published in volume 5 of the *Women's Rights Law Reporter*. An abstract of the original article is followed by recent legal developments.

Rosemary Feurer, "The Meaning of 'Sisterhood': The British Women's Movement and Protective Labor Legislation, 1870-1900" (1988)

31 *Victorian Studies* 233-260
    For annotation, see Chapter 10: **LEGAL HISTORY.**

Thomas Flanagan, "Equal Pay for Work of Equal Value: Some Theoretical Criticisms" (1987) 13 *Canadian Public Policy* 435-444
    The author argues that the serious intellectual problems underlying equal pay for work of equal value -- including, he claims, animism, reification and voluntarism -- make it suspect as a public policy initiative. He analyzes several pieces of Canadian legislation, describes some instances of equal pay being instituted, and looks at the market's influence on the situation.

Jacques Fremont, "Droit Public Assurance-chômage, maternité et adoption: les récents modifications et leur validité" (1982-1983) 17 *Chroniques Sectorielles* 497-506
    For annotation, see Chapter 2: **CONSTITUTIONAL LAW.**

John D. Gibson, "Childbearing and Childrearing: Feminists and Reform" (1987) 73 *Virginia Law Review* 1145-1182
    For annotation, see Chapter 5: **FEMINIST THEORY -- GENERAL.**

Vicki Gottlich, "The Tax Reform Act of 1986: Does It Go Far Enough To Achieve Pension Equity for Women?" (1985) 4 *Wisconsin Women's Law Journal* 1-20
    The author examines private pensions, and the potential impact upon the economic status of older women. She discusses the reason why large numbers of women do not receive pension benefits, which is that pension plans are designed for a male career pattern, and then examines pension legislation to increase the number of women covered, and also to ensure the benefits women receive are a meaningful amount.

Yola Grant, "On Life for Domestic Workers" (1990) 7:4 *Breaking the Silence* 21-23
    The Foreign Domestic Movement Program, an initiative of Employment and Immigration Canada, permits people to enter Canada

to work as domestics. Ninety-five per cent of these are women who face deportation unless they remain continuously employed, are not entitled to unemployment benefits, cannot unionize, cannot refuse to work overtime and must live with the employer. The author discusses their problems including low pay and long working days, and the civil rights ramifications of the exploitation.

Mary W. Gray, "Legal Perspectives on Sex Equity in Faculty Employment" (1985) 41:4 _Journal of Social Issues_ 121-133
This article discusses sex equality in American universities through an analysis of case law concerning hiring, pay, promotion, tenure and termination. The author finds that courts have been inconsistent in their application of the Equal Pay Act of 1963 and Title VII of the Civil Rights Act 1964. She claims that financial and time restrictions make litigation available to only a few, while others may choose not to exercise legal rights for fear of impact on their careers. Internal institutional reform, she concludes, is the only real means of moving toward sex equality.

Ruth A. Harvey, "Equal Treatment of Men and Women in the Work Place: The Implementation of the European Community's Equal Treatment Legislation in the Federal Republic of Germany" (1990) 38 _American Journal of Comparative Law_ 31-71
The author examines two different approaches to creating equality in the work place. The European Economic Community, in its attempts to harmonize the legislation of member states, encourages the pursuit of neutral values which will eliminate differential treatment. The Federal Republic of Germany has enacted legislation on specific needs, but is reluctant to follow the broader approach of the Community.

Penelope Dinneen Hillemann, "Gender and Privacy in the Prisons" (1985) 1 _Wisconsin Women's Law Journal_ 123-140
For annotation, see Chapter 3: CRIMINAL LAW -- SENTENCING AND PRISONS.

Derek Hum, "Fair Wages in the Republic: An Essay on Equal Pay Legislation for the Private Sector" (1986-1987) 16 _Manitoba Law Journal_

203-219

This essay examines "the nature and implications of equal pay legislation as an instrument for eliminating pay differentials between men and women in Canada." The author views this legislation as a response to continuing differentials in earnings, examines sexual discrimination in the workplace and canvasses the ideologies that underlie equal pay legislation.

Russell Juriansz, "Survey of Anti-Discrimination Law" (1984) 16 *Ottawa Law Review* 117-171

This survey covers the period from November 15, 1981 to December 31, 1983 and includes sections on pregnancy, harassment, affirmative action and equal pay amongst others.

Rimma Kalistratova, "Legislatively Guaranteed Equality" (1989) 10 *Canadian Woman Studies* 38-40

For annotation, see Chapter 2: CONSTITUTIONAL LAW.

Leo Kanowitz, "The Law and Sex-Based Employment Discrimination in the United States" (1985) 2 *Comparative Law* 19-28

This article provides an outline of the evolution of restrictions on an employer's freedom to discriminate in employment decisions on the basis of gender. The Equal Pay Act of 1963, Title VII of the 1964 Civil Rights Act and relevant case law are examined. The author advocates the negotiation of collective bargaining agreements and the enactment of new legislation to further the principle of comparable worth.

Sally J. Kenney, "Reproductive Hazards in the Workplace: the Law and Sexual Difference" (1986) 14 *International Journal of the Sociology of Law* 393-414

For annotation, see Chapter 1: ABORTION AND REPRODUCTION.

Kris Kissman, "Brushing Off the Blue Collar Woman?: Has the Women's Movement Ignored the Needs of Working Women?" (1987) 15:1 *Human Rights* 36-41

The author argues that feminists have focused on the integration of women in professional and management roles while neglecting to address the divisions between pink and blue collar jobs. Radical feminists, who largely represent the elite sector of women, exclude class distinctions in their analysis, and in consequence have difficulty dealing with blue collar women. He concludes that feminists must acknowledge that variances exist within groups and that generalizations cannot be made based upon the experience of white, middle class and often professional women alone.

Gail Warshofsky Lapidus, "Interaction of Women's Work and Family Roles in the USSR" (1989) 10:4 _Canadian Women's Studies_ 41-44
The Soviet Union claims the highest representation of women in the labour force of any industrialized society with over 85% of women engaged in full time work or study, and constituting 51% of all workers and employees. The article discusses the dilemma Soviet leadership faces because of the irreplaceable contribution of women in the workplace, and the high value attached to the family. Rising divorce rates and declining birth rates suggest that family and population policies will affect the size and quality of the labour force. Various proposals to alleviate the double burden of Soviet women are canvassed, including assigning reduced work norms without a loss in pay, increasing support services, redistributing female labour resources, improving working conditions for women, and expanding part-time work.

Sylvia A. Law, "Women, Work, Welfare, and the Preservation of Patriarchy" (1983) 131 _University of Pennsylvania Law Review_ 1249-1339
For annotation, see Chapter 4: FAMILY LAW -- GENERAL.

Victoria Lazar, "Not Any Factor Other Than Sex: A Proper Limit to Defending the Equal Pay Act" [1989] _University of Chicago Legal Forum_ 309-329
The U.S. Equal Pay Act of 1963 prohibits employers from using discriminatory pay and benefit scales but allows four exceptions to the requirement of equal pay including a "catch-all" provision for systems based on any factor "other than sex". The legislative history of the Equal Pay Act and its relationship to Title VII is examined and judicial interpretations of the fourth affirmative defence which allows for the

head-of-household rule are analyzed. The author argues that the "head of the household" compensation scheme overwhelmingly benefits men over women, flies in the face of the goals of equal pay legislation and reinforces discriminatory stereotypes about family organization.   She offers legal and policy arguments for rejecting the compensation regime and suggests that alternatives exist for employers seeking to achieve legitimate ends.

G. Legault et E. Tardy, "Les programmes d'accès à l'égalité au Québec: une condition nécessaire mais non suffisante pour assurer l'égalité des femmes" (1986) 17 *Revue de Droit, Faculté de Droit de l'Université de Sherbrooke* **149-189**

The authors argue that the claims for equal rights in law have been an important and valuable objective and that women's organizations have greatly influenced the implementation of legislation and programmes addressing male-female sexuality.   However, they suggest that legal equality is not equality in fact.   Voluntary measures are clearly inadequate to counter systemic discrimination in the workplace as employers oppose positive measures to end discrimination, while supporting equal opportunity in principle.   They conclude that there are inherent limitations in women's claims for equality as greater demands for corrective action create greater opposition.

Marianne Levitsky, "Protecting Workers from Reproductive Hazards" (1986) 1 *Canadian Journal of Women and the Law* **488-497**

For annotation, see Chapter 1: **ABORTION AND REPRODUCTION.**

Sybil Lipschulz, "Social Feminism and Legal Discourse: 1908-1923" (1989) 2 *Yale Journal of Law and Feminism* **131-159**

For annotation, see Chapter 10: **LEGAL HISTORY.**

Gayle M. MacDonald, "Book Review: Jennie Farley, ed., THE WOMAN IN MANAGEMENT: CAREER AND FAMILY ISSUES (1983)" (1987/1988) 2 *Canadian Journal of Women and the Law* **460-462**

For annotation, see Chapter 16: **BOOK REVIEWS.**

Gail Martin, "Landing a Good Blue-Collar Job -- Book Review: Muriel Lederer, BLUE-COLLAR JOBS FOR WOMEN: A COMPLETE GUIDE TO GETTING SKILLED AND GETTING A HIGH-PAYING JOB IN THE TRADES (1979)" (1980) 103 _Monthly Labor Review_ 60-61
For annotation, see Chapter 16: **BOOK REVIEWS**.

Sheryl Gordon McCloud, "Feminism's Idealist Error" (1986) 14 _Review of Law & Social Change_ 277-320
For annotation, see Chapter 4: **FAMILY LAW -- POVERTY**.

Trudy Mills, "The Use of Equal Employment Laws" (1981) 24 _Pacific Sociological Review_ 196
For annotation, see Chapter 7: **JUDGES AND COURTS**.

Barbara J. Nelson, "Comparable Worth: A Brief Review of History, Practice, and Theory -- Book Review: Michael Evan Gold, A DIALOGUE ON COMPARABLE WORTH (1983); Elaine Johansen, COMPARABLE WORTH: THE MYTH AND THE MOVEMENT (1984); Helen Remick, ed., COMPARABLE WORTH AND WAGE DISCRIMINATION (1984); Donald J. Treiman and Heidi I. Hartmann, WOMEN, WORK AND WAGES: EQUAL PAY FOR JOBS OF EQUAL VALUE (1985)" (1985) 69 _Minnesota Law Review_ 1199-1216
For annotation, see Chapter 16: **BOOK REVIEWS**.

Winn Newman, Lisa Newell, and Alice Kirkman, "Pay Me What I'm Worth! Why the Cry for Economic Fairness Goes Beyond Feminism" (1984) 12:1 _Human Rights_ 20-25
American decisions on wage discrimination claims under Title VII of the Civil Rights Act of 1964 and Executive Order 11246 explain the type of evidence required to prove discrimination through either "disparate treatment" or "disparate impact". The authors argue against popular employer excuses such as the "apples and oranges" defence, the "market" defense, and the "cost" and "blame the victim" defenses. The importance of litigation in the fight against sex-based wage discrimination is also explained.

J. Parker, "France: New Equality Law" (1983) 1:28 _Spare Rib_ 12
France's equality legislation known as the "Roudy Law" (after the then Minister for Women's Rights) deals with wage discrimination, but also job training, job seeking, working conditions, recruitment, casual labour, promotions, redundancy and unemployment. The author reports that though some trade unions and women's groups are not entirely happy with it, the law is generally regarded as a big step forward for women's equality.

Marilyn L. Pilkington, "The Canadian Charter of Rights and Freedoms: Impact on Economic Policy and Economic Liberty Regarding Women in Employment" (1988) 17 _Manitoba Law Journal_ 267-289
For annotation, see Chapter 2: CONSTITUTIONAL LAW.

Mack A. Player, "Exorcising the Bugaboo of 'Comparable Worth': Disparate Treatment Analysis of Compensation Differences Under Title VII" (1990) 41 _Alabama Law Review_ 321-376
The Equal Pay Act of 1963 and Title VII of the Civil Rights Act of 1964 both address pay discrimination. The author suggests "a coherent analysis ... of the relative burdens the parties must carry in addressing the issue of the employer's motive for compensation differences."

Diana M. Poole, "On Merit" (1983) 1 _Law and Inequality_ 155-158
For annotation, see Chapter 6: FIRST NATIONS AND RACE.

Mary F. Radford, "Sex Stereotyping and the Promotion of Women to Positions of Power" (1990) 41 _Hastings Law Journal_ 471-535
This article recounts the experiences of Christine Craft, Elizabeth Hishon and Ann Hopkins, three successful professional women who were denied access to the highest levels of power in their respective professions: media, law and accounting. After reviewing current feminist theories on sex discrimination, sex stereotyping in the workplace and the requirements for proving discrimination under Title VII, the author proposes an alternative approach which would "hold employers accountable for allowing deeply imbedded stereotypes to taint their decision making processes."

Charles A. Register and Donald R. Williams, "Some Evidence on the Impact of State-Level Equal Rights Legislation" (1986) 67 _Social Science Quarterly_ 869-876

This article reports the results of a study which examines the effects of state-level Equal Rights legislation on the earnings of women, using 1970 and 1980 Census data. The findings were that there was a modest 3.2% increase in earnings in states having equal rights legislation.

Robin Rogers, "A Proposal for Combatting Sexual Discrimination in the Military: Amendment of Title VII" (1990) 78 _California Law Review_ 165-195

This article examines the reasons for the exclusion of women from combat positions and argues that the justifications for excluding women are unsound, and constitute, as well as encourage, discrimination against women. Although the combat exclusion is unlikely to be abolished, the author suggests that its scope should be narrowed by extending the protection of Title VII of the Civil Rights Act of 1964 to the uniformed military. The author examines the reasons for judicial deference to the military, but concludes that it is appropriate to address this issue through the courts.

Katie Sammons, "Comparable Worth and the Courts: How Fear of the Market Place Is Changing the Face of Title VII" (1986) 23 _Houston Law Review_ 1185-1214

The author discusses opposing views on comparable worth and reviews case law pertaining to Title VII and the market rate defense from the Equal Pay Act's four affirmative defenses. While Courts have both accepted and rejected the notion that a market rate which supports wage discrimination can be a factor "other than sex," the major impact has been in a finding that an employer is not responsible for correcting an economic inequality that it did not create. She concludes that the viability of Title VII as a broad-based prohibition against employment discrimination is in jeopardy.

Ann C. Scales, "Towards a Feminist Jurisprudence" (1981) 56 _Indiana Law Journal_ 375-444

The need for feminist jurisprudence is focused by pregnancy, which is the final and decisive battleground for equality. The author discusses cases which have denied sick and disability leave for pregnancy, and the theories underlying these decisions, and then posits a new vision of equality. She identifies three views of equality: the liberal view which promotes formal equality through law; the assimilationist view in which gender is irrelevant in law and which would require the virtual elimination of pregnancy from social experience; and the bivalent view which specifically emphasizes sex differences. She claims that the notion of discrimination is compromised by forcing a comparison of male/female where none is possible, and argues for labor reforms -- including changes in working hours, flex-time, standard minimum for management and professional, and part-time benefits -- and for social policy which recognizes the value of unpaid private work for males and females.

Vicki Schultz, "Telling Stories About Women and Work: Judicial Interpretations of Sex Segregation in the Workplace in Title VII Cases Raising the Lack of Interest Argument" (1990) 103 _Harvard Law Review_ 1750-1843
For annotation, see Chapter 7: JUDGES AND COURTS.

Mark Seidenfeld, "Some Jurisprudential Perspectives on Employment Sex Discrimination Law and Comparable Worth" (1990) 21 _Rutgers Law Journal_ 269-373
This article analyses three models of sexual inequality -- a conservative model, a liberal model, and a feminist model. The author claims that the American Equal Pay Act is predicated upon the conservative model, which upholds the ideal of separate but "equal" treatment. Title VII, he argues, adopts the liberal model which envisions equality of opportunity and advocates that employment decisions be made in a gender-neutral way. In contrast, the feminist model demands that women's choices and preferences be recognised and accommodated in the workplace. He concludes that the feminist model alone will achieve equality in the workplace, and describes various means for its implementation.

Mary Lyndon Shanley, "Suffrage, Protective Labor Legislation, and Married Women's Property Laws in England" (1986) 12 _Signs: Journal of Women in Culture and Society_ 62-77
For annotation, see Chapter 10: LEGAL HISTORY.

D.M. Shapiro and M. Stelcner, "The Persistence of the Male-Female Earnings Gap in Canada, 1970-1980: the Impact of Equal Pay Laws and Language Policies" (1987) 13 *Canadian Public Policy* 462-476
In evaluating wage discrimination, the authors examine the earnings gap between men and women in Canada and find that "despite the legal, political and ideological commitment to equity in the labour market a large gap in earnings between men and women persists." They also find that the "structural features" of the labour market persist, leaving women segregated by occupation and household division of labour. They report a modest reduction in the earnings gap between women and men and linguistic groups from 1970 to 1980.

Suzanna Sherry, "Employment Discrimination: An Overview of the 1989 Supreme Court Term" (1990) 8 *Law and Inequality* 397-410
The author examines decisions of the United States Supreme Court respecting employment discrimination. She discusses forms of litigation under Title VII, which requires proof of either disparate treatment or disparate impact in employment, and argues that a reform of the test of "business necessity" to "business justification" by the Court will make Title VII cases more difficult for a plaintiff to prove. She concludes, however, that an employer continues to be obligated to use merit as the primary hiring criteria.

Reva B. Siegel, "Book Review: Susan Lehrer, ORIGINS OF PRO-TECTIVE LABOUR LEGISLATION FOR WOMEN (1987)" (1987/1988) 3 *Berkeley Women's Law Journal* 171-187
For annotation, see Chapter 16: BOOK REVIEWS.

Reva B. Siegel, "Employment Equality Under the Pregnancy Discrimi-nation Act of 1978" (1985) 94 *Yale Law Journal* 929-955
For annotation, see Chapter 1: ABORTION AND REPRODUC-TION.

Karen Beck Skold, "Book Review: Carol Tropp Schreiber, CHANG-ING PLACES: MEN AND WOMEN IN TRANSITIONAL OCCUPA-TIONS (1981); Cynthia Fuchs Epstein and Rose Laub Coser, (eds.), ACCESS TO POWER: CROSS-NATIONAL STUDIES OF WOMEN

AND ELITES (1981); Cynthia Fuchs Epstein, WOMEN IN LAW (1981); Judith Hicks Stiehm, BRING ME MEN AND WOMEN: MANDATED CHANGE AT THE U.S. AIR FORCE ACADEMY (1981)" (1982) 8 *Signs: Journal of Women in Culture and Society* 367-372
For annotation, see Chapter 16: BOOK REVIEWS.

Miranda S. Spivack, "A New Coalition is Winning on Family Leave" (September, 1988) *Governing* 66-70

The author claims that while many states are passing legislation allowing for employment leave for care of young children or ailing relatives, this reform has occurred only at a state level and despite intensive business lobbying. She argues for non-gendered family leave implemented on an incremental basis so as not to split the business community, which she concludes the implementation of maternity leave alone would do.

Jane Stackpool-Moore, "From Equal Pay to Equal Value in Australia: Myth or Reality" (1990) 11 *Comparative Labor Law Journal* 273-294

Despite the legal doctrine of "equal pay for work of equal value," the author claims that Australian women suffer discrimination in the workforce. This article addresses factors which contribute to the overall wage differential between men and women in the Australian market and suggests ways to address this imbalance.

Susan Struth, "Permissible Sexual Stereotyping Versus Impermissible Sexual Stereotyping: A Theory of Causation" (1989) 34 *New York Law School Law Review* 679-710

This article discusses the legislative history of Title VII and the case law with respect to the issue of causation - namely, to what extent must the unlawful factor of gender bias have influenced the employment decision for the court to impose Title VII liability. The question of what degree of proof is required to show that the unlawful consideration played a significant part in the decision is also examined. The analysis proposed by the author separates the establishment of a violation -- by applying an "in part" theory of causation -- from the determination of the effect of this on the plaintiff (by applying a "but for" test of causation). In the case of both inquiries, the burden of proof should remain on the employee. She concludes that Title VII requires the employer to

avoid sexual stereotyping in employment decisions, and advocates the
passage of legislation to require preventive measures to be taken.

Katherine Swinton, "Regulating Reproductive Hazards in the
Workplace: Balancing Equality and Health" (1983) 33 *University of
Toronto Law Journal* 45-72
    The author argues that occupational health regulations which
distinguish between men and women in terms of capacity to bear
children can result in the exclusion of women from some jobs, and that
regulations of this sort give rise to serious ethical, scientific, financial and
political issues. She canvasses the roles of government and employers,
and the concerns of employees. Swinton acknowledges that legislated
protections are necessary to shield the foetus. But she concludes that
human rights safeguards are also needed, to prevent indirect employer
discrimination, and to provide for maintenance of a women's income
level should she require temporary removal from a hazardous position.

Deborah M. Tharnish, "Sex Discrimination in Prison Employment: The
Bona Fide Occupation Qualification and the Prisoners' Privacy Rights"
(1980) 65 *Iowa Law Review* 428-445
    For annotation, see Chapter 3: CRIMINAL LAW – SENTEN-
CING AND PRISONS.

Patricia A. Timko, "Exploring the Limits of Legal Duty: A Union's
Responsibilities with respect to Fetal Protection Policies" (1986) 23
Harvard Journal on Legislation 159-210
    For annotation, see Chapter 1: ABORTION AND REPRODUC-
TION.

Gilles Trudeau et Jean-Pierre Villaggi, "Le Retrait Préventif de la
Femme Enceinte en Vertu de la Loi sur la Santé et la Sécurité du
Travail: Où en Sommes-nous?" (1986) 46 *Revue du Barreau* 477-490
    For annotation, see Chapter 1: ABORTION AND REPRODUC-
TION.

Judith P. Vladeck, "Sex Discrimination in Higher Education" (1981) 7

Women's Rights Law Reporter 27-38
   Following an abstract of an article published in volume 4 of the
Women's Rights Law Reporter, the author updates the law for the
intervening years.

   **Marjorie Weinzweig, "Pregnancy Leave, Comparable Worth, and
Concepts of Equality" (1987) 2 *Hypatia: A Journal of Feminist Philosophy*
71-101**
   For annotation, see Chapter 1: **ABORTION AND REPRODUC-
TION.**

   **Mary Whisner, "Gender-Specific Clothing Regulation: A Study in
Patriarchy" (1982) 5 *Harvard Women's Law Journal* 73-119**
   As with any hierarchy, patriarchy needs to distinguish between
member groups, and appearance regulation by gender is a means of
making that distinction. By requiring women to "wear" their gender, the
stage is set for differential treatment.   On the other hand, a woman's
dress can be blamed for instigating and excusing otherwise unacceptable
behaviour on the part of men. The author discusses American case law
under Title VII, which finds clothing regulation at work to be discrimination, as well as other case law illustrating the sexual objectification of
women in institutions such as schools and courts.

   **Robert W. White, Norma J. Shepelak, and Tamila C. Jensen,
"Protesting a Perceived Injustice: Sex Discrimination and the Restoration of Equity" (1988) 2 *Social Justice Research* 25-47**
   The authors apply resource mobilization principles to equity
research. Their data concern a sample of women who filed complaints
about sex discrimination on the job. They study the mobilisation of
non-economic resources, both internal (education, experience) and
external (support from co-workers), to negotiate fair terms and avoid
retaliation for the complaint.

   **Carroll Wetzel Wilkinson, "Women in Non-traditional Fields and
Feminism: An Uneasy Connection?" (1989) 91 *West Virginia Law Review*
153-164**
   The integration of women into male-dominated fields of employ-

ment has come about as the result of feminist thinking, but in the author's view, a tension exists between the occupational pioneers and the members of the women's movement. Some of the reasons offered for this alienation are the existence of unfortunate stereotypes for both groups, disagreement about the place of gender issues in the workplace, and the claims that the totality of one's energy is often required in the pioneering effort. She concludes that the gap must be closed if progress in integration is to continue.

Jane Williamson, "The Struggle Against Sex Discrimination" (1982) 57 *Wilson Library Bulletin* 304-307
   The first step for women in the struggle against sex discrimination is to know what the laws are and what they cover. The author outlines American legislation and leading cases in the area of equal pay, sexual harassment, pregnancy discrimination and affirmative action. She explains how a complaint is made to the Equal Employment Opportunity Commission, when it should be made, and how the complaint will be dealt with.

Affirmative Action

Kathryn Abrams, "Hiring Women" (1990) 14 *Southern Illinois University Law Journal* 487-505
   Part of a Symposium on Gender Bias in Legal Education, this article presents the author's reflections on the legal academy's interest in hiring more women and on its decision to do so through affirmative action. She suggests several reasons why law schools should want to hire more women -- to provide female role models for students, to combat the unconscious sexism with which law schools are often inflicted, to create greater diversity among faculty and to ease what are often unreasonable burdens on the women already employed by law schools. She hedges on the inevitability of affirmative action, prefers instead the terms "hiring for diversity" or "activism in hiring women," and thinks what is really at issue is the re-examination of hiring standards for male bias and disregarding of women's experiences. The article includes a response by

Professor T. B. McAffee and the author's reply.

**Carol Agocs, "Affirmative Action, Canadian Style: A Reconnaissance"
(1986) 12:1 *Canadian Public Policy* 148-163**
 The author argues that Canadians must develop an effective
affirmative action strategy based upon Canadian institutions and values.
The meaning and purpose of affirmative action is explained and the
components of a successful program outlined. Various provincial and
federal voluntary schemes are reviewed and the author argues for
mandatory programs through legislation or contract compliance regulations in the private sector. The current policy of relying on voluntary
compliance has been ineffective in creating occupational equality and
there is evidence that stronger measures are necessary and can be more
effective.

**Jennifer K. Bankier, "Equality, Affirmative Action, and the Charter:
Reconciling 'Inconsistent' Sections" (1985) 1 *Canadian Journal of Women
and the Law* 134-151**
 For annotation, see Chapter 2: **CONSTITUTIONAL LAW.**

**Sandra Burt, "Voluntary Affirmative Action -- Does It Work?" (1986)
41 *Relations Industrielles* 541-551**
 Employers were questioned on their understanding of affirmative
action, and the author concludes that voluntary affirmative action is
unlikely to eliminate systemic discrimination or to remove women from
their historical position as a secondary labour force. Most employers do
not understand the meaning or goals of affirmative action, nor the
barriers to women in employment and may in fact think they are practising affirmative action when they are not. The author doubts that the
social changes resulting from effective affirmative action will be looked
upon favourably by predominantly male employers.

**Richard H. Chused, "The Hiring and Retention of Minorities and
Women on American Law School Faculties" (1988) 137 *University of
Pennsylvania Law Review* 537-568**
 The author analyzes data from 149 American law schools to track
trends in the hiring and granting of tenure to minorities and women

between 1980 and 1987. In the section dealing with women he notes some disturbing developments. Although the growth in the proportion of women in tenured or tenure track positions rose from 10.8 to 15.9%, about one fifth of the schools in 1987, including most of the "high prestige" schools maintained a proportion of women lower than the 1981 national average. The statistics revealed that those schools with less than 12% women were far less likely to grant tenure to women. He notes that there are a large number of women in contract legal writing positions, positions which are generally less prestigious and less likely to lead to tenure. He suggests that a historical "women's job" pattern may be developing. He concludes by urging that there be greater emphasis on promoting faculty diversity.

Rona Davis and Asher Neudorfer, "Affirmative Action in the Work Place" (1988) 2 _National Labour Review_ **12-28**
Examples of inequality in employment still abound, the authors claim, notwithstanding human rights legislation, labor legislation, and the Canadian Charter of Rights and Freedoms. Three broad types of discrimination exist: intentional discrimination, differential discrimination, and systemic discrimination. The authors conclude that mandatory affirmative action legislation is a beginning response to social and economic inequities.

Mary A. Eberts, "Human Rights Tribunal Orders Affirmative Action Program" (1985) 2 _Business and the Law_ **15-16**
After a complaint by Action Travail des Femmes, Canadian National Railways was ordered to institute an affirmative action program under the Canadian Human Rights Act. In 1981, women comprised only 6.11% of the C.N. workforce and a three person Tribunal found that C.N. made no real effort to inform women of opportunities or to change negative attitudes towards women in the workplace. The author reports that C.N. was ordered to discontinue certain employment tests, institute job advertising in newspapers and to hire at least one woman for every four non-traditional position filled in the future.

Ken Feagins, "Affirmative Action or the Same Sin?" (1990) 67 _Denver University Law Review_ **421-451**
For annotation, see Chapter 6: **FIRST NATIONS AND RACE.**

Lucinda M. Finley, "Choice and Freedom: Elusive Issues in the Search for Gender Justice -- Book Review: David L. Kirp, Mark G. Yudolf, and Marlene Strong Franks, GENDER JUSTICE (1986)" (1987) 96 *Yale Law Journal* 914-942
  For annotation, see Chapter 16: BOOK REVIEWS.

Elizabeth Fox-Genovese, "Women's Rights, Affirmative Action, and the Myth of Individualism" (1986) 54 *George Washington Law Review* 338-374
  Part of a Symposium on Civil Rights and Civil Liberties, this article discusses the theory and practice of individualism as evidenced in the American class system, which the author argues promotes the myth of individual mobility and opportunity. Affirmative action, which, she claims, is grounded in this myth, seeks to redress injustices and expand individual opportunity. Concepts like comparable worth short-circuit the market definition of value and confirm women's rights to earn a living and achieve economic equality with men. She uses abortion as an example of feminists claiming radical individualism. She suggests that an age of distributive justice and social rights is beginning and that "bankrupt individualistic principles" will be abandoned.

Carole Geller, "Book Review: Judge Rosalie Silberman Abella, Commissioner, EQUALITY IN EMPLOYMENT: A ROYAL COMMISSION REPORT (Ottawa: Minister of Supply and Services, 1984)" (1985) 5 *Windsor Yearbook of Access to Justice* 425-429
  For annotation, see Chapter 16: BOOK REVIEWS.

Adrian Howe, "'Social Injury' Revisited: Towards a Feminist Theory of Social Justice" (1987) 15 *International Journal of the Sociology of Law* 423-435
  For annotation, see Chapter 5: FEMINIST THEORY -- GENERAL.

Hilary B. Klein, "Book Review: Marjorie Heins, CUTTING THE MUSTARD: AFFIRMATIVE ACTION AND THE NATURE OF EXCELLENCE (1987)" (1989) 11 *Women's Rights Law Reporter* 61 - 66.
  For annotation, see Chapter 16: BOOK REVIEWS.

M. Krauss, "L'action Positive: Réflexions Historiques et Philosophiques" (1985) 16 _Revue de Droit, Faculté de Droit de L'Université de Sherbrooke_ 459-480
The author traces the evolution of the concept of affirmative action and concludes that the modern notion based on allocation of positions as opposed to opportunity is incompatible with liberal values. Although it may be possible to justify it on the basis of desired consequences, he finds current practice not tenable. Affirmative action as it is applied to women is considered in detail.

Nicola Lacey, "Legislation Against Sex Discrimination: Questions from a Feminist Perspective" (1987) 14 _Journal of Law and Society_ 411-420
The difficulties in using and enforcing anti-discrimination statutes in Britain arise from problems of proof and the inadequacy of remedies. Damage awards are low, there are no injunctive powers, the commission is under-resourced and legal aid is not available. The author's feminist critique argues that equality of opportunity is inadequate to transform and that distribution of goods is structured by gender. The proper direction of reform is to abandon equality of opportunity, to strive for equality of results through affirmative action, and to recognize that anti-discrimination legislation is not the only appropriate legal response to oppression, and at best, can only form a small part of a genuine feminist political strategy.

Sylvia A. Law, "'Girls Can't be Plumbers' -- Affirmative Action for Women in Construction: Beyond Goals and Quotas" (1989) 24 _Harvard Civil Rights-Civil Liberties Law Review_ 45-77
The author explores strategies for closing the gulf between the norm of sexual equality and the reality of sex-based discrimination. The protections existing within Title VII of the Civil Rights Act of 1964 are contrasted with the realities of women in the construction industry. She defends the legitimacy of affirmative action including numerical remedies and argues there are three critical components to assuring equal opportunity in construction: enforcement by the executive of federal contract compliance guidelines; vigorous judicial application of Title VII; and well constructed aggressive community-based programs which open opportunities so goals can be met.

Donald E. Lively, "The Supreme Court and Affirmative Action: Whose Classification is Suspect?" (1990) 17 *Hastings Constitutional Law Quarterly* 483-502
    For annotation, see Chapter 6: FIRST NATIONS AND RACE.

Mari J. Matsuda, "Affirmative Action and Legal Knowledge: Planting Seeds in Plowed-up Ground" (1988) 11 *Harvard Women's Law Journal* 1-17
    Just as affirmative action brings new shapes and colours of humanity to law school, legal scholarship should adopt affirmative action to bring the new ideas of "outsiders" to the law. The author argues that a system of legal education which ignores the influence of women and people of colour artificially restricts and stultifies scholarly imagination; and she encourages scholars and law students alike to seek out new perspectives by insisting that the views of outsiders are included on course reading lists, in panel discussions and are considered in scholarly research. The article identifies some of the dangers of scholarly affirmative action, such as under or over-rating a work, appearing patronizing or revealing one's own lack of knowledge. However, the danger of missing out on this important body of knowledge, the author concludes, is a greater risk. She offers examples of her own affirmative action of using outsider literature to explain the underlying rationale for legal concepts.

Kevin Mattson, "The Dialectic of Powerlessness: Black Identity Culture and Affirmative Action" (1990) 84 *Telos* 177-184
    For annotation, see Chapter 6: FIRST NATIONS AND RACE.

Leslie A. Nay and James E. Jones, Jr., "Equal Employment and Affirmative Action in Local Governments: A Profile" (1989) 8 *Law and Inequality:* 103-149
    This article reports the findings of a study of American local government anti-discrimination programs, particularly equal employment opportunity (EEO), affirmative action (AA) and affirmative action in contracting (AAC) programs. The authors report that local government programs are widespread, that EEO and AA programs are more prevalent than AAC programs, that there are regional differences in the prevalence of these programs and that large local governments are more

likely to adopt these programs than are small local governments. They believe that the prevalence of these programs and the ease of their implementation indicate a widespread acceptance of anti-discrimination programs.

David Benjamin Oppenheimer, "Distinguishing Five Models of Affirmative Action" (1988) 4 *Berkeley Women's Law Journal* 42-61

The author laments that proponents of affirmative action programs have allowed the debate to focus too much on quotas instead of on the non-discrimination purposes of such programs. Two court cases are offered as examples of what can happen when the multiple meanings of affirmative action are not distinguished. He offers five models of affirmative action: affirmative action as a quota system favouring women or minorities (most often attacked as "reverse discrimination"); some preference for women and minorities over white men; affirmative action as a self-examination plan to determine whether discrimination is affecting decision-making; outreach plan to include women and minorities in the pool of candidates; and affirmative action as an affirmative commitment not to discriminate. He concludes that affirmative action cases ought to be carefully examined in order to determine whether they can be analyzed as non-discrimination cases.

Barbara A. Owen, "Race and Gender Relations Among Prison Workers" (1985) 31 *Crime and Delinquency* 147-159

This article outlines recent changes to the traditional prison guard structure caused by affirmative action. It claims the guards' racial conflicts parallel the prison culture, while gender conflicts parallel blue collar occupations.

Johnny C. Parker and Linda C. Parker, "Affirmative Action: Protecting the Untenured Minority Professor During Extreme Financial Exigency" (1988) 17 *North Carolina Central Law Journal* 119-134

For annotation, see Chapter 6: FIRST NATIONS AND RACE.

Deborah L. Rhode, "Perspectives on Professional Women" (1988) 40 *Stanford Law Review* 1163-1207

Part of a Symposium on Gender and the Law, this article discusses the informal obstacles to advancement of women in the legal profession, which remain, notwithstanding a lessening of formal barriers. The author provides historical background, sociological and psychological analysis of different male and female vocational decisions, and statistics on law school entry and professional advancement. She discusses legal responses to discrimination, the problems of victimizing the victim, and opposition to affirmative action programs. In particular, she claims that the argument that group treatment compromises the right to be treated as an individual is specious, and argues that since women and minorities are victims of systemic deprivations, affirmative action could right the imbalance. She concludes that assimilation or alteration are the likely outcomes to increased participation by women in the legal profession.

Roberta Edgecombe Robb, "Equal Pay for Work of Equal Value: Issues and Policies" (1987) 13 *Canadian Public Policy* 445-460

The author examines the scope and benefit of equal value legislation against affirmative action and concludes that affirmative action is a necessary complementary policy to equal value but cannot substitute for it because the affirmative action process is so slow. While it assists new entrants into the labour force to get higher paying, traditionally male jobs, affirmative action is less helpful for those currently working and suffering economically from discrimination. An equal value policy is necessary for this group.

Michel Rosenfeld, "Affirmative Action, Justice, and Equalities: A Philosophical and Constitutional Appraisal" (1985) 46 *Ohio State Law Journal* 845-922

For annotation, see Chapter 2: CONSTITUTIONAL LAW.

Susan Ryan, "Australia's Sex Discrimination and Affirmative Action Legislation" (1989) 8 *Journal of the Irish Society of Labour Law* 10-17

The author, a former Minister on the Status of Women in Australia, discusses her two major legislative reforms: the Sex Discrimination Act 1984 and the Affirmative Action (Equal Employment Opportunities for Women) Act 1986. She explains that the nature of the economy and social prejudice had created a sex-segregated workplace in Australia. The respective purposes of the statutes were to challenge existing discrimination and to break down structural discrimination.

Although she concludes that "Australian women now have opportunities...equal to any women in the world," she admits that changes in private attitudes are still needed.

N. Colleen Sheppard, "Affirmative Action in Times of Recession: The Dilemma of Seniority-Based Layoffs" (1984) 42 _University of Toronto Faculty of Law Review_ 1-25

This article canvasses American attempts at reconciling affirmative action with job protection and applies the American experience to the Canadian context and to Canadian Human Rights legislation. Because workers must shoulder the burden of conflicts between seniority and affirmative action whatever the particular outcome, the author argues for greater scrutiny of layoffs based upon business necessity. She concludes that employers should share in the social cost created by their past discriminatory practices.

Elliot E. Slotnick, "Gender, Affirmative Action, and Recruitment to the Federal Bench" (1984) 14 _Golden Gate University Law Review_ 519-571

For annotation, see Chapter 7: JUDGES AND COURTS.

Margaret Thornton, "Affirmative Action, Merit and the Liberal State" (1985) 2 _Australian Journal of Law and Society_ 28-40

The author claims that liberalism disadvantages women as a group, because it perceives merit as apolitical and devoid of social context, and because women as reproductive agents in the private sphere are stigmatized as inferior. Merit-in-practice perpetuates the existing social order and is not objective, value-free, or absolute as posited. The ideology of liberalism, the author concludes, emphasizes individual responsibility for one's success but fails to recognize built in inequities.

Elaine M. Todres, "With Deliberate Care: The Framing of Bill 154" (1986-1987) 16 _Manitoba Law Journal_ 221-226

The Ontario Pay Equity Act guarantees "women in both the public and private sectors that they will finally be entitled to equal pay for work of equal value." The author traces the history of the legislation, including criticisms of it, and concludes that "other initiatives, such as affirmative action and education programs, will also be needed."

Samuel Walker, "Racial Minority and Female Employment in Policing: The Implications of 'Glacial' Change" (1985) 31 *Crime and Delinquency* 555-572
This article examines the changes in police attitude and behaviours as well as public perception of police forces since affirmative action has increased minority membership on police forces. The author claims that litigation is an effective tool for redressing employment discrimination on police forces.

C. Winn, "Affirmative Action for Women: More Than a Case of Simple Justice" (1985) 28 *Canadian Public Administration* 24-46
This is a critical examination of affirmative action for women in the Canadian federal government. The author argues that the gender-gap is not caused primarily by employer discrimination, but rather by the inequality of the family labour burden and by educational segregation. She concludes that affirmative action does injustice to low-income women, low-status men and mothers who work at home, and proposes as alternatives to quota hiring reforms in income tax, pensions, education and job structure.

Sexual Harassment

K. Lee Berthel, "Sexual Harassment in Education Institutions: Procedure for Filing a Complaint with the Office for Civil Rights, Department of Education" (1981) 10 *Capital University Law Review* 585-606
Part of a Symposium on Sexual Harassment, this article deals with federal law on sexual harassment with specific reference to education workers. It also details how to file a complaint and lists all federal and state offices that accept complaints.

Berna L. Brown, "Sexual Harassment in Employment: Procedure for Filing a Complaint with the Ohio Civil Rights Commission" (1981) 10 _Capital University Law Review_ 531-539

Part of a Symposium on Sexual Harassment, this article explains Ohio state and EEOC law on sexual harassment, and details the procedure for filing a complaint with the Ohio Civil Rights Commission.

J. M. Cantin, "Le harcèlement sexuel: une préoccupation majeure dans le monde des relations de travail" (1986) 17 _Revue Générale de Droit_ 271-281

The author discusses definitions of sexual harassment and proposes the use of the "reasonable person" test to determine if conduct is discriminatory. The concept of harassment includes any gender-based words or conduct making the work environment more unpleasant for one sex than the other. The author concludes that it is the responsibility of the employer to punish acts of harassment and that elimination of harassment as opposed to remedies should be the primary concern.

M. Caron, "Aux Frontières du Droit Civil et du Droit Statuaire, un Cas de Harcèlement Sexuel: FOISY c. BELL CANADA" (1985) 19 _Revue Juridique Thémis_ 79-84

The author discusses the effect of the Quebec Charter of Rights on remedies for sexual harassment. The case of FOISY v. BELL CANADA ([1984] C.S. 1164) is used to illustrate problems of the definition of harassment, proof of wrongful behaviour, recourse available to victims and the utility of restoration orders. The author concludes that FOISY has established that the abuse of rights is not merely a contractual matter to be dealt with according to the collective agreement; the Charter creates legal obligations which render sexual harassment a civil offence. Victim rights include: material and moral damages and the right to cessation of the attacks.

Phyllis L. Crocker and Anne E. Simon, "Sexual Harassment in Education" (1981) 10 _Capital University Law Review_ 541-584

Part of a Symposium on Sexual Harassment, this article deals with women as teachers and students, and the sexual harassment specific to these roles. Legal theories for dealing with the problem are outlined, including Title IX, criminal, contract and tort law.

Jill Laurie Goodman, "Sexual Harassment: Some Observations on the Distance Travelled and the Distance Yet to Go" (1981) 10 *Capital University Law Review* 445-468

The author offers a history of women's experience with sexual harassment by describing the many forms that sexual harassment can take and how this extremely common occurrence transcends ethnic origin, occupational lines and geography. She discusses some of the successes and failures of the legal system in addressing the problem and is critical of some of the doubtful and sometimes highly questionable reasoning by the judiciary. Continuing improvement, she concludes, is dependent upon educating judges, and upon changing the law and ultimately fundamental relations between men and women.

Sandy Goundry, "Sexual Harassment in the Employment Context: The Legal Management of Working Women's Experience" (1985) 43 *University of Toronto Faculty of Law Review* 1-42

This article contrasts law's sensitivity to women's experience of sexual harassment with the extent to which sexual harassment as "defined by law," has been "objectified" and "rationalized" out of the realm of that experience. The author argues that law as ideology perpetuates a male vision of socioeconomic reality, and that definitions which ignore women's experience help legitimize and reinforce the status quo. The weaknesses and strengths of law are revealed through an examination of the language of case law and legislation. She considers the American experience, but her analysis focuses on cases under the Ontario Human Rights Code, 1980 with 1981 amendments. Human Rights Boards have failed to articulate a coherent framework of analysis in sexual harassment cases and sexist assumptions and biases pervade their decisions. Alternate remedies in criminal and tort law, union grievances and unemployment insurance claims are briefly discussed.

M. A. Hickling, "Employer's Liability for Sexual Harassment" (1988) 17 *Manitoba Law Journal* 124-157

The author argues that sexual harassment is discrimination and that employers must be held responsible for the acts of their employees who victimize others. She analyzes Canadian decisions on vicarious liability and the "Organic Theory of Liability." She compares Canadian and American approaches and notes recent changes in human rights legislation and a recent Supreme Court of Canada decision that holds employers responsible for providing a healthy work environment free from discrimination.

Jeffrey Higginbotham, "Sexual Harassment in the Police Station" (1988) 57:9 *FBI Law Enforcement Bulletin* 22-26
The author, legal counsel at the Federal Bureau of Investigation Academy, discusses the legal and practical implications for the policing work environment of recent sexual harassment cases arising under Title VII of the 1964 Civil Rights Act in the United States. He provides examples of successful harassment suits and makes suggestions to administrators in the law enforcement workplace on how to avoid such suits, and how to ensure that harassment doesn't take place.

Frances L. Hoffman, "Sexual Harassment in Academia: Feminist Theory and Institutional Practice" (1986) 56:2 *Harvard Educational Review* 105-121
The author argues that sexual harassment is both a manifestation and a cause of the subordination of women and that academic institutions have responded with policies and procedures designed to eliminate the behaviour, and not to eliminate the inequality which causes it. Institutions who by policy prohibit amorous relationships between faculty and students are paternalistic because they assume the less powerful group is incapable of empowerment, and this perpetuates powerlessness and vulnerability. Grievance procedures, she concludes, must also reflect the causation of sexual harassment and be designed to empower rather than protect the victim.

Elaine D. Ingulli, "Sexual Harassment in Education" (1987) 18 *Rutgers Law Journal* 281-323
The author examines sexual harassment in the university context and the role of the professional union in dealing with it. She discusses the problems of setting and enforcing ethical standards, and what the law and the faculty might do to attack the problem, in order to enhance the academic and intellectual environment. She describes the way academics as compared to legal professionals learn ethics. The article includes appendices of sexual harassment policies and procedures.

Marlene Kadar, "Sexual Harassment: Where We Stand; Research and Policy" (1983) 3 *Windsor Yearbook of Access to Justice* **358-374**
The author is critical of wording which limits the scope of the offense of sexual harassment, and which creates evidentiary difficulties for the victim. After reviewing existing legal remedies, she concludes these do not address its social cause. She argues that unions should be capable of dealing with the causes, that under the duty of fair representation, are obliged to defend the interests of every member regardless of sex, and that sexual harassment is a workplace hazard which ought to be addressed at the bargaining table and through membership education. The trade union movement combined with outside women's organizations are key to the eradication of sexual harassment.

Linda J. Krieger and Cindi Fox, "Evidentiary Issues in Sexual Harassment Litigation" (1985) 1 *Berkeley Women's Law Journal* **115-139**
The article examines whether the past sexual behaviour of a harassment plaintiff may be introduced as evidence for the defence and under what circumstances the harasser's conduct towards other women is admissible by the plaintiff. The authors discuss American statute and common law and review various attempts at introducing such evidence. They conclude that the sexual history of the plaintiff is neither discoverable nor admissible at trial while the past conduct of the defendant towards other women is in several circumstances admissible and directly relevant to proving the essential elements of sexual harassment. They conclude that whenever such evidence is admitted, fair procedures must be taken to limit the possibilities for abuse.

L. Lamarche, "Définition du Harcèlement Sexuel Prohibé sur les Lieux de Travail en Droit Canadien" (1986) 2 *Canadian Journal of Women and the Law* **113-134**
The author identifies two types of sexual harassment which attract legal attention: activities or behaviour imposed on women under threat of dismissal or other sanction and pervasive sexual innuendo or advances which do not result in sanctions for non-compliance. She reports that although both forms have been recognized in American law, to date Canadian courts and administrative boards have been ineffective in combatting the second type. She proposes alternative means such as workers compensation claims, confrontation of the harasser, and the introduction of preventive health and safety provisions into the workplace

to deal with harassment.

Jan C. Leventer, "Sexual Harassment and Title VII: EEOC Guidelines, Conditions, Litigation, and the United States Supreme Court" (1981) 10 _Capital University Law Review_ 481-197

Part of a Symposium on Sexual Harassment, this article follows the history of the Equal Employment Opportunities Commission (EEOC)'s position on sexual harassment as a form of employment discrimination, reviews recent litigation approving EEOC guidelines, and reprints the guidelines.

Susan Littler-Bishop, Doreen Siedler-Feller, and R.E. Opaluck, "Sexual Harassment in the Workplace as a Function of Initiator's Status: The Case of Airline Personnel" (1982) 38:4 _Journal of Social Issues_ 137-147

In this study, female flight attendants were asked to record how often they had been subject to sexual harassment, the personnel status of the initiator, and their affective responses to hypothetical situations. The kinds of harassment were divided into sexual looking, sexual comment, and sexual touch. The number of harassment incidents were found to be closely related to status; pilots (highest status) were found to initiate incidents more often than ticket agents (equal status) or cleaning personnel (lower status). The strongest affective reactions, however, were to hypotheticals where the initiator was of lower status, although there tended to be more consistent responses for all status where the hypothesized behaviour was more serious.

Joy A. Livingston, "Responses to Sexual Harassment on the Job: Legal, Organizational, and Individual Actions" (1982) 38:4 _Journal of Social Issues_ 5-21

The women's movement raised public awareness about the serious nature of sexual harassment on the job, as a legitimate problem requiring solution. This article canvasses remedial measures including legal redress, grievance procedures, employee education schemes, organizational support services and individual action. Statistical evidence of effectiveness is offered. The author argues for a more comprehensive approach within a larger framework, which recognizes the unequal power between men and women.

Catharine MacKinnon, "Introduction to Symposium: Sexual Harassment" (1981) 10 *Capital University Law Review* i-vii

MacKinnon's introduction to the Capital Symposium on Sexual Harassment notes that the acceptance of the term and concept of sexual harassment marks the first time that women's point of view of a situation has been perceived as definitive of that situation. She discusses the relativity of points of view, noting that the differences between the male and female perspectives result in different doctrinal requirements in law. The progress and failures in regard to the integration of sexual harassment concepts into sex discrimination doctrine and equal protection theory are briefly discussed. MacKinnon poses a final question about how best to ensure that the law against sexual harassment remains part of women's demand to control their own sexuality, and does not become a "request for paternal protection."

Michael Marmo, "Arbitrating Sex Harassment Cases" (1980) *Arbitration Journal* 35-40

The author discusses typical sexual harassment cases which come for arbitration, remedies available to the employee and the problems women face in seeking remedies. He examines the union's role in the process, and management responses to the problem.

P. J. Murray, "Employer: Beware of 'Hostile Environment' Sexual Harassment" (1987/88) 26 *Duquesne Law Review* 461-484

The author focuses on sexual harassment in a hostile environment, and discusses many aspects of harassment, including verbal abuse, suggesting that the courts adopt an objective victim standard to assess behaviour. Such a standard will further the Title VII objective of eliminating workplace discrimination. She discusses the responsibilities of the employer and victim, and recommends a framework to eliminate sexual harassment.

Catherine A. O'Neill, "Sexual Harassment Cases and the Law of Evidence: A Proposed Rule" [1989] *University of Chicago Legal Forum* 219-248

The author draws an analogy between rape and sexual harassment, and suggests that a version of Federal Rule of Evidence 412 be created for application to sexual harassment. In the United States, Rule 412 prohibits the admission, in most cases, of evidence of a rape victim's previous sexual history, and she argues that a similar rule would be justified in civil trials for sexual harassment. The article examines the history and purpose of Rule 412, the possible benefits and problems of extending a similar rule to sexual harassment, and concludes with an appendix model version of the rule.

E. Polansky, "Sexual Harassment at the Workplace: The Behaviour That Our Culture Condones and the Law Prohibits Makes it Profoundly Difficult to Enforce Title VII" (1980) 8 _Human Rights_ 14-19

This article discusses the historical development of the concept of "sexual harassment", particularly the growing recognition, in the 1970's, of sexual harassment as a significant problem. The author describes the analogy between sexual harassment and rape, noting the similarities in their effects on the victim and the motives of the perpetrator. She also addresses the legal issue of whether sexual harassment in the United States constitutes sex discrimination for the purposes of Title VII of the CIVIL RIGHTS ACT of 1964.

Timothy Reilly, Sandra Carpenter, Valerie Dull, and Kim Bartlett, "The Factorial Survey: An Approach to Defining Sexual Harassment on Campus" (1982) 38:4 _Journal of Social Issues_ 99-109

This article reports the findings of a survey of under-graduate students and faculty at the University of California to assess perceptions of sexual harassment in hypothetical situations. The authors found that the behaviour and the intentions of the male instructor were the most relevant factors in consensus between male and female respondents with respect to the situation between student and faculty: the more extreme the behaviour, the more likely there was to be consensus as to whether the behaviour was harassment. There was more disagreement when the student and the instructor had a past relationship or the student's behaviour was "suggestive".

Claire Robertson, Constance E. Dyer, and D'Ann Campbell, "Campus Harassment: Sexual Harassment Policies and Procedures at Institutions of Higher Learning" (1988) 13 _Signs: Journal of Women in Culture and Society_ 792-813

The article presents the results of a survey of 668 American universities and colleges, both public and private, with respect to the methods used to handle sexual harassment complaints, institutional policies and procedures, including the different definitions of sexual harassment, and an analysis of the effectiveness of these policies and procedures. The survey found that the larger institutions were more likely to have harassment policies in place, and that a significant portion of public institutions, which are required by law to do so, do not. The authors present a series of recommendations for effective sexual harassment policies. These include the need to educate personnel and administrators, the importance of consistently applied sanctions, and regular publication of the institution's policies, procedures, and the number of complaints filed and resolved.

Ann Schneider, "Sexual Harassment Brief Bank and Bibliography" (1985) 8 *Women's Rights Law Reporter* 267-301
     This article digests 182 sexual harassment cases from the mid-1970's through 1985, and indexes them by subject. It is accompanied by a three page bibliography of law review articles, books, and pamphlets on sexual harassment.

Beth E. Schneider, "Consciousness about Sexual Harassment Among Heterosexual and Lesbian Women Workers" (1982) 38:4 *Journal of Social Issues* 75-97
     For annotation, see Chapter 12: LESBIANISM AND SEXUAL ORIENTATION.

J. Clay Smith Jr., "Prologue to the EEOC guidelines on Sexual Harassment" (1981) 10 *Capital University Law Review* 471-479
     Part of a Symposium on Sexual Harassment, this article outlines the history of the development of the Equal Employment Opportunity Commission (EEOC)'s definition of sexual harassment as well as the public and private influences on the definition. It also examines early court decisions and categorizes current sexual harassment complaints before the EEOC.

Amy Somers, "Sexual Harassment in Academe: Legal Issues and Definitions" (1982) 38:4 *Journal of Social Issues* 23-31

For annotation, see Chapter 9: LEGAL EDUCATION.

Martha Sperry, "Hostile Environment Sexual Harassment and the Imposition of Liability Without Notice: A Progressive Approach to Traditional Gender Roles and Power Based Relationships" (1990) 24 _New England Law Review_ 917-952
This comment examines the factors at play in court decisions concerning sexual harassment in the workplace. The author outlines earlier American cases, including the first recognition of sexual harassment as gender discrimination, and discusses the imposition of vicarious liability for sexual harassment on employers in a recent Massachusetts case. The author approves of this development, but concludes that further steps must still be taken in order to redress inequality in the workplace.

Marcy Strauss, "Sexist Speech in the Workplace" (1990) 25 _Civil Liberties Law Review_ 1-51
For annotation, see Chapter 2: CONSTITUTIONAL LAW.

Verta A. Taylor, "How To Avoid Taking Sexual Harassment Seriously: A New Book That Perpetuates Old Myths -- Book Review: Mary Coeli Meyer, Inge M. Berchtold, Jeannenne L. Oestreich, and Frederick J. Collins, SEXUAL HARASSMENT (1981)" (1981) 10 _Capital University Law Review_ 672-684
For annotation see Chapter 16: BOOK REVIEWS.

Joan Vermeulen, "Employer Liability Under Title VII For Sexual Harassment By Supervisory Employees" (1981) 10 _Capital University Law Review_ 499-530
Part of a Symposium on Sexual Harassment, this article deals with the strict and vicarious liability of employers and the constructive knowledge theory. It provides a review of early court decisions.

Russell W. Wittenburg, "Sexual Harassment: A Jurisprudential Analysis" (1981) 10 _Capital University Law Review_ 607-624
Part of a Symposium on Sexual Harassment, this article deals with

the politics and the effectiveness of sexual harassment law. It focuses on employer liability, punishment, and remedies.

CHAPTER 9
LEGAL EDUCATION

Kathryn Abrams, "Hiring Women" (1990) 14 *Southern Illinois University Law Journal* 487-505
For annotation, see Chapter 8: LABOUR AND EMPLOYMENT -- AFFIRMATIVE ACTION.

Edward A. Adams, "A Battle for Yale Law School's Soul? Offer to a Feminist Draws Fury (Catharine A. MacKinnon)" (1988) 10 *National Law Journal* 3-4
This article discusses the controversy surrounding the appointment of Professor MacKinnon, a leading feminist legal theoretician, as a visiting faculty member to Yale Law School. The debate focused on whether feminist legal theory is merely political or scholarly. Much of the concern focused on the perception of an ideological split in the faculty between liberal and conservative faculty members.

Marina Angel, "Women in Legal Education: What it's Like to be Part of a Perpetual First Wave or the Case of the Disappearing Women" (1988) 61 *Temple Law Review* 799-846
The author combines both her personal experience as a law student, lawyer, and professor, with statistical information about the progress of women in law school settings in the United States. The article illustrates the problems of institutional bias in the granting of tenure, focusing particularly on the five law schools at which the author has studied or taught: Columbia, University of Pennsylvania, Rutgers-Camden, Hofstra, and Temple.

Taunya Lovell Banks, "Gender Bias in the Classroom" (1988) 38 *Journal of Legal Education* 137-146
In her survey of five law schools, the author found continuing sexism in legal education. Expanding her 1986 pilot study, she found emerging patterns of behaviour. The voluntary participation of male and

female students is significantly different, and differs with the year and age of the student. In four out of five schools the students reported sexist, racist, homophobic and anti-religious comments. She asks to what extent male and female students truly receive equal education. The classroom environment, structure and language, she claims, all exclude women and make them feel inferior. Although the silencing tactics are exacerbated for women, she suggests that they also injure sensitive male students and indeed the legal system as whole.

Taunya Lovell Banks, "Gender Bias in the Classroom" (1990) 14 _Southern Illinois University Law Journal_ 527-543
    For annotation, see Chapter 6: **FIRST NATIONS AND RACE.**

David Barnhizer, "The Revolution in American Law Schools" (1989) 37 _Cleveland State Law Review_ 227-269
    The author discusses the shifts in the focus of legal scholarship and in the curriculum of law schools. He considers the impact of, among other things, feminism, Critical Legal Studies, sociological research, political science and political economy, structuralism, the legal skills movement, and constitutional interpretation. In his opinion, modern legal interpretation stems either from a concept of positive justice or from a recognition of unjust conditions. He argues that the latter, "negative," strategy is no longer useful because awareness of injustice and of bias now exists. He concludes with the prediction that the constructive intellectual activities now occurring in law schools will have a "ripple effect," and extend to every aspect of legal practice.

Kathleen S. Bean, "The Gender Gap in the Law School Classroom - Beyond Survival" (1989) 14 _Vermont Law Review_ 23-56
    This article explores the problem of gender bias in the law school classroom. The author analyses the hostility she has encountered from students who expect a law teacher to be male and discusses ways of dealing with such bias.

Leslie Bender, "A Lawyer's Primer on Feminist Theory and Tort" (1988) 38 _Journal of Legal Education_ 3-37
    For annotation, see Chapter 5: **FEMINIST THEORY -- GEN-**

ERAL.

M. H. Berlin, "Note on the Scales–Johnson Syllabus" (1986) 16 _New Mexico Law Review_ **433-438**

Part of a Symposium on Legal Education, this is a response to the Scales/Johnson article (K. Johnson and A. Scales, An Absolutely, Positively True Story: Seven Reasons Why We Sing (1986) 16 New Mexico Law Review 433), contained in the same volume. The author claims that the Scales and Johnson approach to teaching law is unrealistic, and argues that because their roles are different, equality between student and teacher does not exist in the classroom, and that to deny that, is to reject the teacher's responsibility. As a non-lawyer, the author has a "sense of awe for the western legal tradition," and she finds the idea of rejecting it unsettling, even if it really is a projection of the white male hierarchical structure, as claimed by Scales and Johnson.

K. Lee Berthel, "Sexual Harassment in Education Institutions: Procedure for Filing a Complaint with the Office for Civil Rights, Department of Education" (1981) 10 _Capital University Law Review_ **585-606**

For annotation, see Chapter 8: **LABOUR AND EMPLOYMENT – SEXUAL HARASSMENT.**

Christine Boyle, "Criminal Law and Procedure: Who Needs Tenure?" (1985) 23 _Osgoode Hall Law Journal_ **427-440**

Part of a Symposium on Canadian Legal Scholarship, this article discusses the purpose of tenure, and in so doing, presents a brief and impressionistic analysis of recent Canadian criminal law articles. She argues that most advocate the status quo, basing their discussion on the assumption that male equals human. She points to the limitations of this kind of analysis in assessing not only gender related issues such as wife-battering and rape, but the gender cost of such values as freedom of expression and privacy. She comments on some of the leading feminist writers and indicates areas of feminist research that still require study. She concludes that those who need tenure are not those who advocate the status quo because they are not at risk. Rather, tenure is needed for those who advocate change and new ideas.

Christine Boyle, "Teaching Law As If Women Really Mattered, or, What About the Washrooms?" (1986) 2 *Canadian Journal of Women and the Law* 96-112

The author discusses gender bias in the law school, where the status quo is presented as neutral, but where in fact sex inequality is reflected in the materials and classroom conduct because masculine is valued over feminine. Alternatives for change are viewed as political, and reformist educators are caught in a double bind as they are faced with student resistance, tenure problems, accusations of radicalism and incompetence, and ugly backlash situations.

Naomi R. Cahn and Norman G. Schneider, "The Next Best Thing: Transferred Clients in a Legal Clinic" (1987) 36 *Catholic University Law Review* 367-393

This article addresses the problems of transferring cases in the legal clinic setting, and suggests means by which the transfer can be made easier for both the client and the students. The authors look at some of the factors, such as race, sex and class, that may complicate the process.

Patricia A. Cain, "Teaching Feminist Legal Theory at Texas: Listening to Difference and Exploring Connections" (1988) 38 *Journal of Legal Education* 165-181

The author describes a feminist legal theory class which combines discussion with consciousness-raising. She includes a detailed description of the curriculum materials and methodology, excerpts from student journals, examples of "hard cases" and underlying themes.

W. C. B. Chang, "Zen, Law and Language: Of Power and Paradigms" (1986) 16 *New Mexico Law Review* 543-572

Part of a Symposium on Legal Education, this article compares what the author considers to be the similar methods employed when teaching law and zen, and in the context of the Johnson and Scales article (K. Johnson and A. Scales, An Absolutely, Positively True Story: Seven Reasons Why We Sing (1986) 16 *New Mexico Law Review* 433), discusses how comparative philosophical methodology can be used to illustrate problems in legal philosophy. As an example, the author presents the problem of a legal paradox - the doctrine of stare decisis in conflict with the courts' theoretical freedom to change the law. Using the case ROBINSON v. ARIYOSHI 753 F.2d 1468, and applying the zen process, he argues that it is possible either to force an anomaly into the present paradigms, create a new paradigm, or to regard the anomaly as "mu": not right, not wrong. He says that the zen concept of "mu" relates to false duality, something which he says exists extensively in the law.

Richard H. Chused, "The Hiring and Retention of Minorities and Women on American Law School Faculties" (1988) 137 *University of Pennsylvania Law Review* **537-568**
    For annotation, see Chapter 8: LABOUR AND EMPLOYMENT -- AFFIRMATIVE ACTION.

Lorraine Code, "Stories People Tell" (1986) 16 *New Mexico Law Review* **599-606**
    Part of a Symposium on Legal Education, this article is in response to the Johnson and Scales work (K. Johnson and A. Scales, An Absolutely, Positively True Story: Seven Reasons Why We Sing (1986) 16 *New Mexico Law Review* 433), and discusses the nature of reality and what we can know for certain. The author compares modern psychological case histories with Johnson and Scales' approach, noting that there is only a limited degree to which we can claim to know and understand other people's experiences. The stories people tell inform us about their experiences -- a subjective truth that will be different from the objective "truth" of theory. She argues that it may be that an experiential analysis will reveal that the objective theory is flawed, and the experience a more accurate gauge of truth, as long as we listen carefully to the stories people tell.

Mary Irene Coombs, "Crime in the Stacks, or A Tale of a Text: A Feminist Response to a Criminal Law Textbook" (1988) 38 *Journal of Legal Education* **117-135**
    The author analyzes Perkins and Boyle, CRIMINAL LAW (3d ed., 1982) and claims that an identifiable attitude permeates the book. The text includes the doctrine of coercion of wives by husbands and husbands' authority to discipline wives (which it treats with great seriousness); presents women as defined by sexual behaviour; and describes rape as aggravated fornication. She thinks the textbook is capable of causing harm, because uninformed students may accept its vision. A letter to the

authors, with quotations of problem text, elicited a non-helpful response. However, a petition sent to the publisher resulted in revisions to the text. This experience underlines the need to apply feminist sensitivities and methodologies to a variety of materials, and the need for women students and faculty to join voices.

Mary Irene Coombs, "Non-Sexist Teaching Techniques in Substantive Law Courses" (1990) 14 *Southern Illinois University Law Journal* **507-526**

Part of a Symposium on Gender Bias in Legal Education, this article proposes what the author terms "a gender sensitive approach" to teaching law which incorporates anti-sexism, gender awareness and a feminist approach to teaching. She illustrates how the first two elements of her approach would impact on curriculum, course materials and class-room dynamics, and concludes with a discussion of what it means to be a feminist professor, using as an example the teaching of rape law. The article includes a response by Professor W. R. Schroeder.

Phyllis L. Crocker and Anne E. Simon, "Sexual Harassment in Education" (1981) 10 *Capital University Law Review* **541-584**

For annotation, see Chapter 8: **LABOUR AND EMPLOYMENT – SEXUAL HARASSMENT.**

Tove Stang Dahl, "Taking Women as a Starting Point: Building Women's Law" (1986) 14 *International Journal of the Sociology of Law* **239-246**

The author argues that since traditional law is based upon men's experience and needs, the development of women's law must take women as its starting point. The article describes the twelve year development of women's law as an academic discipline at the University of Oslo in Norway. Its goal is to offer feminist instruction at all stages of legal study, to make law more relevant to women and to build women's law into a research discipline. The author discusses justice and freedom as the values most relevant to women's law. When legal doctrine and empirical data are crossed with these values, at least four areas of concern are presented: the unjust distribution of money; time and work in society; the restraints to women's self-determination; and restraints on self-realization.

Clare Dalton, "Where We Stand: Observations on the Situation of Feminist Legal Thought" (1987) 3 _Berkeley Women's Law Journal_ 1-13

The author examines "feminist enlightenment" within the context of the existing "mainstream malaise" in law school. She explains how the focus of law courses has moved from an equality model of women's issues to a feminist jurisprudential approach and finally toward an expansion of women's issues into the curriculum at large. She considers the benefits and drawbacks of various approaches of dealing with women's reality within legal education. Recognizing aspects of legal education and practice as "important creators and sustainers of the culture of gender as well as the culture of law," she asserts "the importance of studying the treatment of women, women's realities and women's concerns."

Richard F. Devlin, "Legal Education as Political Consciousness-Raising or Paving the Road to Hell" (1989) 39 _Journal of Legal Education_ 213–229

This article describes the author's experiences when he assigned an anti-pornography memorandum and moot exercise to first year law students. The author discusses the political, social, and educational reaction of the students as well as faculty, and concludes that a strict legal and rational way of looking at such issues often causes problem for the students.

Richard L. Devlin, "Towards An/Other Legal Education: Some Critical and Tentative Proposals to Confront the Racism of Modern Legal Education" (1989) 38 _University of New Brunswick Law Journal_ 89-120

For annotation, see Chapter 6: FIRST NATIONS AND RACE.

Cynthia Fuchs Epstein, "Rationales and Realities: Social Change, Women and the Law" (1988) 37 _DePaul Law Review_ 367-377

For annotation, see Chapter 11: LEGAL PRACTICE.

Nancy S. Erickson, "Legal Education: The Last Academic Bastion of Sex Bias?" (1985-86) 10 _Nova Law Journal_ 457-464

Speaking at a symposium on Transforming Legal Education: A

Symposium of Provocative Thought, the author recounts the "blatant sex bias" in course materials, in teaching methods, and in the law which she encountered as a law student in the 1970's, canvasses early attempts to eliminate sex bias in the traditional law school curriculum, criticizes the legal academy for failing to undertake a systematic study of sex bias in legal education, and reports on two such projects then underway, one of which -- "Sex Bias in the Criminal Law: Bring the Law School Curriculum into the 1980's" -- she heads. She goes on to describe this project which has since made its final report: see, Erickson and Taub, "Final Report: Sex Bias in the Teaching of Criminal Law" (1990) 42 *Rutgers Law Review* 309-606.

Nancy S. Erickson, "Sex Bias in Law School Courses: Some Common Issues" (1988) 38 *Journal of Legal Education* 101-116
    The author argues that a rethinking and reformulation of law school courses will include identification of sex-bias. Choice of course offerings and elimination of sex-bias in courses, both in materials and presentation is not, she claims, a superficial undertaking. It requires wrestling with fundamental legal issues, but will illuminate them as well.

Nancy S. Erickson and Nadine Taub, "Final Report: 'Sex Bias in the Teaching of Criminal Law'" (1990) 42 *Rutgers Law Review* 309-605
    The Report claims that traditional legal education fails adequately to address gender-related issues and that this failure contributes to the alienation of women in law school. It is based upon an assessment of the treatment of gender-related issues in seven criminal law casebooks and upon a survey of criminal law teachers. The authors contrast the results of the assessment -- namely, that casebooks either omit entirely or treat superficially gender-related topics -- with the survey results and conclude that at least some of the exclusion of gender topics in the classroom is due to the lack of textbook coverage. The Report suggests ways in which topics of particular interest to women can be included in criminal law courses and provides a bibliography for use by textbook authors and criminal law teachers.

Mary Jo Eyster, "Analysis of Sexism in Legal Practice: A Clinical Approach" (1988) 38 *Journal of Legal Education* 183-193
    The author supervises a Brooklyn Law School civil litigation clinic

in New York City. She describes how she integrates confrontation of sexism and racism into the clinic setting.

Mary Jo Eyster, "Integrating Non-Sexist/Racial Perspectives Into Traditional Court and Clinical Settings" (1990) 14 *Southern Illinois University Law Journal* 471-486
For annotation, see Chapter 6: FIRST NATIONS AND RACE.

Jay M. Feinman, "Change in Law Schools" (1986) 16 *New Mexico Law Review* 505-512
Part of a Symposium on Legal Education, this article attempts to define the process of reform and innovation in legal education. Referring to Johnson and Scales' article (K. Johnson and A. Scales, An Absolutely, Positively True Story: Seven Reasons Why We Sing (1986) 16 *New Mexico Law Review* 433), the author discusses the difficulty of integrating theory and practice, of combining educational experimentation with thoughtful and substantive course objectives, and of institutionalizing these changes.

Lucinda M. Finley, "A Break in the Silence: Including Women's Issues in a Torts Course" (1989) 1 *Yale Journal of Law and Feminism* 41-72
The author argues that women's issues ought to be integrated into the basic law school curriculum in order to help women feel less alienated in law school, to increase male student awareness of gender issues, and to overcome the societal tendency to trivialize women's issues. She discusses several areas in tort law that reflect gender concerns, such as intra-familial immunity, action for loss of consortium, and sexual harassment. She also analyzes how traditional standards, such as the reasonable person standard, contain gender bias, and suggests areas of women's experience that could be used to further enrich a torts course.

James C. Foster, "Book Review: Seyla Benhabib and Drucilla Cornell, FEMINISM AS CRITIQUE: ON THE POLITICS OF GENDER (1987)" (1988) 38 *Journal of Legal Education* 471-473
For annotation, see Chapter 16: BOOK REVIEWS.

David Fraser, "What's love got to do with it? Critical legal studies, feminist discourse, and the ethic of solidarity" (1988) 11 *Harvard Women's Law Journal* 53-81
    For annotation, see Chapter 5: FEMINIST THEORY -- GENERAL.

Mary Frug, "Re-Reading Contracts: A Feminist Analysis of a Contracts Casebook" (1985) 34 *American University Law Review* 1065-1140
    The author examines a contracts casebook [see: J. Dawson, W. Harvey, and S. Henderson, Contracts Casebook (1982) 4th ed.] from a feminist perspective, and demonstrates the gender bias inherent in the text. She claims that this bias affects the reader's understanding of both contract law and the law in general. She argues that gender bias in the contracts casebook is only an instance of the larger problem, which is gender bias in legal education generally, and recommends that her evaluation of the casebook serve as a model for further analysis of texts and teaching.

Meredith Gould, "The Paradox of Teaching Feminism and Learning Law" (1983) 7 *ALSA Forum* 270-289
    The author claims that feminist pedagogy is necessary in the law school as more women attend and are faced with the problems inherent in traditional law school pedagogy. Feminist pedagogy puts the theoretical validity of women's social experience into practice. She outlines strategies to infuse feminist issues into legal education. These include analysis of cases of gender inequality; discussion of socio-cultural context of cases; and development of methodological skills of analysis to reveal the social, cultural and historical context of legal activity.

Catharine W. Hantzis, "Kingsfield and Kennedy: Reappraising the Male Models of Law School Teaching" (1988) 38 *Journal of Legal Education* 155-164
    Because feminist pedagogy is largely uncharted territory, the author examines the male models of Kingsfield (as in the movie, PAPER-CHASE) and Kennedy (see: Kennedy, "Legal Education as Training for Hierarchy" (1982) D. Kairys, ed., THE POLITICS OF LAW 40) and then offers a female model in which student stereotyping is avoided, a

caring attitude to students is developed and different experiences are offered. She suggests, however, that this is a reformist and not a reconstructionist activity, and concludes that this raises the serious issue of legal education's perpetuating and legitimating existing institutions which are the actual source of the problem.

Didi Herman, "Legal Education, Feminism, and the 'Well-Intentioned Man': A Response to Richard Devlin" (1990) 40 _Journal of Legal Education_ **257-260**
This article is a student response to R. Devlin's "Legal Education as Political Consciousness-Raising or Paving the Road to Hell" [(1989) 39 _Journal of Legal Education_ 213-229]. The author criticizes Devlin for his portrayal of students as inexperienced scholars, and of himself as the knowledge holder, and admonishes him not to use the classroom as a place for his own personal discovery of feminism.

J. Highwater, "Vigilante Law" (1986) 16 _New Mexico Law Review_ **595-597**
Part of a Symposium on Legal Education, this article discusses what George Will calls the "indignation industry", a media creation for people who love to feel outraged but never bother to think for themselves. The author links stupidity of such people to the vigilante elements of law, and praises Johnson and Scales (K. Johnson and A. Scales, An Absolutely, Positively True Story: Seven Reasons Why We Sing (1986) 16 _New Mexico Law Review_ 433), for their attempt to replace vigilantism with creativity.

Suzanne Homer and Lois Schwartz, "Admitted but Not Accepted: Outsiders Take an Inside Look at Law School" (1989-90) 5 _Berkeley Women's Law Journal_ **1-74**
In an attempt to ascertain whether men and women experience law school differently, the authors administered a nineteen page questionnaire to the students at Boalt Hall (University of California at Berkeley). The response rate was 78%. The questionnaire, which is appended to the article, focused on self-esteem as the primary variable and organizing principle. They comment on recent studies at Yale and Stanford, the feminist legal literature in the area, and the lack of diversity in the faculty, which continues to be largely male and white.

W. Hurst, "Hurst Story" (1986) 16 _New Mexico Law Review_ 585-586
Part of a Symposium on Legal Education, this article discusses the Johnson and Scales syllabus (K. Johnson and A. Scales, An Absolutely, Positively True Story: Seven Reasons Why We Sing (1986) 16 _New Mexico Law Review_ 433), and the methods used to discover and confront the problems of injustice in the law. The author suggests some additions to the syllabus to alert students to the fact that some of these problems do not fit neatly into the syllabus analysis.

Elaine D. Ingulli, "Sexual Harassment in Education" (1987) 18 _Rutgers Law Journal_ 281-323
For annotation, see Chapter 8: **LABOUR AND EMPLOYMENT -- SEXUAL HARASSMENT.**

Karl Johnson and Ann C. Scales, "An Absolutely, Positively True Story: Seven Reasons Why We Sing" (1986) 16 _New Mexico Law Review_ 433-478
Part of a Symposium on Legal Education, this article provides an impressionistic and lyrical account of the authors' own, and their students' experiences and reactions to the teaching methodology used in their non-traditional first year law course in jurisprudence. The article touches upon philosophy, rock music, feminism, civil rights, law school, and creativity; it discusses what it is to be a law student, a law teacher, and a human being. Three appendices include a description of the course, the syllabus, and a description of the teaching method.

Emily Joselson and Judy Kaye, "Pro Se Divorce: A Strategy for Empowering Women" (1983) 1 _Law and Inequality_ 239-275
For annotation, see Chapter 4: **FAMILY LAW -- MARRIAGE AND DIVORCE.**

C. D. Kelso, "Goings-On at the University of New Mexico School of Law" (1986) 16 _New Mexico Law Review_ 587-588
Part of a Symposium on Legal Education, this article questions the effectiveness of the Johnson and Scales syllabus (K. Johnson and A. Scales, An Absolutely, Positively True Story: Seven Reasons Why We Sing (1986) 16 _New Mexico Law Review_ 433), and notes that the real test

will lie in the results and the kind of lawyers the students become in the real world. The author claims that Johnson and Scales' insights are not new, merely rediscovered, and cautions that law schools shouldn't be used just for self-improvement or to promote reform movements.

O. H. King, "I Sing Because I'm Happy: Some Random Thoughts on 'An Absolutely Positively True Story: Seven Reasons Why We Sing'" (1986) 16 _New Mexico Law Review_ 535-541
Part of a Symposium on Legal Education, this article is a response to the Johnson/Scales article (K. Johnson and A. Scales, An Absolutely, Positively True Story: Seven Reasons Why We Sing (1986) 16 _New Mexico Law Review_ 433), which questions many of its claims regarding the law and law schools. The author defends the law as a liberator, and regards the Johnson and Scales approach as an attack upon law's values.

Philip C. Kissam, "The Decline of Law School Professionalism" (1986) 134 _University of Pennsylvania Law Review_ 251-324
The author claims that the law school is a professional community in which the professors and students share common values, methods and attitudes. He suggests that the way law has been studied is now in decline and that structural changes are occurring as legal inquiry moves beyond formalism and realism towards a more contextual and critical study with more emphasis on history, the social sciences and legal theory. He identifies a number of changes which will contribute to a reconstruction of the law school community including increased specialization of faculty, students who want less hostility in the classroom, the introduction of woman's voice, and external pressures from the public and the profession.

Mari J. Matsuda, "Affirmative Action and Legal Knowledge: Planting Seeds in Plowed-up Ground" (1988) 11 _Harvard Women's Law Journal_ 1-17
For annotation, see Chapter 8: **LABOUR AND EMPLOYMENT -- AFFIRMATIVE ACTION.**

D. J. McCarthy, Jr., "Some Brief Reflections on Johnson and Scales, 'An Absolutely, Positively True Story: Seven Reasons Why We Sing'"

(1986) 16 *New Mexico Law Review* 607-612

Part of a Symposium on Legal Education, this article criticizes the Johnson and Scales article (K. Johnson and A. Scales, An Absolutely, Positively True Story: Seven Reasons Why We Sing (1986) 16 *New Mexico Law Review* 433) as amateurish pop psychology based on "customary legal education trashing", and he dismisses as a fad their attempts at changing legal education. He suggests that the article contains some valuable insights, including the need for law teachers to convey to their students a more expansive view of the lawyer's role. He argues, however, that Johnson and Scales' experimental course ignores the substantive subject matter required in a professional school.

Sheila McIntyre, "Gender Bias Within the Law School: 'The Memo' and its Impact" (1987-88) 2 *Canadian Journal of Women and the Law* 362-407

The author chronicles the incidents of sexism and anti-feminism which she observed and experienced during her first year of teaching, and which led her to write a memo which she distributed first to her colleagues and later to the press. She reproduces the actual memo, with factual observations and analysis of each incident, and describes how it polarized opinion in the faculty. In the epilogue, she questions whether the memo harmed more than it empowered, and discusses some of its effects on personal life and on the university.

Carrie Menkel-Meadow, "Feminist Legal Theory, Critical Legal Studies, and Legal Education or 'The Fem-Crits Go to Law School'" (1988) 38 *Journal of Legal Education* 61-85

The author argues that feminist critical scholars ("fem-crits") are dissatisfied with the Critical Legal Studies (CLS) agenda, because CLSers are committed to different methods and processes. Both conventional teaching methodology and CLS, she claims, aim to "break down" legal discourse, the former through analysis, the latter through deconstruction (trashing). Feminist method, on the other hand, seeks to "break up" through conversations and shared experiences, aiming for empowerment.

G. Minda, "Phenomenology, Tina Turner and the Law" (1986) 16 *New Mexico Law Review* 433-446

Part of a Symposium on Legal Education, this article describes phenomenology as an analytic method which uses subjective experience to describe and critique kinds of discourse, in this case legal discourse. Suggesting that the Johnson-Scales syllabus (K. Johnson and A. Scales, An Absolutely, Positively True Story: Seven Reasons Why We Sing (1986) 16 *New Mexico Law Review* 433) may be phenomenological, the author discusses the impact and power of the language of legal discourse in defining "truth" and in dividing reality into discrete elements. The alternative voice of rock and roll and the counter culture, he says, may provide a phenomenological focus that could be used to encourage creativity, new understanding of differences, and new ways to use the law to build and preserve relationships in order to create a peaceful world.

Martha Minow, "Feminist Reason: Getting It and Losing It" (1988) 38 *Journal of Legal Education* **47-60**
The author describes the problem of the production of knowledge within the presumed neutrality of academia. In established academic institutions, what counts as theory meets the criteria of coherence, value neutrality and abstraction, yet those requirements embody a false universalism that feminists criticize. To be credible in academia, a feminist approach must resemble the object of attack. She suggests that in consequence, there is a risk of becoming embroiled in what is criticized, becoming entranced by what should be demystified. Feminists, she argues, cannot re-vision the world with the tools that are given.

J. Moon, "An Essay on Local Critique" (1986) 16 *New Mexico Law Review* **433-453**
For annotation, see Chapter 5: FEMINIST THEORY -- GENERAL.

Mary Jane Mossman, "Feminism and Legal Method: The Difference It Makes" (1985) 3 *Wisconsin Women's Law Journal* **147-168**
For annotation, see Chapter 5: FEMINIST THEORY -- GENERAL.

Mary Jane Mossman, "Feminism and Legal Method: The Difference It Makes" (1986) 3 *Australian Journal of Law and Society* **30-51**
For annotation, see Chapter 5: FEMINIST THEORY -- GEN-

ERAL.

Mary Jane Mossman, "'Otherness' and the Law School: A Comment on Teaching Gender Equality" (1985) 1 *Canadian Journal of Women and the Law* 213-218

The author argues that woman as "Other" is still an apt characterization of women in law schools. Although there have been some efforts to redress the situation through analysis of the maleness of legal standards and values, they are mostly piecemeal, ad hoc, and peripheral to the main curriculum. She illustrates her point by describing challenges to her Women and the Law course at Osgoode Hall Law School at York University in Toronto. In order to transform "otherness", she urges that we not under-estimate the radical intent of women's studies which aim to reconstruct the normative tradition. Feminists seek fundamentally to change the legal system. Mossman believes that understanding "otherness" is central to understanding law and society.

Mary O'Brien and Sheila McIntyre, "Patriarchal Hegemony and Legal Education" (1986) 2 *Canadian Journal of Women and the Law* 69-95

The authors argue that traditional legal education instills the values and reinforces the interests of patriarchal capitalism. They point to law school curriculum's emphasis on law for the elite, to hierarchical classroom dynamics, to the fetishization of "objectivity" and "hard" law over "subjectivity" and "soft" law, to the doctrine/policy and public/private dichotomies as aspects of this process. They also argue that legal education serves a hegemonic function by declaring the mere presence of women as evidence of democracy, while in practice masculinizing women law students in male values and language. They conclude that counter-hegemonic activity by women law students is possible in women's experience of "soft," "private" realm courses and issues, because that experience can create a critical standpoint and an ethical consciousness to resist hardness and undermine capitalist/patriarchal values.

Johnny C. Parker and Linda C. Parker, "Affirmative Action: Protecting the Untenured Minority Professor During Extreme Financial Exigency" (1988) 17 *North Carolina Central Law Journal* 119-134

For annotation, see Chapter 6: FIRST NATIONS AND RACE.

Toni Pickard, "Experience as Teacher: Discovering the Politics of Law Teaching" (1983) 33 _University of Toronto Law Journal_ 179-214

The author examines the power dynamics of the law school classroom, and the ways that these dynamics confirm the patriarchal hierarchy and imbue students with the professional attitudes they develop. She describes NALT (Non-Adversarial Lawyering Tasks), an experimental program she undertook to explore the emotional dynamics of the classroom, the effect of these dynamics on the intellectual content, and the outcome of denying their existence.

Judith Resnik, "Complex Feminist Conversations" [1989] _University of Chicago Legal Forum_ 1-6

The author introduces the symposium, Feminism in the Law, by sharing some of her experiences as a female law faculty member, particularly her experience of being encouraged to ignore women's issues and to concentrate on the "real stuff" like torts, contracts, procedure and property. She discusses the trivialization of women and women's work, the "proximity" of feminists to feminist issues, and experiences of anger. The risks of voicing anger about experiences of marginalization, trivialization and subordination, she claims, are enormous. She concludes with the caution that feminists must take care not to speak from an "imperial position," as some men do, in articulating a universal women's experience; and the perception that women from different classes, races, sexual preferences and "modes of being" must also be heard.

Deborah L. Rhode, "The 'Woman's Point of View'" (1988) 38 _Journal of Legal Education_ 39-46

Part of a Symposium on Women in Legal Education, this article discusses feminist ambivalence with respect to requests from within the legal academy for the "woman's point of view" and provides the author's cautions on the implications of "woman's point of view" for legal, social, and feminist theory. The author argues that such requests are often either reductionist -- because they deny the differences among women -- or trivial and self-serving. She concludes that invitations of this sort are best viewed by feminists as an opportunity to challenge the assumption that any single view can capture the diversity of women's experiences and interests.

Ann Robinson, "Thémis Retrouve l'usage de la Vue" (1989) 3
***Canadian Journal of Women and the Law* 211-233**
    This article describes the discrimination faced by women in the law
faculties of Quebec. Despite the large influx of women into the law
school, there is a notable lack of feminist teachers and feminist research.
The author recounts numerous incidents which reflect the enduring
sexism of the institutions and their failure to deal with the denigration of
women students and teachers within them.

Kim Rosser, "Law and Gender: The Feminist Project in Action" (1988)
13 *Legal Service Bulletin* 233-235
    This article discusses the "Women and the Law" courses being
offered in many law schools. Focusing on a "Law and Gender" course
offered at the University of New South Wales Law School, the author
analyzes the way in which feminist jurisprudence is taught in law school.
She notes that these courses are generally optional, and that their
students tend to be those already aware of feminist issues in the law.
She suggests that the schools which offer these courses may be less likely
to integrate feminist perspectives into their other courses. She concludes
that in order for feminist jurisprudence to become accepted in the legal
and academic community, it will have to be incorporated into standard
law school courses, or failing that, specialized courses will have to be
compulsory.

Sharon Elizabeth Rush, "Understanding Diversity" (1990) 42 *Florida*
***Law Review* 1-24**
    Part of a Symposium on Women and the Law: Goals for the 1990s,
this article examines the meaning of and need for various diversities in
law school faculties -- namely, facial diversity, hardship diversity, and
ideological diversity. Women, the author claims, often fit into all three
definitions of diversity, although women, men of colour, and marginalized
men will all be necessarily represented in a diverse faculty. She concludes with the recommendation that facial diversity should be the
primary goal of any affirmative action within law faculties because this
type of diversity acknowledges that oppressed peoples speak with different voices, and thus are likely to encompass other diversities.

Arthur E. Ryman, "Women and the Bar Exam: Thinking Like a

Woman Lawyer" (1987-1988) 27 _Drake Law Review_ 79-82
This article discusses the differences between women's and men's failure rates on Bar exams, focusing on the results in Iowa in 1986-87. The author raises several reasons that may explain the differences, despite "anonymous" papers, including writing style, feminine handwriting, and differences in problem-solving approaches. He makes reference to Carol Gilligan's work (Gilligan, IN A DIFFERENT VOICE (1982)), and argues that women's different way of thinking can infuse new insights into the law. He concludes that there is a need for funded research to discover how to bring these differences into the legal education system, rather than forcing the male voice onto female law students and lawyers.

Elizabeth M. Schneider, "Task Force Reports on Women in the Courts: The Challenge for Legal Education" (1988) 38 _Journal of Legal Education_ 87-95
Several American states have appointed task forces to study women in the courts. The report of the New York task force documents many substantive areas of law and the environment in the courtroom as the locus of women's experience of discrimination. This article outlines the changes that law schools must make to effect a difference in gender bias. The author argues that changes must be made to the curriculum, casebooks, classroom dynamics and research agendas.

Ann Shalleck, "Report of the Women and the Law Project: Gender Bias and the Law School Curriculum" (1988) 38 _Journal of Legal Education_ 97-99
Part of a Symposium on Women in Legal Education, this article reports on the annual workshops on the treatment of women's rights in the law school curriculum convened by the Association of American Law Schools. The article suggests ways to bring a feminist perspective to courses and how to change the form of classroom discussion to ensure that not all dialogue is channelled through the professor. It recommends both methods to validate students' emotional and personal responses to course material and ways in which the feminist perspective can highlight the operation of power relations in the study of law.

Amy Somers, "Sexual Harassment in Academe: Legal Issues and

Definitions" (1982) 38:4 *Journal of Social Issues* 23-31

This article analyzes the legal state of affairs with respect to sexual harassment in the United States, and reports that the precedents that have considered sexual harassment have generally done so within the context of the sex discrimination laws. These laws, for the purposes of the education setting, fall under Title IX of the Education Amendments of 1972. The author outlines the process involved in dealing with a complaint, and canvasses the sanctions possible against individuals and institutions. She also discusses some of the criticisms directed at the guidelines established under Title IX by the Office of Civil Rights.

Paul J. Spiegelman, "Integrating Doctrine, Theory and Practice in the Law School Curriculum: The Logic of Jake's Ladder in the Context of Amy's Web" (1988) 38 *Journal of Legal Education* 243-270

The author claims that there has been little curriculum change in the law school since Langdell's case method, and that in any move toward reform, there is conflict between the theorists (more sophisticated abstraction) and the practice-oriented (more concrete learning) faculty. A complicating factor is that the traditionalists are not invited into the process of reform while the reformers are unable to agree on the competitive and cooperative orientations in legal education. The justice of Gilligan's Jake is compatible with traditional legal education which embodies interference with rights of others, unequal treatment and atomistic and competitive dispute resolution by adjudication. The caring of Gilligan's Amy is best taught by experiential learning techniques in small groups which increases the intellectual rigor of student thinking. He gives specific proposals for including both Jake and Amy in teaching and provides direction for needed changes. He suggests that as part of the debate over theory and practice, the discourse could be changed.

Michele Stolls, "A Feminine Perspective of Law School" (1987) 26 *New York State Bar Journal* 30(3)

The author suggests that women in law school are in a transitional stage, "one stage beyond defensive feminism - several stages before the goal of natural femininity". Once incorporated into every level of legal practice, she argues, women will no longer be compelled to assimilate and this will eventually result in the feminization of law students and practitioners.

Janet Taber et al., "Gender, Legal Education, and the Legal Profession: An Empirical Study of Stanford Law Students and Graduates" (1987-88) 40 *Stanford Law Review* 1209-1297
For annotation, see Chapter 11: LEGAL PRACTICE.

Esmeralda Thornhill, "Black Women's Studies in Teaching Related to Women: Help or Hindrance to Universal Sisterhood?" (1982) 16 *Fireweed* 77
For annotation, see Chapter 6: FIRST NATIONS AND RACE.

Carl Tobias, "Gender Issues and the Prosser, Wade, and Schwartz Torts Casebook" (1988) 18 *Golden Gate University Law Review* 495-527
This article provides a gender analysis of W. PROSSER, J. WADE AND V. SCHWARZ; CASES AND MATERIALS ON TORTS (8th ed.). The author notes that women who appear as characters in the casebook are generally presented in a stereotypical and unflattering manner. He finds the most serious deficiencies in the casebook, however, are a result of poor organization and a tendency to ignore tort issues which are of particular importance to women, such as wife-battering and marital rape. He presents a more detailed analysis of gender bias in a section dealing with the intentional torts chapters. He suggests that it may be possible to use the casebook to highlight gender issues, with the help of supplementary materials, but he cautions that more subtle forms of gender bias in the book and the classroom may be difficult to identify.

Carl Tobias, "Respect for Diversity: The Case of Feminist Legal Thought" (1989) 58 *University of Cincinnati Law Review* 175-182
The author argues that tenure and appointment disputes involving women in legal theory and feminist legal thought bring into question the institutional commitments of law schools to diversify. He reports that schools have rejected or discouraged teaching applications from women who have produced outstanding theoretical and practical work and have thereby deprived students of the challenge and intellectual stimulation of expertise in important fields of law. The criteria for judging contributions for publication in areas as complex as gender issues should be whether the work stimulates constructive thinking rather than whether the issue is settled or the reader is persuaded. Under this view, writing in an area of feminist legal theory would be as valuable as writing in the

areas of tax or constitutional law. He concludes that there is ample
room in law school for traditional legal scholarship and much more.

**Catherine Weiss and Louise Melling, "The Legal Education of Twenty
Women" (1988) 40 *Stanford Law Review* 1299-1369**
Part of a Symposium on Gender and the Law, this article documents the experience of twenty women at Yale Law School in 1987 who
found legal education alienating and who organized a women's group to
confront the alienation. After reporting their analysis of the problem --
alienation, they think, is a matter of domination rather than difference
and impoverishes the intellectual and emotional life of the law school --
the authors make a number of recommendations for change, including
an ethic of personal authenticity, more women faculty members,
curriculum changes, a more communal classroom environment, and acknowledgement of pre-law knowledge and experience.

**Leigh West, "Book Review: Ronald Chester, UNEQUAL ACCESS:
WOMEN LAWYERS IN A CHANGING AMERICA (1985)" (1985) 5
Windsor Yearbook of Access to Justice 407-410**
For annotation, see Chapter 16: **BOOK REVIEWS.**

**Stephanie M. Wildman, "The Classroom Climate: Encouraging Student
Involvement" (1989) 4 *Berkeley Women's Law Journal* 326-334**
Prior socialization and the method of teaching law both contribute
to the silence of women in class. The author was a "silent woman" in law
school and she offers practical suggestions for students and teachers to
increase class participation by women. She reports both success and
failure in her attempts to introduce feminist concepts and discussion of
women's life experiences into legal education. She concludes that changing the classroom climate is difficult when you feel isolated and suggests
that the boundaries of permissable discourse in law school can be
expanded by practising on each other's oppressions.

**Stephanie M. Wildman, "The Question of Silence: Techniques to
Ensure Full Class Participation" (1988) 38 *Journal of Legal Education*
147-154**
The author claims that the silence problem in the classroom is part

of a larger cultural phenomenon in which society does not see the voiceless. Silence is a socialized role for women and it interferes with women's ability to learn substantive material and wastes time for practice in verbal agility. Wildman suggests classroom teaching techniques which give students a chance to talk in order to change students' experiences at a fundamental level. She urges a challenge to the male version of law school which is engrained in the collective unconscious.

Vivian Wilson, "How Women Betray Themselves" (1985-86) 10 *Nova Law Journal* 889-894

This comment, part of a Symposium entitled Transforming Legal Education: A Symposium of Provocative Thought, discusses liberalism and female law professors who are the unappreciative beneficiaries of victories won by 'older, more daring women'. The author emphasizes the centrality of consciousness-raising in the development of feminist theory and analysis, and discusses organizational structure and the method and the theory of social change.

K. C. Worden, "A Student Polemic" (1986) 16 *New Mexico Law Review* 573-504

Part of a Symposium on Legal Education, this article focuses on ways in which students may work to change the legal education system. The author criticizes both the lack of student interest and involvement in changing legal education, and the system's exclusion of the student's point of view when considering reform. She presents several basic and simple classroom tactics that students can use to change "the boredom, the alienation, and the disempowerment of the law school experience." The article was written in response to the Scales/Johnson syllabus (K. Johnson and A. Scales, An Absolutely, Positively True Story: Seven Reasons Why We Sing (1986) 16 *New Mexico Law Review* 433).

K. C. Worden, "Overshooting the Target: A Feminist Deconstruction of Legal Education" (1985) 34 *American University Law Review* 1141-1156

The author argues that the powerful political strategy of ideological abuse in legal education contributes to the subjugation of the female voice in law. She examines the difference debate -- Gilligan's Amy/Jake analysis -- and cites examples of classroom situations and moot court experience which exemplify the debate, especially in the requirement to learn to speak male as a second language and learn it fluently. Black letter law epitomizes the notion that the male voice of rationality is the only form of reasoning appropriate for legal analysis. She concludes, however, that there is difficulty -- even in feminist analysis -- in breaking free from the male voice because it is internalized through socialization. She suggests unveiling its assumptions as a useful and energizing means to social change.

CHAPTER 10
LEGAL HISTORY

Rosalie Silberman Abella, "The Critical Century: The Rights of Women and Children from 1882-1982" (1984) 18 *Law Society Gazette* 40-53

The author claims that this has been a century of benign neglect in the development of women's and children's rights. She treats the changing status of women in society through legislation and case law, and detects a move from restriction to the private domain to an ever-growing participation in public affairs. She suggests that changes such as political enfranchisement and ownership of property must be coupled with attitudinal changes so women's equality is achieved and society as a whole can benefit.

Barbara Allen Babcock, "Clara Shortridge Foltz: First Woman" (1988) 30 *Arizona Law Review* 673-719

This is a biographical account of the life of Clara Shortridge Foltz, the first woman to attend law school, the first woman lawyer in California, the first woman notary public, first woman counsel to a legislative committee and the first woman deputy district attorney. This trail blazing feminist overcame the obstacles and biases against her pursuit of her goals, partly through her dedicated commitment to all aspects of the women's movement.

Constance B. Backhouse, "Married Women's Property Law in Nineteenth-Century Canada" (1988) 6 *Law and History Review* 211-257

For annotation, see Chapter 4: FAMILY LAW -- PROPERTY.

Constance B. Backhouse, "'To Open the Way for Others of my Sex'; Clara Brett Martin's Career as Canada's First Woman Lawyer" (1985) 1 *Canadian Journal of Women and the Law* 1-41

The first woman to be admitted to the Bar in the British Commonwealth was called to the bar in the province of Ontario in 1897. This article describes her persistence in lobbying for changes to the law to allow her to study, and later to be admitted to the Bar in the face of bitter opposition from the Benchers of the Law Society of Upper Canada. After becoming the first female student-at-law, she endured constant scrutiny by the press, and encountered persistent "uncollegial behaviour" in her fellow students. Martin practised law, and became a community activist in a number of causes of interest to the women's movement.

Christine Ball, "Female Sexual Ideologies in Mid to Late Nineteenth-Century Canada" (1985-1986) 1 *Canadian Journal of Women and the Law* 324-337
    For annotation, see Chapter 5: FEMINIST THEORY -- SEXUAL-ITY.

Norma Basch, "The Emerging Legal History of Women in the United States: Property, Divorce, and the Constitution" (1986) 12 *Signs: Journal of Women in Culture and Society* 97-117
    For annotation, see Chapter 4: FAMILY LAW -- PROPERTY.

Norma Basch, "Marriage and Property in Nineteenth-Century New York" (1983) 2:3 *American Historical Review* 374-393
    For annotation, see Chapter 4: FAMILY LAW -- PROPERTY.

L. Berzins and S. Cooper, "The Political Economy of Correctional Planning for Women: The Case of the Bankrupt Bureaucracy" (1982) 24 *Canadian Journal of Criminology* 399-416
    For annotation, see Chapter 3: CRIMINAL LAW -- SENTEN-CING AND PRISONS.

M. Boivin, "L'évolution des droits de la femme au Québec: un survol historique" (1986) 2 *Canadian Journal of Women and the Law* 53-68
    This article contains a survey of the significant milestones in the legal history of the rights of Quebec women from 1867 to 1985. The author focuses on the juridical incapacity of married women and notes that although formal equality has now been attained, equality in fact re-

mains to be achieved.

Eileen Boris, "Homework and Women's Rights: The Case of the Vermont Knitters, 1980-1985" (1987-88) 13 *Signs: Journal of Women in Culture and Society* 98-120
    For annotation, see Chapter 8: LABOUR AND EMPLOYMENT -- GENERAL.

Brenda Boswell, "The Perpetuation of Wife Assault" (1983) 4 *Canadian Woman Studies* 69-71
    For annotation, see Chapter 3: CRIMINAL LAW -- BATTERING.

Julia Brophy, "Parental Rights and Children's Welfare: Some Problems of Feminists' Strategy in the 1920s" (1982) 10 *International Journal of the Sociology of Law* 149-168
    For annotation, see Chapter 4: FAMILY LAW -- CUSTODY.

Margaret A. Burnham, "An Impossible Marriage: Slave Law and Family Law" (1987) 5 *Law and Inequality* 187-225
    For annotation, see Chapter 6: FIRST NATIONS AND RACE.

June K. Burton, "Human Rights Issues Affecting Women in Napoleonic Legal Medicine Textbooks" (1987) 8 *History of European Ideals* 427-434
    For annotation, see Chapter 1: ABORTION AND REPRODUCTION.

M. Caron, "Les Travaux du Comité pour l'élimination de la Discrimination à l'égard des Femmes" (1985) 2 *Revue Québecoise de Droit International* 295-303
    For annotation, see Chapter 2: CONSTITUTIONAL LAW.

Martha Chamallas and Linda K. Kerber, "Women, Mothers and the Law of Fright: A History" (1990) 88 *Michigan Law Review* 814-863

This article explores whether the law of torts is actually gender neutral. By examining the development of the law of fright-based injuries, the authors demonstrate how certain torts have become feminized, and that the means by which damages were restricted had an unequal gender effect. The doctrines which deal with emotional injuries were developed from cases in which women were frequently the plaintiffs, and recovery was denied because the "reasonable man" would not have suffered damage in the same circumstances. They conclude with a feminist analysis of DILLON v. LEGG 68 Cal 2d 728 (1968), which presents an expanded doctrine that will make it easier for women to recover damages.

Lucie Cheng, "Women and Class Analysis in the Chinese Land Revolution" (1988-89) 4 *Berkeley Women's Law Journal* **62-93**
    For annotation, see Chapter 4: FAMILY LAW -- PROPERTY.

Richard H. Chused, "Gendered Space" (1990) 42 *Florida Law Review* **125-161**
    Part of a Symposium on Women and the Law: Goals for the 1990s, this article discusses the political importance of gendered spaces by examining nineteenth century writing about the women's temperance movement's "invading" of saloons. Both the nature of space, and of the people who occupy that space, influence political discourse. Thus, temperance intrusions of male saloons expanded the range of space in which women could engage in political discourse, forced men to pay attention to women's concerns, and established women's ability to alter the shape of their environments. The author argues that analysis of the social expectations which were challenged by temperance women, more than modern discrimination theory and its interface with legal challenges, will assist in a theory of gender and law. He carries out this form of analysis in a discussion of modern American equal protection litigation, and concludes that notwithstanding appropriate cultural and social analysis by feminists and academics, judicial interpretive writing misconstrues signals about the ways men and women relate, and also ignores the long history of white men segregating and structuring spaces for their own benefit.

Richard H. Chused, "Married Women's Property and Inheritance by

Widows in Massachusetts: A Study of Wills Probated Between 1800 and 1850" (1986) 2 *Berkeley Women's Law Journal* 42-88
   For annotation, see Chapter 4: FAMILY LAW -- PROPERTY.

   Elizabeth B. Clark, "Religion, Rights, and Difference in the Early Woman's Rights Movement" (1985) 3 *Wisconsin Women's Law Journal* 29-57
   For annotation, see Chapter 5: FEMINIST THEORY -- GENERAL.

   R. Collette-Carrière, "La Victimologie et le Viol: un Discours Complice" (1980) 13:1 *Criminologie* 60-79
   For annotation, see Chapter 3: CRIMINAL LAW -- RAPE.

   Clare Collins, "Book Review: Joan Sangster, DREAMS OF E-QUALITY: WOMEN ON THE CANADIAN LEFT, 1920-1950 (1989)" (1990) 19:1 *Resources for Feminist Research/ Documentation sur la Recherche Féministe* 8
   For annotation, see Chapter 16: BOOK REVIEWS.

   Mary Irene Coombs, "Agency and Partnership: A Study of Breach of Promise Plaintiffs" (1989) 2 *Yale Journal of Law and Feminism* 1-23
   For annotation, see Chapter 4: FAMILY LAW -- MARRIAGE AND DIVORCE.

   John D'Emilio, "Making and Unmaking Minorities: The Tensions Between Gay Politics and History" (1986) 14 *New York University Review of Law and Social Change* 915-922
   For annotation, see Chapter 12: LESBIANISM AND SEXUAL ORIENTATION.

   Karen Davis and Sue Schneider, "Women and the Law: 15th National Conference" (1984) 14:6 *Off Our Backs* 1-4
   This is a report of discussions at the Women and the Law Conference, which dealt with economic issues such as social program-

ming, child care and employment, civil rights, women in prison, lesbian battering, and law in a different voice. The articles are largely descriptive.

Carol Anne Douglas, "Feminist Jurisprudence" (1983) 13 *Off Our Backs* 16

This article reports on a workshop on feminist jurisprudence at which Catharine MacKinnon, LaDoris Hordel and Nadine Taub were the speakers and Phyllis Segal was the moderator.

Virginia G. Drachman, "'My 'Partner' in Law and Life': Marriage in the Lives of Women Lawyers in Late 19th- and Early 20th-Century America" (1989) 14 *Law and Social Inquiry* 221-250

This is one of three essays in a Symposium on Women in Legal Practice: Issues of Past, Present and Future. It looks at women lawyers in the 1880s and the 1910s and examines how they balanced career and marriage. The author brings together the history of women and the history of the legal profession, and looks beyond the discrimination model to "examine a broad range of issues, including ... female culture ...", using as a "starting point the notion of separatism." She uses letters of members of the Equity Club which tell the stories of women lawyers in the 1880s, and information gathered by the Bureau of Vocational Information for the later group.

E. Dwyer, "Varieties of Female Deviance: Insane Women in Nineteenth Century New York" (1980) 2:2 *Canadian Criminology Forum* 29-34

This article discusses whether the institutionalization of women has been used as a means of social control. Through a study of case files from a Utica institution for the years 1868-69, the author identified a group of 32 women and 56 men. Although she notes distinct differences between men and women diagnosed with the same illnesses, she found no evidence that institutionalization was routinely used as a way to control non-conforming women. The women admitted were generally in need of treatment, having been admitted after suicide attempts, acts of violence, or other activity recognizable as the result of mental illness.

Rosemary Feurer, "The Meaning of 'Sisterhood': The British

**Women's Movement and Protective Labor Legislation, 1870-1900" (1988)
31 _Victorian Studies_ 233-260**

The author describes the social and political climate in England
during the late 19th century, the feminist and labour movements, and
their views on gender and class. She reports that protective labour
legislation split the women's movement, because feminists were con-
vinced that trade union women had been duped by the men.

**Estelle B. Freedman, "Sentiment and Discipline: Women's Prison
Experiences in Nineteenth Century America" (1984) 16:4 _Prologue: The
Journal of National Archives_ 249-259**

For annotation, see Chapter 3: **CRIMINAL LAW -- SENTEN-
CING AND PRISONS.**

**Marina Fuccilli, "Feminist Legal Issues Conferences (Australia)" (1986)
11 _Legal Service Bulletin_ 142**

This is a report on the 1986 Conference on Feminist Legal Issues
held at Macquarie University, Australia. It includes a short summary of
the conference papers: Mossman, Feminism and Legal Method; Stubbs,
Positivism and the Law; Erika, Patriarchy and the State; Martin, IVF:
Towards a Feminist Critique; Graycar, Women in the Legal Profession
(subsequently published in (1987) 3 _Australian Journal of Law and
Society_).

**Mary Ellen Gale and Nadine Strossen, "The Real ACLU" (1989) 2
Yale Journal of Law and Feminism 161-187**

The authors, who have had a long association with the American
Civil Liberties Union, provide a feminist history of the organization
which supports their argument that it is feminist, although not exclusively. They seek to refute Andrea Dworkin's assertions of fact and theory
("The ACLU: Bait and Switch" (1989) 1 _Yale Journal of Law and
Feminism_ 37), which describes the ACLU as anti-feminist. They discuss
the ACLU commitment to free speech and explore its continuing pursuit
of equality rights.

**Shelley Gavigan, "Petit Treason in Eighteenth Century England:
Women's Inequality Before the Law" (1989-1990) 3 _Canadian Journal of_**

Women and the Law 335-374
    For annotation, see Chapter 3: CRIMINAL LAW -- EVIDENCE.

Ruth Bader Ginsburg, "Remarks on Women Becoming Part of the Constitution" (1988) 2 *Law and Inequality* 19-25
    For annotation, see Chapter 2: CONSTITUTIONAL LAW.

Ruth Bader Ginsburg and Barbara Flagg, "Some Reflections on the Feminist Legal Thought of the 1970s" [1989] *University of Chicago Legal Forum* 9-21
    For annotation, see Chapter 5: FEMINIST THEORY -- GENERAL.

Jan M. Glasgow, "Marital Rape Exemption: Legal Sanction of Spouse Abuse" (1980) 18 *Journal of Family Law* 565-585
    For annotation, see Chapter 3: CRIMINAL LAW -- RAPE.

Regina Graycar, "Feminism Comes to Law: Better Late Than Never" (1986) 3 *Australian Feminist Studies* 115-119
    The author describes two conferences held in 1986, one at Macquarie, Australia called Feminist Legal Issues, and the other in London organized by the European Conference on Critical Legal Studies, called Feminist Perspectives on Law: Theory and Practice. She outlines the main debates in feminism and law, criticizes the conference formats, and gives some interesting aspects of the presentations.

Robert L. Griswold, "Sexual Cruelty and the Case for Divorce in Victorian America" (1986) 11 *Signs: Journal of Women in Culture and Society* 529-541
    For annotation, see Chapter 4: FAMILY LAW -- GENERAL.

Souad Halila, "From Koranic Law to Civil Law: Emancipation of Tunisian Women Since 1956" [1984] *Feminist Issues* 23-44
    This article traces the historical developments that led to the emancipation of Tunisian women. The author argues that emancipation

was dictated by socio-economic factors which led to the breakdown of social patterns and reflected the tension between traditional and modern values. She concludes that despite this conflict, emancipation has produced substantive legal and personal gains for Tunisian women.

Patricia J. Higgins, "Women in the Islamic Republic of Iran: Legal, Social, and Ideological Changes" (1985) 10 _Signs: Journal of Women in Culture and Society_ 477-494

Although women participated in the revolution which successfully removed the Shah from power, the author argues, this participation occurred in sex-segregated groups with the women veiled. Post-revolution public confrontation over veiling, women's lack of participation in the judiciary and the military, and a proposed review of marriage and family law was quickly diffused because of concern that internal dissension weakened the revolution. However, the basic reason for minimal resistance by Islamic women is that the ideology of sex roles supported by Iranian officialdom is consistent with that held by the majority in Iran. Furthermore, some Iranian women have more access to political power, and do not aspire to the same equality rights and opportunities as do Western feminists. She concludes that the roles of men and women in Iran are based on separate but overlapping male and female spheres, and any equality in power and status will ensue within this structure.

Joan Hoff-Wilson, "The Unfinished Revolution: Changing Legal Status of U.S. Women" (1987) 13 _Signs: Journal of Women in Culture and Society_ 7-36

Notwithstanding the use of the words "person" and "individual" in the American Constitution and Bill of Rights, historically the United States Supreme Court has systematically discriminated against women. The author examines models of equality employed by feminists and by the Courts, alliances between feminists and conservatives, and concludes that while progress has been made, women have not yet achieved "complete equal rights with white males" even two hundred years after drafting the federal constitution. She specifically challenges feminists to consider the question of equal versus special treatment, and whether it is equality or justice for both sexes which is being sought.

Allen Hunter, "The Role of Liberal Political Culture in the Construc-

tion of Middle America" (1987) 42 *University of Miami Law Review* 93-126
   For annotation, see Chapter 5: FEMINIST THEORY -- GENERAL.

Flora Johnson, "Verbatim: Words Between the Sexes -- Book Review: Casey Miller and Kate Swift, WORDS AND WOMEN: NEW LANGUAGE IN NEW TIMES (1976)" (1980/81) 9 *Student Lawyer* 64-65
   For annotation, see Chapter 16: BOOK REVIEWS.

Chris Kehoe, "Legislative Alert!" (1980) 4:6 *Longest Revolution* 4-5
   The article discusses legislation passed in California with respect to non-gender specific sexual assault laws, funding for battered women shelters, and establishment of a DES information program. The author also discusses forthcoming legislation regarding child support enforcement, regulations requiring equal athletic opportunities for male and female students, and mandatory advice of medically viable alternatives to mastectomy.

Marian Leslie Klausner, "Redefining Pornography as Sex Discrimination: An Innovative Civil Rights Approach" (1984-85) 20 *New England Law Review* 721-777
   In this note, which is part of a Symposium on Pornography, the author traces the history of American obscenity law, and examines the alternative of the municipal ordinance, which recognizes pornography as a form of sex discrimination. Appended to the article are several examples of such ordinances.

H. Lane Kneedler, "Sexual Assault Law Reform in Virginia -- A Legislative History" (1982) 68 *Virginia Law Review* 459-505
   For annotation, see Chapter 3: CRIMINAL LAW -- RAPE.

Tamar Lewin, "Feminist Scholars Are Having Second Thoughts on Law and Order" (1988) 134 *Chicago Daily Law Bulletin* 1 (6 col.)
   This article surveys the influence that feminism is having on the law, and the effect of Gilligan's theories on approaches to difference.

Barbara S. Lindemann, "'To Ravish and Carnally Know': Rape in Eighteenth-Century Massachusetts" (1984) 10 *Signs: Journal of Women in Culture and Society* 63-82

This article is an historical study of rape in eighteenth-century Massachusetts which explains and analyzes the frequency and patterns of rape prosecution. The author discusses the evidentiary rules and narrow definitions of rape in patriarchal law as well as the cultural norms which minimized the occurrence of rape. Factors such as marital status and the presence of employer/employee relationships also affected findings of rape. She views rape law as a method of male control over women designed to serve men rather than protect women.

Sybil Lipschulz, "Social Feminism and Legal Discourse" (1989) 2 *Yale Journal of Law and Feminism* 131-159

This article examines the social feminist political vision of the 1920's and their "equality-through-difference" approach, known as "industrial equality." The author argues that advocacy of protective labour legislation was shaped during this time, separating earlier litigation from that of the twenties. She reports their equality through difference campaign was hampered by their dependence on male lawyers, who did not understand feminist ideals, and who saw women as inferior beings requiring protection. She concludes that their failure in ADKINS v. CHILDREN'S HOSPITAL, 261 U.S. 525 (1923) caused fear and demoralization in the movement, and forced feminists to return "to old ideas that worked," that is, women in need of protection.

Vera Mackie, "Feminist Politics in Japan" (1988) (Ja/Fe) *New Left Review* 53-78

The author reviews the history and current status of feminism in the world's most advanced capitalist state, beginning with the "Imperial Legacy" from 1868-1898 when patriarchal power and traditional woman's roles were explicitly linked to Imperial power, and continuing with the development of women's organizations and the early influence of socialists and suffragettes. The most "liberal" constitution in the world was adopted in 1947 under General MacArthur in the hopes that granting women's suffrage might dilute traditional militarism. Following this, other groups such as Fighting Women were formed, links with Asian feminists were developed and information was disseminated through private publication. She concludes that a liberal constitution is useless without affirmative action, adequate childcare and welfare services.

**Catharine MacKinnon, "Sex Equality and Nation-Building in Canada:
The Meech Lake Accord" (1990) 25 *Tulsa Law Journal* 735-757**
   Part of a Symposium on Feminist Jurisprudence, this article
provides the testimony the author gave to the Ontario Legislature's
Select Committee on Constitutional Reform, when it was considering the
Canadian constitutional amendment, commonly called the Meech Lake
Accord.

**L. Mailhot, "L'histoire des Femmes dan le Droit et dans la Magistra-
ture: Les Pionnières" (1986) 2:2 *Monde Juridique* 10, 21, 44-45**
   This is a short tribute to women pioneers in the law which focuses
on Emily Murphy and Helen Kinnear. Biographical sketches comprise
the largest part of the essay.

**Alice Mantel, "Book Review: Ellen Boneparth, ed., WOMEN,
POWER AND POLICY; A COLLECTION OF ESSAYS WRITTEN
FROM A FEMINIST PERSPECTIVE (1983)" (1986) 11 *Legal Service
Bulletin* 28**
   For annotation, see Chapter 16: BOOK REVIEWS.

**Isabel Marcus, "Locked In and Locked Out: Reflections on the History
of Divorce Law Reform in New York State" (1988/89) 37 *Buffalo Law
Review* 375-483**
   For annotation, see Chapter 4: FAMILY LAW -- MARRIAGE
AND DIVORCE.

**Deborah L. Markowitz, "In Pursuit of Equality: One Woman's Work
to Change the Law" (1989) 11 *Women's Rights Law Reporter* 73-97**
   The article is an account of Ruth Bader Ginsburg's struggle to
show the Supreme Court of the United States that legislated sex discrimination was part of a scheme of sex role allocation that was
hampering social change.   After detailing her career, the author
concludes that it was largely because of Ms. Ginsburg's successful
litigation strategy that the Supreme Court in 1976 adopted an "inter-

mediate level of scrutiny" for constitutional challenges to sex-based classifications.

Lorna R. Marsden and Joan E. Busby, "Feminist Influence Through the Senate: The Case of Divorce, 1967" (1989) 14:2 _Atlantis_ 72-80
Since the first woman senator was appointed in 1930, there have been twenty-five women appointed to the Senate of Canada. The authors list the women's organizations with which female senators have associated, and focus specifically on Senator Muriel Fergusson's association with the National Council of Women of Canada and the Council's possible influence on the hearings of the Special Senate-House of Commons Committee on Divorce in 1967. Senator Fergusson, the only woman on the committee, supported the NCWC submissions, the content of which were ultimately reflected in the legislation. They conclude that women's organizations have effectively exerted their influence through members in the Senate.

Thurgood Marshall, "Justice Thurgood Marshall's Remarks on the Bicentennial of the U.S. Constitution" (1987) 13 _Signs: Journal of Women in Culture and Society_ 2-6
For annotation, see Chapter 6: FIRST NATIONS AND RACE.

Mari J. Matsuda, "The West and the Legal Status of Women: Explanations of Frontier Feminism" (1985) 25 _Journal of the West_ 47-56
The author gives an historical account of the origin of women's rights within the law of western frontier states in the nineteenth and early twentieth centuries. She argues that it was the west that led the way in women's rights: women were offered the right to vote as early as 1869 in Wyoming; and property rights and family law reform including women's separate control of earnings during marriage and equal custody of children, often existed long before such rights were available to other American women. She discusses explanations for the West's receptivity to improving women's status and suggests they fall into four general categories -- the geographic explanation or "frontier theory," and economic, political and ideological explanations. She concludes that the best explanation is the coalescence of these factors with nineteenth century feminism and Western receptiveness to change primary. These early victories, she suggests, softened resistance in the east and inspired a vision

of feminism in its broadest social context.

A. Anne McLellan, "Legal Implications of the Persons Case" (1989) 1:1 *Constitutional Forum: Forum Constitutionnel* 11-14
For annotation, see Chapter 2: **CONSTITUTIONAL LAW.**

Martha Minow, "Forming Underneath Everything That Grows: Toward a History of Family Law" [1985] *Wisconsin Law Review* 819
The author argues that family law is underneath any exploration of the experience of women in a subordinate legal role. The traditional outline of the family progressing from patriarchal to egalitarian is deeply flawed because the cult of domesticity fails to account for the interaction between law and society, where social roles mediate change and reinforce norms. There are vast numbers of working women, volunteers, organizers and reformers with stories untold in history because hidden by reference to family roles and connections to others in patterns of obligation. Women who engaged in economic and political activities pushed at the edges of social roles as family members, and showed the strength and power of a united front of women.

Martha Minow, "Rights of One's Own in her Own Right: The Life of Elizabeth Cady Stanton -- Book Review: Elisabeth Griffith, IN HER OWN RIGHT: THE LIFE OF ELIZABETH CADY STANTON (1984)" (1985) 98 *Harvard Law Review* 1084-1099
For annotation, see Chapter 16: **BOOK REVIEWS.**

James C. Mohr, "Feminism and the History of Marital Law: Basch and Stetson on the Rights of Wives -- Book Review: D.M. Stetson, A WOMAN'S ISSUE: THE POLITICS OF FAMILY LAW REFORM IN ENGLAND (1982); N. Basch, IN THE EYES OF THE LAW: WOMEN, MARRIAGE AND PROPERTY IN NINETEENTH-CENTURY NEW YORK (1982)" [1984] *American Bar Foundation Research Journal* 223-228
For annotation, see Chapter 16: **BOOK REVIEWS.**

L. J. Moran, "A Study in the History of Male Sexuality in Law:

Non-Consummation" (1990) 1:2 *Law and Critique* 155-171

The author examines the history of marriage nullity actions for a husband's non-consummation, and suggests that this case law is both indicative of differing views of male sexuality, and of production of a knowledge of the male body. This knowledge is confined to the juridical, where the act, capacity, duty, right and remedy are interrelated and answer the question, "what is he by nature?" Consummation within this paradigm is an embedded power relation, an area where government may be deployed, and crucial for development of male heterosexuality within the institution of marriage.

Martha J. Morgan, "Founding Mothers: Women's Voices and Stories in the 1987 Nicaraguan Constitution" (1990) 70 *Boston University Law Review* 1-107

This article explores constitution-making from women's perspectives through a study of the drafting and adoption of the 1987 Nicaraguan Constitution in order to re-think, from a feminist perspective, the nature and importance of the events that comprise constitution-making and the significance of participation by women on the constitutional process, and, more particularly, to test the premises underlying the "stories" metaphor used by feminists to argue for a grounded and constitutive jurisprudence. The author details how Nicaraguan women participated in the constitutional process, and the effect their participation had on the constitution, on Nicaraguan society generally, and on the women themselves, and their continued influence on public discourse and policy during the early stages of the constitution. She concludes that women's participation in constitution-making does make a difference, and that there is much to learn from the experiences of these women, especially "the promise of a new understanding of the role of law in the struggle to reconstruct gender and of the relationships between equality and difference, unity and diversity, and community and individuality."

F. L. Morton, "Sexual Equality and the Family in Tocqueville's Democracy in America" (1984) 17 *Canadian Journal of Political Science* 309-324

Tocqueville's third tier remedy to the "problem of democracy" is the democratic family, where a "different but equal" regime between the sexes exists. The author argues that this regime requires men's dominance over women.

Dorothy Nelson, "Symposium on Women's Rights in International Law" (1987) 9 *Whittier Law Review* 393-398

As a presenter in the Symposium on Women's Rights in International Law, the author gives examples of how different customs and value systems affect women in third world countries. Differences and similarities between women are identified in her account of her conversation with Mrs. Sadat in 1975 about the need for equal education as a prerequisite to world peace. She gives a brief history of the development of women's rights in America and discusses how international covenants might be used to bring about the same results as the Equal Rights Amendment.

Mary Beth Norton, "The Constitutional Status of Women in 1787" (1988) 6 *Law and Inequality* 7-15

Part of a Symposium on the American Constitution and Equality, this article takes a historical perspective and explains that while gender neutral words were used when writing the constitution, this was more because the family was the basic unit of society and not because of any attempt to afford women the same constitutional protections as men. The constitution was based on Lockean philosophy more than equality considerations.

Karen O'Connor, "She Shall Overcome" (1988) 15 *Human Rights* 24

This is a chronology of the development of women's rights organizations in the United States. The author claims that both the older, more traditional strain of the women's movement represented by the National Organization for Women and the younger, more liberal strain had their roots in the civil rights movement. The NAACP provided the model for future organizations and "blazed the way" in the area of women's rights litigation.

Frances Olsen, "From False Paternalism to False Equality: Judicial Assaults on Feminist Community, Illinois: 1869-1895" (1986) 84 *Michigan Law Review* 1518-1541

This article examines the feminist debate over what women should emphasize in the struggle for equality: their similarities to men or their differences from men. The author argues that choosing between gender-blind and gender-conscious policies misfocuses attention because the application of "special treatment" versus "equal treatment" brings different results depending on the context of the issue. Two 19th century Illinois decisions illustrate the differing results. She claims that IN RE BRADWELL, 55 Ill. 535 (1869), a case refusing to allow women to practice law, is an instance of false paternalism while RITCHIE v. PEOPLE, 155 Ill. 98 (1895), a case which threw out an eight hour working day for women, is an instance of false equality.

Maureen Orth, "The Ginny Foat Case and the Future of the Women's Movement -- Book Review: Ellen Hawkes, FEMINISM ON TRIAL; The Ginny Foat Case and the Future of the Woman's Movement" (1986) 132 _Chicago Daily Law Bulletin_ 2
For annotation, see Chapter 16: BOOK REVIEWS.

G. Parker, "The Legal Regulation of Sexual Activity and the Protection of Females" (1983) 21 _Osgoode Hall Law Journal_ 187-244
The author traces the history of regulation of sexual activity from ancient cultures, which regarded sexual offenses as akin to property offenses; to the middle ages, which treated the "ravishment" of women lightly; to the Victorian era, which saw the rise of moral prohibitions against prostitution and rape. She reports that before Confederation, little Canadian law dealt with sexual behaviour and that the first fifty years following the passage of the Canadian Criminal Code witnessed the rise of laws prohibiting defilement of females, contributing to immorality and delinquency, and seduction under promise of marriage.

Donna M. Peizer, "A Social and Legal Analysis of the Independent Practice of Midwifery: Vicarious Liability of the Collaborating Physician and Judicial Means of Addressing Denial of Hospital Privileges" (1986) 2 _Berkeley Women's Law Journal_ 139-240
This article examines midwifery as an alternative to physician controlled births. The author discusses the difficulty in obtaining physician backup, the denial of hospital privileges to midwives, and the problem of liability. She reviews both dependent and independent models of making midwifery services available, and concludes that the story of midwifery is the story of women's loss of control over childbirth.

Stephen S. Pistono, "Rape in Medieval Europe" (1989) 14:2 *Atlantis* 36-42

The author discusses the historical, legal and social attitudes towards rape, and describes several historical accounts of rape, including the rape of a young woman by her husband's friend while he was overseas, and the self-mutilation practised by some nuns to avoid rape by Viking invaders. Although some medieval sources consider rape a crime of passion, the author claims that the evidence clearly indicates that it was a brutal and violent expression of class and power struggles. He also discusses the problems victims faced when trying to bring charges, noting that in many areas the burden of proof fell on the complainant, and that in others, victims were expected to claw their own faces and grovel on the ground as proof of their humiliation. Unlike civil authorities which considered the father or husband to be the victim of the crime, the Church saw the woman as the victim of the crime, and was a factor in changing public attitudes.

Debra Ratterman, et al., "17th National Conference on Women and the Law" (1986) 16:6 *Off Our Backs* 12-16

The authors report on the highlights of the 17th National Conference on Women and the Law held in Chicago, March 20-23, 1986 and attended by 1200 women. The theme, "In Our Own Voices: A Call to Action" celebrated the diversity of the feminist movement and encouraged a move toward action. Included in the many workshops were three "Agendas for Action" focusing on increasing minority enrolment in law school, especially of women of colour, preserving low-income housing and aiding incarcerated women. Workshops included panel discussions on prostitution, disabilities, lesbian politics and ideology, feminist jurisprudence, low-income women and native child welfare law.

Deborah L. Rhode, "Equal Rights in Retrospect" (1983) 1 *Law and Inequality* 1-72

This article gives an overview of the ratification campaign for the Equal Rights Amendment and offers insight with respect to the dimension of "symbolic politics," and with respect to the significance of the equal rights controversy. The author argues that the ERA failed because of an ambivalence about the meaning of equality and the method of attaining it in a society marked by economic and sexual inequality, and because proponents lacked the ability to counteract opposition strategies. Her analysis "identifies a poverty of both social theory and practical politics within the feminist camp." In consequence, she claims, supporters were unable to offer convincing arguments for constitutional change, and failed to show the ERA as a "step toward suppression of gender hierarchies rather than gender differences." The article focuses on the Illinois campaign and the "Stop ERA" movement launched by Phyllis Schlafly.

Deborah L. Rhode, "It May have been Fruitless, but in the Long Run, the Tough Fight over the ERA may have been the Best Thing to Happen to Feminist Politics Since the Suffragette" (1984) 12 *Student Lawyer* **12-15**
    The fact that the Equal Rights Amendment encompassed only state and not private action was lost on many observers as the debate became more a dispute over "cultural dominance" than constitutional equality. The author provides a history of the struggle, and attempts to explain why the women's movement failed to rally support from women in traditional roles and those on low incomes, despite outrageous and insightful rhetoric from ERA opponents. In the long run, she concludes, the instruction in the "mechanics of realpolitik" and the "political truths" distilled from the struggle may be enduring fruits of ERA for the women's movement.

Theresa Roth, "Clara Brett Martin -- Canada's Pioneer Woman Lawyer" (1984) 18 *Law Society Gazette* **323-340**
    On February 2, 1897 Clara Brett Martin broke through the barriers that had prevented women from entering the legal profession in Canada. She fought for the introduction and passage of two separate Bills allowing her first to be admitted to the Law Society as a student and then to be called to the Bar. As Martin herself said, "If it were not that I set out to open the way to the bar for others of my sex, I would have given up the effort long ago." This article provides a history covering Martin's entire life, giving a detailed account of her struggle for admission, the forces of support and opposition, as well as her experiences and successes as a student and then a barrister. Martin believed that equal educational rights were key to reducing women's subordination.

Tammy Dunnet Sagel, "Leaders Among the Women Lawyers in Ontario" (1986) 20 *Law Society Gazette* **242-247**

This article profiles the historical and present day struggles and achievements of women in the legal profession by examining several case histories from Clara Brett Martin, the first woman called to the Bar in the British Commonwealth, to those in practice today. The author concludes that the contribution of women in law to the advancement of the women's movement in general is an important and substantial one.

Sue Scheider, "Women and the Law: 15th National Conference" (1984) 14:6 *Off Our Backs* 1-3
This is a series of articles on the conference, including an overview of the finances and organization, a report on the keynote address given by Angela Davis, a panel on the legal problems of women in prison, and a presentation on violence against women by women.

Mary Lyndon Shanley, "Suffrage, Protective Labor Legislation, and Married Women's Property Laws in England" (1986) 12 *Signs: Journal of Women in Culture and Society* 62-77
The author examines three areas of law which have affected women in the last two centuries: suffrage, protective labor laws, and marital property laws. She argues that liberal historians have misrepresented the impact of such legislation on women, and that reform in the area of married women's property, which seems to provide for equality, in fact still retains male privilege.

Suzanna Sherry, "Two Hundred Years Ago Today" (1988) 2 *Law and Inequality* 43-61
Part of a Symposium on the American Constitution and Equality, this article discusses the problems and conflicts which preceded the signing of the American constitution. The author believes that the reason the constitution is still a valid document, despite the problems surrounding its agreement, is that it is open-ended, and flexible and was constructed so that its interpretation was left to future generations.

Reva B. Siegel, "Book Review: Susan Lehrer, ORIGINS OF PRO-TECTIVE LABOUR LEGISLATION FOR WOMEN (1987)" (1987 / 1988) 3 *Berkeley Women's Law Journal* 171-187
For annotation, see Chapter 16: **BOOK REVIEWS**.

Amy Dru Stanley, "Conjugal Bonds and Wage Labor: Rights of Contract in the Age of Emancipation" (1988/89) 75 *Journal of American History* 471-500
During the Post-Bellum period in the United States, when contract rights were highlighted as a freedom right, married women's right to contract was severely limited. The author analyzes the contradiction between contract rights and the marriage relation, and explores how it came to "express a profoundly gendered conception of freedom."

Susan Staves, "'The Liberty of a She-Subject of England': Rights Rhetoric and the Female Thucydides" (1989) 1 *Cardozo Studies in Law and Literature* 161-184
The author discusses the power of rights rhetoric to promote the liberation of women, focusing on a biographical sketch of Catherine Macaulay, an 18th century historian. She notes that although Macaulay's position was left-leaning, supporting such important political rights as the right to petition, she did not promote women's rights. By analyzing the rights rhetoric of the Glorious Revolution, she attempts to address the contemporary debate over whether rights talk is a liberal trap which contributes to the isolation and alienation of women.

Carolyn Strange, "'The Criminal and Fallen of Their Sex': The Establishment of Canada's First Women's Prison, 1874-1901" (1985-86) 1 *Canadian Journal of Women and the Law* 79-92
This article traces the history of Canada's first prison for women, the Andrew Mercer Reformatory, along with the ideological precepts upon which the institution was founded. The author discusses the futile attempt to "transfer maternal reform into a penal setting" by establishing an "ordinary, well constructed household" made up of cells and dungeons. The maternalistic efforts of the first "mistress" of the institution could not overcome the reality of the setting in order to reform morally and "reclaim the criminal and fallen" women.

Victor L. Striel and Lynn Sametz, "Executing Female Juveniles" (1989) 22 *Connecticut Law Review* 3-59
Of the sixteen thousand lawful executions in the history of the United States, 398 (or 2.5%) have been of women; and of that group, ten (or 0.06%) have been of women under eighteen years of age at the time

of their crimes. This article examines the death penalty for crimes committed by female juveniles. The authors provide an analysis of violent crime by female juveniles and of sentencing patterns, a case-by-case history of the execution of female juveniles along with an analysis of recent death sentences, and a comparison of condemned female juveniles as against both female adults and condemned male juveniles. The article also offers an analysis of constitutional issues in capital punishment for female juveniles, including gender bias and juvenile status. The authors conclude that there is an almost total refusal to apply the death penalty to female juveniles due both to a strong, constitutionally based rejection of the death penalty for juveniles and to an even stronger, culturally based rejection of the death penalty for women.

D. Sudell, "'Rise of Right' Discussed at Women and Law Conference" (1981) 8 *Gay Community News* 1-2
For annotation, see Chapter 12: **LESBIANISM AND SEXUAL ORIENTATION.**

Lee E. Teitelbaum, "Family History and Family Law" [1985] *Wisconsin Law Review* 1135-1181
The author argues that legal developments in the late nineteenth and early twentieth centuries belie the accepted view of the family as within the private sphere, and beyond governmental interference. He argues that this period is characterized by increasing public intervention in child rearing, in education and custody, and in marriage and spousal support. He concludes it is difficult objectively to identify the family as private in any form; and that the family is instead a combination of private and public elements which compels a reassessment of the history of the family.

Lee E. Teitelbaum, "The Legal History of the Family -- Book Review: Michael Grossberg, GOVERNING THE HEARTH: LAW AND THE FAMILY IN NINETEENTH-CENTURY AMERICA (1985)" (1987) 85 *Michigan Law Review* 1052-1070
For annotation, see Chapter 16: **BOOK REVIEWS.**

Irene Thery, "The Interest of the Child and the Regulation of the Post-Divorce Family" (1986) 14 *International Journal of the Sociology of Law* 341-358

The author traces the history of divorce in France, and examines the 'interest of the child' concept, the post-divorce family, and the usual custodial parent. She reports that the "feminisms" of France have not been influential in resolving the important issues, and that associations of fathers "are fighting the legislation and criticising dominant legal practice."

Frances Wasoff, "Legal Protection From Wifebeating: The Processing of Domestic Assaults by Scottish Prosecutors and Criminal Courts" (19-82) 10 *International Journal of the Sociology of Law* 187-204

This paper examines two major periods of law reform with respect to both family law and domestic violence, and concludes that the response of the criminal law has remained largely unchanged. Because of under-reporting and under-recording of domestic assaults, the role of the judicial system is marginalized; however, it plays an important symbolic and declarative role. The author recommends institutional improvements to challenge the basis of violence within the family.

John de P. Wright, "Admission of Women to the Bar: An Historical Note" (1982) 16 *Law Society Gazette* 42-45

This piece briefly traces the opposition faced by Clara Brett Martin, the first woman admitted to the Bar in the British Commonwealth, and how the battle to admit women was won in the U.S. This history, the author thinks, illustrates the rationalization for the prejudice against women entering the profession.

CHAPTER 11
LEGAL PRACTICE

Barry D. Adam and Kathleen A. Lahey, "Professional Opportunities: A Survey of the Ontario Legal Profession" (1981) 59 *Canadian Bar Review* 674-686

This article reports the results of a survey of Ontario female lawyers five years after graduation, namely, that while the survey group is not under-represented in elite and large firms, the income gap between men and women is statistically significant.

M. Avery, "Legal Action for Women: Streets and Statutes" (1987) 17:11 *Off Our Backs* 24-25

For annotation, see Chapter 4: **FAMILY LAW -- POVERTY**.

Martha W. Barnett, "Women Practicing Law: Changes in Attitudes, Changes in Platitudes" (1990) 42 *Florida Law Review* 209-228

Part of a Symposium on Women and the Law: Goals for the 1990s, this article examines women's increased participation in legal practice, specifically in large firms, which she claims are the place where "the seeds of change often germinate." Notwithstanding women's significant access to the legal profession, the author claims, there are still problems: sexual harassment in law firms still exists, and formerly overt discrimination is now covert and subtle. She reports findings by the American Bar Association Commission on Women in the Profession that men generally either believe no gender bias problem exists or regard it as trivial, whereas women generally perceive gender discrimination to be a serious problem. Concerns include law firm's acquiescence when clients refuse female lawyers, women's lack of mentors, more rigorous scrutiny of women's work and work-style, and the different and more negative impact practising law has on women's lives. She concludes with recommendations for change in both legal education and practice in order to humanize the practice of law.

**Barbara P. Billauer, "View From A Law Firm: Success v. Family"
(1989) 16:1 *Human Rights* 44-47**

The author claims that women must put much extra energy into the
practice of law to be recognized as a good lawyer and then much more
in order to overcome the hostile office environment designed to keep
them from reaching beyond the glass ceiling.   This effort depletes
emotional and energy reserves, and ultimately coerces women into making a choice between career and womanhood. Law schools do not prepare women for the rigors of a male-dominated profession and the reality that lawyering is "forensic strife - civilized psychological warfare," and
there are few successful women role models to mentor young women
entering the profession.   She thinks women must first prepare and
protect themselves for reality, obtain power and then work for change.

**Nancy Blodgett, "I Don't Think That Ladies Should be Lawyers"
(1986) 72 *American Bar Association Journal* 46**

The American Bar Association urges law schools to admit more
female students and hire more female professors, on the premise that the
problems women face in practice will diminish with growing numbers.
The author believes the situation is improving and that gender bias is
losing its force as the expanding presence of women lawyers and judges
brings the issue to the foreground.

Jack Burden, "The Feminist Touch" (1985) 9:3 *Canadian Lawyer* 23-26

This is an interview with a Montreal labour lawyer who is a partner
in a six person firm and a member of the national steering committee of
the National Organization of Women and the Law. She notes stereotyping in the kind of law women are expected to practice and the
systemic barrier that the long work day presents. She does not foresee
any visible impact of larger numbers of women in practice until
networking and collective actions are common, there are more women
judges and patriarchal attitudes are changed.

**David L. Chambers, "Accommodation and Satisfaction: Women and
Men Lawyers and the Balance of Work and Family" (1989) 14 *Law and
Social Inquiry* 251-287**

This is the second of three essays in a Symposium on Women in
Legal Practice: Issues of Past, Present and Future. University of Mich-

igan Law School graduates from the late 1970s were surveyed after five, seven and ten years as to their balancing of career and child raising and satisfaction with career. Following a review of the research concerning multiple roles and work satisfaction, the author describes the survey instrument and ponders the results which show that women with children and career are more satisfied than any other category of lawyer.

Lissa M. Cinat, "Book Review: Jill Abramson and Barbara Franklin, WHERE THEY ARE NOW: THE STORY OF THE WOMEN OF HARVARD LAW 1974 (1986)" (1987) 85 _Michigan Law Review_ 1204-1209

For annotation, see Chapter 16: **BOOK REVIEWS.**

Virginia G. Drachman, "'My 'Partner" in Law and Life': Marriage in the Lives of Women Lawyers in Late 19th- and Early 20th-Century America" (1989) 14 _Law and Social Inquiry_ 221-250

For annotation, see Chapter 10: **LEGAL HISTORY.**

Cynthia Fuchs Epstein, "Rationales and Realities: Social Change, Women and the Law" (1988) 37 _DePaul Law Review_ 367-377

The article offers the author's reflections on the tensions created by the enormous changes the legal profession has undergone in the last two decades, and especially the entry of women which the author claims has revolutionized attitudes in legal practice and legal education. The article concludes with the author's statement of cautious optimism regarding the future both of the profession and of women in the profession.

Cynthia Fuchs Epstein, "The Short Unhappy Life of Feminist Law Firms" (1980) 8 _Student Lawyer_ 23-28

The first "women's law firms" were started in New York in 1973, but to the author's knowledge, none exist today. These were feminist firms comprised solely of women lawyers and dedicated to the promotion of feminist ideals. Their structures were egalitarian and non-hierarchical and although established for profit, emphasis was on social welfare. The article reviews the aspirations of the women involved in two such firms and the problems encountered which resulted in dissolution.

James C. Foster, "Antigones in the Bar: Women Lawyers as Reluctant Adversaries" (1986) 10 _Legal Studies Forum_ 287-313
  The adversarial process is a metaphor for legal combat in the male world of law, which is formal and rational. In order to succeed, women must silence their voice of care and be reluctant adversaries. In order for the system, a patriarchy with psycho-sexual roots, to change, the author thinks the reluctance must continue.

Delee Fromm and Marjorie Webb, "The Work Experience of University of Alberta Law Graduates" (1985) 23 _Alberta Law Review_ 366-378
  The authors report on a survey of University of Alberta law graduates from 1975 and 1980, which found differences between men and women in the type of law they practised, their partnership status, their income, the number of hours worked and the benefits such as club memberships and bonuses. Women made substantially less money, were fifty percent less likely to be partners, held more government jobs, worked less hours and enjoyed fewer benefits.

S. V. N. Hodgson and Burt Pryor, "Sex Discrimination in the Courtroom: Attorney Gender and Credibility" (1985) 71:2 _Women Lawyers Journal_ 7-8
  For annotation, see Chapter 7: **JUDGES AND COURTS.**

Deborah K. Holmes, "Structural Causes of Dissatisfaction Among Large-Firm Attorneys: A Feminist Perspective" (1990) 12 _Women's Rights Law Reporter_ 9-28
  This article draws on interdisciplinary research and writing, and on Carol Gilligan's IN A DIFFERENT VOICE (1982), to discuss the structure of large law firms. The author identifies hierarchy, bureaucratization and specialization, overwork, moral conflict, and childrearing as structural barriers to satisfaction of individual lawyers. She reports that female lawyers fare less well than male, in that women generally have more trouble finding jobs, earn less, and are not as easily accepted either socially or professionally as are males. She concludes that not only male and female lawyers, but also law firms, suffer when working conditions are too rigid and outdated, and recommends structural changes to an organizational model more closely resembling a closely held corporation.

Judy Kaye, "Women Lawyers in Big Firms: A Study in Progress Toward Gender Equality" (1988) 57 *Fordham Law Review* 111-126

The author claims that large law firms are a "superb example of our halting progress toward gender equality in the workforce." While the influx of women into the profession has had a progressive effect on the legal issues affecting women, it is time for women to stand not only as lawyers but as "women lawyers". She warns that any notion of equality which ignores the unique qualities of pregnancy, abortion and reproduction implies that women can only be equal insofar as they are like men. Problems such as increasing work pressures, family responsibilities and career advancement are reviewed in this context.

Janet Kee, "Portrait of a Young Woman as Lawyer" (1986) 34 *Canadian Lawyer* 32-33

This is a ten year stock-taking of seven female law school graduates who formed the women's caucus in law school and later were associated with the National Association of Women in the Law. The author reports that they share an appreciation of the privileges and mobility which they claim comes with legal training, and that they are "using legal smarts to earn a living, and liking it." There are personal stories of each woman.

Jennifer A. Levine, "Preventing Gender Bias in the Courts: A Question of Judicial Ethics" (1988) 1 *Georgetown Journal of Legal Ethics* 775-794

For annotation, see Chapter 7: JUDGES AND COURTS.

Thomas Lyon, "Sexual Exploitation of Divorce Clients: The Lawyer's Prerogative" (1987) 10 *Harvard Women's Law Journal* 159-201

For annotation, see Chapter 4: FAMILY LAW -- MARRIAGE AND DIVORCE.

Nancy S. Marder, "Gender Dynamics and Jury Deliberations" (1987) 96 *Yale Law Journal* 593-611

For annotation, see Chapter 7: JUDGES AND COURTS.

Linda B. Matarese, Mona J. E. Danner and Rita J. Simon, "A Survey of Gender Bias Among Corporate/Securities Lawyers: Does It Exist?"

[1989] *Journal of the Legal Profession* **49-72**

This article reports the findings of a survey of gender bias among lawyers in the Corporation, Finance and Securities Law Section of the District of Columbia Bar Association. The survey consisted of a self-administered questionnaire, and was sent to a random sample of 192 men and 192 women of the 1,055 men and 383 women holding active, non-judicial membership in the Corporate-Securities bar. Thirty per cent of the men and 49% of the women responded. The authors report that while the Corporate/Securities bar is less gender biased than the general population, gender bias does exist, and they point to responses of women lawyers to the survey's questions regarding the possibility of making partner or managing partner as evidence of this. They also report that while women lawyers overwhelmingly preferred a life style combining marriage, children and career, the majority were, in fact, single or divorced and childless. They note also that while survey respondents endorsed the possibility for child rearing, the same respondents felt that job flexibility should result in fewer promotions.

Carrie Menkel-Meadow, "The Comparative Sociology of Women Lawyers: The 'Feminization' of the Legal Profession" (1986) 24 *Osgoode Hall Law Journal* 897-918

Using worldwide data on the increasing participation of women in law, and feminist theory from different perspectives, the author explores the impact of more women in law. She reports that substantive law has already been influenced especially in law reform of women's issues and that differences in approach, practice and substance may broaden the practice of law. She concludes that future study of the significance of women in the law is needed, not only from the perspective of quantitative sociology.

Carrie Menkel-Meadow, "Excluded Voices: New Voices in the Legal Profession Making New Voices in the Law" (1987) 42 *University of Miami Law Review* 29-53

The author argues that groups are excluded from law-making and practice because of the patriarchy of law. She suggests, however, that in the epistemology of exclusion, there are two caveats about "women's knowing". The first is that exclusions may produce characteristics not truly women's, but if they are worthwhile they should not be rejected simply because they are borne of oppression. The second is that one of the difficulties of tokenism is the danger of reification of differences. It is important for women to rethink the world from woman's point of view, to take their own experiences seriously and to challenge the conventional order of things. The structure of knowledge is changing constantly, and law is a dynamic process. It is possible to learn from other disciplines like social psychology, game theory and economics.

Carrie Menkel-Meadow, "Exploring a Research Agenda of the Feminization of the Legal Profession: Theories of Gender and Social Change" (1989) 14 _Law and Social Inquiry_ 289-319
This is the third essay in the Symposium on Women in Legal Practice; Issues of Past, Present and Future. The author aims to "deconstruct the current work on women in the legal profession." She argues that the focus of research must change, and that the questions we ask must change. She enumerates some of the questions that need to be asked, and suggests that the socially constructed difference that women bring to the profession needs to be examined for its influence on practice of law.

Carrie Menkel-Meadow, "Portia in a Different Voice: Speculations on a Women's Lawyering Process" (1986) 1 _Berkeley Women's Law Journal_ 39-63
The author thinks it possible that the legal profession will be transformed with the increased presence of women. Two developments in feminist scholarship offer insights: the first is the change of knowledge base and methodology and the understanding of what it means to be a lawyer where the norm is male; the second is the theoretical and empirical research in psychology and sociology including the difference debate which affect style of argument and role virtuosity. These developments have implications for legal education and the appointment of judges. She concludes that it is a fallacy to use part of the male legal world to describe the whole. Other voices such as those of women, homosexuals and the disabled require study.

Roma Mitchell, "Consideration of Gender in Changes in the Law" (1985) 1 _Australian Feminist Studies_ 41-53
For annotation, see Chapter 7: JUDGES AND COURTS.

Mary Jane Mossman, "Book Review: Ronald Chester, UNEQUAL ACCESS: WOMEN LAWYERS IN A CHANGING AMERICA (1985)" (1986) 2 *Canadian Journal of Women and the Law* 178-189
For annotation, see Chapter 16: BOOK REVIEWS.

New York Task Force on Women in the Courts, "Report of the New York Task Force on Women in the Courts" (1987-88) 15 *Fordham Urban Law Journal* 11-198
For annotation, see Chapter 7: JUDGES AND COURTS.

Rose Pearson and Albie Sachs, "Barristers and Gentlemen: A Critical Look at Sexism in the Legal Profession" (1980) 43 *Modern Law Review* 400-414
This article discusses sexism in the legal profession, which ensures the perpetuation of male dominance. The authors argue that this sexism was present historically when legal professionals, as both interpreters and enforcers of constitutional law, placed obstacles in the way of feminist challenges to women's voting, holding public office, gaining access to education, and entering the legal and other professions. However, they claim, such obstacles are still present, though they are perhaps more subtle at present. Many women lawyers develop a "masculine disposition" in order to deal with the patterned sexism in the profession. The authors challenge members of the legal profession to do individual and collective self-examination of sexist practices, including a critique of current legal professional styles, in order to be responsive to changing social patterns.

Miriam I. Pickus, "Book Review — Ronald Chester, UNEQUAL ACCESS: WOMEN LAWYERS IN A CHANGING AMERICA (1985)" (1986) 84 *Michigan Law Review* 1052-1057
For annotation, see Chapter 16: BOOK REVIEWS.

Nancy Polikoff, "Lesbian Mothers, Lesbian Families: Legal Obstacles, Legal Challenges" (1986) 14 *New York University Review of Law and Social Change* 907-914
For annotation, see Chapter 12: LESBIANISM AND SEXUAL ORIENTATION.

Deborah L. Rhode, "Perspectives on Professional Women" (1988) 40 *Stanford Law Review* 1163-1207
For annotation, see Chapter 8: **LABOUR AND EMPLOYMENT -- AFFIRMATIVE ACTION.**

Debourah Ruble Round, "Gender Bias in the Judicial System" (1988) 61 *Southern California Law Review* 2193-2220
For annotation, see Chapter 7: **JUDGES AND COURTS.**

Tammy Dunnet Sagel, "Leaders Among the Women Lawyers in Ontario" (1986) 20 *Law Society Gazette* 242-247
For annotation, see Chapter 10: **LEGAL HISTORY.**

Lorraine Schmall, "Book Review: Catharine MacKinnon, FEMINISM UNMODIFIED (1987)" (1987) 73 *American Bar Association Journal* 80-81
For annotation, see Chapter 16: **BOOK REVIEWS.**

Elizabeth Schneider (moderator); Mary C. Dunlap, Michael Lavery, and John De Witt Gregory (participants), "Lesbians, Gays and Feminists at the Bar: Translating Personal Experience Into Effective Legal Argument -- A Symposium" (1988) 10 *Women's Rights Law Reporter* 107-141
For annotation, see Chapter 12: **LESBIANISM AND SEXUAL ORIENTATION.**

Joan Norman Scott, "A Woman's Chance for a Law Partnership" (1987) 71 *University of Southern California* 119-122
This article reports the findings of a study designed to reveal the factors that influence women's obtaining law partnership. The author reports that larger firms in the study had almost as many female first year associates as male; and she surmises that firms are unlikely to invest such a high proportion of their training in women only to pass them over as partners. She concludes, however, that pregnancy and parenting responsibilities are likely to interfere in a woman's ability to meet high billing quotas.

Faith A. Seidenberg, "The Bifurcated Woman: Problems of Women Lawyers in the Courtroom" (1985-86) 1 *Canadian Journal of Women and the Law* 219-225

For annotation, see Chapter 7: JUDGES AND COURTS.

Melinda Siddons, "Women in Law: Then and Now, Where are We?" (1985) 59 *Law Institute Journal* 1156-1159

The author reports the results of a survey of the "great women in the profession." She finds that women have problems fulfilling their families' expectations, and that whereas males see their careers as a primary goal, women make primary providing care for personal or family needs. She concludes that women are their own worst enemies with respect to successful law practice.

Stephen J. Spurr, "Sex Discrimination In The Legal Profession: A Study of Promotion" (1990) 43 *Industrial and Labor Relations Review* 406-417

Although the proportion of lawyers who are women has grown significantly in recent years, this study reports evidence of discrimination against women in promotion to partnership in major law firms in the United States in 1964-1973 and 1980. The author finds that women were about one-half as likely as men to achieve partnership in those years, notwithstanding that they did not significantly differ from men in academic distinction, in the rank of their law school, or in productivity.

G. S. Swan, "Gender Discrimination in Employment of Attorneys: Feminists Sharpen the Issues" (1983) 8 *Journal of the Legal Profession* 139-159

This article reports that marriage is a more significant factor than gender in determining the income of female lawyers. The author explores the sociological phenomena of "hypergamy" (marriage of a woman into a higher social group) and "homogamy" (the marriage of equal status partners). She also discusses the effect of unequal distribution of labour in the household in evaluating marriage as a strong income-determining factor.

Janet Taber, et al., "Gender, Legal Education, and the Legal Profes-

sion: An Empirical Study of Stanford Law Students and Graduates"
(1987-88) 40 _Stanford Law Review_ 1209-1297

In a study of gender difference in the way students experience law
school, the authors looked at the reasons for attending (prestige and
income vs. service commitments); participation in class discussions;
reaction to the Socratic method of study and the subtle silencing of
women; satisfaction with the law school experience; and performance in
school. They compared the 1980 study results with 1960 results and
found that the male/female disparity was reduced. In searching for the
reasons for this change, the authors suggest that Gilligan's female voice
may be more integrated and the practice of the law school adapted to
accommodate it; that women have changed and perhaps their indoctrina-
tion and socialization has made it possible for them to be more
successful with the male voice; and that women are more realistic in
their expectations, thus less disappointed with the experience.

F. Taschereau, "Situation de la Femme Juriste" (1982) 16 _Law Society_
Gazette 293-294

This is a report on a meeting of the Quebec bar on the numbers
and status of Quebec women lawyers. It includes issues such as
representation in the judiciary, existing work structures and disparity with
men in both employment stability and remuneration.

E. Vogt, "The Case for Female Barristers, Esq." (1983) 41 _Advocate_
367-369

Male lawyers in British Columbia acquire the title "Esquire" when
called to the bar, whereas women lawyers do not. "Esquire" is gender
specific and is synonymous with "gentleman." According to the author,
some women, not wanting to be assimilated with men and wanting to
practice law on their own terms, may be insulted if "Esquire" was
accredited to all barristers. In legal practice, the title is a recognition of
a status, "a title of honour associated with the function of being an officer
of the court." The author recommends the female equivalent, "Esquiress"
which is also abbreviated as "Esq.," and reports that in the U.S., all
barristers before the Supreme Court are referred to by "Esq.," regardless
of gender.

Patricia M. Wald, "Breaking the Glass Ceiling" (1989) 16:1 _Human_

Rights 40(5)

Findings of the American Bar Association Commission on Women in the Profession prompt the author to ask whether it is possible to rid the legal profession of "the ugly residue of gender discrimination" and shatter the glass ceiling excluding talented women from top management? In her view, the problem begins in law school with teaching methods, attitudes towards female students and the lack of tenured women faculty. A "gender-based two-tiered career track" is emerging. The author discusses the high expectations of law firms and the effect on family life.

Lorraine E. Weinrib, "Women in the Legal Profession: Old Issues, Current Problems" (1990) 24 *Law Society Gazette* 71-77

The author claims that the increased number of women in the legal profession has not resulted in the reappraisal of old issues nor a change in the profession. The problem, in her view, is "culture" and not biology, a culture which begins with how women are treated in law school and continues in practice with the selection procedure of law firms, the fields women are slotted into and the discrimination they face in the profession. Child care, as distinct from reproduction, also creates barriers, especially when exacerbated by husbands and colleagues. She is optimistic that new roles are evolving and that new flexibility will eventually allow women to achieve.

Leigh West, "Book Review: Ronald Chester, UNEQUAL ACCESS: WOMEN LAWYERS IN A CHANGING AMERICA (1985)" (1985) 5 *Windsor Yearbook of Access to Justice* 407-410

For annotation, see Chapter 16: **BOOK REVIEWS.**

John de P. Wright, "Admission of Women to the Bar: An Historical Note" (1982) 16 *Law Society Gazette* 42-45

For annotation, see Chapter 10: **LEGAL HISTORY.**

CHAPTER 12
LESBIANISM AND SEXUAL ORIENTATION

Katherine Arnup, "'Mothers Just Like Others': Lesbians, Divorce, and Child Custody in Canada" (1989) 3 *Canadian Journal of Women and the Law* 18-32

This article discusses child custody case law where lesbianism is a factor, and includes an historical analysis of divorce and custody law during the past two centuries. Lesbian mothers continue to face discrimination, notwithstanding the liberalization of divorce law in the recent past. The author concludes that discrimination such as that faced by lesbian mothers is generally applicable to all mothers who behave in non-traditional ways. A lesbian mother, because she represents a continuing challenge to the structures of heterosexuality and the nuclear family, fares badly in the judicial system.

Elvia Rosales Arriola, "Sexual Identity and the Constitution: Homosexual Persons as a Discrete and Insular Minority" (1988) 10 *Women's Rights Law Reporter* 143-176

The author examines the need to shift from a focus on conduct to a focus on identity in order fully to protect the rights of lesbian women and gay men. She begins with an evaluation of the weaknesses inherent in the argument that homosexuality is primarily sexual conduct that can be protected by the constitutional right to privacy, and suggests that in the light of recent events in the United States, the courts could recognize gay people as a "discrete and insular minority" and invoke the "equal protection" clause of the Constitution. Although she is hopeful about this method of potentially stopping discrimination, she concludes that changes in social attitudes are what is really necessary.

Lisa Bloom, "We Are All Part of One Another: Sodomy Laws and Morality on Both Sides of the Atlantic" (1986) 14 *New York University Review of Law and Social Change* 995-1016

Part of a Symposium on Sex, Politics and the Law, this article examines the moral debates in which sodomy law reform has traditionally

been framed, proposes an alternative moral theory which could ground
sodomy law reform, canvasses the British debate leading to the 1967
Sexual Offenses Act which decriminalized sodomy in England and Wales,
and assesses sodomy law challenges in American cases in terms of the
different moral theories. The author argues that "the territory covered
by both sides in the traditional sodomy law morality debate is barren,"
and that "ultimately a richer moral theory, feminist morality, should
supplant the older terms of analysis on both sides of the Atlantic."

   Susan B. Boyd, "The Politics of Custody" (1987) *Breaking the Silence*
8-10
      For annotation, see Chapter 4: **FAMILY LAW -- CUSTODY.**

   Patricia A. Cain, "Feminist Jurisprudence: Grounding the Theories"
(1989) 4 *Berkeley Women's Law Journal* 191-214
      The author argues that while no feminist jurisprudence exists now,
we do have both feminist legal theory through which to question existing
masculine jurisprudence and feminist litigation that strives to restructure
the system. Any feminist theory derived from feminist method which is
uninformed by critical lesbian experience is incomplete. She offers some
general thoughts about current trends in feminist legal scholarship and
discusses the "invisibility" of the lesbian experience. She identifies three
stages of feminist legal scholarship -- formal equality and reproductive
rights; women are different from men; and postmodernism -- reviews the
influence, if any, lesbian experience has had on each, and concludes that
feminist legal theory is deficient because it has not listened to those who
do not speak from the "dominant discourse". Feminists must understand
the institution of heterosexuality and the role it plays in supporting the
patriarchy; she challenges women to consider their sexuality and
recognize the different standpoints women have.

   Mary Anne Coffey, "Of Father Born: A Lesbian Feminist Critique of
the Ontario Law Reform Commission Recommendations on Artificial Insemination" (1986) 1 *Canadian Journal of Women and the Law* 424-433
      The author claims that the role of feminists in the reproductive
debate is to question the increase or decrease in the empowerment of
women through public policy initiatives. Policy proposals tend to be
written for and by men; they re-enforce the norm of the heterosexual

family, and deny lesbian existence. She challenges the "malestream" definition of socially acceptable reproduction, and proposes a re-definition of artificial insemination as a non-medical fertilization alternative to achieve pregnancy.

Carrie Costello, "Book Review: Harriet Alpert, ed., WE ARE EVERYWHERE: WRITINGS BY AND ABOUT LESBIAN PARENTS (1988)" (1989) 12 _Harvard Women's Law Journal_ 287-296
     For annotation, see Chapter 16: BOOK REVIEWS.

John D'Emilio, "Making and Unmaking Minorities: The Tensions Between Gay Politics and History" (1986) 14 _New York University Review of Law and Social Change_ 915-922
     Part of a Symposium on Sex, Politics and the Law, this article tracks the political shifts in the gay and lesbian movement from the original radicalism of gay liberation to the current liberalism of gay rights. The author explains this shift in terms of the gay and lesbian movement's adoption of the traditional minority group model of social change through law and, on the basis of an interpretation of the work of gay and lesbian historians with respect to the nature of human sexuality, argues that this model is an inappropriate basis for gay and lesbian political strategy because it "implies acceptance of a sexual paradigm that itself shapes and strengthens the oppression" which gays and lesbians are fighting against.

David S. Dooley, "Immoral Because They're Bad, Bad Because They're Wrong: Sexual Orientation and Presumptions of Parental Unfitness in Custody Disputes" (1989-1990) 26 _California Western Law Review_ 397-424
     The author discusses child custody cases involving lesbian women and gay men, and reports that presently a presumption of unfitness is employed in custody determinations. He examines levels of constitutional scrutiny for American legislation, and argues that the presumption of unfitness fits within the ambit of the "quasi-suspect" class, which requires intermediate scrutiny. The factors which suggest this level of judicial scrutiny are that sexual orientation is an immutable trait, that lesbian women and gay men are labelled with incorrect stereotypes, that lesbian women and gay men have been historically discriminated against, and that lesbian women and gay men are a politically powerless minority. He

concludes that within the ambit of this classification, the presumption of unfitness would fail an equal protection constitutional challenge, and courts would be less able to unfairly favour heterosexual parents.

Mary C. Dunlap, "Brief AMICUS CURIAE, BOWERS v. HARD-WICK" (1986) 14 _New York University Review of Law and Social Change_ 949-972

Part of a Symposium on Sex, Politics and the Law, this article introduces an amicus curiae brief written on behalf of the Lesbian Rights Project, and other organizations working for women's rights, and filed with the United States Supreme Court in BOWERS v. HARDWICK 106 S. Ct. 2841 (1986). The author reports that the brief was unorthodox in several respects, including, in particular, its forthright argument that "because gay men and lesbians constitute an oppressed minority worthy of constitutional protection," the Court was required by law to render a decision which would legitimate gay and lesbian persons and relationships. The brief is reproduced following the introduction.

Nan Feyler, "The Use of the State Constitutional Right to Privacy to Defeat State Sodomy Laws" (1986) 14 _New York University Review of Law and Social Change_ 973-994

Part of a Symposium on Sex, Politics and the Law, this article examines ways in which law criminalizing sodomy between consenting adults can be defeated on state constitutional right to privacy grounds, given the United States Supreme Court decision in BOWERS v. HARDWICK 106 S. Ct. 2841 (1986), denying privacy protection under the federal constitution. The author discusses the need for sodomy law reform, examines the case law of states with an explicit constitutional right to privacy, and offers theoretical and methodological approaches for the legal argument in terms of state constitutions.

Alissa Friedman, "The Necessity for State Recognition of Same-Sex Marriage: Constitutional Requirements and Evolving Notions of Family" (1987-88) 3 _Berkeley Women's Law Journal_ 134-170

This article argues that statutes denying two members of the same sex the right to marry interfere with fundamental rights to marriage, family and procreation and should, in consequence, be subjected to strict judicial scrutiny under the due process clause of the fourteenth amendment of the American constitution. The author provides a history of lesbian and gay couples' attempts to procure marriage licenses, examines state interests in distinguishing between same-sex and opposite-sex marriages and concludes that the laws cannot survive strict scrutiny because the interests of same-sex and other-sex families are essentially identical and because distinctions between them in terms of license to marry is, in consequence, invidious and irrational.

Jewelle Gomez, "Repeat After Me: We Are Different. We Are the Same" (1986) 14 _New York University Review of Law and Social Change_ **935-941**
Part of a Symposium on Sex, Politics and the Law, this article offers the author's reflections on being black and lesbian in America.

Robert Goodman, "Substantive Due Process Comes Home to Roost: Fundamental Rights, GRISWOLD to BOWERS" (1988) 10 _Women's Rights Law Reporter_ **177-208**
In BOWERS v. HARDWICK 106 S. Ct. 2841 (1986), the U. S. Supreme Court held that states could enforce legislation prohibiting consensual sodomy by adult homosexuals. The author contrasts this decision with earlier decisions holding similar state legislation invalid for violating the constitutional right to privacy. Because the modern Supreme Court has previously held that the due process clause of the Constitution not only protects procedural rights, but also limits the substantive content of legislation, the author concludes that the decision in BOWERS inexplicably upsets the reasoning of the precedents. The result is that after BOWERS, the personal beliefs and policy concerns of the court will determine the definition of substantive due process.

Sandra J. Grove, "Constitutionality of Minnesota's Sodomy Law" (1984) 2 _Law and Inequality_ **521-556**
The article questions the social/sexual function of sodomy statutes in a male-dominated society and argues that the Minnesota statute and its use by law enforcement agencies serves the institution of forced heterosexuality. The author claims that sodomy laws codify the social belief that male sexual aggression is acceptable towards women and children but unacceptable when directed towards men, and that they punish lesbians for refusing to be the objects of such aggression. She

suggests that the preferred constitutional challenges are the cruel and unusual punishment challenge, the establishment of religion challenge, and the freedom of expression challenge. To argue the privacy doctrine, she concludes, would risk adding more governmental sanction to male dominance and strengthen stereotypical and male-oriented gender conceptions.

Gregory M. Herek, "The Social Psychology of Homophobia: Toward a Practical Theory" (1986) 14 *New York University Review of Law and Social Change* 923-934

Part of a Symposium on Sex, Politics and the Law, this article examines theories with respect to homophobia which guide lesbian and gay practice in the struggle to eliminate homophobia. The author identifies the conflicting strategies which present theories inform, proposes a theory of homophobia as a social psychology which serves a variety of psychological functions, and concludes that heterosexuals in America are homophobic for many different reasons having to do with the heterosexual individual's social interactions and personal experiences. He goes on to recommend that gays and lesbians adopt strategies appropriate to each of the attitudes which cause homophobia and to suggest that the best strategy is "for lesbians and gay men to come out, to disclose their sexual orientation."

Mitchell Karp, "The Challenge of Symbolism" (1986) 14 *New York University Review of Law and Social Change* 943-947

Part of a Symposium on Sex, Politics and the Law, this article argues that the failure of gays and lesbians to understand that they are symbols has been "the bane of the lesbian and gay movement." The contradiction between lesbian and gay status as "negative symbols" in the eyes of potential allies, and gay and lesbian self-conception as progressive, the author claims, has blocked formation of the coalitions necessary to confront institutional racism and sexism.

Sylvia A. Law, "Homosexuality and the Social Meaning of Gender" [1988] *Wisconsin Law Review* 187-235

The author examines laws criminalizing homosexual behaviour, and claims that they articulate cultural values, namely, condemnation and contempt for gay men and lesbian women. She also argues that such laws also perform the more ideologically important function of preserving and reinforcing the social meaning attached to gender, and of enforcing the existence of the patriarchal family premised on differentiated social roles of men and women.

Leigh Morgan Leonard, "A Missing Voice in Feminist Legal Theory: The Heterosexual Presumption" (1990) 12 _Women's Rights Law Reporter_ 39-49

The author criticizes feminist legal theory particularly, and patriarchal society in general, for routinely denying lesbian existence. She argues that feminist legal theoreticians, with the exceptions of Catharine MacKinnon and Sylvia Law, dichotomize "woman" and "lesbian" and that lesbian existence is either omitted, referenced by a token allusion, or sexualized. She concludes with process recommendations for inclusion of lesbian existence, and argues for the fundamental importance of such inclusion, namely, that heterosexism is the principal means of oppression of women in our society.

Margaret Leopold and Wendy King, "Compulsory Heterosexuality, Lesbians, and the Law: The Case for Constitutional Protection" (1985-1986) 1 _Canadian Journal of Women and the Law_ 163-186

The authors argue that the struggle for lesbian rights is central to the women's movement, because without such rights, feminists cannot hope to change sex roles and attitudes toward women. They examine the heterosexist bias of Canadian law, focusing on family law and human rights legislation, and explore the role of s. 15(1) of the Canadian CHARTER OF RIGHTS AND FREEDOMS as a possible guarantee of equality for women as lesbians, not simply for women as females.

Nancy Polikoff, "Lesbian Mothers, Lesbian Families: Legal Obstacles, Legal Challenges" (1986) 14 _New York University Review of Law and Social Change_ 907-914

Part of a Symposium on Sex, Politics and the Law, this article discusses the conservative nature of lawyer advocacy and client demeanour required in lesbian and gay causes, especially in custody matters. The author argues that courtroom success for gay men and lesbians in custody actions turns on their appearing both personally and through their counsel "to be part of the mainstream with middle class values, middle-of-the-road political beliefs, repressed sexuality, and sex-role stereotyped behaviour." She goes on to accuse gay and lesbian lawyers of complicity in this non-affirming process and to articulate a radical challenge to gay and lesbian lawyers to fit lesbian families within the existing legal system without preserving or perpetuating patriarchy.

Nancy Polikoff, "This Child Does Have Two Mothers: Redefining Parenthood to Meet the Needs of Children in Lesbian-Mother and Other Nontraditional Families" (1990) 78 _Georgetown Law Journal_ 459-575
The author points out the difficulties of assessing the rights and responsibilities of lesbian mothers upon relationship dissolution, specifically with respect to planned lesbian families. She recommends that courts explore the reality of children's lives in making such determinations, and articulates the hazards of attempting to make individual children's lives fit within the traditional family form.

Adrienne Rich, "Compulsory Heterosexuality and Lesbian Existence" (1980) 5 _Signs: Journal of Women in Culture and Society_ 631-660
The author claims that feminist theory cannot afford to tolerate lesbianism, make token allusions to lesbianism, or expect a mirror image of heterosexual or homosexual male relations in lesbian relationships. It is important to question whether or not women would choose heterosexual coupling/marriage, instead of simply presuming heterosexuality, because male power over women is manifested as enforced heterosexuality. She argues that lesbianism is a continuum: all women move in and out of the continuum, whether or not they identify themselves as lesbian. She concludes that woman-identification is untarnished by romanticism, and is therefore a source of energy and a springboard of power: women's choice of women as allies, companions, and community is a potential liberating force for all women.

David A. J. Richards, "Constitutional Privacy and Homosexual Love" (1986) 14 _New York University Review of Law and Social Change_ 895-905
Part of a Symposium on Sex, Politics and the Law, this article examines the application of the constitutional right to privacy to homosexual love. The author's analysis supports the continued recognition of a constitutional right to privacy; he argues that this right properly applies to consensual homosexuality, both because homosexual

relationships are a form of the basic right to intimate association, and because coercive abridgement of these relationships cannot be justified constitutionally. He concludes that "the criminalization of homosexuality is, at bottom, a grievous harm to the spiritual lives of people who deserve more from their constitutional traditions than unjust contempt."

Beth E. Schneider, "Consciousness about Sexual Harassment Among Heterosexual and Lesbian Women Workers" (1982) 38:4 _Journal of Social Issues_ 75-97
This article discusses sexual harassment, women's identity, and women's sexual identity in the workplace. A survey of 237 lesbians and 144 heterosexual working women explored four indicators of consciousness of sexual harassment: experiences and reactions to daily approaches, attitudes about the problem of sexual harassment, understanding of the term sexual harassment, and the willingness to use the term sexual harassment. The results revealed that lesbians were more likely to use the term sexual harassment, and that despite the fact that the majority of the women experienced and disliked sexual approaches at work, there was a definite gap in their willingness to use the term. The author concludes with suggested areas for further research.

Elizabeth Schneider (moderator); Mary C. Dunlap, Michael Lavery, and John De Witt Gregory (participants), "Lesbians, Gays and Feminists at the Bar: Translating Personal Experience Into Effective Legal Argument -- A Symposium" (1988) 10 _Women's Rights Law Reporter_ 107-141
This paper is the transcript of a symposium held at Brooklyn Law School in April 1986. The discussion was based on the idea that legal practice is not and should not be independent of personal experience. The participants concluded that a lawyer's recognition of the relationship between her personal experiences and her shaping of a legal argument will lead to a better understanding of her client's and her needs.

Annamay T. Sheppard, "Lesbian Mothers II: Long Night's Journey Into Day" (1985) 8 _Women's Rights Law Reporter_ 219-245
This article reviews changes in medical and legal views toward homosexuality over the last fifteen years, and the custody claims that lesbian mothers have made. The author urges heterosexual men and

women to work toward women's right of sexual choice, so that sexual orientation no longer counts in custody cases.

D. Sudell, "Rise of Right' Discussed at Women and Law Conference" (1981) 8 _Gay Community News_ 1-2

This article is a report on the twelfth annual National Conference on Women and the Law held in Boston in April, 1981. Conference participants claimed that the November 1980 election of Ronald Reagan signalled the advent of New Right legislation and policies which would have a severe impact on lesbians and other women, especially low income and third world women.

Gina Torielli, "Protecting the Nontraditional Couple in Time of Medical Crises" (1989) 12 _Harvard Women's Law Journal_ 220-236

In 1983, a car accident left Sharon Kowalski physically and mentally impaired. A dispute arose about custody and visitation rights between Kowalski's parents and the woman she was living with who claimed they were in a "life partnership." The author argues that the case illustrates the need to protect people in relationships other than heterosexual marriage. To achieve that end, she discusses nontraditional couples' legal rights and how they can add to those rights by using contracts to express their wishes.

CHAPTER 13
PORNOGRAPHY

"Anti-Pornography Laws and First Amendment Values" (1984) 98 *Harvard Law Review* 460-481
For annotation, see Chapter 2: CONSTITUTIONAL LAW.

Maryann Ayim, "Pornography and Sexism: A Thread in the Web" (1985) 23 *University of Western Ontario Law Review* 189-196
The author argues that a full understanding of the nature and effect of pornography is impossible without a consideration of its social context. She identifies four features of this context: sex role stereotypes, patterns of family violence against women, economic oppression and linguistic oppression. Sex discrimination is systemic and may be amenable only to systemic solutions. She concludes that censorship may be the only measure effective in countering pornography and that it may aid rather than hinder freedom.

J. Bakan, "Pornography, Law and Moral Theory" (1985) 17 *Ottawa Law Review* 1-31
The author contrasts liberalism and legal moralism, the theories which inform the contemporary debate on pornography. She claims feminist theory is a species of liberalism; feminists suggest pornography is harmful, and the provocation thesis and direct harm thesis are primary feminist arguments. Current law reflects legal moralist concerns, which is that pornography should be restricted to the extent that it can be shown to create either psychological or physical harm. Because feminist arguments are liberal arguments, she asserts that they cannot be met by merely evoking liberal principles of freedom of speech or individual liberty.

Gordon B. Baldwin, "Pornography: The Supreme Court Rejects A Call for New Restrictions" (1985) 2 *Wisconsin Women's Law Journal* 75-83

This article discusses the decision by the United States Supreme Court in declaring unconstitutional the Indianapolis Ordinance declaring pornography a civil action issue. The author relates the involvement of Catharine MacKinnon in the drafting of the ordinance, which was aimed at "sexually explicit subordination of women" as a form of sex discrimination. He criticizes the ordinance as an unwarranted intrusion on free speech, and applauds the Court's decision, and concludes that conventional obscenity laws, zoning regulations, and private pressures are more effective and constitutionally sound methods of controlling pornography.

Margaret A. Baldwin, "Pornography and the Traffic in Women: Brief on Behalf of Trudee Able-Peterson, et al., Amici Curiae in Support of Defendant and Intervenor-Defendants, VILLAGE BOOKS v. CITY OF BELLINGHAM" (1989) 1 *Yale Journal of Law and Feminism* **111-154**

This is a legal brief on the relationship between pornography and prostitution filed in a case challenging a Bellingham, Washington anti-pornography ordinance. The consensus among experts is that women in prostitution are the main victims of pornography. This brief is directed at convincing the court of the necessity of remedies such as the anti-pornography ordinance to women vulnerable to sexual abuse, exploitation and discrimination through prostitution. The author graphically documents the reality of prostitution and the use of pornography to normalize sexual practices common in the trade and to batter prostitutes into fear and compliance. She reports that male customers typically model their demands on pornography.

Chrisje Brants and Erna Kok, "Penal Sanctions as a Feminist Strategy: A Contradiction in Terms? Pornography and Criminal Law in the Netherlands" (1986) 14 *International Journal of the Sociology of Law* **269-285**

The authors discuss the philosophical underpinnings of penal sanctions, and whether they are appropriate to furthering feminist goals. Using the issue of pornography as a case study, they examine the debate that took place in the Netherlands over whether pornography should be criminalized. Noting that feminists found themselves the unlikely allies of conservative religious groups, "involved in a crusade against sex and other immoralities," the authors argue that feminists joined the debate at the wrong level. They analyze the different functions of penal sanctions, including deterrence, symbolism and ideology, and conclude that the battle over pornography should have been conducted from an ideological perspective, using the discrimination sections of the Dutch Penal Code.

Paul Brest and Ann Vandenberg, "Politics, Feminism, and the Constitution: The Anti-Pornography Movement in Minneapolis" (1987) 39 *Stanford Law Review* 607-661
 For annotation, see Chapter 2: CONSTITUTIONAL LAW.

Beverley Brown, "Debating Pornography: The Symbolic Dimensions" (1990) 1:2 *Law and Critique* 131-154
 Part of a Symposium on Sex and Difference, this article examines the symbolic dimension of the pornography debate with respect to fundamental political values and shifting political policies. The author argues that the dominance of liberal political discourse obscures the symbolic dimension to the extent that feminist discourse is unintelligible unless mediated through liberalism. She concludes that the legislative focus on "a limited class of serious harms" is inappropriate to feminism because it is primarily concerned with sex rather than sexism, and ignores the symbolic nature of pornography.

E. Edward Bruce, "Prostitution and Obscenity: A Comment Upon the Attorney General's Report on Pornography" [1987] *Duke Law Journal* 123-139
 The Attorney General's Report on Pornography accepted and attempted to provide data in support of the U.S. Supreme Court position on obscenity, which focuses on the impact and social value of the material in question. The author describes the current American obscenity law and the findings of the Report. He then argues for adoption of an alternative approach: that state laws banning prostitution be extended to cover pornography. Under such a regime, any sexual act which involves payment to the performers would be prohibited, courts would no longer need to assess the social value of the material, and concerns about freedom of expression would disappear, since only actions traditionally regarded as criminal would be unlawful.

David Bryden, "Between Two Constitutions: Feminism and Pornography" (1985) 2 *Constitutional Commentary* 147-189

The Minneapolis Ordinance, which is reproduced in full, passed over protests of civil libertarians. The author suggests that the idea that pornography violates women is likely to endure, as well as the notion that a legal definition provides justification for enforcement. He reviews and criticizes the feminist analysis of pornography; claims that it flourishes despite illegality; and discusses more effective ways to enforce with more powerful sanctions.

Edward A. Carr, "Feminism, Pornography, and the First Amendment: An Obscenity-Based Analysis of Proposed Antipornography Laws" (1987) 34 *UCLA Law Review* 1265-1304

For annotation, see Chapter 2: CONSTITUTIONAL LAW.

Coalition Against Media Pornography, "NOT Dealing with Pornography: A Federal Government Ritual" (1987) *Breaking the Silence* 14-15

Bill C-114 which was to amend the Canadian CRIMINAL CODE and the CUSTOMS TARIFF ACT died on the order paper. The author discusses some of the definitional problems with the Bill which could be viewed as a "statement against sexuality, not pornography." Following a short history of recent developments in the struggle against pornography, the coalition suggests amendments and calls upon activists to work against attempts to "water down the meaning of degrading, sexually violent pornography that shows physical harm."

Susan G. Cole, "Book Review: Varda Burstyn, ed., WOMEN A-GAINST CENSORSHIP (1985)" (1985) 1 *Canadian Journal of Women and the Law* 226-239

For annotation, see Chapter 16: BOOK REVIEWS.

Ruth Colker, "Legislative Remedies for Unauthorized Sexual Portrayals: A Proposal" (1984-85) 20 *New England Law Review* 687-720

For annotation, see Chapter 2: CONSTITUTIONAL LAW.

Park Elliot Dietz and Alan E. Sears, "Pornography and Obscenity Sold in 'Adult Bookstores': A Survey of 5132 Books, Magazines, and Films in Four American Cities" (1988) 21 *University of Michigan Journal of Law Reform* 7-46

Part of a Symposium on Pornography, this article reports the results of an investigation by members of the Attorney-General's Commission on Pornography, in which Commission staff surveyed material sold in pornographic outlets in four major cities in the United States. While the survey focused on the "imagery" of the front cover of magazines, books, and films, limiting the comprehensiveness of the data, the authors report that the material available for sale is wide-ranging and depicts aspects of sexual behaviour considered unhealthy even by those with "sexually liberal attitudes and values." The authors conclude that nation-wide distribution of pornography is part of a "campaign of sexual misinformation that pornographers have waged on Americans" for two decades.

Edward Donnerstein, Cheryl Champion, Cass R. Sunstein, and Catharine MacKinnon, "Pornography: Social Science, Legal, and Clinical Perspectives" (1986) 4 *Law and Inequality* 17

Part of the Seventh Annual Conference of the National Association of Women Judges, the presenters provide various perspectives on pornography. Donnerstein discusses his research on the effects of violent pornography on male attitudes to rape and violence against women. Champion focuses on the relationship between pornography and the continuum of fantasy and reality of offenders under treatment. Sunstein discusses the application of principles of free expression to the regulation of pornography, distinguishing harm-based from viewpoint-based regulation. MacKinnon points out the inadequacies of obscenity law in controlling pornography, noting the effective silencing of its victims. She concludes that toleration of pornography is inconsistent with both equality and free speech.

Andrea Dworkin, "Against the Male Flood: Censorship, Pornography, and Equality" (1985) 8 *Harvard Women's Law Journal* 1-29

This article proposes that censorship is directed toward acts not ideas, and that pornography is the sexual exploitation of women as a class through inequality and abuse. The subordination of women is distinct from other forms of discrimination because sex is the medium of oppression. The author identifies four components of subordination in pornography: hierarchy, objectification, submission and violence. Equality for women, she concludes, requires material remedies, available through anti-pornography laws which alter the power relationship allowing women to be heard and to act against the harm done to them.

Andrea Dworkin, "Pornography is a Civil Rights Issue for Women" (1988) 21 _University of Michigan Journal of Law Reform_ **55-68**
Part of a Symposium on Pornography, this article is a transcript of Dworkin's testimony before the Attorney General's Commission on Pornography in 1986. In it she describes the effect of protecting pornography as "free speech" as a silencing of women. The American Civil Liberties Union, lawyers, media, writers, politicians as well as consumers are all identified as participants in the pornography industry. Dworkin points out that there is no affirmative responsibility to open the channels of communication to pornography's victims, who remain powerless. A list of specific recommendations to reduce the harm caused by pornography is included.

Robyn Eckersley, "Whither the Feminist Campaign? An Evaluation of Feminist Critiques of Pornography" (1987) 15 _International Journal of the Sociology of Law_ **149-175**
This article traces and evaluates the recent history of pornography within the women's movement and the difficulty of translating theoretical insights into political awareness and legal change. The author submits that criminal law reform in the area of pornography will not serve the practical or strategic ends it has in the areas of rape and domestic violence. She identifies four problems relevant to the feminist position: the fatalism of biological determinism, the introduction of conservative moralism, feminine vs. feminist erotica and the search for a causal link between pornography and violence. Pornography's contribution to men's image of women is considered.

Daniel Farber and David Bryden, "The Minneapolis Civil Rights Ordinance, with Proposed Feminist Pornography Amendments" (1985) 2 _Constitutional Commentary_ **181-189**
This is, as the title suggests, a copy of the civil rights ordinance incorporating the Dworkin - MacKinnon anti-pornography amendments, reprinted by the editors of the periodical. Included are descriptions of

pornography's specific harms to women as a class which illuminate the underlying rationale of the amendments. The ordinance also contains a description of the conditions under which women have a civil cause of action for harm caused by pornography.

Ian Freckelton, "Book Review: A.B.W. Simpson, PORNOGRAPHY AND POLITICS (1983)" (1986) 11 _Legal Service Bulletin_ 29-30
    For annotation, see Chapter 16: BOOK REVIEWS.

Leah Fritz, "Book Review -- Andrea Dworkin, PORNOGRAPHY: MEN POSSESSING WOMEN (1981)" 1981 6:1 _Longest Revolution_ 14
    For annotation, see Chapter 16: BOOK REVIEWS.

Jeffrey M. Gamso, "Sex Discrimination and the First Amendment: Pornography and Free Speech" (1986) 17 _Texas Tech Law Review_ 1577-1602
    For annotation, see Chapter 2: CONSTITUTIONAL LAW.

Beth Gaze, "Pornography and Freedom of Speech: An American Feminist Approach" (1986) 11 _Legal Service Bulletin_ 123-127
    For annotation, see Chapter 2: CONSTITUTIONAL LAW.

Judith M. Hill, "Pornography and Degradation" (1987) 2 _Hypatia: A Journal of Feminist Philosophy_ 39-53
    Adopting a Kantian approach to the question of pornography and degradation, the author argues that by perpetuating derogatory myths about women, for financial gain, the pornography industry treats women as a class as a means only and not as individuals who are ends in themselves. Pornography, she claims, in this way degrades all women, as members of this class, by imputing to them less than full human status.

Eric Hoffman, "Feminism, Pornography, and Law" (1985) 133 _University of Pennsylvania Law Review_ 497-534
    This article details and evaluates feminist legal proposals on pornography. The author outlines the constitutional history of obscenity

regulation and contrasts the liberal and conservative perspectives that are prevalent in current judicial opinions. Feminist arguments incline strongly in the direction of regulation. He acknowledges a role for the law in defining social values. However he argues that, given the history of the state as male-dominated, the value of anti-pornography legislation may be outweighed by considerations of political strategy.

Patricia Hughes, "Tensions in Canadian Society: The Fraser Committee Report" (1986) 6 *Windsor Yearbook of Access to Justice* 282-323
The author claims that both pornography and prostitution reflect deep-seated assumptions about women and their role in society, and that neither phenomenon can be addressed adequately without profound changes in those assumptions. The article examines the Fraser Committee's mandate to develop legal responses to these problems, and assesses the Report against its guiding principles and socio-political themes. The Committee reveals a feminist understanding, which is somewhat marred by the ambivalent status they accord pornography as protected expression. The author argues the Committee failed to appreciate that the state is 'male-ist' and therefore, to be treated warily. She concludes, however, that compared to current legislation regarding prostitution and pornography, the Committee demonstrates a far more sophisticated perception of the political and societal oppression of women reflected in pornography and prostitution.

Nan D. Hunter and Sylvia A. Law, "Brief Amici Curiae of Feminist Anti-Censorship Taskforce, et al., in AMERICAN BOOKSELLERS ASSOCIATION v. HUDNUT" (1988) 21 *University of Michigan Journal of Law Reform* 69-136
The authors, who wrote the Feminist Anti-Censorship Taskforce (FACT) Brief, claim their view represents a continuation of the nineteenth-century goal of women's rights activists to gain sexual self-determination as an essential aspect of liberation. They claim the ordinances drafted by MacKinnon and Dworkin in Minneapolis (Minneapolis Minn., Ordinance Amending Title 7, Chs. 139, 141 Minneapolis Code of Ordinances Relating to Civil Rights, December 30, 1983) and Indiana (The Indianapolis Ordinance, Indianapolis, Ind., City-County General Ordinance No. 35, June 11, 1984) seek to protect women by restricting male sexual freedom by imposing the old female "sexual purity" standard to men as well as to women. They acknowledge the "contradictory

strands" in feminist approaches to sexuality, and argue that feminist
analysis is far from complete. They argue, however, that the Brief by
FACT ensures open discussion of sexual explicitness and claim that such
materials have not only repressive, but also liberating qualities. The
FACT Brief is reproduced as an Appendix to the article; and the article
is part of a Symposium on Pornography.

Caryn Jacobs, "Patterns of Violence: A Feminist Perspective on the
Regulation of Pornography" (1984) 7 _Harvard Women's Law Journal_ 5-55
     This article proposes that the current legal approach to obscenity
reflects the conservative goal of combating moral corruption rather than
preventing harm to women. Citing recent studies which show a link
between violent pornography and violent behaviour, the author views
pornography as both a symptom and cause of the vitality of patriarchal
society. She claims that the law's recognition that obscenity regulation
can be used to alleviate the exploitation of children should be extended
to adults. She suggests a compendious approach to pornography regulation through criminal statutes, nuisance statutes, zoning laws, tort suits,
libel suits, taxation, and victims' aid funding.

Marian Leslie Klausner, "Redefining Pornography as Sex Discrimination: An Innovative Civil Rights Approach" (1984-85) 20 _New England
Law Review_ 721-777
     For annotation, see Chapter 10: **LEGAL HISTORY.**

Kathleen A. Lahey, "The Canadian Charter of Rights and Pornography: Toward a Theory of Actual Gender Equality" (1984-5) 20 _New
England Law Review_ 649-685
     For annotation, see Chapter 2: **CONSTITUTIONAL LAW.**

Daniel Linz and Edward Donnerstein, "Methodological Issues in the
Content Analysis of Pornography" (1987-88) 21 _University of Michigan
Journal of Law Reform_ 47-54
     Part of a Symposium on Pornography, this article is a response to
the paper by Dietz and Sears -- published in the same volume -- entitled
"Pornography and Obscenity Sold in 'Adult Bookstores': A Survey of
5132 Books, Magazines and Films in Four American Cities". The au-

thors criticize the Dietz and Sears study on a number of methodological grounds. They claim that "adults only" bookstores do not provide a complete picture of the American pornography market. They also raise concerns about the reliability and consistency of the researchers who actually coded the materials into the various content categories.

Angela A. Liston, "Pornography and the First Amendment: The Feminist Balance" (1985) 27 _Arizona Law Review_ 415-435
   For annotation, see Chapter 2: CONSTITUTIONAL LAW.

Marilyn J. Maag, "The Indianapolis Pornography Ordinance: Does the Right to Free Speech Outweigh Pornography's Harm to Women?" (1985) 54 _University of Cincinnati Law Review_ 249-269
   For annotation, see Chapter 2: CONSTITUTIONAL LAW.

Catharine MacKinnon, "Not a Moral Issue" (1984) 2 _Yale Law & Policy Review_ 321-345
   The author argues that pornography protected by the First Amendment free speech provisions under the legal doctrine of obscenity does not take into consideration the gender and power issues central to pornography and leaves women silenced in the liberal state. She criticizes the morality and practice of pornography and obscenity and claims that the status of women is at stake in this argument.

Catharine MacKinnon, "Pornography, Civil Rights, and Speech" (1985) 20 _Harvard Civil Rights-Civil Liberties Law Review_ 1-70
   For annotation, see Chapter 2: CONSTITUTIONAL LAW.

Catharine MacKinnon, "Pornography: Not a Moral Issue" (1986) 9 _Women's Studies International Forum_ 6-78
   This is a reprint of the author's "Not a Moral Issue" in (1984) 2 Yale Law and Policy Review 321.

Kathleen E. Mahoney, "Obscenity, Morals and the Law: A Feminist Critique" (1985) 17 _Ottawa Law Review_ 33-71

The author argues that conservative and liberal approaches to obscenity can be traced to male-defined concepts of justice and individual rights, and that feminist analysis of law constitutes a fresh appraisal. She cites feminist analysis of obscenity law as an example. According to that analysis, one must look beyond non-interference and autonomy, and recognize the values of interdependence and concern for real harm to real people. Current law ignores cultural harm and injury to women created by pornography. The author concludes that the civil action approach proposed by MacKinnon and Dworkin must be revived.

Michael I. Meyerson, "The Right to Speak, The Right to Hear, and the Right Not to Hear: The Technological Resolution to the Cable/Pornography Debate" (1987-88) 21 *University of Michigan Journal of Law Reform* 137-200

Part of a Symposium on Pornography, this article reviews the regulation of pornographic programming on cable television in light of U.S. Supreme Court decisions dealing with the balancing of privacy in the home and free speech. The Court distinguishes between obscene material, which may be banned entirely in the public interest, and indecent material, which may be regulated only to protect unwilling adult viewers and children. Only cable TV pornography material which is obscene may be legally regulated. The author argues that the solution is inherent in the nature of cable television, since each viewer can be given the means to block out programming which he personally finds offensive, without limiting the free access of others. He does not deal with the question of the depiction of pain or humiliation, but rather talks in broad terms of material which by its language or images would be offensive to most adults.

Selene Mize, "A Critique of a Proposal by Radical Feminists to Censor Pornography Because of its Sexist Message" (1988) 6 *Otago Law Review* 589-614

For annotation, see Chapter 2: CONSTITUTIONAL LAW.

Deana Pollard, "Regulating Violent Pornography" (1990) 43 *Vanderbilt Law Review* 125-159

For annotation, see Chapter 2: CONSTITUTIONAL LAW.

Robert C. Post, "Cultural Heterogeneity and Law: Pornography, Blasphemy, and the First Amendment" (1988) 76 *California Law Review* 297-335
  For annotation, see Chapter 2: CONSTITUTIONAL LAW.

Mathias Reimann, "Prurient Interest and Human Dignity: Pornography Regulation in West Germany and the United States" (1987-88) 21 *University of Michigan Journal of Law Reform* 201-253
  For annotation, see Chapter 2: CONSTITUTIONAL LAW.

Elizabeth Spahn, "On Sex and Violence" (1984-85) 20 *New England Law Review* 629 - 647
  For annotation, see Chapter 2: CONSTITUTIONAL LAW.

Christina Spaulding, "Anti-Pornography Laws as A Claim for Equal Respect: Feminism, Liberalism and Community" (1988-89) 4 *Berkeley Women's Law Journal* 128-165
  For annotation, see Chapter 2: CONSTITUTIONAL LAW.

Cass R. Sunstein, "Pornography and the First Amendment" [1986] *Duke Law Journal* 589-626
  For annotation, see Chapter 2: CONSTITUTIONAL LAW.

Bruce A. Taylor, "Hard-Core Pornography: A Proposal for a Per Se Rule" (1987-88) 21 *University of Michigan Journal of Law Reform* 255-281
  For annotation, see Chapter 2: CONSTITUTIONAL LAW.

Rene L. Todd, "Book Review: Donald A. Downs, THE NEW POLITICS OF PORNOGRAPHY (1989)" (1990) 88 *Michigan Law Review* 1811-1821
  For annotation, see Chapter 16: BOOK REVIEWS.

Rosemarie Tong, "Women, Pornography, and the Law" (1987) 73(5) Academe: *Bulletin of the American Association of University Professors* 14

For annotation, see Chapter 2: **CONSTITUTIONAL LAW.**

D. Turley, "The Feminist Debate on Pornography -- An Unorthodox Interpretation" (1986-87) 8 *Socialist Review* 81
This article chronicles the pornography debate leading to the Minneapolis ordinance drafted by MacKinnon and Dworkin, which crystallized the differences in the feminist movement. The author rejects the argument that female sexuality has been constructed by men, and claims that sexual practices do not have to be a reflection of politics. He argues that pornography reflects the male - female dynamic, but as a symptom, not the cause, and that inequitable distribution of wealth and power between men and women in society is the cause of the dynamic.

Mark Tushnet, "The New Politics of Pornography Regulation -- Book Review: G. Hawkins and F. Zimring, PORNOGRAPHY IN A FREE SOCIETY (1988); S. Gubar and J. Hoff, FOR ADULT USERS ONLY: THE DILEMMA OF VIOLENT PORNOGRAPHY (1988)" (1989) 58 *University of Cincinnati Law Review* 183-198
For annotation, see Chapter 16: **BOOK REVIEWS.**

Nancy W. Waring, "Coming to Terms With Pornography: Toward a Feminist Perspective on Sex, Censorship, and Hysteria" (1986) 8 *Research in Law, Deviance & Social Control* 85-112
For annotation, see Chapter 5: **FEMINIST THEORY -- SEXUALITY.**

Robin West, "The Feminist-Conservative Anti-Pornography Alliance and the 1986 Attorney General's Commission on Pornography Report" [1987] *American Bar Foundation Research Journal* 681-711
The traditional debate about pornography centres upon whether pornography has value or should be banned, with liberals and conservatives disagreeing over the meaning and source of value. The author claims that the feminist challenge to the debate centres around women's experience of pornography as victimizing and oppressive as well as liberating and transformative. She cautions of the dangers to feminism of the feminist/conservative alliance, which she identifies as confusion, co-optation, and   distraction. She concludes that feminists need to

explore women's contradictory experiences of pornography. Until recently, women's experiences of pornography were private, subjective, and silent; breaking that silence will, she thinks, change pornography's content and the meaning of the debate.

CHAPTER 14
PROSTITUTION

M. Avery, "Legal Action for Women: Streets and Statutes" (1987) 17:11 *Off Our Backs* 24-25
For annotation, see Chapter 4: FAMILY LAW -- POVERTY.

Margaret A. Baldwin, "Pornography and the Traffic in Women: Brief on Behalf of Trudee Able-Peterson, et al., Amici Curiae in Support of Defendant and Intervenor-Defendants, VILLAGE BOOKS v. CITY OF BELLINGHAM" (1989) 1 *Yale Journal of Law and Feminism* 111-154
For annotation, see Chapter 13: PORNOGRAPHY.

Katharine T. Bartlett, "Porno-Symbolism: A Response to Professor McConahay" (1988) 51 *Law and Contemporary Problems* 71-77
This is a response to John McConahay's "Pornography: The Symbolic Politics of Fantasy," both of which are part of a symposium on vice. The author argues that McConahay marginalizes the significance of feminist analysis of prostitution and misses its critical insights.

Neil T. Boyd, "Sexuality and the State: A Comment on Moral Boundaries in the Physical Realm" (1989) 7 *Canadian Journal of Family Law* 353-366
For annotation, see Chapter 5: FEMINIST THEORY -- SEXUALITY.

Belinda M.M. Cheney, "Prostitution - A Feminist Jurisprudential Perspective" (1988) 18 *Victoria University of Wellington Law Review* 239-258
The author begins by analyzing the reasons why women become prostitutes, and identifies economic factors and the socialization process which causes women to view their value as residing primarily in their bodies. She discusses the feminist analysis of prostitution, and the law's

role in legitimating the public/private dualism that supports men's exploitation of women. She examines several alternatives to the current New Zealand regime governing prostitution, and claims that decriminalization with controls, and concurrent social and economic reforms to equalize socially constructed differences between men and women, is the most favourable choice.

Belinda Cooper, "Prostitution: A Feminist Analysis" (1989) 11 *Women's Rights Law Reporter* **99-119**
The author applies radical feminist insights about the nature of society and the law to prostitution, and criticizes both "conservative moralist discomfort" and more liberal treatments of prostitution. She claims that even if prostitution is under the control of women and not criminalized, it creates a negative view of women. However, because many women continue to turn to prostitution for financial reasons, she urges support for decriminalization, and recommends that legislation be drafted in part by prostitutes with their own empowerment as the goal.

Jody Freeman, "The Feminist Debate Over Prostitution Reform: Prostitutes' Rights Groups, Radical Feminists, and the (Im)possibility of Consent" (1989-90) 5 *Berkeley Women's Law Journal* **75-109**
The author urges feminists of all stripes to unite to work for the decriminalization of prostitution as a short-term goal. She reviews the laws of New York, Nevada and Canada, the liberal and radical feminist positions on prostitution, and the views of prostitutes themselves through statements of rights organizations like CORP, COYOTE, NTFP and WHISPER. She argues that while it is proper for feminists to develop a theory of consciousness and to discuss consent, they must find a solution to the daily abuse experienced by the prostitute.

Susanne Kappeler, "The International Slave Trade in Women, or, Procurers, Pimps and Punters" (1990) 1:2 *Law and Critique* **219-235**
The author examines various aspects of sex slavery and trafficking -- white slave trade, international trafficking in women, child prostitution, and prostitution of boys -- and identifies the unifying factor in all as that of adult "male agency of sex trading." She claims that within patriarchal society, social gender defines two sexes: the adult male, the sexual subject; and all others, the sexual object. Sexual slavery is sexual by vir-

tue of the gendered male power, and the author claims that slavery, possession and trade are intrinsic to this power. She concludes with the
caution that as western women are, with recently acquired legal status,
attempting to gain sexual and economic subject status, men are bonding
internationally to form a multinational traffic in women to maintain
global dominance of men.

**John Lowman, "Notions of Formal Equality Before the Law: The
Experience of Street Prostitutes and Their Customers" (1990) 1:2 *Journal
of Human Justice* 55-76**

For annotation, see Chapter 3: CRIMINAL LAW -- SENTEN-
CING AND PRISONS.

**Anita L. Morse, "Pandora's Box: An Essay Review of American Law
and Literature on Prostitution" (1985) 4 *Wisconsin Women's Law Journal*
21-62**

The author canvasses literature regarding prostitution, which she
claims demonstrates that the United States has created its own version
of prostitution, which is a marketplace version of women's sex and
sexuality controlled by men. She discusses theories of regulation,
examines these theories within contemporary literature on women's
sexuality and prostitution, and concludes that any notion of women acting
sexually freely must be tempered by accounts of domination and
subjugation of women in sexuality and in sex roles.

**Marcia Neave, "The Failure of Prostitution Law Reform" (1988) 21(4)
Australian and New Zealand Journal of Criminology 202-213**

Prostitution remains a thriving business in New South Wales, where
a report estimates eighteen thousand men seek the services of prostitutes
per week. The author argues that current law attempts to reconcile the
notions that prostitution is necessary, that prostitutes are deviant, and
that containment is the essential strategy of law and enforcement policy,
because containment permits the symbolic assertion of traditional
morality, while ensuring the availability of women who supply services
discreetly. She concludes with the following principles for reform:
recognize that the prime cause of prostitution is the sexual and economic
inequality of women; repeal criminal laws penalizing prostitution and
related activities; and design law to empower prostitutes so they can

exercise greater control over the circumstances of their work.

Carole Pateman, "Defending Prostitution: Charges against Ericsson" (1982-83) 93 *Ethics* 561-565

This article is a response to Ericsson's free market, liberal contractarian defence of prostitution as a morally acceptable service occupation whose only problem is the hypocrisy that surrounds it. (See L. O. Ericsson, "Charges Against Prostitution: An Attempt at a Philosophical Assessment" (1980) 90 *Ethics* 335-366.) She argues that Ericsson excludes the patriarchal dimension of society from his analysis, and fails to substantiate his claim that prostitution is the free sale of sexual services. She claims that prostitution differs from the provision of other services in that it involves the sale of the self. She rejects the claim that it is a natural feature of human life and she identifies in his analysis an implicit generalization of human behaviour based on the masculine self.

Margaret Jane Radin, "Market-Inalienability" (1987) 100 *Harvard Law Review* 1849-1936

Market-inalienability refers to things that cannot be traded on the market. This article provides a general theory of market-inalienability designed to fill theoretical gaps not filled by either traditional liberalism or modern economic analysis. The author bases her theory on "our best current understanding of the concept of human flourishing." The concept of "commodification", where all things are commodities and alienable, and that of "noncommodification", where the market is abolished, are both considered and rejected. She applies her theory to three instances of contested commodification of sexuality and reproduction: prostitution, baby-selling, and surrogacy. She concludes that market-inalienability is justified for baby-selling, and provisionally for surrogacy, but that prostitution ought to regulated by a regime of incomplete commodification.

Pasqua Scibelli, "Empowering Prostitutes: A Proposal for International Legal Reform" (1987) 10 *Harvard Women's Law Journal* 117-157

The author claims that prostitutes are the most oppressed group of women and that three approaches to prostitution are possible. The first, prohibition, would render prostitution illegal and subject to penalty under criminal law. The rationale for this approach is to reduce prostitution; and it is based on moral views, which, in the author's view, alienate and marginalize the prostitute and commodify sexuality. Moral feminists, who object to the commodification of women's bodies as a harm to all women, support this view. The second approach is regulation, which would allow but limit prostitution by zoning and licensing. In this regime, prostitutes pay taxes but receive no employment benefits. The third option is abolition of all regulation and recognition of the prostitute's right to choose work. Under this regime, prostitution is legal, but pimping and the coercion of women into prostitution is prohibited. Although it is difficult to implement, the author argues that abolitionism is the most desirable approach to prostitution. She concludes that it is essential for prostitutes to control their lives and work as long as the social need for prostitution remains.

Laurie Shrage, "Should Feminists Oppose Prostitution?" (1989) 99 _Ethics_ 347-361

The sex industry, or prostitution, is structured by engrained attitudes and values which are oppressive to women. Criminalization of prostitution brings oppression and harassment, whereas decriminalization of sex sale brings domination and degradation by men. The author argues that prostitution is not inherently wrong, but that prostitution is wrong because it epitomizes and perpetuates a system of patriarchal ideology. She concludes that not all nonconformist acts challenge conventional morality, and that overcoming discriminatory structures in family, work outside the home, and political institutions present the strongest challenge to cultural presuppositions sustaining prostitution.

CHAPTER 15
BIBLIOGRAPHIES

Benjamin N. Cardozo School of Law, "Women's Annotated Legal Bibliography" (New York: Clark Boardman Co., 1984)

Benjamin N. Cardoza School of Law, "Women's Annotated Legal Bibliography" 2nd ed. (Buffalo, New York: William S. Hein & Co., 1988)

Julie Brewer, "Bibliography of Resources on American Law and Literature on Prostitution" (1988) 4 *Wisconsin Women's Law Journal* 63-93

Rebecca Cook, "The International Right to Nondiscrimination on the Basis of Sex (Bibliography)" (1989) 14 *Yale Journal of International Law* 161-181

Phyllis L. Crocker, "Annotated Bibliography on Sexual Harassment in Education" (1982) 7 *Women's Rights Law Reporter* 91-106

Nancy S. Erickson, Joan M. Black, Catherine Heid, Julia David, and Nan Still, "Bibliography: Sex Bias in the Teaching of Criminal Law" (1990) 42 *Rutgers Law Review* 507-605

Kathy Garner, "Gender Bias in Legal Education: An Annotated Bibliography" (1990) 14 *Southern Illinois University Law Journal* 545-571

Paul M. George and Susan McGlamery, "Women and Legal Scholarship: A Bibliography (Working Draft)" (Los Angeles: Law Center, University of Southern California: 1990)

Regina Graycar, "Yes, Virginia There is Feminist Legal Literature: A Survey of Some Recent Publications" (1986) 3 *Australian Journal of Law and Society* 105-138

Anthony P. Grech and Daniel J. Jacobs, "Women and the Legal Profession: A Bibliography of Current Literature" (1989) 44 *Record of the Association of the Bar of the City of New York* 215-229

Carole L. Hinchcliff, "American Women Jurors: A Selected Bibliography" (1986) 20 *Georgia Law Review* 299-321

Shelley K. Hubner, "The Perilous Path to Partnership for Women Attorneys in Private Firms" (1989) 9 *Legal Reference Services Quarterly* 11-72

Lorraine K. Lorne, "Bibliography: Women and the Law" (1984) 63 *Michigan Bar Journal* 501-506

Carrie Menkel-Meadow, "Mediation Bibliography" (1984)

Elizabeth R. Morrissey, "Contradictions Inhering in Liberal Feminist Ideology: Promotion and Control of Women's Drinking (With Bibliography)" (1986) 13 _Contemporary Drug Problems_ 65-87

K. Munro, Lillian MacPherson, and F. C. De Coste, "Feminist Legal Literature in Family Law: An Annotated Bibliography" (1991) 7 _Canadian Family Law Quarterly_ 87-123

Barbara M. Pawloski, "Bibliography: Forcible Rape -- An Updated Bibliography" (1983) 74 _Journal of Criminal Law & Criminology_ 601-625

Betty-Carol Sellen and Patricia Young, "Feminists, Pornography and the Law : An Annotated Bibliography of Conflict, 1970-1986" (Hamden, Conn.: Library Professional Publications, 1987)

Elizabeth A. Sheehy and Susan B. Boyd, "Canadian Feminist Perspectives on Law: An Annotated Bibliography of Interdisciplinary Writings" Special Publication, _Resources for Feminist Research / Documentation sur la Recherche Féministe_ (Toronto: Ontario Institute for Studies in Education, 1989)

Beth Lynn Stanton, "Sexual Harassment: A Bibliography" (1981) 10 _Capital University Law Review_ 697-708

CHAPTER 16
BOOK REVIEWS

<hr style="width:40%"/>

Kathryn Abrams, "Kitsch and Community -- Book Review: Robert Bellah, HABITS OF THE HEART (1985); Benjamin Barber, STRONG DEMOCRACY (1984); and Michael Walzer, EXODUS AND REVO-LUTION (1985)" (1986) 84 *Michigan Law Review* 941-962

Kitsch is the insipid smile which covers an unacceptable human existence. HABITS OF THE HEART reflects the precarious state of inquiry into community. The authors describe the home as the first arena of conflict, and express concern that there is an erosion of communitarian impulses. In the reviewer's opinion, they fail to address the special issues of work for women. The two other books, the reviewer suggests, present the genesis of a new politics. Addressing the question of community, they propose the transformation of liberal democratic norms into political participation.

Elizabeth S. Anderson, "Women and Contracts: No New Deal -- Book Review: Carole Pateman, THE SEXUAL CONTRACT (1988)" (1990) 88 *Michigan Law Review* 1792-1810

In this book, the author argues that social contracts are patriarchal in origin, and that they continue to legitimate patriarchal domination. The reviewer criticizes the author for "mistakenly" supposing that the only conception of a contract is the current one of "self-interested bargaining," suggests that Pateman confuses "possessive contractarianism" with other forms of contractarian theory, and concludes that while the book demonstrates that possessive contractarianism is patriarchal in nature, further non-ideological analysis is required to evaluate other forms of contract.

Donna E. Arzt, "Book Review: R. Mamonova, ed., WOMEN AND RUSSIA: FEMINIST WRITINGS FROM THE SOVIET UNION (1984); C. Hansson and K. Liden, MOSCOW WOMEN: THIRTEEN INTERVIEWS (1984)" (1985) 8 *Harvard Women's Law Journal* 265-273

The author reviews the first two books by Soviet women written "in their own voices, that focus on women's roles, sex discrimination and sexuality". WOMEN AND RUSSIA is a collection of essays, interviews, fiction and poetry written for publication in underground feminist manuscripts while MOSCOW WOMEN is a book of thirteen interviews with women who talk about their daily lives. The latter does not purport to "encapture feminist ideas" but, the reviewer thinks, complements the other book to give a more complete picture of women's lives in the Soviet Union. Both books criticize the state system of daycare and the horrible conditions for birth and abortion in hospital. In the reviewer's opinion, WOMEN AND RUSSIA exposes the hypocrisy of a regime that constitutionally guarantees equality but does not provide it.

Marie Ashe, "Book Review: Barbara C. Gilpi, Nancy Hartsock, Clare Novak, and Myra Strober, eds., WOMEN AND POVERTY (1986)" (1987) 89 *West Virginia Law Review* 1183-1189
The reviewer discusses two thrusts of this book -- the PSID (Panel Study of Income Dynamics), which exposes the systemic second class economic status of women, and then the notion of comparable worth as a solution to the problem.

Marie Ashe, "Review Essay: Conversation and Abortion -- Book Review: Mary Ann Glendon, ABORTION AND DIVORCE IN WESTERN LAW (1987)" (1987) 82 *Northwestern University Law Review* 387-402
Glendon's work provides a comparative account of abortion regulation in twenty Western nations and recommends that the United States borrow from European, generally French and West German, models. The reviewer finds the author's proposals disappointing and identifies her comparative method as the source of difficulty. Comparison, she suggests, is inherently incapable of resolving an issue like abortion that requires not merely reform or reformulation, but re-visioning. This is so, she claims, because comparison is incapable of criticism; and Glendon's work is deficient precisely because it does not move beyond an essentially non-critical account of varying rhetorics to inquire whether a different abortion rhetoric is possible. The review concludes by suggesting the form a healing and constructive discourse about abortion might take.

Martha J. Bailey, "Book Review: Howard H. Irving and Michael Benjamin, FAMILY MEDIATION: THEORY AND PRACTICE OF DISPUTE RESOLUTION (1987)" (1989) 3 *Canadian Journal of Women and the Law* 303-312

The reviewer criticizes this book, which surveys the history, research, and writing with respect to family mediation, for implicit and explicit male-defined bias and bias toward joint custody. She argues that the authors fail to understand the inequalities faced by women in both society and mediation, make false claims about women's success rate in custody litigation, and use a definition of empowerment which is, at best, non feminist. She concludes with the recommendation that mediation such as that presented in the book is detrimental to women and must be challenged.

Katherine T. Bartlett, "MacKinnon's Feminism: Power on Whose Terms? -- Book Review: Catharine MacKinnon, FEMINISM UN-MODIFIED (1987)" (1987) 75 *California Law Review* 1559-1570

MacKinnon's theory is that men have power over everything of value in society, even the power to decide what does and does not have value. The book is a collection of her speeches and each speech seeks to demonstrate that everything of relevance to women fits her theory of power. MacKinnon rejects equal treatment or special treatment as strategies for change. The reviewer finds that contradictions permeate MacKinnon's description of reality, but acknowledges that an important part of women's experience is the existence of contradictory truths. The reviewer comments that MacKinnon also missed the opportunity to discuss the role of power in women's hands, and what women intend to do with power, because that affects the terms on which they acquire it. The transformation of values, she argues, must coincide with and stimulate the undoing of gender oppression.

Virginia Bartley, "Book Review: Shiela Kieran, THE FAMILY MATTERS (1986)" (1989) 3 *Canadian Journal of Women and the Law* 317-323

This book describes the history of family law in Ontario for two centuries, and has as its focus the progress women have made during that time. The book gives biographies of various women who were instrumental in effecting legal reform. The reviewer concludes that the book, because is fails to deal with the new legal challenges in family law, is only a beginning document to an important discussion.

Beth Bernstein, "Difference, Dominance, Differences: Feminist Theory, Equality, and the Law -- Book Review: Zillah Eisenstein, THE FEMALE BODY AND THE LAW (1989)" (1989-90) 5 *Berkeley Women's Law Journal* **214 - 226**
    Eisenstein tries to move the feminist debate beyond sameness/difference and subordination/dominance to "a pluralist, multiple, and open-ended notion of 'differences'" using the post-modern technique of deconstruction. She discusses sexual equality through the pregnant body, pornography, abortion, and sexual freedom. The reviewer claims that the author is not entirely successful in making clear how the "radically egalitarian world" is to be reached.

Christine Boyle, "Book Review: Judith Rowland, RAPE: THE ULTIMATE VIOLATION (1986)" (1986) 14 *International Journal of the Sociology of Law* **428-432**
    The reviewer praises this book for its gripping accounts of trials which raise fundamental questions about the criminal justice system, but she is critical of its analysis, finding it to be sloppy and often inaccurate. However, she feels that its most significant impact is its presentation of the author's experience as a prosecutor with the San Diego District Attorney's Office, and her growing understanding of rape trauma syndrome. It describes her frustrations and successes as she struggles to learn, understand and make changes to the built in gender bias in the criminal justice system.

Susan J. Brown, "Book Review: Catherine A. MacKinnon, TOWARD A FEMINIST THEORY OF THE STATE (1989)" (1990) 24 *University of British Columbia Law Review* **146-149**
    The reviewer claims that MacKinnon's analysis becomes problematic when she says that sexuality is central to women's oppression, because this statement "oversimplifies women's experience." The reviewer thinks that MacKinnon's claim that gender hierarchy is the dominant hierarchy leaves the "power differences between women ... largely unexplained."

Sarah E. Burns, "Apologia for the Status Quo -- Book Review: David

L. Kirp, Mark G. Yudolf, and Marlene Strong Franks, GENDER JUSTICE (1986)" (1986) 74 *Georgetown Law Journal* 1769-1797
The reviewer criticizes this book because it fails to take feminist legal theory seriously and because it in consequence ends up blaming the victim for existing imbalances. The authors propose a process-oriented approach to the individual exercise of choice, which would purge impediments and allow the individual to determine the relevance of gender. The book covers a wide range of subjects such as free will, the benign attitude of male decision makers, sex-based distinctions, and the serious pursuit of gender neutral law which would treat men and women the same. The reviewer suggests that the authors' underlying assumptions defeat equal choice for women, and that there is no factual evidence for some of their claims.

Claudia Card, "Women's Voices and Ethical Ideals: Must We Mean What We Say? -- Book Review: Eva Feder Kittay and Diana T. Meyers (eds.), WOMEN AND MORAL THEORY (1987)" (1988) 99 *Ethics* 125-135
This book, a collection of papers, explores the implications of Gilligan's challenge to ethical theory and the centrality to moral development of autonomy, universality and appeal to principle. The reviewer thinks that violence is a good organizing focus for the work, but that nuclear violence is not covered adequately. She claims that the illusion of female non-violence arises from stereotypes of women's relationships with men and that there is a serious lack of critical scrutiny of what disadvantaged women say, a relative silence on the underside of women's ethics.

Ruth E. Chang, "Book Review: Christine Delphy, CLOSE TO HOME: A MATERIALIST ANALYSIS OF WOMEN'S OPPRESSION (1984)" (1988) 11 *Harvard Women's Law Journal* 269-278
This book examines three interrelated themes with respect to women's oppression: the economic analysis of housework; the new metaphysic of world interpretation offered as a substitute for dominant patriarchal ideology, which ensures continued oppression; and the need for incisive inquiry into such issues as the relationships between men and women, women intellectuals, and feminism. The reviewer argues that the radical conclusions in the book are vigorously asserted, but are not backed up by empirical data.

Monique Charlebois, "Book Review: Lenore J. Weitzman, THE DIVORCE REVOLUTION: THE UNEXPECTED CONSEQUEN-CES FOR WOMEN AND CHILDREN IN AMERICA (1985)" (1989) 3 *Canadian Journal of Women and the Law* 287-315

The reviewer argues that because the debate about no-fault divorce and mandatory joint custody is still alive in Canada, this book is of immense importance. The book clearly documents the devastating impact of California's no-fault legislation: decreased support orders, imbalanced sharing of property and income, and imbalanced custody negotiations. Changing the law without a change in societal attitudes and financial situations of men relative to women does not improve the lives of women. She concludes the value of the book lies in its demonstration that sex-neutral laws which fail to take inequalities into account actually transform those inequities or create new ones. However, the reviewer criticizes THE DIVORCE REVOLUTION for its failure to recommend no more than minor legal reform in the face of such devastating consequences.

Phyllis Chesler, "Book Review: Miriam M. Johnson, STRONG MOTHERS, WEAK WIVES: THE SEARCH FOR GENDER EQUALITY (1988)" (1989) 3 *Canadian Journal of Women and the Law* 280-286

The reviewer examines this book in relation to radical feminist theory on motherhood, custody, and equality, and agrees with the author's conclusions that male dominance will only be eliminated by retaining gender specificity. Equality in parenting will reinforce dominance unless men and women are truly equal, and the author's conclusions about male parenting as different from female mothering are applauded by the reviewer. However, she criticizes the book's ten-tativeness and concludes that the author did not draw the inescapable conclusions from the data and her own analysis.

Lissa M. Cinat, "Book Review: Jill Abramson and Barbara Franklin, WHERE THEY ARE NOW: THE STORY OF THE WOMEN OF HARVARD LAW 1974 (1986)" (1987) 85 *Michigan Law Review* 1204-1209

The book reports on a survey of seventy-one female graduates of the Harvard Law School class of 1974, and concludes that these women have not found the fulfilment they sought. The author finds the conclusions trite, without sound analysis and claims that the authors minimize the seriousness of the study and the problems of the graduates. She suggests, however, that the book is satisfying for the experiences portrayed and that it points to the need for constructive change in attitudes and in the institutions which restrict the full achievement of women in the profession.

Elizabeth B. Clark, "Book Review: Michael Grossberg, GOVERNING THE HEARTH (1985)" (1985) 2 *Wisconsin Women's Law Journal* 159-167

This book is an historical examination of American family law during the nineteenth century, which discusses laws with respect to courtship and marriage, as well as reproduction and parenthood. The reviewer applauds the author's discussion of the complex relationship between the family, courts, and the state, especially his discussion of the growth of the "judicial patriarchy." She thinks the book an important descriptive work, but states that the author failed to adequately explore the implication of his theories with respect to the issue of the nature of rights in an interventionist state, and suggests that the problem is less that of judicial intervention into the family, than it is the understandings of ideologies of the intervening judges. The review concludes that the author's acceptance of the liberal assumption that the family is secured by the perfection of individual rights is not correct, and that the interests of the individual and the family must be viewed as separate and potentially conflicting.

Lorraine Code, "Book Review: Katherine O'Donovan, SEXUAL DIVISIONS IN LAW (1985)" (1986) 2 *Canadian Journal of Women and the Law* 190-198

The book explores the public/private dichotomy which is the framework and central focus for the study of sexual divisions. The author traces the historical roots of the divisions, notes that legal thinking changes as ideology changes, and claims that feminist legal reform must go beyond liberalism because its conceptual apparatus is too impoverished to generate reform. The reviewer finds the author intelligent and subtle, but criticizes her concentration on heterosexual marriage to the exclusion of single/lesbian women. There are ways of life, she concludes, which evade traditional family altogether as well as deviations within it.

Susan G. Cole, "Book Review: Varda Burstyn, ed., WOMEN A-
GAINST CENSORSHIP (1985)" (1985) 1 *Canadian Journal of Women
and the Law* 226-239

This review is a critique of the central thesis in WOMEN
AGAINST CENSORSHIP, namely, that censorship will be used by the
state to harm radicals and those committed to social change. The
reviewer argues that the book fails to acknowledge the real harm done
to women by pornography by dwelling on abstract threats which are not
informed by real experiences with censorship. She warns of the danger
of pornographers co-opting the arguments of civil rights feminists to their
own advantage.

Ruth Colker, "Feminism, Sexuality, and Self: A Preliminary Inquiry
Into the Politics of Authenticity -- Book Review: Catherine MacKinnon,
FEMINISM UNMODIFIED (1987)" (1988) 68 *Boston University Law
Review* 217-264

The reviewer describes MacKinnon's book as a woman's search for
authenticity, her sexual self, questions whether MacKinnon has used feminist methodology to probe these questions and urges women to be
especially attentive to their sexual selves, which must not be over-empha-
sized but rather seen as part of a fuller self. She claims that MacKinnon
fails to use experiential discourse, but rather selectively validates
women's voices. By so doing she does not provide the tools for
determining authentic voices. The reviewer states that there is an
underlying unjustified assumption about women in the book, that it raises
fundamental questions, and that resolutions must be sought elsewhere.

Clare Collins, "Book Review: Joan Sangster, DREAMS OF E-
QUALITY: WOMEN ON THE CANADIAN LEFT, 1920-1950 (1989)"
(1990) 19:1 *Resources for Feminist Research / Documentation sur la Recherche Féministe* 8

This book examines Canadian women's activities within the
Communist Party of Canada (CPC) and Cooperative Commonwealth
Federation (CCF) from 1920 until 1950. The reviewer applauds the
author's "generous use of oral testimony" because it provides a richly
detailed view not only of the leadership but also of the grassroots of each
party. However, the reviewer claims the book lacks an overarching
analysis, as well as a statement of the author's theoretical approach, and
concludes that the book is of most assistance in providing detailed data

which will be ultimately useful for further analysis.

Drucilla Cornell, "Beyond Tragedy and Complacency -- Book Review: Roberto Unger, POLITICS (1987)" (1987) 81 _Northwestern University Law Review_ **693-717**

Unger states that the form of social organization is made, not given, and proposes comprehensive political and economic programs for all levels of social life, remaking the collective project by imagining transformation where compassion is essential to political community. The reviewer criticizes the book for its masculine bias, particularly for its conception of the subject as self-conscious will and rational intentionality.

Rose Laub Coser, "The Women's Movement and Conservative Attacks -- Book Review: Sylvia Ann Hewlett, A LESSER LIFE: THE MYTH OF WOMEN'S LIBERATION IN AMERICA (1986)" [1987] _Dissent_ **259-262**

This book is about the privilege and responsibility of motherhood. The reviewer criticizes the author's scholarship on a number of issues and claims that the author "talks herself into a frenzy, proceeds by exaggeration, and ignores contrary evidence." The book advocates laws for the protection of women based upon their ability to bear children, "our most important natural resource." The reviewer finds Hewlett's arguments fanatical in their disdain for feminists who are referred to as "anti-children and anti-motherhood." The worst part of the book, the reviewer concludes, is the chapter denouncing the fight to pass the Equal Rights Amendment.

Carrie Costello, "Book Review: Harriet Alpert, ed., WE ARE EVERYWHERE: WRITINGS BY AND ABOUT LESBIAN PARENTS (1988)" (1989) 12 _Harvard Women's Law Journal_ **287-296**

The reviewer evaluates this book as a potent challenge to homophobia and heterosexism. She concludes that two themes emerge from the book: first, that ordinary domestic happiness is evident in most of the lesbian relationships discussed in the book; and second, that lesbian families structurally and ideologically are different from the idealized heterosexual norm, and thus a challenge thereto.

Dawn H. Currie, "Book Review: Lydia O'Donnell, THE UNHER-
ALDED MAJORITY: CONTEMPORARY WOMEN AS MOTHERS
(1985)" (1989) 3 _Canadian Journal of Women and the Law_ 313-316
This book is the report of a case study of 75 mothers, which is
written from an experiential perspective. The reviewer praises the book
for challenging earlier feminist characterizations of motherhood as
restrictive personally or socially, but criticizes the failure of the book to
deal with the issue of why mothering is still devalued after two decades
of feminist struggle.

T. Brettel Dawson, "Book Review: Catharine MacKinnon, FEMIN-
ISM UNMODIFIED (1987)" (1988) 20 _Ottawa Law Review_ 241-249
The reviewer claims MacKinnon's arguments are political, not
biological and describe the dynamics of socially structured relations. She
is hesitant, however, with what MacKinnon provides as a theoretical basis
for criticism. To the reviewer, "unmodified" may mean "polarized." The
centrality of sexuality to theory is unique to MacKinnon, and in the
reviewer's opinion, her views are contradictory and paradoxical, which
reveals the internal contradictions of heteropatriarchal inequality.

Janet Drysdale, "Book Review: Sylvana Tomaselli and Roy Porter,
RAPE (1986)" (1989-1990) 3 _Canadian Journal of Women and the Law_
644-647
The reviewer views the book positively with respect to the range of
approaches taken in the essays contained in it; indeed, she thinks it a
"multidisciplinary primer on rape." However, she criticizes the book for
its failure to effectively utilize feminist theory, notwithstanding that the
academic work in the book builds upon the foundation laid by feminist
authors. The reviewer concludes that the book would have benefitted
from a more critically developed review of feminist theory about rape.

Jean Bethke Elshtain, "Ordinary Scholarship; Book Review: Judith N.
Shklar, ORDINARY VICES (1984)" (1985) 94 _Yale Law Journal_
1270-1284
The author is an 'unabashed celebrant of liberal democracy' whose
discourse on vice pre-supposes the possibility of discourse on virtue.
Vices are defects, corruptions and depravities which conjure up the
notion of lapse and active repudiation. The reviewer notes that the

author offers no explanation of the framework that locates vices as primary, and she forges no links between the personal and public dimensions of cruelty, hypocrisy, snobbery, betrayal, and misanthropy. The author asserts a connection between personal character and liberal government, 'keeping its hands off our characters' and presumes features of American culture. According to the reviewer, she ignores the force of family and the changing face of male/female relations, refuses to press hard cases, or to draw political implications of her own claims.

Susan Erickson, "Book Review: Josephine Donovan, FEMINIST THEORY: THE INTELLECTUAL TRADITIONS OF AMERICAN FEMINISM (1985); Claire Duchen, FEMINISM IN FRANCE: FROM MAY '68 TO MITTERAND (1986)" (1985) 4 *Wisconsin Women's Law Journal* 117-128

The reviewer examines American anti-discrimination litigation from the perspectives of feminism discussed in Donovan's book, which she thinks is a good contribution to feminist thought. She then contrasts AMERICAN FEMINISM with French feminism, as presented in FEMINISM IN FRANCE. She concludes that the question of what constitutes woman's voice is an unanswered dilemma, and that the response has been widely disparate forms of feminism, but argues that both solidarity and diversity are important within and between feminisms.

David L. Faigman, "Discerning Justice When Battered Women Kill -- Book Review: Charles P. Ewing, BATTERED WOMEN WHO KILL: PSYCHOLOGICAL SELF-DEFENSE AS LEGAL JUSTIFICATION (1987)" (1987) 39 *Hastings Law Journal* 207-227

This book review essay examines the Battered Woman Syndrome as a self-defence claim, and rejects the "psychological self-defence" test presented in the book reviewed as unworkable and unrelated to the woman's actual claim, and as based on male stereotypes. The author argues instead for a re-examination of the reasonableness test for justifiable use of force, and recommends that evidence of battering before the killing is necessary only to determine whether the woman acted reasonably under the circumstances.

Lucinda M. Finley, "Choice and Freedom: Elusive Issues in the Search for Gender Justice -- Book Review: David L. Kirp, Mark G. Yudolf, and

Marlene Strong Franks, GENDER JUSTICE (1986)" (1987) 96 _Yale Law Journal_ 914-942

GENDER JUSTICE, the reviewer claims, is an ardent defense of nineteenth century conventional liberalism seemingly untouched by recent feminist writing. Justice is defined as "enhancing choice for individuals" and the authors "value self-determination over collective determinations of sex roles." The reviewer outlines the arguments in support of their "liberty and choice approach" and how they apply it to Supreme Court equality cases. She argues that the authors overlook the ways in which power, domination and social construction of gender affects choice. She focuses on three aspects of the book in her argument: that the choice principle is not outcome neutral, consistent or coherent as presented; that the book fails to probe the meaning of "choice" in a society where race, class, ethnicity and sex have great impact; and the ways in which feminist methodology offers more constructive approaches to gender justice than classic liberalism.

Lucinda M. Finley, "The Nature of Domination and the Nature of Women: Reflections on Feminism Unmodified -- Book Review: Catharine MacKinnon, FEMINISM UNMODIFIED (1987)" (1988) 82 _Northwestern University Law Review_ 352-386

The reviewer examines MacKinnon's theories, and the nature of the controversy among feminists and non-feminists with which the author's comments were met. She posits that the book, because it is a collection of speeches, is easily accessible, and that while the style of writing has minor drawbacks (occasionally tendentious, polemic, and repetitive), the controversy arises because of MacKinnon's fundamental challenge to the nature of male power and control over what constitutes knowledge in society, especially as it relates to pornography. MacKinnon has effectively removed the traditional liberal argument that pornography is a matter of personal private choice and is victimless, and she starkly challenges the law to stop accepting the objectification and subordination of women. The reviewer concludes with a challenge to women to reexamine thoughts about men, women, sexuality and desire, and how the disproportionate power of men has constructed our notions of knowledge and ignored women's experience.

James C. Foster, "Book Review: Seyla Benhabib and Drucilla Cornell, FEMINISM AS CRITIQUE: ON THE POLITICS OF GENDER

(1987)* (1988) 38 *Journal of Legal Education* 471-473
The reviewer thinks that the feminist perspective is essential to legal education in the post-modern world, and he notes that this book, containing an introduction and eight essays, presents valuable alternative paths for legal education beyond the restrictions of the case study method. Feminism has gone beyond deconstruction and exposing gender bias, and has begun the process of reconstruction to "incorporate what patriarchy leaves out". He particularly notes the chapter by Judith Butler, "Variations on Sex and Gender" as challenging and exciting in its approach to understanding the work of Simone de Beauvoir, Monique Wittig and Michel Foucault. He concludes that the book is a compelling and insightful synthesis of contemporary social theory.

Siegrun F. Fox, "Rights and Obligations: Critical Feminist Theory, the Public Bureaucracy, and Policies for Mother-Only Families -- Book Review: Kathy E. Ferguson, THE FEMINIST CASE AGAINST BUREAUCRACY (1984); Wendy McElroy, FREEDOM, FEMINISM AND THE STATE (1986); Lenore J. Weitzman, THE DIVORCE REVOLUTION (1985); Ruth Sidel, WOMEN AND CHILDREN LAST (1986); Irwin Garfinkel and Sara McLanahan, SINGLE MOTHERS AND THEIR CHILDREN (1986)" (1987) 47 *Public Administration Review* 436-440
The reviewer canvasses five books, two which offer a "radical critique of women's relationship to the state" and three of which "confront the problem of poverty among women and their children." Ferguson's book, which calls for the elimination of bureaucracies, has four major weaknesses, including method, simplistic approach to public administration and radical feminist theory, and dichotomous thinking. Wendy McElroy's collection of articles "promotes a libertarian, individualist version of feminist thought." Although it includes works from the last two centuries which are not available in other anthologies, it does not deal in a balanced way with the state. The two existential modes described in these books, woman as care giver and woman as autonomous person, have not yet been reconciled in public policy. The remaining three books all look at the poverty of women. Weitzman's book is intended to educate the courts and others of the effects of their decisions on women; Sidel's is an unimaginative look at the problem, while Garfield and McLanahan offer new insights and radical solutions to the condition of women and children.

Nancy Frank, "Book Review: Eleanor M. Miller, STREET WOMEN (1986)" (1985) 4 *Wisconsin Women's Law Journal* 129-133

The book reports the findings of a study of street women, which the reviewer claims is a richly textured and important contribution to criminology and especially to the study of female crime. The author makes an argument that the duality of the present labour market (i.e. with an "affluent track" and a "second track" of low-skill jobs), has been important in the increase of female crime, which the reviewer concludes is both interesting and a positive addition to current theories of the causation of female crime.

Ian Freckelton, "Book Review: A.B.W. Simpson, PORNOGRAPHY AND POLITICS (1983)" (1986) 11 *Legal Service Bulletin* 29-30

Simpson's book, the reviewer claims, is unashamedly partisan on the question of pornography. It suggests that the Williams Committee (England) Report be left unadopted, and that the law should intervene only to prevent harm. It is facile and propagandistic on the feminist reaction to the committee report, satirizes Dworkin and Brownmiller, and does not fairly confront the feminist concern that pornography depicts women in unequal, dehumanized roles. The book, she concludes, is essentially nostalgic propaganda.

Leah Fritz, "Book Review: Andrea Dworkin, PORNOGRAPHY: MEN POSSESSING WOMEN (1981)" 1981 6:1 *Longest Revolution* 14

The reviewer discusses both Dworkin's book and the outrage expressed by patriarchal press, and applauds the book for its detailed description of the contents of pornography. She claims that Dworkin has advanced by several years women's "right to know" about the contents of pornography, and that Dworkin's "incisive" analysis allows the reader to assimilate otherwise "indigestible" data. She argues that it is essential for women's struggle to come to terms with the meaning and pervasiveness of misogyny, and thinks that Dworkin's book assists greatly in the struggle.

Carole Geller, "Book Review: Judge Rosalie Silberman Abella, Commissioner, EQUALITY IN EMPLOYMENT: A ROYAL COMMISSION REPORT (1984)" (1985) 5 *Windsor Yearbook of Access to Justice* 425-429

Abella was appointed in 1983 to recommend measures to achieve equality for women, native people, visible minorities and persons with disabilities in eleven Crown corporations. The Abella Report concludes that voluntary "affirmative action" has not been effective and recommends a mandatory approach requiring public and private employers to adopt "employment equity" programs. The reviewer is concerned that "employment equity" and "affirmative action" are considered the same, and argues that affirmative action is a preferable group remedy. She claims also that the report's definition of "equality" is severely limiting, as it accepts an "individualistic equal opportunity to compete model" instead of a group based "fair share" model which would ensure equitable results in the workplace.

Susie Gibson, "Book Review: Susan Edwards (ed.), GENDER, SEX AND THE LAW (1985)" (1986) 14 *International Journal of the Sociology of Law* 423-428

Edward's book is a collection of essays which the reviewer praises for abandoning the early feminist tendency of interrogating law as if it were a homogeneous social process discriminating against women as a distinctive homogeneous group. Instead, the reviewer encounters in the book's essays the inconsistent and contradictory nature both of legal process generally and of gender decisions in law in particular. She also praises the book for shifting the emphasis from doctrinal exegesis to the production of distinctively feminist theories of law form and legal process.

Donna Greschner, "Book Review: Kenneth H. Fogarty, EQUALITY RIGHTS AND THEIR LIMITATIONS IN THE CHARTER (1987)" (1988) 2 *Canadian Journal of Women and the Law* 463-467

The reviewer criticizes the book for its traditional approach to equality rights under the Canadian Charter of Rights and Freedoms; for the complete absence of discussion of dominance and oppression as a source of inequality; and for the author's outspoken disapproval of s. 28 of the Charter. The author's inability to see beyond the sameness/difference paradigm, she concludes, makes this an unsatisfactory book.

Catharine W. Hantzis, "Is Gender Justice a Completed Agenda? The Feminization of America: How Women's Values are Changing Our

Public and Private Lives -- Book Review: Elinor Lenz and Barbara Myerhoff, THE FEMINIZATION OF AMERICA (1985)" (1987) 100 *Harvard Law Review* 690-713

The reviewer thinks this book is a premature celebration of women's success in entering the public sphere and in transforming both public and private spheres to produce more egalitarian relationships. The authors argue that the dominant male culture has begun to be transformed by the infusion of "female culture" and that this near complete transformation allows us to move "beyond feminism." In the reviewer's opinion, the authors reach their controversial conclusion that "enough change" has occurred by ignoring contrary statistical evidence in favour of selective anecdotal evidence which does not support their claim. She agrees that some change has occurred, but female oppression, which lies at the roots of "female culture," has persisted in the face of greater choice for women. Theories of transformation lead us to draw false assurances for the future.

Angela P. Harris, "Categorical Discourse and Dominance Theory -- Book Review: Catharine A. MacKinnon, TOWARD A FEMINIST THEORY OF THE STATE (1989)" (1989-90) 5 *Berkeley Women's Law Journal* 181-196

The reviewer claims that MacKinnon's book is an instance of categorical discourse, which she defines as a division of "human beings into two internally homogenous categories, men and women." The reviewer then discusses the uses and limits of categorical discourse under several headings, including consciousness-raising, sexuality, politics, feminism, and Marxism.

Mark Harris, "Book Review: Catharine A. MacKinnon, TOWARD A FEMINIST THEORY OF THE STATE (1989)" (1990) 27 *Harvard Journal on Legislation* 294-302

The reviewer admires MacKinnon's "cogent and passionate exposition of feminist thought," and describes her post-Marxist stance, her equation of sex with power, and her proposals for reform. He comments on her occasional rhetoric, her difficult writing style, her attack on objectivity and the "lingering problem in the way feminist theory calls itself into question ... [and] feminist practice into question," and her odd tone of defeatism and ambivalence.

Winifred L. Hepperle, "Book Review: Betty Medsger, FRAMED: THE NEW RIGHT ATTACK ON CHIEF JUSTICE ROSE BIRD AND THE COURTS (1983)" (1984) 14 _Golden Gate University Law Review_ 505-517

The thesis of Medsger's book is that the new right is determined to destroy the independent state and the federal courts in the United States, and that the press is an unwitting partner in this program with its reporting of an investigation of the Court, which took place in 1978. The reviewer criticizes the book for its "bitterness and myopia" and for the things that it leaves out. This review is part of the Symposium Issue: National Association of Women Judges.

Joan Heifetz Hollinger, "Blest Be the Tie That Binds -- Book Review: Mary Ann Glendon, THE NEW FAMILY AND THE NEW PROPER-TY (1981)" (1983) 81 _Michigan Law Review_ 1065-1082

The reviewer finds Glendon's nuts and bolts description of the legal aspects of family and economic structures in America and Western Europe thorough albeit conservative, but is critical of her solutions, which are religious and spiritual, rather than economic and political.

Judith L. Hudson, "Book Review: Jane J. Mansbridge, WHY WE LOST THE ERA (1986)" (1988) 86 _Michigan Law Review_ 1408-1413

The author distils the essence of ERA activists' platforms, and describes the context in which the struggle took place. She lists the arguments against the ERA, and how they gained support among conservative forces and homemakers who saw it as a further devaluation of their lifestyles. The reviewer thinks the book well researched, readable, thoughtful and often insightful, although primarily descriptive and analytical, rather than political.

Ellen Jacobs, "Book Review: Ann Ferguson, BLOOD AT THE ROOT: MOTHERHOOD, SEXUALITY AND MALE DOMINANCE (1989)" (1990) 19:1 _Resources for Feminist Research / Documentation sur la Recherche Féministe_ 5-6

The reviewer criticizes this book for an understanding of feminism which is limited by a "particular socialist standpoint," and which is linked to male intellectual theory and male ideology. Furthermore, the author's linking of sexuality and motherhood in her analysis of sex/affective production within Marxist theory ignores lesbian women, and women who refuse a motherhood or reproductive role.

Flora Johnson, "Verbatim: Words Between the Sexes -- Book Review: Casey Miller and Kate Swift, WORDS AND WOMEN: NEW LAN-GUAGE IN NEW TIMES (1976)" (1980/81) 9 _Student Lawyer_ 64-65

The author confesses to being a "languagesnob", conservative about changing words in her vocabulary. Yet as a feminist, she finds it difficult to defend the use of language with a male bias. WORDS AND WOMEN: NEW LANGUAGE IN NEW TIMES has assisted her in being able to resolve this conflict. The book outlines the historic origins of words such as "man" and how man has evolved from a generic term referring to the whole human race to its present totally masculine meaning. "Woman" on the other hand comes from "wifman" an old English term meaning an adult female person. Other examples are given and suggestions made in finding alternatives to terms comprised of traditionally masculine words.

Nannerl O. Keohane, "Feminist Scholarship and Human Nature -- Book Review: Mary Ann Warren, THE NATURE OF WOMAN: AN ENCYCLOPEDIA AND GUIDE TO THE LITERATURE (1980); Susan Okin, WOMEN IN WESTERN POLITICAL THOUGHT (1979); Rosemary Reuther and Eleanor McLaughlin, WOMAN OF SPIRIT: FEMALE LEADERSHIP IN THE JEWISH AND CHRISTIAN TRADITIONS (1979); Susan Griffin, WOMAN AND NATURE (1978); Elizabeth Wolgast, EQUALITY AND THE RIGHTS OF WOMEN (1980)" (1982) 93 _Ethics_ 102-113

This article is comprised of individual reviews of five books. Warren's NATURE OF WOMAN is an overview of major themes in contemporary philosophy and social theory, and has an explicitly feminist perspective. The reviewer thinks it is weakened by its excluding fiction or poetry, from which, in her view, the best understanding of human nature and women may come. Okin's WOMEN IN WESTERN POLITICAL THOUGHT enquires whether woman's nature is different from man's? Political and ethical philosophy's use of the masculine as generic is profoundly significant for maternity and female sexuality. Reuther and McLaughlin's WOMAN OF SPIRIT challenges orthodoxy as defined by the male fathers of the church. They give examples from history of spirited women who have creatively made a difference in the world. Griffin's WOMAN AND NATURE fuses poetry and prose with the history of ideas. It rejects traditional analytical categories for sensual imagery, and explores and celebrates the profound connectedness of women and nature. Wolgast's EQUALITY AND THE RIGHTS OF WOMEN is argued in the familiar tradition of philosophical analysis. It asserts that men and women are different in important ways, and that distributive justice requires different treatment for fairness, and claims that differences of sex are more profound than those of race and class. All five books demonstrate the double-bind of the difference debate.

Hilary B. Klein, "Book Review: Marjorie Heins, CUTTING THE MUSTARD: AFFIRMATIVE ACTION AND THE NATURE OF EXCELLENCE (1987)" (1989) 11 *Women's Rights Law Reporter* 61 - 66.
    The book considers current assumptions about what it means to be qualified, with reference to the personnel practice at Boston University's School of Theology, the trial of Nancy Richardson's case, and recent decisions of American courts. The reviewer thinks that the affirmative action debate is successfully presented in the book, but claims the debate should be discussed within the context of the larger issue of whether any view of merit is valid. She concludes that the author's limited view is that of the legal system, and that as long as the rulers make the rules and decide who joins them, equality will not result.

Teresa LaFramboise and Elizabeth Anne Parent, "Book Review: Patricia Albers and Beatrice Medicine (eds.), THE HIDDEN HALF: STUDIES OF PLAINS INDIAN WOMEN (1983); Gretchen M. Bataille and Kathleen Mullen Sands, AMERICAN INDIAN WOMEN: TEL-LING THEIR LIVES (1984); Beth Brant (ed.), A GATHERING OF SPIRIT: WRITING AND ART BY NORTH AMERICAN INDIAN WOMEN (1984); Rayna Green, NATIVE AMERICAN WOMEN: A CONTEXTUAL BIBLIOGRAPHY (1983)" (1985) 10 *Signs: Journal of Women in Culture and Society* 782-784
    The reviewers state that all the reviewed books are important to the American Indian feminist tradition of "retraditionalization." In their view, each book's author states "idealistically" that women in Indian societies are already liberated. The books depict traditional Indian collaborative sex roles, the alternative sex roles found in different tribes, and the stress of multiculturalism. The reviewers conclude that all point to the potential for both sexes to cooperate in protecting the rights of all.

Nora Jane Lauerman, "Book Review: Lenore J. Weitzman, THE DIVORCE REVOLUTION: THE UNEXPECTED SOCIAL AND ECONOMIC CONSEQUENCES FOR WOMEN AND CHILDREN (1985)" (1986) 2 *Berkeley Women's Law Journal* 246-257

The reviewer praises the book for sharply focusing on the efficacy of changes in law which were made in part in the name of equality between men and women. Weitzman's book explores the impact of California's no-fault divorce law in several areas, including property division, alimony, custody and child support, and concludes that the economic impact of divorce is usually quite disparate, with men being enriched and women impoverished.

Sylvia A. Law, "Equality: The Power and Limits of the Law -- Book Review: Zillah R. Eisenstein, FEMINISM AND SEXUAL EQUALITY (1984)" (1986) 95 *Yale Law Journal* 1769-1788

The author claims that liberalism, capitalism, and patriarchy are tightly interdependent, and that a challenge to gender inequality is a challenge to the institutions it supports. She argues that formal equality has failed to empower women, and has implicitly devalued traditional women's work/lives, and that the patriarchal family and prevailing economic structures must be challenged. The reviewer applauds the author's theory of feminism, and her statement that feminists now need to move from theory to action to power.

Nancy Lemon, "Book Review: Cynthia K. Gillespie, JUSTIFIABLE HOMICIDE: BATTERED WOMEN, SELF-DEFENSE, AND THE LAW (1989)" (1989-90) 5 *Berkeley Women's Law Journal* 227-235

Women who kill men are more likely to be responding to violence against them than are men who kill men. Therefore, they are more likely to be acting in self defence. However, the law of self defence has not been available to them. The author of the reviewed work argues that the American criminal justice system is biased in favour of the batterer; she traces the history of the self defence law, outlines its requirements, and makes six recommendations for legal change. The reviewer questions her subjective test proposal, and applauds the accessibility of her language.

Lori Leu, "Book Review: Ellen Hawks, FEMINISM ON TRIAL: THE

GINNY FOAT CASE AND ITS MEANING FOR THE FUTURE OF THE WOMEN'S MOVEMENT (1986); Jean Harris, STRANGER IN TWO WORLDS (1986)" (1987) 10 *Harvard Women's Law Journal* 327-333

This article reviews these two very different books dealing with women's treatment in the legal system. Noting the contrasts between Foat's and Harris' approaches, the reviewer suggests that individual responsibility for criminal activity will not occur until society changes its perception of women. Foat, a feminist, exploited those myths by presenting herself at trial as the passive victim of society, a strategy that resulted in her acquittal. Harris, on the other hand, a woman committed to "traditional feminine values," accepted responsibility for her actions, and was convicted. The review provides brief summaries of the books and some analysis.

Christine A. Littleton, "Book Review: C. A. MacKinnon, FEMINISM UNMODIFIED (1987)" (1989) 41 *Stanford Law Review* 751-788

The reviewer discusses MacKinnon's focus on methodology, rather than substance, as a means of defining her position in the feminist movement. She explores MacKinnon's critique of liberal feminism as a form of assimilation, due to liberalism's concern with the individual. The reviewer summarizes MacKinnon's views on rape, sexual harassment and pornography, and her proposals for change, which she claims is through believing women's own accounts of sexual use and abuse by men.

Scott Lyall and Anita Szigeti, "Book Review: Catharine A. MacKinnon, TOWARD A FEMINIST THEORY OF THE STATE (1989)" (1990) 48 *University of Toronto Faculty of Law Review* 185-190

MacKinnon "wants to show us the importance of power in cultural institutions like law, the family and the productive industries of art and scholarship." The reviewers discuss MacKinnon's insistence that the reader feel the issues, her rejection of the escape to authenticity, and her reliance on consciousness-raising as an investigative method. In grappling with the criticism that MacKinnon's work does not speak for all races and classes, the reviewers note that her work "moves beyond a substantive critique of the law and attempts to explain its structural significance. ... her project is to demonstrate the ways in which law and legal reasoning operate against women."

Gayle M. MacDonald, "Book Review: Jennie Farley, ed., THE WOMAN IN MANAGEMENT: CAREER AND FAMILY ISSUES (1983)" (1987/1988) 2 *Canadian Journal of Women and the Law* 460-462

The book is a collection of papers from a conference held at Cornell University in April, 1982 and offers personalized glimpses into "life in the fast lane" and the difficulties women managers face. Rather than placing the blame for these problems at the "corporate door", the book serves as a guide to help women cope and adapt to the increasing demands and challenges of the working environment. Advice and anecdotal remedies address issues such as balancing career and family, racial and sexual discrimination, systemic discrimination, how women learn to "fit in" to a company and strategies for "getting more women hired and heard within the corporate structure."

Catharine MacKinnon, "Complicity: An Introduction to Andrea Dworkin -- Book Review: Andrea Dworkin, RIGHT WING WOMEN (1983)" (1983) 1 *Law and Inequality* 89-93

The reviewer begins by discussing the context of the legalization of abortion in ROE v. WADE (410 U.S. 113 (1973)), and Dworkin's radical analysis of abortion policies. In this book, she reports, Dworkin discusses the reasons that anti-feminism is a woman's response to a woman's situation -- namely, that the Right offers a better deal in a universe men control.

Catharine MacKinnon, "Toward Feminist Jurisprudence -- Book Review: Ann Jones, WOMEN WHO KILL (1980)" (1982) 34 *Stanford Law Review* 703-737

The reviewer argues that it is necessary to redraw the subjective/objective division as a test for reasonableness in criminal law. Subjective does not mean personal, except insofar as the personal is political; and women's subjective point of view as damaged is part of both the problem and the solution in criminal law as it deals with women. The reviewer applauds the issues the book raises -- for instance, race, sex, and class -- but criticizes the author for her formalist analysis.

Catharine MacKinnon, "Unthinking ERA Thinking -- Book Review: Jane J. Mansbridge, WHY WE LOST THE ERA (1986)" (1987) 54 *University of Chicago Law Review* 759-771

Mansbridge claims that the ERA was lost because its proponents did not play the conventional political game conventionally enough. The reviewer criticizes both the book and the ERA effort for assuming that politics as usual sets the ground rules for politics for women. This assumption, she argues, neither faces the misogyny of the status quo, nor comprehends that sex inequality is a problem of male dominance. The real damage of sexism, she concludes, is what women were dealing with the night the ERA was defeated.

Sue Mahan, "Book Review: Russel P. Dobash, R. Emerson Dobash, and Sue Goutteridge, THE IMPRISONMENT OF WOMEN (1986)" (1988) 79 *Journal of Criminal Law & Criminology* 560-563
The reviewer describes this book as an integration of historical information and contemporary data designed to present a critical analysis of women's prisons. According to the reviewer, the authors identify three factors -- material, social, and ideological -- that are important to the analysis. The authors' feminist perspective touches on the perception of women criminals as mad and their behaviour as part of their biological and sexual character. The reviewer disputes the authors' contention, that women's prisons have different problems than men's, noting that studies have shown that both male and female inmates voice the same complaints. The book also discusses the results of the therapy model, frequently used as a justification for separate prisons.

Kathleen E. Mahoney, "Book Review: A. Alan Borovoy, WHEN FREEDOMS COLLIDE: THE CHASE FOR OUR CIVIL LIBER-TIES" (1988) 28 *Alberta Law Review* 715-729
Borovoy discusses the collisions of freedoms that he finds to be inevitable in a democratic society. He takes a strong liberal approach to civil liberties, based on a view of society as a group of autonomous individuals with whom the state should interfere as little as possible. The civil liberties issues discussed are freedom of expression, police powers, equality and involuntary civil commitment; the book also discusses a number of examples of the misuse of civil liberties ideals. The reviewer discusses Borovoy's underlying assumptions and shows how his conclusions arise from the failure of dominant white male-oriented liberal theory to address the problem of oppression suffered by minority groups.

Alice Mantel, "Book Review: Ellen Boneparth, ed., WOMEN, POWER AND POLICY; A COLLECTION OF ESSAYS WRITTEN FROM A FEMINIST PERSPECTIVE (1983)" (1986) 11 *Legal Service Bulletin* 28

The book is an examination of the women's movement in the United States in the 1960's, which is organized in three parts: an overview of legislative changes in the U.S. context; a review of sexuality and crime, including female victims and offenders, pornography, battered women and women in the criminal justice system with differences in colour and class; and a survey of the differences between male and female voters on foreign policy and political representatives. The reviewer thinks this is an important survey of the conditions of women, which provides a basis for the reassessment of the goals and strategies for the future.

Isabel Marcus, "A Sexy New Twist: Reproductive Technologies and Feminism -- Book Review: L. Andrews, BETWEEN STRANGERS: SURROGATE MOTHERS (1989); E.H. Baruch, A.F. D'Anano, Jr. and J. Seager, (eds.), EMBRYOS, ETHICS, AND WOMEN'S RIGHTS: EXPLORING THE NEW REPRODUCTIVE TECHNOLOGIES (1988); S. Cohen and N. Taub, (eds.), REPRODUCTIVE LAWS FOR THE 1990'S (1989); G. Corea et al., (eds.), MAN-MADE WOMEN: HOW NEW REPRODUCTIVE TECHNOLOGIES AFFECT WO-MEN (1988); M.A. Field, SURROGATE MOTHERHOOD: THE LEGAL AND HUMAN ISSUES (1988); R.D. Klein, INFERTILITY: WOMEN SPEAK OUT ABOUT THEIR EXPERIENCES OF RE-PRODUCTIVE MEDICINE (1989); E. Martin, THE WOMAN IN THE BODY: A CULTURAL ANALYSIS OF REPRODUCTION (1987); B.K. Rothman, RECREATING MOTHERHOOD: IDEOL-OGY AND TECHNOLOGY IN A PATRIARCHAL SOCIETY (1989); P. Spallone, BEYOND CONCEPTION: THE NEW POLITICS OF REPRODUCTION (1989); M. Stanworth, (ed.), REPRODUCTIVE TECHNOLOGIES, GENDER, MOTHERHOOD AND MEDICINE (1987)" (1990) 15 *Law and Social Inquiry* 247-269

The author gives a brief history of feminist thought regarding reproduction. She then reviews ten books dealing with modern reproductive technologies, including both scholarly works and what she calls "confessional narratives." She concludes that the possibility of separating reproduction from sex has not led to liberation; on the contrary, all the books reviewed evince a "sense of beleaguerment, if not siege."

Otwin Marenin, "Nations not Obsessed with Crime -- Book Review: Freda Alder, NATIONS NOT OBSESSED WITH CRIME (1984)" (1985) 31 *Crime and Delinquency* 332-333

Part of a special issue on Rape, this is a review of a book which attempts to examine and explain low crime rates in ten countries. The reviewer criticizes the book for its lack of meaningful patterns, for its lack of solutions, and for its failure to support its claim that crime rates are kept low by informal control mechanisms.

Sally Markowitz, "Book Review: Kristin Luker, ABORTION AND THE POLITICS OF MOTHERHOOD (1984)" (1985) 2 *Wisconsin Women's Law Journal* 151-157

This book demonstrates the historical linking of abortion with the doctor's claim that medicine should be a profession subject to strict licensing, in which only doctors have "scientific" knowledge about when foetal life becomes human, and the dangers of pregnancy. The author examines the abortion-rights debate, and claims that both pro- and anti-abortionists, because they view the personhood of the foetus to be a "fact to be discovered," support each other's system of values. The reviewer thinks the book is an excellent starting point for understanding the issue of abortion, but criticizes the book for not making specific connections between women's material position, general ideological framework, and position with respect to abortion.

Gail Martin, "Landing a Good Blue-Collar Job -- Book Review: Muriel Lederer, BLUE-COLLAR JOBS FOR WOMEN: A COMPLETE GUIDE TO GETTING SKILLED AND GETTING A HIGH-PAYING JOB IN THE TRADES (1979)" (1980) 103 *Monthly Labor Review* 60-61

This book is helpful, the reviewer claims, for those who want to enter the blue-collar labour market. The title is descriptive of the contents, and the reviewer especially likes the forty-page appendix containing a glossary and information on apprenticeships. The text is "peppered" with comments from women in blue-collar jobs; these are particularly illuminating to women intending to follow in their footsteps. While the focus is on the higher pay available in blue-collar jobs, the reviewer prefers more stress on the fulfilment and satisfaction gained through use of one's agility, strength, intelligence and other qualities.

Janice Dickin McGinnis, "Book Review: Christine L. M. Boyle et al., A FEMINIST REVIEW OF CRIMINAL LAW (1985)" (1987) 21 *University of British Columbia Law Review* 241-246
The reviewer critically discusses the Review, published by the Status of Women Canada in 1985, noting the amount of popular media attention given to it. She points out some "glaringly inaccurate" references to gender identification, and a few other seemingly careless flaws in the Review, but unlike the popular media, she finds some interesting and challenging ideas about women and criminal law. In particular, she discusses the Review's concern with the rights of "private property" in potential conflict with the "security of the person," the application of special women's legal defenses, and the issue of honest belief in consent as it relates to rape.

Martha Minow, "Consider the Consequences -- Book Review: Lenore Weitzman, THE DIVORCE REVOLUTION: THE UNEXPECTED SOCIAL AND ECONOMIC CONSEQUENCES FOR WOMEN AND CHILDREN IN AMERICA (1985)" (1986) 84 *Michigan Law Review* 900-916
The book examines California's no-fault divorce law, which, according to its author, has had devastating economic consequences for women. The reviewer agrees with the author, identifies the consequences of the reform as a drastic reduction of financial security for women and children, and questions why these consequences were surprising. She discusses how to reduce surprise in the next reform, by examining the broad social conditions of male/female inequality. She concludes that formal equality in a narrow realm, that of divorce and custody, and the consequent privileging of individual freedom over partnership in marriage, exposes the powerless to the will of the more powerful.

Martha Minow, "The Properties of Family and the Families of Property -- Book Review: Mary Ann Glendon, THE NEW FAMILY AND THE NEW PROPERTY (1981)" (1982) 92 *Yale Law Journal* 376-395
The reviewer praises Glendon's work on family, employment,

property, and security, but finds her analyses overly dependent on legal method, and suggests that the interplay between law and society must be examined.

Martha Minow, "Rights of One's Own in her Own Right: The Life of Elizabeth Cady Stanton -- Book Review: Elisabeth Griffith, IN HER OWN RIGHT: THE LIFE OF ELIZABETH CADY STANTON (1984)" (1985) 98 _Harvard Law Review_ **1084-1099**

Griffith's book provides a comprehensive picture of the life and legacy of Stanton, the nineteenth century American women's rights reformer, and focuses on Stanton's search for a role model that would sustain her efforts to change women's place in society without losing the respect traditionally accorded to women. The reviewer criticizes the work for failing to discuss the development of Stanton's ideas, including why she, an abolitionist, opposed the fourteenth amendment and how she, a natural rights exponent, proclaimed the superiority of women over at least some men. The review goes on to correct these deficiencies, and to suggest that an understanding of Stanton's experience can contribute to contemporary debates over women's rights and the problem of social and legal change generally.

Martha Minow, "Speaking of Silence -- Book Review: Kristin Bumiller, THE CIVIL RIGHTS SOCIETY: THE SOCIAL CONSTRUCTION OF VICTIMS (1988)" (1988) 43 _University of Miami Law Review_ **493-511**

Bumiller's book claims that anti-discrimination law is disempowering and inhibits challenges by those whom it is supposed to help, both because it assigns victim status to those who assert their rights, and because it promotes silence by many who have anti-discrimination claims in order to avoid the pain of the victim role. The reviewer argues that silence is produced by a number of reasons in addition to that identified by the author, including self-blame, failure to recognize the harm as legal, the uncertainty and burden of litigation, the social stigma associated with complaining, and the ethic of submission and self-sacrifice. She agrees with the author's assessment that the problem is not merely a faulted law, but has to do, instead, with the very nature of anti-discrimination law as law. Unlike the author who concludes that the law can never empower those it treats as victim, the reviewer thinks that something can be done about silence, and she concludes her essay with a discussion of the ways in which antidiscrimination law can be reconceived so as to make empowerment possible.

James C. Mohr, "Feminism and the History of Marital Law: Basch and Stetson on the Rights of Wives -- Book Review: D.M. Stetson, A WOMAN'S ISSUE: THE POLITICS OF FAMILY LAW REFORM IN ENGLAND (1982); N. Basch, IN THE EYES OF THE LAW: WOMEN, MARRIAGE AND PROPERTY IN NINETEENTH-CENTURY NEW YORK (1982)" [1984] *American Bar Foundation Research Journal* **223-228**

Both books discuss the effect of femininism on the Anglo-American doctrine of coverture. Stetson concludes that feminists had a general influence on the development of divorce and matrimonial property law in England, but variable impact on specific decisions. The reviewer finds that Stetson's arguments are weak, particularly in the application of conflict resolution theory. Basch's book is a skilfully crafted and scholarly analysis of three important New York statutes of the mid-1850's. The reviewer presents his own thesis, which is that marital law may not be at the base a feminist issue. Rather, particularly in the nineteenth century, its development is better understood in the socio-economic terms of contract and commercial law.

Mary Jane Mossman, "Book Review: John Eekelaar and Mavis Maclean, MAINTENANCE AFTER DIVORCE (1986)" (1989) 3 *Canadian Journal of Women and the Law* **293-302**

The author reviews a book examining the history of maintenance payments post-divorce in England, then compares the findings with recent research in the United States and Australia. She concludes with suggestions for research which should be done in Canada.

Mary Jane Mossman, "Book Review: Katherine O'Donovan, SEXUAL DIVISIONS IN LAW (1985)" (1986) 36 *University of New Brunswick Law Journal* **221-225**

The author of this book uses the term 'sex' but deals more with gender, and the distinction between social and biological characteristics is, the reviewer suggests, therefore crucial to the book's argument. The book is divided into several sections: the philosophical dimensions of the public/private dichotomy, especially for the liberal tradition; law's wide-ranging and challenging role in practice; law reform in the public/private dichotomy; and measurement of the efficacy of the equality principle. The reviewer submits that there must be a conflation of public and private, a recognition of communitarian value, and family responsibilities and obligations within society. We must, she concludes, develop a language of domestic and social concern.

Mary Jane Mossman, "Book Review: Ronald Chester, UNEQUAL ACCESS: WOMEN LAWYERS IN A CHANGING AMERICA (1985)" (1986) 2 _Canadian Journal of Women and the Law_ 178-189
   The reviewer thinks that UNEQUAL ACCESS is an important book because it presents "herstories" of women law graduates from three part-time American law schools in the 1920's and 1930's. The book is based upon sample interviews with women graduates; and because it is an oral history, there are many voices telling individual and often quite different stories. The reviewer, however, criticizes the book for failing to take into account the impact of sex upon the careers of the women and for failing to provide an analysis of their lives from the perspective of the women themselves. None of the women voiced real concern about their acceptance by the profession and in fact sometimes they asserted that there were no problems for women lawyers. She asks whether the lives of such women could be considered "struggles" if they themselves did not recognize them as such, and inquires whether it is their perception, or the author's, that is skewed.

Barbara J. Nelson, "Comparable Worth: A Brief Review of History, Practice, and Theory -- Book Review: Michael Evan Gold, A DIALOGUE ON COMPARABLE WORTH (1983); Elaine Johansen, COMPARABLE WORTH: THE MYTH AND THE MOVEMENT (1984); Helen Remick, ed., COMPARABLE WORTH AND WAGE DISCRIMINATION (1984); Donald J. Treiman and Heidi I. Hartmann, WOMEN, WORK AND WAGES: EQUAL PAY FOR JOBS OF EQUAL VALUE (1985)" (1985) 69 _Minnesota Law Review_ 1199-1216
   The reviewer gives a history and definition of comparable worth and then examines managerial practices and economic theory associated with pay equity through an examination of four books on the topic. The books are, she thinks, best at giving an overview of the history, theory and politics of pay equity. She concludes with an examination of the theoretical issues underlying personnel processes.

Susan Moller Okin, "Feminism, the Individual and Contract Theory --
Book Review: Carole Pateman, THE SEXUAL CONTRACT (1988)"
(1990) 100 *Ethics* 658-669
    Liberal social contract theories assume the voluntariness of the
contracting parties.   Pateman argues that social and employment
contracts depend on the pre-existence of what she calls the sexual
contract, which governs men's rights of access to women's bodies. The
sexual contract is the source of patriarchal rights, but patriarchal rights
extend to all aspects of life. It is therefore impossible, she concludes,
that social or political contracts could ever include women. She finds
Pateman's description of the sexual contract and her analysis of male
political theorists' works compelling, but takes issue with her analysis of
psychoanalytic theories. She argues that social contracts are still of value
to society, and that work must be done within the existing liberal
framework to equalize the power of men and women.

    Maureen Orth, "The Ginny Foat Case and the Future of the Women's
Movement – Book Review: Ellen Hawkes, FEMINISM ON TRIAL;
The Ginny Foat Case and the Future of the Woman's Movement" (1986)
132 *Chicago Daily Law Bulletin* 2
    Foat was a feminist activist in NOW, and an accused murderer.
The book describes the politics of feminism in the 1970s, and the trial.
The reviewer bemoans the fact the writer never had access to Foat
herself.

    Christine A. Pagac, "Susan Moller Okin, JUSTICE, GENDER AND
THE FAMILY (1989)" (1990) 88 *Michigan Law Review* 1822-1827
    In her book, Okin argues that the current institution of family is
unjust and criticizes major theories of justice which have ignored injustice
within the family. The reviewer suggests that while the book's concept
is powerful, the author too "blithely" dismisses the traditionalists and
naively proposes that changing the law will change society, and criticizes
the author's theory as not sufficiently developed, and not having provided
an adequate explanation of how to create a more just family.

    Lynn M. Paltrow, "Book Review: Rita Arditti, Renate Duelli Klein
and Shelley Minden, TEST-TUBE WOMEN: WHAT FUTURE FOR
MOTHERHOOD? (1984)" (1985) 8 *Women's Rights Law Reporter*

303-307

This is a collection of feminist articles about reproductive technologies. The reviewer finds the tone of the work -- which views women as powerless victims who are "empty vessels for men's use" -- unbalanced.

Carole Pateman, "Sex and Power -- Book Review: Catharine MacKinnon, FEMINISM UNMODIFIED: DISCOURSES ON LIFE AND LAW (1987)" (1990) 100 *Ethics* 398-407

The reviewer applauds MacKinnon's insistence that feminism deal with a specific problem -- namely, the political problem of men's power over women -- through an approach different from other political theories. She has difficulty, however, with MacKinnon's discussion of the equality and difference debate, and her claim that "sexual difference is nothing more than an artifact of men's power." She asserts "MacKinnon's major claim ... is that what is at issue in the present structure of social relations is sexual subordination," but finds her lack of clarity in using the terms sex and gender confusing. She canvasses MacKinnon's arguments on abortion, privacy and pornography and concludes that MacKinnon's concentration on "unpleasant facts" is necessary.

Helen Patey, "Book Review: Marcia Westkott, THE FEMINIST LEGACY OF KAREN HORNEY (1986)" (1986/1988) 2 *Canadian Journal of Women and the Law* 455-459

The reviewer focuses on Westkott's fusion of Horney's early and later work, which she notes, provides the author with a framework in which to construct a social psychology for women. Horney challenged the Freudian theory of penis envy, arguing that women want to be men not because of penis envy but because of repressed ambition. In her analysis, the conflict of women who must try to reconcile the masculine ideal of "woman" with their own internal female identities results in "powerless responsibility," leading to suppressed anger and neuroses. The reviewer describes Westkott's expansion of these ideas into the area of moral choice as fascinating, and concludes that the book is an important contribution to feminist writing.

Teresa Godwin Phelps, "Stories of Women in Self-Defense -- Book Review: Cynthia K. Gillespie, JUSTIFIABLE HOMICIDE: BATTERED WOMEN, SELF-DEFENSE, AND THE LAW (1989)" (1989)

2 Yale Journal of Law and Feminism 189-197

In JUSTIFIABLE HOMICIDE, the author traces the history of the law of self defence, finds it reflects patriarchal values and is designed for men, and argues that it must be extended to include women. The book is sprinkled with the stories of the two hundred battered women who murdered, whom the author studied. Although Gillespie's proposals for reform are modest and not original, the reviewer praises the book because it "seeks to remove the sexism that hears only men's stories and adheres to the reasonable man standard."

Miriam I. Pickus, "Book Review: Ronald Chester, UNEQUAL ACCESS: WOMEN LAWYERS IN A CHANGING AMERICA (1985)" (1986) 84 *Michigan Law Review* 1052-1057

The book is a compilation of stories of twentieth century women in the legal profession, in which the author argues that women's access to power positions in law has not improved significantly and recommends female solidarity. The reviewer praises the book because its narratives provide the reader with a glimpse of the lives and struggles of women pioneers, and gives a sense of power and pride in their accomplishments.

Barbara Raffel Price, "Book Review: Freda Adler, THE INCIDENCE OF FEMALE CRIMINALITY IN THE CONTEMPORARY WORLD (1981); S. K. Mukherjee and Jocelynne A. Scutt, (eds.), WOMEN AND CRIME (1981); Dorothy Zeitz, WOMEN WHO EMBEZZLE OR DEFRAUD: A STUDY OF CONVICTED FELONS (1981)" (1982) 8 *Signs: Journal of Women in Culture and Society* 718-721

These three books deal with the issue of female criminality, and each discusses the differences between male and female crime. Adler's book is valuable for its international crime information and its analysis of the "striking consistencies" in female crime throughout these countries. WOMEN AND CRIME is the proceeding of an Australian Conference dealing with sexism in criminal law, young women, female crime rates, and women in prison. The book by Zeitz discusses the differences, especially in motivation, of women who embezzle versus men who do so. The reviewer claims a similarity between countries with respect to sex-role socialization and forms of female crime, and concludes that analysis of female crime will result in a better general theory of both male and female crime, therefore legitimizing the study of female crime by male criminologists.

Rosemary Pringle, "Book Review: Carol Smart, FEMINISM AND THE POWER OF LAW (1989)" (1990) 18 *International Journal of the Sociology of Law* 229-232

Smart has reservations about the power of law to provide solutions for women's situation, but is also concerned that this power not be under-rated. The reviewer thinks that Smart "has provided an intelligent critique of a very wide range of writings, and taken a controversial stance on legal change." Her one reservation is that Smart's "caution ... could paralyse strategic action around the law."

Katharine E. Renison, "Book Review: Marion Boyd, ed., HANDBOOK FOR ADVOCATES AND COUNSELLORS OF BATTERED WOMEN (1985)" (1986) 2 *Canadian Journal of Women and the Law* 214-218

The reviewer thinks this handbook is extremely helpful in developing an effective response to domestic violence, because it outlines the social, economic, emotional, and legal factors which must be considered. The handbook includes information about the cycle of violence, a critique of anti-feminist explanations of violence, and information about criminal or civil actions available within the legal system. The reviewer criticizes the handbook for its omission of information specific to immigrant women, and points out that such women are doubly bound, due to non-acceptance by their cultural communities on leaving the family home.

Andrew Ross, "Politics Without Pleasure -- Book Review: Catharine MacKinnon, FEMINISM UNMODIFIED (1987)" (1988) 1 *Yale Journal of Law and the Humanities* 193-201

The reviewer criticizes MacKinnon's view that pornography is the articulation of patriarchal domination. Finding this perspective reductionist, polemical and inflexible, he discusses MacKinnon's opposition to liberal feminism and Freudian insights. He regards her position as locked in a circle of aggression and rejects her epistemology of pleasure.

Kim Lane Schepple, "The Re-Vision of Rape Law -- Book Review: Susan Estrich, REAL RAPE: HOW THE LEGAL SYSTEM VICTIMIZES WOMEN WHO SAY NO (1987)" (1987) 54 *University of Chicago Law Review* 1095-1118

The reviewer contrasts the view that rape is a very serious crime which should be severely punished, with the nightmarish experiences the rape victim often has in the criminal justice system and the unlikelihood that a rapist will be punished. Estrich's book, she claims, dissolves the apparent contradiction by pointing out that the system sees two kinds of rape - real rape and simple rape. Real rapes are by strangers and are accompanied by violence, while simple rapes, generally dismissed as trivial by the law, are those where the rapist knows the victim, acts alone, and doesn't use brutal force or a weapon. Estrich argues that what is necessary is a re-visioning of rape and of men and women's interaction generally. The reviewer concludes that the book empowers women and gives a direction to their struggle with the legal system.

Lorraine Schmall, "Book Review: Catharine MacKinnon, FEMINISM UNMODIFIED (1987)" (1987) 73 *American Bar Association Journal* 80-81

This short review of FEMINISM UNMODIFIED focuses on the issues raised by the text which would be of interest to practising women lawyers, such as child care, job structure in the legal profession and the discomfort of living with a feminist perspective. The review touches on rape statistics, anti-pornography ordinances, abortion and privacy rights of women on welfare.

Ferdinand Schoeman, "Book Review: L.D. Houlgate, FAMILY AND STATE: THE PHILOSOPHY OF FAMILY LAW (1988)" (1989) 99 *Ethics* 651-655

Houlgate proposes a view of family life which he calls the "communal model." The most important feature of this model is that the members of the community can claim care and nurturing as their right. The reviewer accepts Houlgate's characterization of the family as a social practice and as a relationship defined by rules. However, he takes issue with Houlgate's assertions that utilitarianism is the overarching principle in settling disputes about the family and that the state recognizes parental authority over children only because the parents promote the child's welfare. The reviewer argues that the family is an economic and social unit which promotes a wide variety of values. Judges should supplement Houlgate's perspective with a respect for the parents' interests in family life.

Paul Schwartz, "Baby M in West Germany -- Book Review: Michelle Stanworth, REPRODUCTIVE TECHNOLOGIES: GENDER, MOTHERHOOD AND MEDICINE (1987); and Goerhard Amendt, DER NEUE KLAPPERSTORCH: DIE PSYCHISCHEN UND SOZIALEN FOLGEN DER REPRODUKTIONSMEDIZIN (1987)" (1989) 89 *Columbia Law Review* 347-367

This review compares the legal response to reproductive practice and medicine in the U.S. and the Federal Republic of Germany through a review of two books which the reviewer thinks reflect the American and German responses. Individual choice is central to the American legal perspective; the concern of German law is with the impact of reproductive choice on social values. The reviewer analyzes the results of the two perspectives in the context of surrogate motherhood, and proposes an additional norm based on the family as an instrument creating persons capable of participating in democracy.

Mary Lyndon Shanley, "Book Review: Josephine Donovan, FEMIN-IST THEORY: THE INTELLECTUAL TRADITIONS OF AMERI-CAN FEMINISM (1985); David L. Kirp, Mark G. Yudof, and Marlene Strong Franks, GENDER JUSTICE (1986)" (1987) 13 *Signs: Journal of Women in Culture and Society* 175-178

The reviewer found FEMINIST THEORY to be a helpful collection of feminist writings, and states it will make feminist theory more accessible to traditionally trained philosophers, political theorists, and historians who are unaware of feminist theory. Unlike FEMINIST THEORY, GENDER JUSTICE is original theory which attempts to build a theory of justice encompassing gender differences. The reviewer argues this to be a failed attempt, thinks the book oversimplified and based on distortion of feminist writing, and concludes that the goal of individual liberty cannot be reached in a society which is as systematically unequal as is present day society.

Reva B. Siegel, "Book Review: Susan Lehrer, ORIGINS OF PRO-TECTIVE LABOUR LEGISLATION FOR WOMEN (1987)" (1987/1988) 3 *Berkeley Women's Law Journal* 171-187

This book is an ambitious historical account of the politics surrounding the sex-based regulatory regime. "Drawing on a rich array of sources", the book attempts to make political sense of the controversy by examining the motives and attitudes of proponents and opponents of regulating women's employment and by devoting particular attention to the debate which divided the women's movement after the passage of the nineteenth amendment.   The reviewer has difficulty with Lehrer's "hindsight" analysis that the legislation served the interests of the business class and was enacted to subordinate women in the market. In the reviewer's opinion, Lehrer's own evidence does not support the adequacy and accuracy of her account.   The reviewer thinks the author artificially divides the women's movement between "social reformer" proponents and "feminist" opponents (the National Women's Party), and ignores the fact that women who were divided over the legislation had also fought together for women's suffrage.

Karen Beck Skold, "Book Review: Carol Tropp Schreiber, CHAN-GING PLACES: MEN AND WOMEN IN TRANSITIONAL OC-CUPATIONS (1981); Cynthia Fuchs Epstein and Rose Laub Coser, (eds.), ACCESS TO POWER: CROSS-NATIONAL STUDIES OF WOMEN AND ELITES (1981); Cynthia Fuchs Epstein, WOMEN IN LAW (1981); Judith Hicks Stiehm, BRING ME MEN AND WOMEN: MANDATED CHANGE AT THE U.S. AIR FORCE ACADEMY (1981)" (1982) 8 *Signs: Journal of Women in Culture and Society* 367-372
     The reviewer thinks it important to evaluate the progress of affirmative action programs in halting the equation of "power" with "maleness"; and she discusses these books in relation to the changing of the equality debate from one of gender segregation as a problem of sex roles to one of gender segregation as connected to power. The books deal with the changing roles of women in blue-collar positions, science, law, and the military. The reviewer concludes that they collectively provoke questions about women's entry into male domains, and illustrate that women in elite positions have made tangible gains, which to some extent have been of benefit to all women. However, she cautions that it remains an open question whether these changes will in fact alter the power imbalance between the sexes, and recommends an explicit link in research between work environment gender segregation and issues of power and hierarchy.

J.C. Smith, "Book Review: Catharine A. MacKinnon, TOWARDS A FEMINIST THEORY OF THE STATE (1989)" (1990) 69 *Canadian Bar Review* 597-601
     The reviewer claims that MacKinnon's book is "the single most

important book in the new jurisprudence," particularly as "her perspective has the potential of social revolution." He goes on to describe the main thrusts of the book, notes how recent Canadian jurisprudence has taken the feminist position seriously, and concludes that male sexuality must be explored in the new jurisprudence.

Barbara Stark, "Book Review: Malvina Halberstam and Elizabeth F. Defeis, WOMEN'S LEGAL RIGHTS: INTERNATIONAL COVENANTS; AN ALTERNATIVE TO THE ERA? (1987)" (1990) 12 *Women's Rights Law Reporter* **51-57**

The book includes a concise but comprehensive survey of international covenants available for challenging gender discrimination; and the reviewer thinks it an important step toward the realization of human rights in the United States. She identifies the book's major strength as its placement of American rights law into an international context, because this allows some perspective on the strengths and weaknesses of the American notion of rights.

Cass R. Sunstein, "Feminism and Legal Theory -- Book Review: Catharine MacKinnon, FEMINISM UNMODIFIED (1987)" (1988) 101 *Harvard Law Review* **826-848**

The reviewer describes MacKinnon's work as a work of three parts -- the first theoretical and general, including a distinctive approach to sex discrimination; the second deals with applications including rape, abortion, sexual harassment, and athletics; and the third consists of six essays on pornography. He challenges MacKinnon's ends, as many women do not seek the same changes; her means, as she does not specify which institutions to change; and her approach to pornography. MacKinnon's claim is not that pornography is perversion of sexuality, but rather that pornography helps to constitute sexuality, which is socially constructed. Sunstein considers these brilliant insights even though at times polemical and one-sided and drawn with insufficient empirical evidence. However, he concludes that within the decade MacKinnon's work will be taken as substantially correct within legal culture.

Nadine Taub, "Book Review: Lenore J. Weitzman, THE DIVORCE REVOLUTION: THE UNEXPECTED SOCIAL AND ECONOMIC CONSEQUENCES FOR WOMEN AND CHILDREN IN AMERICA

(1985)" (1988) 13 *Signs: Journal of Women in Culture and Society* 578-583
    The book presents the results of a ten-year study designed to ascertain the impact of California's no-fault divorce law. The author reports that women are worse off relative to men after divorce with no-fault than they were before. The reviewer praises the book for making known the economic consequences of divorce for women and children. However, she questions the causal relation which the book maintains between the adoption of no-fault divorce and women's post divorce difficulties, and suggests that the problem is really due to the manner in which California judges choose to enforce the law. She concludes that, on the whole, the book is another reason to speculate about the meaning of gender equality and the law's ability to help in achieving it.

    Verta A. Taylor, "How To Avoid Taking Sexual Harassment Seriously: A New Book That Perpetuates Old Myths -- Book Review: Mary Coeli Meyer, Inge M. Berchtold, Jeannenne L. Oestreich, and Frederick J. Collins, SEXUAL HARASSMENT (1981)" (1981) 10 *Capital University Law Review* 672-684
    Part of a Symposium on Sexual Harassment, this book review is critical of the gender free perspective of the text, which the reviewer thinks renders the book androcentric. She criticizes the book's methodology, its selective historical account of sexual harassment, and the solutions it proposes.

    Lee E. Teitelbaum, "The Legal History of the Family -- Book Review: Michael Grossberg, GOVERNING THE HEARTH: LAW AND THE FAMILY IN NINETEENTH-CENTURY AMERICA (1985)" (1987) 85 *Michigan Law Review* 1052-1070
    The reviewer praises the book as indispensable to both historians and legal theorists. He discusses Grossberg's observations within the context of republicanism in the United States, its relationship to the patriarchal family, and the consequent view of the family in individualistic terms, which has led, he claims, to increased use of rights-talk with respect to families. The reviewer commends the book both for the data it presents and for the questions it provokes.

    Jim Thomas, "Criminal Justice -- Book Review: Allison Morris, WOMEN, CRIME AND CRIMINAL JUSTICE (1987)" (1988) 38

Journal of Legal Education 437-450

This article reviews a selection of books. The review dealing with WOMEN, CRIME AND CRIMINAL JUSTICE suggests that Morris' focus is too narrow, and that she over-generalizes by faulting previous research for its male patriarchal bias. The reviewer suggests that similar criticism could be levelled at most research on the grounds of race or class bias, as well as gender. He states, however, that her thesis is well argued and documented, and that the annotated bibliography which is included would be useful to those interested in further research.

Rene L. Todd, "Book Review: Donald A. Downs, THE NEW POLITICS OF PORNOGRAPHY (1989)" (1990) 88 _Michigan Law Review_ 1811-1821

In his book, the author asserts that radical feminist anti-pornography legislation must give way to protection of speech under the first amendment. He then attempts a compromise, by suggesting that only violent obscenity be restricted by pornography laws. The reviewer attacks this argument, and suggests that the author understands neither the irreconcilability of obscenity law and anti-pornography law, nor the theoretical basis of radical feminism.

Mark Tushnet, "The New Politics of Pornography Regulation -- Book Review: G. Hawkins and F. Zimring, PORNOGRAPHY IN A FREE SOCIETY (1988); S. Gubar and J. Hoff, FOR ADULT USERS ONLY: THE DILEMMA OF VIOLENT PORNOGRAPHY (1988)" (1989) 58 _University of Cincinnati Law Review_ 183-198

The reviewer introduces his review of the two books with a survey of the sexualized violence against women to be found in music videos. In response to Hawkins and Zimring's conclusion that ambiguity in defining pornography renders it impossible to assess the harms it causes, the reviewer suggests that a redefinition in itself will have important social effects. The second part of the article is a response to accounts of the nature of the ambiguity of pornography by Linda Williams, Richard Miller and Robin West. The reviewer concludes that the difficulty in regulating pornography stems from its inherent ambiguity.

Shauna Van Praagh and Barbara Austin, "Book Review -- Lorraine Code and Christine Overall, eds., FEMINIST PERSPECTIVES:

PHILOSOPHICAL ESSAYS ON METHOD AND MORALS (1988)" (1989) 47 *University of Toronto Faculty of Law Review* 1016-1019

FEMINIST PERSPECTIVES, a Canadian collection of philosophical essays, is a collaborative effort, divided into two parts, the first a feminist methodology and the second a feminist morality. The reviewers applaud the content and concept of the book which "embodies the feminist process," by looking at the world from a variety of perspectives instead of one.

Virginia L. Warren, "How Radical is Liberalism? -- Book Review: James S. Fishkin, JUSTICE, EQUAL OPPORTUNITY, AND THE FAMILY (1983)" (1984) 82 *Michigan Law Review* 761-780

The reviewer finds the text to be a comprehensive critique of the liberal view of social justice. Fishkin links liberalism with family autonomy, and postulates that its major failing is that it has ignored the role of the family. Overall the review is positive, however, the reviewer notes the author's absence of solutions.

Joanna K. Weinberg, "The Politicization of Reproduction -- Book Review: Sherrill Cohen and Nadine Taub, REPRODUCTIVE LAWS FOR THE 1990s (1989)" (1989-90) 5 *Berkeley Women's Law Journal* 197-213

Concluding that the world depicted in Margaret Atwood's HANDMAID'S TALE is close to that articulated by the U.S. Supreme Court, the reviewer contends that REPRODUCTIVE LAWS FOR THE 1990s requires close attention. She juxtaposes the broad examination of reproductive issues in the book against the "shrill clamour" of the Supreme Court in WEBSTER v. REPRODUCTIVE HEALTH SERVICES, and considers the "intersection of social and legal issues in the regulation of women's ability to choose pregnancy or abortion." She concludes with a discussion of autonomy.

Leigh West, "Book Review: Ronald Chester, UNEQUAL ACCESS: WOMEN LAWYERS IN A CHANGING AMERICA (1985)" (1985) 5 *Windsor Yearbook of Access to Justice* 407-410

Chester's book provides an oral history of women who entered the American legal profession during the 1920's and 1930's. The reviewer finds this study to be less comprehensive than earlier ones, although a number of observations, especially with respect to the clustering of women in civil service positions and their absence in powerful and prestigious law firms, confirms the earlier studies. Overall, she thinks oral chronicles such as this offer reliable and accurate data and provide a base against which the progress of women in gaining access to power in the profession can be compared.

Christina B. Whitman, "Law and Sex -- Book Review: Catharine MacKinnon, FEMINISM UNMODIFIED (1987)" (1988) 86 *Michigan Law Review* 1388-1403

MacKinnon claims that any modification of feminism weakens feminism. Common criticisms of MacKinnon's work are that she must hate men and that she must not like sex. In the reviewer's opinion, the fact that they are made supports MacKinnon's basic thesis because they espouse a contempt for women and suggest that a woman who hates men is irrational and lacking in judgment. MacKinnon's personal message for women, the reviewer suggests, is not about better sex, but rather is a demand that women in power see what they have in common with less powerful women. MacKinnon is from an empowered group; her message is that women all have in common the fact of being victims. She appeals to moments when powerful women share their vulnerability. MacKinnon's intolerance of feminists who do not share her perspective, however, causes the reviewer to conclude that she has borrowed the tools of male dominance.

Joan C. Williams, "Feminism and Post-Structuralism -- Book Review: Zillah R. Eisenstein, THE FEMALE BODY AND THE LAW (1988)" (1990) 88 *Michigan Law Review* 1776-1791

The author categorizes The Female Body and the Law as "part of a broad attack on essentialism in both feminist theory and women's history." She states that the author is seeking to deconstruct both the male/female and difference/sameness dichotomies, and that this deconstruction is vitally important to feminism. She concludes, however, that Eisenstein's adoption of post-structuralism leads to confusion between biological sex and social gender, and her attention is directed away from the two central tasks of showing that "difference" is based on false conceptions of gender and that "sameness" cannot occur in a system of gender privilege.

Conna Wood, "Book Review: Mary Eaton, JUSTICE FOR WOMEN?: FAMILY, COURT AND SOCIAL CONTROL (1986)" (1988) 79 *Journal of Criminal Law & Criminology* 261-263

JUSTICE FOR WOMEN describes a 1980-82 case study that focused on the treatment of women offenders in a Magistrate's Court close to London. The reviewer raises several criticisms of this book, noting a lack of substantiation for Eaton's claims, and the absence of adequate definitions of key concepts. She also lists some methodological problems in the study, and complains about poor organization.   In general, the reviewer thinks the book a poor choice for instructional purposes and found that, although it was interesting in parts, it left the reader without a clear understanding of how magistrate's court reinforces gender differences and contributes to women's subordination.

Jennifer Wriggins, "Book Review: Catharine MacKinnon, FEMINISM UNMODIFIED (1987)" (1987) 10 *Harvard Women's Law Journal* 353-356

According to the reviewer, MacKinnon's provocative, insightful speeches on women's status, role and treatment have three underlying themes: that social relationships where men dominate and women submit are sexual in nature; that the inequality of power based on gender and on which social status is based determines who is permitted to do what to whom; and that pornography is the key means of actualizing the first two themes.   She thinks the book explores the role of law in feminism and feminist causes and provides a critique of liberalism, dominance theory and the sexualization of hierarchy in conditions of inequality. She concludes that MacKinnon has moved beyond substantive criticism into an analysis of the structure of law and legal reasoning, and that the work is brilliant and creative because few authors rival MacKinnon in revealing assumptions and ideologies hidden in the law.

Judith T. Younger, "The Supreme Court and the American Family -- Book Review: Eva R. Rubin, THE SUPREME COURT AND THE AMERICAN FAMILY (1986)" (1987) 4 *Constitutional Commentary* 173-176

The reviewer criticizes the book's attempt to show that traditional family ideals have shaped the Supreme Court's decisions regarding abortion, illegitimacy, maternity leave, and contraception, and questions these issues as family issues, and cites cases whose dicta is both pro- and anti-family values.

CHAPTER 17
SYMPOSIA

=====

"Symposium on Sexual Harassment" (1980-81) 10 *Capital University Law Review* 445-708 (i-viii)

"A Symposium on Reproductive Rights" (1982) 7 *Women's Rights Law Reporter* 169-299

"Sexuality, Violence, and Pornography" (1984) 7 *Humanities in Society* 1

"Symposium: National Association of Women Judges" (1984) 14 *Golden Gate University Law Review* 464-666

"Symposium on Pornography" (1984-85) 20 *New England Law Review* 629-777

"Symposium: Papers From the 1986 Feminism and Legal Theory Conference" (1987) 3 *Wisconsin Women's Law Journal* 1-274

"Symposium on Canadian Legal Scholarship" (1985) 23 *Osgoode Hall Law Journal* 427-572.

"Special Issue: Rape" (1985) 31 *Crime and Delinquency* 163-331

"Symposium: Seventh Annual Conference of the National Association of Women Judges" (1986) 4 *Law and Inequality* 1-169

"Transforming Legal Education: A Symposium of Provocative Thought" (1986) 10 *Nova Law Journal* 255-894

"Sex, Politics and the Law: Lesbians and Gay Men Take the Offensive -- A Symposium" (1986) 14 *New York University Review of Law and Social Change* 891-1016

"Review Symposium on Weitzman's Divorce Revolution -- Lenore J. Weitzman, THE DIVORCE REVOLUTION: THE UNEXPECTED CONSEQUENCES FOR WOMEN AND CHILDREN IN AMERICA (1985)" [1986] *American Bar Foundation Research Journal* 759-797

"Symposium: Issues in Procreational Autonomy" (1986) 37 *Hastings Law Journal* 697-1006

"Symposium on Women's Rights in International Law" (1987) 9 *Whittier Law Review* 393-443

"Feminist Moral, Social, and Legal Theory: A Symposium" (1987) 56 *University of Cincinnati Law Review* 459-550

"Women's Conflict With Man's Law" (1987) *Breaking the Silence* 5

"Symposium: Excluded Voices: Realities in Law and Law Reform" (1987) 42 *University of Miami Law Review* 1-158

"Symposium: Pornography" (1987-88) 21 *University of Michigan Journal of Law Reform* 1-281

"Symposium: The Civil Liberties and Human Rights Implications of United States International Population Policy" (1987-88) 20 *New York University Journal of International Law and Politics* 1-354

"Women in Legal Education -- Pedagogy, Law, Theory, and Practice" (1988) 38 *Journal of Legal Education* 1-194

"Symposium: The American Constitution and Equality" (1988) 2 *Law and Inequality* 27-61

"Symposium: Women and the Constitution" (1988) 6 *Law and Inequality* vii-62

"Symposium on Vice" (1988) 51 *Law and Contemporary Problems* 1-386

"USC Symposium on Judicial Election, Selection, and Accountability" (1988) 61 *Southern California Law Review* 1555

"Women's Symposium" (1989) 15 _New England Journal on Criminal and Civil Confinement_ 171-241

"Symposium on Feminism and Political Theory" (1989) 99 _Ethics_ 219-406

"Voices of Experience: New Responses to Gender Discourse" (1989) 24 _Harvard Civil Rights-Civil Liberties Law Review_ 1-172

"Symposium on Reproductive Rights" (1989) 13 _Nova Law Review_ 329-624

"Women in Legal Practice: A Symposium" (1989) 14 _Law and Social Inquiry_ 221-319

"Review Symposium: Critical Empiricism and Sociolegal Studies" (1989) 14 _Law and Social Inquiry_ 3-166

"Symposium: Women in Legal Practice -- Issues of Past, Present, and Future" (1989) 14 _Law and Social Inquiry_ 221-322

"Symposium: Children, Family and the Law" (1989-1990) 26 _California Western Law Review_ 223-424

"Symposium on Feminist Jurisprudence" (1990) 25 _Tulsa Law Journal_ 657-798

"Symposium on Poverty, Legislation, and Law" (1990) 16 _Journal of Legislation_ 127-214

"Symposium: Women and the Law: Goals for the 1990s" (1990) 42 _Florida Law Review_ 1-228

"Symposium: Employment Law Discrimination" (1990) 8 _Law and Inequality_ 387-436

"Symposium: Gender Bias in Legal Education" (1990) 14 _Southern Illinois University Law Journal_ 469-571

"Symposium: Sex and Difference" (1990) 1:2 _Law and Critique_ 131-248

AUTHOR INDEX

JOURNAL INDEX

TOPICAL INDEX